A. P. H.

Other books by
A. P. HERBERT

*please see the bibliography
at the end of this book*

A. P. H.

His Life and Times

by

Sir Alan Herbert, C.H.

HEINEMANN : LONDON

William Heinemann Ltd

15–16 Queen Street, Mayfair, London W1X 8BE

LONDON MELBOURNE TORONTO

JOHANNESBURG AUCKLAND

First published 1970

© Sir Alan Herbert 1970

Reprinted 1971

434 32750 6

Printed Offset Litho and bound in Great Britain
by Cox & Wyman Ltd,
London, Fakenham and Reading

TO
MY DEAR WIFE
FOR OUR 56th ANNIVERSARY

CONTENTS

ACKNOWLEDGEMENTS

The author and publishers are grateful to all those who granted permission for the inclusion in this book of letters addressed to A. P. Herbert by the following:

C. R. Attlee
Stanley Baldwin
J. M. Barrie
Hilaire Belloc
Arnold Bennett
Winston S. Churchill
John Galsworthy
Rudyard Kipling
G. B. Shaw
H. G. Wells

ILLUSTRATIONS

PREAMBLE

FIRST, a thousand genial maledictions on my dear friends Jean and Derek Tangye, the tough, contented exiles of Dorminack, the little cottage on a Cornish cliff, where I have spent so many healthy happy days. On one of their brief darts up to London, in one of those seductive Savoy rooms that can see the river, they urged me to write a book of recollections, to mark my eightieth birthday.

They are authorities on the arts of recollection. When I first met the tiny twinkling Jean Nicol, not long before War Two, she was the Queen of Public Relations at the Savoy Hotel, and a magnet to many. Derek, after a lively miscellaneous life, which had recently ranged from Military Intelligence to William Hickey, was weary of the Big City, of telephones and cocktail-parties. They tore up their roots, discarded the Big City, and fled to the small old cottage (no telephone) the other side of Penzance. There they started a flower farm, and quite on their own had a rough time with Nature – and Economics. The first battles over, they found time for writing. Jean did a sprightly but informing work, *Meet Me at the Savoy*, and a nice novel, *The Regina Hotel*. Derek has done a hugely successful series of finely written books about their joys and struggles, and the processions of Nature by the Cornish sea. The first was *A Gull on the Roof* (I believe the gull was named after me) and the sixth – the sixth – *A Cornish Summer* – is about to leave the nest.

So they should know. But I resisted strongly. I had written enough about me, I said – Parliament in *Independent Member*, the divorce affair in *The Ayes Have It*, the Thames and World War Two in *The Thames*. But two of those are out of print, they said, and you have not covered your long theatrical adventures or your many causes and conflicts since you left the House of Commons. 'I don't,' I said, 'want to be like one of Gilbert's customary spinsters, I forget which, who sang *"There will be too much of me in the coming by-and-by"*.'

I thought I had won. But, at the literary party to which we went, given by the great Hatchard's, they tackled and brought down an innocent publisher and, bless them all, here we are.

It will be some excuse if some of this work amuses some of the old, if it helps some of the 'causes' still unwon, and most if it encourages (or deters) the Young. I have broken many good rules. I have not stuck to my last – often I have been busy at two or three lasts at the same time. Chesterton – was it? – wrote about Belloc:

Mr Hilaire Belloc
Is a case for legislation *ad hoc*:
He seems to think nobody minds
His books being all of different kinds.

The poet was right; people do mind: and my modest books have been of far more different kinds than the splendid Belloc's. Apart from novels, I have written books, large and small, about the entertainment tax, about sun-dials, about Royal Commissions, about renaming the stars, about the history of Summer Time, about the attitude of the Anglican Church to the marriage of divorced persons, about authors and the Public Libraries, about Parliament, and Parliamentary procedure, about the Thames, its history and administration, about the football pools, about justice in the eighteenth century, about the rigging and running of sailing barges, about the first seven years of 'Space', about the Law (four or five), about the War Story of Southend Pier, about a greyhound, about the right use of English, the first 'Family' series for the B.B.C. (Mr Pewter), a historical work about Napoleon on Elba, not to mention about twenty volumes of verse and, I think, fifteen librettos, and, I should say, a million articles about almost everything from Jamaica to the moon. I should have a pension from the printers, and an award for 'productivity'. But how can such a chameleon expect a steady, respectful gaze from anyone?

Also, I have ignored the advice I often give to the Young with artistic or literary aspirations. In these harsh mechanical times, regular money is the thing. Till you have got a foothold on the foothills of Parnassus, arrange to win some bread lower down. Join Equity, young lady, by all means, and fight for a place on screen or stage, but learn typing and even shorthand, so that if Fate is foul, you can fall back into some secretarial job, if only for a time. Above all, unless you are Ian Fleming and one or two others, do not expect to make a living *out of books alone*. I earned some 'regular money' for about a year and a half as a private secretary to Sir Leslie Scott just after War One, and in Parliament I drew £400, and later £600 a year. But in fifty years that is the only 'regular money' I have earned. Even with *Punch* I have never had a contract. I had a small start from my father, but for fifty years I have by God's grace kept going – just – as a free-lance, with a wife and four children. I still offer the same advice to the Young. But here they may find evidence that works both ways. A free-lance is not free from anxiety – but he has some fun.

My warm thanks to Priscilla Hunt, who has nursed me for ten years, and to Caroleen Conquest. A.P.H.

FEBRUARY 28, 1970

THE SHALLOW END

MY first cry, the doctor said, was 'I told you so'. The second was: 'No speeches, I hope?'

I can never recall my birthday without thinking of the Mansion House. About seventy years later it provoked my rashest sally in an after-dinner speech. I was invited to the annual banquet of the Worshipful Company of Clockmakers in the famous Egyptian Hall. I hate the laborious white-tie rig and many-course meals, but the Warden of the Company, Sir Harold Spencer Jones, then Astronomer Royal, had been kind to me in a strange way, and I went. As an amateur student of the stars I try to be accurate if I mention the heavenly bodies in a book. I am annoyed by stage-designers who, precise about everything else, sprinkle their back-cloths with stars as from a pepper-pot. Why not buy a star-map, seek advice, and draw a genuine constellation or two? In my book *Why Waterloo?*, the story of Napoleon on Elba, I had a careful description of the departure of the Emperor's little fleet from the island on 26 February 1815. I could tell what stars were about from a gadget I invented myself. At eight o'clock the Emperor (that was still, by the Treaty, his title) went aboard the *Inconstant*, a gun was fired and the fateful voyage began. Sirius, the brightest star, was over the meridian of Porto Ferraio. High in the West were great Orion and his flanking henchmen, Aldebaran and Procyon, Castor and Pollux, Capella and the Pleiades, a noble escort. But the planets were too difficult, and, without much hope, I wrote to the Astronomer Royal. They sent me an elaborate plan of the courses of Jupiter and Venus throughout the ten months of Napoleon's stay. Venus, it turned out, was a morning star, and rose astern of the fleet about midnight. I might so easily have written: 'Venus, sinking in the West, beckoned Napoleon home.' But the pertinacious pursuit of accuracy, not always successful, has always been a vice of mine.

I was so warmly impressed by the astronomers' courtesy and craft that it seemed a small return to tackle the white tie and travel to the Mansion House. There were the usual well-decorated guests of City Company dinners, Ambassadors, a Bishop, the Lord Mayor of London

– and the Clockmakers' ladies. Oliver Lyttelton (now Lord Chandos) and the delightful Priscilla Tweedsmuir, M.P., made witty speeches. I had prepared a rather serious little speech about the glories of Greenwich, Greenwich Mean Time, and so on. I thought 'This is going to be damned dull'. But the speaker before me gave me a cue. 'The Lord Mayor of London,' he said, 'was born on Christmas Day.' This, for reasons not clear to me, was received with applause. I rose and recited, in my Mansion House voice, probably in the wrong order, the exhausting roll of addresses: 'Warden, Your Grace, Your Excellencies, My Lord Mayor, Sheriffs and Aldermen, My Lords, Ladies and Gentlemen' at the end of which one feels that one has made a speech already:

'I am delighted to hear that the Lord Mayor was born on Christmas Day. But I believe that I can beat that. For I was born on 24 September; and I have always proudly reckoned —'

At this point I thought to myself: 'This is the end of A.P.H. If I say what is in my mind there will be a horrid hush and I shall have to leave the Mansion House on all fours.' But it was too late to stop, and I went on:

'I have always proudly reckoned that I must have been conceived on Christmas Eve.'

To my relief there was loud laughter for about two minutes. There was a brief break in the middle for finger-counting, and then they laughed again, while I waited with a solemn face, gazing at the Corinthian pillars, to say my 'tag-line' – all this was genuinely impromptu – 'which of course, explains my beautiful nature'.

'A solemn face' – here is a tip, my boy: never show the slightest sign that you are amused by your own attempts at merriment.

Yes, I was born on 24 September 1890, and I hope to be eighty when this work appears, which will be more than I deserve – and much more than my old friend Nancy Astor expected. How often she promised me, with other wine-lovers, an early and horrible end – and imagination, memory and reason would be gone long before that. (Well, she may still turn out right in substance though wrong in time.)

I vowed long ago that if I ever presumed to publish any account of my life the childhood story should stop at my birthday. I promised myself that I would not write a book beginning 'My earliest memory is of hay-fever'. But perhaps I was wrong. Child-life in 1890–1900 was so different in many ways from child-life today that, here and there, it may rouse a ripple of interest, and, even – who knows? – approval.

Then, on my odious earliest memory, I can offer advice and comfort, and that is an opportunity not to be lightly thrown away. First, the fever is hereditary – my mother had it, and one of my brothers, and two of my children get it badly. Second, you may boast that it attacks only those with sensitive and delicate natures; you never heard of a heavy-weight boxer who complained of hay-fever. Third – and here is a real comfort – it is perhaps the only affliction that grows milder as you grow older. As a boy I suffered much – put to bed in the darkest room on a hot summer's day, with streaming, itching eyes which you must not rub, interminable sniffing and sneezing, an obstinate cough at night, and asthma. Suffering is a true word, though to others you may seem to have no more than a laughably unseasonal cold. All are enjoying the sun, the flowers, even the hay, but you are wretched and hate them. I do not wonder that Americans, who take the plague seriously, run away to the tops of mountains. At my private school my cough was so tiresome to the world at night that I was put away alone in the sanatorium. At Winchester my hay-cough was diagnosed as whooping-cough: I was sent into the sanatorium, and duly caught whooping-cough from the boys already there.

Hay-fever was an extra misery on the Gallipoli Peninsula in War One. On either side of the communication trenches the poppy and the cornflower flourished, and I used to sneeze all the way to the front-line and back. I was Battalion Scout Officer. One night the Staff desired some particular piece of reconnaissance in No Man's Land, and I was detailed. I was a fool, I suppose, and afterwards I blamed myself severely. I should have said: 'I'm sorry, I have hay-fever.' But how would this have been received by the Staff, by my Colonel? To the rest of the world hay-fever is a joke. So, on a quiet night, with two of my scouts I crawled forth. All went well for some way. There were no flowers in No Man's Land, but suddenly I sneezed: the Turks opened rapid fire, and one of my scouts was hit. He was hit in the femoral artery. I remember terribly how the other scout and I dragged the poor fellow back through the hole in the wire into the front trench. He died later. I ceased to be Scout Officer: and hay-fever is no joke to me.

But for many years now I have had no more than a little itch in the eyes for a week or two. So if you have the plague, hope on.

During the agitation that surrounded my 'Marriage Bill' (later the Matrimonial Causes Act 1937) a speaker for the Catholic Truth Society said in Hyde Park: 'And who is the man – what kind of man is it that is trying to tear up the institution of Christian marriage by the roots, etc. etc.? Look at his nose. That will tell you.' I am not against the Jews – indeed, I have many Jewish friends and I am all for Israel – but like the Catholics I prefer the Truth, and the Truth is that my mother came from a long line of Anglican bishops, and my father from a family of Irish Catholics (the P. is for Patrick). My mother was Beatrice Selwyn, and George and John Selwyn, Bishops of Melanesia,

New Zealand, and Lichfield, were among her ancestors. When I visited New Zealand in 1925 (I represented *Punch* at the Third Imperial Press Conference) many I met said that they recognized 'the Selwyn nose'. One day my brother Sidney, who was in some cathedral with his wife, looked across at a recumbent figure in stone and said: 'Look! there's Alan.' They walked over, and it was a Selwyn. So I laughed heartily when I heard the Hyde Park story about my nose.

Some years later I feebly consented to take part in an absurd debate about divorce (with, it turned out, an audience of teenagers) on television at Manchester. My opponent was to have been a Roman Catholic priest called Heenan, but he was made a Cardinal, and withdrew. The man who replaced him sat opposite to me in the train to Manchester. We discovered this, in the British way, towards the end of the journey. I told him the Hyde Park story, thinking that it would amuse him. It did. He said: 'I know. That was me.'

About my father's side of the family I am not so clear. His name was Patrick Coghlan Herbert Herbert (yes, two Herberts). He was, I have always understood, one of a family of thirteen, one of 'the Herberts of Muckross' in County Kerry, four miles from Killarney. Muckross, I believe, is a beautiful place, with a lake, but I am ashamed to say that I have never been there. My father, on a signet ring, wore the crest of the Pembrokes, who are Herberts too: but I have never gone into that. What is certain is that he was at Trinity College, Dublin, in the days of Oscar Wilde, that after that he came to England and spent his life as a Civil Servant in the old India Office.

I remember with unashamed hostility one of his Civil Servant friends. My two brothers and I were born at Ashstead Lodge, on the corner of Ashstead Common, between Epsom and Leatherhead. Two or three favourite India Office men would come down sometimes for lunch on Sunday. Before lunch we three boys were exposed to the public view for a minute or two, and then whisked back to the nursery. A small Civil Servant called Newmarch – I can see him now, with a moustache that did not suit him – said to me: 'Come along, my little man, come to Uncle Newmarch.' I duly went to him. He took my hands and hoisted me aloft, the idea being that I should perch gloriously on his left shoulder. Unfortunately, he was not skilled at this sort of thing. He flung me over the left shoulder so that I fell head-first on to a brass fender behind him. I spent many weary hours on a 'back-board', and since this episode I have never felt that my head was stuck on in the right place. Never let bachelors play with your children.

I am sure I had a happy childhood at Ashstead. We had a nice garden, a lawn, and a splendid shrubbery for bandits, ambushes and so on. But I can recall few positive pleasures. My mother died of consumption when I was seven and we did not see much of her: but we had a devoted nanny, who lived to look after some of my own children. I was mildly beaten by my father now and then with a large strap for refusing to eat cold boiled mutton or failing to finish my semolina. There were three major nursery foods in those days – semolina, tapioca and sago – without which no child could hope to grow up and be a big man like Daddy. I read in an Analytical Table of Cereal Foods the other day that the detested three had small nutritional merit. Sago and tapioca have some iron but no vitamins at all: semolina did not get a place in the list. My father did not put much zest into the beatings, but he had to obey the nursery. I could have endured much worse to avoid eating cold boiled mutton.

In middle-age I went for fun to a phrenologist in Fleet Street. He told me to my surprise, that I had the qualities necessary for a successful commercial career; the Epsom Bun Story perhaps supports him.

When I was six they sent me to an Infant School in Epsom. Mick, the gardener, drove me in a pony-trap. On the first day we stopped in a traffic-jam (yes, we had traffic-jams then) opposite a gorgeous cake-shop which I had visited with my mother. In the window was a magnetic pile of shiny round Penny Buns. I felt that before this big new experience I must have a Penny Bun. I slipped down, went into the shop and said 'May I have a Bun, please?' 'Certainly, my little man. And how is your dear mother? Maureen, help the little fellow into the trap.' There was no tawdry talk about payment. I marched out with my bun, and young Maureen, with whom Mick the gardener discussed County Kerry and so on and, I think, fell instantly in love. I would not swear who suggested that we make another stop on the way home, but we did. I thought that this was a good arrangement. So, for many weeks, the pleasant routine persisted. Sometimes, on the way home, Mick had a bun too.

Then one awful Sunday I heard grave words passing between my father and mother, '259 penny buns! What is all this? I don't remember seeing a single penny bun in the house.'

So the Idyll of the Buns came to a cruel end. Mick had to content himself with a wave of his whip to Maureen as we passed. As for me, the sages of today, I suppose, could here detect a deep-seated and justified trauma which set the little fellow against Society and the System for the rest of his days. In fact I found my parents' attitude reasonable enough. I was let off with a lecture, and privately, I believe, held up to the Civil Servants as a master of cool effrontery. The odious Newmarch used to cry, 'Hello, Bun Boy' with a friendly leer (but I was not now allowed within five yards of the dangerous man). The worst mischief of this affair was still to come. Maureen married the invaluable Mick and carried him back to Ireland.

Not much to say, then, for my first seven years, which is just as well.

I do not even remember vividly my mother's death at the end of them. She was a good and gentle person, a well-named Beatrice. We were brought up in the Church of England, and duly went to church with her, but in spite of her episcopal ancestry she did not plant any strong seeds of religion in us. I loved the singing – 'The day Thou gavest', some of the Psalms – but the rest did not mean much to me. At that age I do not know why it should: but it is a good thing to be given the chance, to learn the drill, and all my own children had the same opportunity. I found religion quickly enough at moments on the Gallipoli Peninsula, when high-velocity shells approached in France, or doodle-bugs in London. So you may call me a foul-weather worshipper, if you will. Maybe, but I am glad that I am formally entitled to be one of that inferior species.

Now and always, I can say firmly, we three brothers were fond and happy together, and I am quite unable to exhibit any fashionable and instructive family troubles.

I was the delicate first-born, promising brains – my father used to tell Mr Newmarch that one day I should be Lord Chancellor, provided people didn't drop me on my head. Was not my mother's father, George Selwyn, that fine countenance on the staircase, a Lord of Appeal? Sidney Jasper was robust and broad, more of a Herbert, with a face made for the Navy and the shoulders of a Rugby forward. He did go into the Navy through the long routine of those days, Osborne (at twelve), and Dartmouth, and he did play Rugger for the Navy. But he had brains as well. He served in submarines in the 1914 war. He was one of the first twelve seaman officers selected by Lord Fisher to specialize in engineering. He went down in the *Hood*, 1941, then Captain (E) to the Squadron. He had often tried to explain to me his own plans for making H.M. ships less 'sinkable', and the trouble he was having trying to impress those on high. I have no idea of the worth of his plans: but they went down with him in the suddenly-sunk *Hood*.

I do not remember Owen William Eugene quite so well. He, too, was more Herbert than Selwyn. He went through Sandhurst and Woolwich into the Regular Army and was posted missing (a Gunner) at Mons in 1914. So I am the one survivor of the Herberts of Ashstead, Surrey.

At about the age of eight we dispersed to different preparatory schools. Mine was the Grange, Folkestone – you could see the large green grounds as the train passed through Folkestone Central. In those days if you went to school, you went to school – and stayed there. There were no half-term outings, or week-ends at home, no visits from parents. For a child of eight uprooted from his home a term of twelve or thirteen weeks was long and lonely. Yet I should have enjoyed the Grange more than I did. It was well run by a good old scholar called Hussey. Harold Nicolson was there two years before me. C. D. Burney, afterwards Commander Sir Charles, the distinguished officer who invented the paravane (for mine-sweeping), was in my dormitory. We did not think the food was good: but how many schoolboys have thought it good? There was some mild bullying but not for me – except from a rather brutal music-master, who gave his pupils tough 'clacks' over the ear on a cold Monday morning. My chief offence was that I tended to 'practise' Gilbert and Sullivan instead of Czerny's detestable Exercises. But I did learn to play the piano, for which I have ever been grateful, I learned a lot of Latin, and English. I won many prizes. At the Grange and Winchester I acquired in all twenty-four shinily-bound volumes, the Lettres de Madame Sévigné and so on – and two King's Medals – a horrid boy. At the Grange I had some athletic pretensions too. I was a darting inside-right, very proud of the velvet cap the First Eleven wore. It may sound smug, but I remember vividly how one behaved when one scored a goal in those far days. You did not fling your arms in the air, in arrogant exultation, even if it was the goal that won the match. None of your fellows approached you, patted, slapped or embraced you, even your captain. You quietly trotted back to your place, with your modest eyes directed to the ground, as if you were almost ashamed to have attracted special attention. Applause was rightly left to the spectators. I am sorry to see that the disgusting ecstasies of the professional footballer are beginning to invade the cricket field. A famous international batsman comes in. All expect, and many hope, that he will make a hundred. A good ball, or a poor stroke, gives a catch to slip or wicket-keeper, and he is out for two. By the fielding-side, at least, the fall of the hero might be observed in respectful silence, unless the ball or the catch deserves a decorous clap or two. But no, four or five players leap into the air, many pairs of arms are extended to the heavens, there is back-slapping and happy huddling. It is not only the childish self-applause that I deplore. There emerges a note of malignance from the jubilation, as if they are saying: 'Ha! that will teach him to bat against us!' However, the cricketers have still some way to go. I have not seen Cowdrey kiss a wicket-keeper yet – but I have seen those arms go up. It is not cricket, I feel, to crow.

Here again I can support my square opinions with some smug personal testimony. I was the school's top bowler, and if I did not take seven wickets in a match against some other school I was disappointed: but I never leapt aloft or was slapped on the back by mid-off. Many years later I had the honour to address the Surrey County Club, then Champions, at an Oval dinner. I told them how I bowled in my youth, 'off-breaks, very slow and cunning, in a style afterwards adopted by

Laker and Locke' who sat very near. But, alas, these particular powers deserted me at Winchester. I, also, by the way, used to win the hurdle race. Altogether, if I was not happy at the Grange I must have been hard to please.

If it is of interest to anyone I never heard a word about sex at the Grange. Nor did I ever hear a word about sex from my father or mother or anyone in authority over me. Last year, when I had the honour to be made an honorary Freeman of the Borough of Hammersmith, I said: 'Mr Mayor, my wife and I have lived in this Borough for nearly fifty-four years. It must be a healthy neighbourhood. For we have four fine children, fourteen grandchildren, and five great-grandchildren. How all this happened without the slightest assistance or instruction from the B.B.C., I am unable to explain.'

After my mother's death we moved to London, to a tall Victorian dwelling in Argyll Road (No. 4) off High Street, Kensington. It had an enormous basement where a cook and a housemaid, I think a 'parlour-maid' too, worked and gossiped and made tea with our faithful nanny, Miss Deacon. There was never a whisper in those days, even in our modest circumstances, of any difficulty about 'help in the home'. I remember hearing that the cook got £22, but whether that was for a month or a year I wouldn't wager. 'The servants' seemed quite happy, and if one went another came. To us boys it was all as natural and assured as the visits of the postman.

Here my first positive memories of domestic pleasure begin: and what simple joys they were! We had no gramophones, no cinemas, no radio, no television. But I am sure we never made the complaint so often heard today that there was 'nothing to do'. There was much to do. For one thing, we made our own music, hammering away, all three of us, at the piano in the dismal drawing-room, Gilbert and Sullivan, favourite songs like 'The Trumpeter' or 'Until'. Sometimes we played duets. I do not think we read much, but at first there was the *Boy's Own Paper* and G. A. Henty, the splendid *Strand Magazine* and Sherlock Holmes. The big cultural event of the year was the last day of the Christmas holidays when our father always took us to Drury Lane to see the pantomime, with Dan Leno and Herbert Campbell in their prime (I must have been thirteen or fourteen when I saw my first play – Lewis Waller as an escaped convict at the *Adelphi*).

The pantomime, and sometimes the Military Tournament, were the only organized entertainments of the year. There were no parties. We entertained ourselves. We had our five-shilling 'Brownie' cameras, wonderful little things; we did our own developing and printing and carefully pasted our masterpieces into 'Albums'. We marched to the Round Pond in Kensington Gardens, and launched our three small boats on that lake of delight. There were evenings of agony when someone's boat collided with another and was stuck in the middle, or the wind fell and all had to be left deserted in the dusk. I think I had the first of my few mild feelings of envy when I watched the old men launching their beautiful models, great cutters and schooners almost as tall as themselves.

We went to Drury Lane, and to the Kensington Museums, by the No. 9 horse-bus. The Red Bus was always a good adventure. We scampered up the stairs, wet or fine (the top was not covered), eager to get the front seats just behind the driver, who had cheerful talk for all, but especially for boys. We were not so fond of the Underground Railway, for the simple reason that in early days most of the trains were driven by steam, and some of the stations, especially Baker Street, I know not why, were suffocating caverns of smoke. I can still see the smoke surging out through those sloping channels at Baker Street, the coughing porters, the passengers with handkerchiefs over their mouths which were black when they reached the street. I remember the excitement when the first Twopenny Tube, the Central London Railway, electric, smokeless, swift, was opened, though I forget the date.

I remember seeing electric 'broughams' in Hyde Park, but the thought of a Herbert motor-car never occurred to us. Our ambition was to have a bicycle: and, by degrees, on birthdays, we all got bicycles. My father was an earnest bicyclist, a member of the Cyclists' Touring Club. In winter he sometimes took a small cottage near Esher. In summer we always went to the sea-side – to Bognor (not yet Regis), to Colwyn Bay, to Rhyl, to Tenby, to Sea View, to Frinton, to Whitby, to Newquay, to Minehead. All the bicycles went too and there were long and solemn family 'rides', our father like the flagship pedalling with dignity, the brothers, like a destroyer escort, skirmishing ahead or astern. I remember our delight when the 'free wheel' came in. Before that, when coasting down a hill you had to put your feet inelegantly under the handlebars, while the pedals still flew round. The great thing about a bicycle is that you can stop to pick a wild flower or look at a bird, which seldom seems in order in a motor-car. We loved our bicycles and did not sigh for broughams.

There was family bathing too. At more than one of the 'resorts' we used that strange invention the 'bathing-machine'. This was a sort of hut on four wheels which was drawn out through the shallows by a horse till you reached a depth convenient for entering the water. But the main idea behind the 'machine' was not convenience but decency. There was a great High Court case (*Blundell* v. *Catterall**) in 1821. The question was: 'Is there, or is there not, a Common Law right to

* 5 B and Ald. 268.

cross the foreshore for the purpose of bathing in the sea?' The King's
Bench by a majority (Mr Justice Best admirably dissenting) held that
there was not, though it was conceded generously that 'bathing in the
waters of the sea is generally speaking a lawful purpose'. But Mr
Justice Best went further: 'Bathing in the sea if done with decency is
not only lawful, but proper, and often necessary for many of the
inhabitants of this country. There must be the right to cross the shore
in order to bathe as for any lawful purpose. The universal practice of
England shows the right of way over the sea-shore to be a Common
Law right. All sorts of persons who resort to the sea either for business
or pleasure have always been accustomed to pass over the unoccupied
parts of the shore with such *carriages* as were suitable to their respective purposes, and no lord of a manor has ever attempted to interrupt
such persons. . . . Men have from the earliest times bathed in the sea;
and unless at places or at seasons when they could not, consistently
with decency, be permitted to be naked, no one ever attempted to
prevent them.' But the brave Best also said: '*I believe the use of
machines is essential to the practice of bathing. Decency must prevent all females and infirmity many men from bathing except from a
machine.*'*

So you undressed in the damp and chilly machine, and when you
were dressed again the horse came back for you if its rider was kindly
disposed. I forget when the 'machine' departed, but as late as the
1920's I remember a campaign by the Corporation of Eastbourne
against 'macintosh bathers', who instead of using the Corporation's
nice huts undressed with furtive contortions under a raincoat. I wrote
a Misleading Case about the row and quoted Mr Justice Best.

But when in this unmanly manner we entered the sea at last we were
content to swim, or dive, if we had the chance. We did not expect
Daddy to hire expensive motor-boats to tow us round the bay. One
must resist the temptation to deride other people's pastimes, but
'water-ski-ing' causes so much noise, nuisance, and danger to others
that I dare to say it is one of the silliest. Some of the experts array
themselves from head to foot in rubber suits in case they fall in the
water: but a sea-sport in which you insulate yourself from the sea
does not seem to me to make sense. I once saw Sir B. and Lady D.,
thus protected, leave the gangway of their great yacht and make in
turn a stately progress round a Mediterranean bay. It was a graceful
and assured performance: but when it was done each retired into the
yacht without having touched the lovely dark blue water at all. In my
barbarous youth there was nothing like this.

Roller-skating was our other London sport. I specialized in skating
backwards. Years later, at Oxford, when I got my first chance on the

* *Uncommon Law* – page 219.

ice, I found that I could go backwards beautifully but forwards not at all.

Such were our simple pleasures – and, of course, there was the thrilling water chute at the Earl's Court Exhibition. My generation, and later ones too, should be grateful that we were born when we were, and saw that great mushroom, the modern world, appear. In our time Man has made more great strides – forwards and backwards – than in any other seventy years in his history. We have watched his principal wonders grow from minute seeds to monsters; so to us they are wonders still. I can remember the scratchy cylinder they called a 'phonograph', long before the gramophone was heard of. I remember talk about the 'cat's whiskers' and 'the crystal set'. I remember some eager fellow thrusting ear-phones at me. I heard some crackles and a word or two, and I said loftily: 'Very interesting. But I don't think anything much will come of it.' What a prophet! 'It' was the birth of radio, the magic that brought those voices down from the Moon. The three brothers spent too much of their pocket-money on a pilgrimage to Brooklands to see Monsieur Paulhan fly upside down – on which today no boy would spend a penny. I remember the first talkie – London went mad – the theatre, the book, even the gramophone was doomed. I have still to be persuaded that television is really possible, but to the young it is the most natural thing. I hate the coming of 'Space' in general, but I did not fail to goggle for one minute at the Apollo 11 pictures. The grandsons next door would not come out of the garden to see the rocket go up. For many months they had wallowed in 'Dr Who', much more remarkable. While my wife and I were suffering that most painful of the waits, before the 'lift-off' from the Moon, I went out into the garden: and there on the tideway, was my fifth granddaughter, bless her, sailing her *Mirror* about. She was happy, so why should anyone complain? But I thought 'How odd that we old stuffies should still retain the capacity for wonder, and imaginations that can be torture: while the Young seem to have lost them! And how fortunate are we!'

In 1958 (I *think*) I expressed some of these thoughts in verse, but rather more crossly, because the Angry Young Men were raging, and running down their fathers, who had left them so many miraculous toys. At the Oxford Encaenia (Commemoration Day) Mr Harold Macmillan, Hugh Gaitskell, Lord Beveridge, Mr Justice Owen, Chief Justice of Australia, a Scandinavian scientist, whose name I forget, Poulenc, the French composer, and Shostakovich, the Russian composer, received honorary degrees – 'Doctor of This and That'. I had the honour to be No. 6 on the list, a Doctor of Civil Law. At the traditional banquet in Christ Church Hall, attended by all the Honorands, in their new gowns and hoods (very hot), I sat opposite to

Shostakovich, a small, friendly man. I urged him to celebrate this great
day with an Oxford Symphony, but he said he thought some Comrade
had done one already. There is generally one speech only, but I was
asked to follow Mr Macmillan. Often, pitted against the great, Norman
Birkett, for example, or Robert Menzies, I would retaliate in verse.
That night, in the beautiful dark Hall, lit by candles only, I delivered
my long piece, I am proud to say, without using the script: and I
believe it pleased the learned scholars who for fifteen years had
suffered their eccentric Member, and now had done me this great
honour. Some of the last part went like this:

"And now, with terror treading on my tongue,
May I address the Less Contented Young?
I am not one of those who moan and mourn
'It was without our leave that we were born!'
And therefore claim the right to sit and wince
At almost everything that's happened since.
Cheer up, young Tristram, and control your tongue,
For too much anger stupefies the young.
If worldly comforts are a worthy sign
Your generation's miles ahead of mine . . .
We had no gramophone. Oh, how you'd laugh
If you could see the early 'phonograph!'
We had no 'wireless'. Almost I forget
Head-phones, cat's whiskers, and the 'crystal set'.
But I remember saying, I admit,
'I do not think that much will come of it.'
No moving pictures, boys. I saw them come,
And then – can you believe it? – they were dumb!
Yes, yes, I swear, they used to print below
'The hero here is saying so-and-so'.
At last the photographs began to speak
And London had hysterics for a week.
But television, Mervyn, even then
Was not conceived by ordinary men:
Nay, though today I regularly 'view',
I don't believe it's possible, do you?
No motor-buses. Horses dragged us round,
And smoke and sulphur filled the Underground.
No flight. I saw brave Bleriot come over
(A great mistake, I think) from France to Dover.
It took five weeks to Sydney in a ship:
Today, they tell me, it's a weekend trip.
No radar nursed the steamer in a mess:
No radio could flash the SOS.
No penicillin eased the doctor's toil,
And if you had a boil – you had a boil . . .

{ 12 }

Nor did the dentist send us off so soon
But gassed us with a frightening balloon:
And I don't think that angry little men
Got off with 'local anaesthetics' then.
All sorts of ills are easily dismissed
Which would have put us on the danger list.
The surgeons, with a rare, and recent, knack,
Take any organ out, and put it back:
And marvels move among us, old and young,
With but one kidney or a lonely lung.
Mothers receive such long and loving care
That angry babes are easier to bear.
You turn a tap, you poor 'frustrated' kid,
And all the Elements do what you bid.
The siren and the sage of every land
Attend your dwelling place at your command.
All these delights you take for granted, rather –
And have the cheek to criticize your father.
When I was young, dear Cyril, one would meet
The beggar and the blind in every street:
Nor could the humblest of the island race
Proceed to Oxford, or the other place.
All these great wonders of the world you scorn
Have happened, little men, since I was born.
How dare you, then, you bunch of bitter weeds,
Affront your fathers and decry their deeds?
No British young, since British young were new,
Have had such boons and benefits as you.
The talk of war 'unsettles' you, I see:
I've served in two, my lads, and suffered three.
We did not whine and whimper at our doom:
We did not cry 'Frustration!' in the womb.
We saw, and shared, some grandeur in the grime.
Cheer up, my lads – you'll understand in time."

There was a lot more. On the other hand I like to recall some verses
I wrote in 1940 (*Sunday Graphic* 28 July – and in *Siren Song*).

THESE ARE THE BOYS

These are the boys of whom we said
   'They are not what their fathers were;
They have no heart and little head;
   They slouch, and do not cut their hair.'

Yet these like falcons live and die;
   These every night have new renown:
And while we heave a single sigh
   They shoot a brace of bombers down.

{ 13 }

{ 2 }

THE DEEP END

TRULY equalitarian schooling, it seems to me, must produce something like a swimming-bath with no deep end, in which old and young, swimmer and non-swimmer, can march happily about together in three feet of water. In my Election Address of 1935 I wrote: 'There are certain desirable studies which can only be kept alive by the continued existence of private schools for particular sections of society. I have in mind especially the study of Latin and Greek. . . .' There are other special benefits which the best Public Schools have to offer. If the State took them over and kept them exactly as they are, prefect system, examinations, Latin and Greek, chapel and all, I should not object, for this would save many good parents much anxiety and money. But this is unlikely. The prefect system would be undemocratic, the examinations would be cruel and barbarous, compulsory chapel would be intolerable, any intensive study of Latin and Greek, even if reserved for the few, as I think it should be, would be untechnological, retrograde, a waste of public money. Even if half the pupils came from 'working-class' homes the whole thing would be 'socially divisive'. Finally the boarding system would be condemned as undesirable: the scholars would be dispersed to comprehensive schools nearer the pupils' homes, and the school buildings would be handed over to housing estates. So I hope the State will keep its clumsy fingers off them, so long as the old standards survive and anyone can afford to pay for them.

I went to Winchester College in the autumn of 1904 and left after the Christmas term (Short Half) in 1909. I have heard much of Eton, and admire the school greatly: but of Winchester only can I give positive evidence. First of all, there was a healthy tradition of work. For one thing, after, I think, two years, you could be 'super-annuated' – strange phrase, meaning asked to go – if your work was not up to Winchester standards. But more than that, more than any admonitions from the dons, there was a strong urge to work, a respect for work, among the boys or 'men'. If you went to the top of your 'division' you received as much applause as if you had taken five wickets. I was,

I confess, revealed as a 'jig', or clever boy, very soon, rushed to the top of my 'div' and won prizes. But I got no sneers from older men who were stuck at the bottom. On the other hand the prefects kept an eye on those who slacked at work as well as those who were frivolous or lazy in the field. All this was assisted by the structure of the house. No boys had private studies, as, I believe, at Eton. There was one large hall called Toy Room, in which each man – there were forty of us – had his own 'toys'. The 'toys' were small spaces, about three feet wide and deep, with a seat and a flap for writing. Here you pinned your photographs on the wooden partitions, here you kept your books and treasures, here was your own tiny citadel and, if you wished, you could draw a curtain across it against the world, but there was no ceiling so you could not shut out its noise. The evening's 'preparation' period – I think, from 7 p.m. to 9 p.m. – was called Toy Time. All worked quietly alone, the housemaster rarely appeared, but one of the prefects, who had slightly larger 'toys' with real doors, was always on duty, to keep order and quiet and assist the young, if necessary. I remember one Toy Time one Michael Heseltine, a prefect, afterwards a lofty Civil Servant, came to my 'toys' and asked how I was getting on. I must, I think, have confessed my love for W. S. Gilbert's work: for later the prefect presented me with the collected verse of C. S. Calverley, of whom I had never heard. That, without doubt, began my verse-career, which has been so large a part of my life. I began to scribble at once.

All this, by the way, is a big mark for the 'boarding' system. Here were schoolboys doing their 'prep', as schoolboys must all over the world. They were doing it without formality or interference in their own private places, but in ordered peace and quiet, and with a sense of common effort to carry them on. All about them were busy too – that young upstart Jones junior on the other side of the partition might well be stealing a march on you with those quite impossible sums. Fight on! This fruitful tranquillity was guaranteed, I think, five nights in the week. How different from the boy who does his 'prep' at home, in competition with television, gramophone, a noisy sister or chatty visitors, and no one present perhaps who can assist him with his sums!

I remember two other literary events at Toy Time. I was in Cook's House, up the hill, formerly du Boulay's. Arthur Kemball Cook was a large round, genial, lovable man, a fine scholar, a good speaker, mad about Ruskin, and a perpetual pipe-smoker. During my last two years I was senior prefect, and, mindful of the help I had from Heseltine, I took my tutelage duties at Toy Time very seriously. It was whispered to me that Robert Nichols, about three years junior to me, wrote poetry. Old Cook said once in an after-dinner speech that Nichols used to leave his poems about, but that I gave orders for them not to be found. This was unjust. In fact, I nursed the poet and drew him out, I asked to see his work and praised it, even if I did not understand or like it. I was ahead of the world in perceiving a superior talent. He was never happy, I do not know why – nobody bullied him: and one evening he was not in his toys. He had not been seen all day. I had the house searched in vain, and knocked at last at the housemaster's door. No answer, which did not surprise me. Since his wife died the old man often seemed very far away. I knocked again. 'Come in.' I pushed the door open, and a great cloud of tobacco smoke poured out. I could hardly see the great head, lost in Ruskin and smoke. 'Please, sir,' I faltered, 'Nichols senior has run away.' There was a pause while the old man dragged himself from Ruskin to reality: and then the deep voice boomed: 'Send him to me at once.' The poet returned next day.

Cook was succeeded in my time by Charles Little, straight from Rugby, a good man, but stricter than we liked, after 'old Cook's' gentle reign. One evening he said to me: 'Herbert – I found Nichols senior reading a play by Bernard Shaw. You'll stop that, won't you?' I suppose I said: 'Yes, sir' but I fear that I did nothing. Even then, sixty years ago, I was shocked. He did not say '*Mrs Warren's Profession*'. He said: 'A Play by Bernard Shaw.' I think it was *Major Barbara*.

These glimpses, I hope, may suggest that there was some virtue in the prefect system. But there is more. It seems elementary that where you have forty strangers living and working together someone must control and counsel, whether you call him a prefect, a monitor, a lance-corporal, or a shop-steward. The housemaster cannot do what is wanted for, like the colonel, he is too far away. He makes the rules, the prefects see that they are carried out. We were no tyrants: I see us rather as guides and guardians to the young. There was some mild fagging, though the word was not in our dictionary, but I do not remember resenting it as a new man or revelling in it as a prefect. Making tea for the prefects in the library was a good education. I remember no bullying or 'brocking': if there had been the prefects would have stopped it.

The foes of the Public School laugh heartily if you claim that the prefects usefully learn the gifts of leadership. But it is true. Also, by the way, the others learn to be led. The gift of obedience to reasonable commands is by no means to be despised. The evidence mounts that at some of the new Universities there are too many who have learned neither to lead nor to be led. Nor, as some seem to think, is leadership no longer necessary because we have dispersed the Empire.

How many a promising young soldier, threatened with promotion to lance-corporal, is secretly as apprehensive as he is proud? Is he man enough for the job? Has he the knowledge, the understanding, the tact, the temper, the strength to be firm, the sense to be forbearing? When I was made a prefect in my third year, I by no means regarded myself as a leader of men, and thought it a poor appointment. But I believe I did pretty well. It certainly did me good.

Discipline was founded largely on the ancient body of customs which governed the whole school, the 70 scholars in College, and the 400 Commoners in the ten Houses. So no house was an island by itself. 'A bad notion', a thing not done, was a bad notion everywhere. Every 'new man' was attached to an older man who taught him his 'notions', all the rules and customs, all the weird words, and set him on the proper path. In this way he became not a Cookite, merely, but a Wykehamist.

Corporal punishment was available to the Headmaster (but not to the housemaster) and, I think, to all prefects; as I feel, in reserve, it should be. 'Boy must not beat boy' say the reformers. But if Boy is given the authority of Man why not, in due degree, some of his powers? Better a beating, instant humiliation, than expulsion, permanent shame. One may never be heard of in the home, the other may haunt a family for generations. Better then, I say, that Boy beat Boy than that Boy sneak to Headmaster unless the fault is plainly beyond forgiveness or cure. Oh yes, I know some of the objections but these come generally from too-earnest students of sex, who think that every British boy may become a Rousseau.

In my time the awful thing was rare. Certainly there were none of the orgiastic prefectual beatings I have read about in best-selling books. I never met anyone who was birched by the great Dr Burge, or his successor Monty Randall. I was not beaten by anyone; and in my two years as head of the house I chastised one boy only, and that with doubt and trepidation. I laugh when I think of it now. Freddie Someone was in my Gallery (dormitory) where nine 'men' were going to bed. He was a friend of mine, but he had deliberately defied some rule of dormitory discipline – I forget what, nothing wicked – before the whole gallery, and notice had to be taken. But Freddie was 'as tall as I was and only about a year my junior, and when I said, for the first time, 'Bend over' I was by no means confident that he would obey. If he had not, the whole authority of the senior prefect, and all the prefects, would have tottered, and inwardly I quaked. But Freddie, I think, was thinking in the same way, he had been 'trying it on', and was ready to repent. My six strokes were far from being 'six of the best': but Honour was saved and Discipline maintained. I had no more trouble. What a brutal scene!

But if there had been a bad case of bullying it would have been a different story. The prefects would have got together and the punishment would have been far from formal; and how much better than running to the housemaster, who could do nothing but give the bully a 'pi-jaw'. How sad that so many reformers insist on interfering in things they know nothing about.

One of the easy epithets the enemies fling at the Public Schools is 'socially divisive'. As I have hinted, a swimming-bath is socially divisive: those snobs who can swim and dive tend to monopolize the deep end while those poor fellows who can't are cruelly segregated in the shallows. A Petty Officers' Mess is socially divisive: so are the great Trade Unions, especially those which exclude the White-Collar workers.

May I here wave one more flag for the boarding system? Your 'comprehensive' schools (of which I know nothing) may be splendid: but they are local – and for day-boys. A great boarding-school like Winchester brings together 470 boys, not from every class, maybe, but from every county, every corner of the Kingdom, and keeps them together to work, to play, to eat and sleep for more than half the year. You cannot tell me that the result is a hot-house for special plants. Through their far-flung, many-minded parents, mostly in the humane professions, they must at least have a wider view of the world than the day boys of the best of schools.

If we must use such words, I prefer to say that in my time at least Winchester was 'socially educative'. They laugh at 'the team-spirit' taught at the Public Schools. But is not the team-spirit the same thing, fundamentally, as their beloved 'social conscience' – the persuasion that you must not regard yourself alone but spare a thought for Others? One way and another, I believe we did acquire a sharp sense of duty to our neighbours. It was a bad notion to be selfish or superior. The House of Commons is full of Etonians, the Civil Service of Wykehamists. No day school can have bred so many public servants.

My family life was sheltered. Some, I suppose, would call us, idiotically, bourgeois. I might well have remained impregnably bourgeois. But Winchester had a Mission in a poor part of Southampton. We heard sermons about this, contributed to collections, and I went on one of the visits. A small experience, no doubt, but it impressed me. I became aware that domestic servants do not grow like flowers in every home: and this kind of thought followed me to Oxford. Nearly every vacation I made frequent visits to the Oxford House Mission in Bethnal Green, helped humbly in clubs and did odd jobs. I enjoyed especially, at Children's Country Holiday Fund time, escorting up to a hundred yelling children, all bent on suicide, from Bethnal Green to Paddington or Euston. In 1914, when I had done with Oxford, I planned to spend a year at Oxford House and do some real service, but the war stopped that. My wife-to-be was running a club for Oxford House in the early months of the war, and on the last day of 1914 we were married at the Red Church in Bethnal Green Road. I had enlisted in the Navy, and wore bell-bottomed trousers: but they dragged me out of the ranks and made an infantry officer of me. In War Two I enlisted in the Navy again; they tried again to make an officer of me – a Naval Air Force editor – but I stubbornly remained in the ranks. For all this I expect neither earthly praise nor heavenly profit. I merely make the point that a Public School is not always 'socially divisive'.

My dear wife, who has made her entrance prematurely, was – is – a Quilter – Gwendolen Harriet Quilter. In War One her initials G.H.Q. on the railway luggage-rack would attract respectful attention. Her father was Harry Quilter, the artist and collector who used to have rows with Whistler and others. Roger Quilter, that charming, graceful melodious composer, was her cousin. There was talk at one time of our doing a work for the stage together – and I wish we had. I had better make it plain at once that Gwen is a very good wife, mother and grandmother – and a splendid cook, a painter and a musician. I don't suppose I have been the best of husbands, but we did celebrate our Golden Wedding nearly six years ago, and I am beginning to worry about my speech for the Diamond.

Then on Sundays there were two (compulsory) attendances at Chapel. This, I suppose, would be the first thing to go if the 'State' took over: yet it is not wholly irrelevant to social conscience etcetera. Few of us were deeply interested in theology, and the Holy Ghost was a trouble to many. But no one can sit in a beautiful chapel, listening to a fine organ and good singing (especially those pure and soaring boy sopranos) without receiving some spark, some warm glow, in the spirit. The organ rolling round the roof may make a boy say to himself: 'I will be better. I will work harder. I will be kinder to that boring boy who likes me.' To sing a grand old hymn in company is to feel yourself a member of something more important than yourself. To me at least Chapel was always a pleasure: except for a single term, I always wore a surplice, a member of the Choir. I made a stately descent through all the ranks. Soprano, Contralto, Tenor (for not very long) and Bass. Once a term the whole school attended a service in the great Cathedral. Compulsory? Yes. How ghastly!

At Winchester, at last, I heard something about sex – but not again from anyone in authority and not, directly, from any person. No man, woman, or boy ever explained to me 'the facts of life'. We brothers never mentioned them. No one ever got as far as the bees and butterflies. The great secrets came to me slowly by eavesdropping when I was about fifteen. Such prolonged ignorance would now be condemned as a barbarous failure by society – indeed, I suppose it would be impossible today when sex shouts everywhere. But I am not quite sure. If innocence is so precious as they say perhaps the longer it survives the better. It certainly helped me in the early days. I was considered attractive and classed as a 'tart': but my innocence was, rather incredulously, respected. 'Not before the new man.' When knowledge burst, it was exciting, pieced together from hints and whispers, from this clue, this sensation, and that, like the end of a detective story, and at last the grand mysterious experiment. I remember being asked, almost reverently, if this had happened yet, and then being welcomed warmly into the ranks of men. But my innocence still clung protectively, and for a long time – not for ever – it was complained that I was 'pi'.

All this was better, I believe, than these clinical lectures to the young before they are needed or can really be understood. But I do concede that every housemaster at a Public School should assume that any of his new boys may have had parents as reticent as mine, and deliver his own little lecture on the troubles of boys in a world of boys. Such troubles, in my house, at least, were not acute nor common. There were some innocent sentimental passions, as in a girls' school, rough talk and some knockabout fun: there was too little privacy for serious vice to persist. This is forgotten by the foes of the boarding school. From what I read in the papers the virtue of boys and girls who stay at home is not invariably inviolate. The boarding school may be safer. Certainly, while I was at school no boy became a father.

It will be, I fancy, a shocking confession that my wife was the first woman I kissed. I have kissed one or two since, but no more of that. I disapprove of those who kiss and tell.

The life in those days was fairly Spartan. We were up at 6.15 a.m. and every 'man' took a cold shower (compulsory) every day of the year. After that, for the houses up the hill, it was five to seven minutes' walk or trot, down to the first class at School, which was at 7 a.m. Then the walk back before breakfast, the first bite of the day. I wonder if the Welfare State, when it takes over, will keep this up. (My son tells me that it has gone already. Well, I must confess that there were many wintry snivelly mornings when one wished for other arrangements: but no one ever said so.)

'Our Game', the native Winchester game of football, which we played in Short Half, the Christmas term, is a fast and splendid game, but it was tough – rougher, some Rugger players have said, than their own great game, because of the weird equipment. Winchester is more than 500 years old: and very far back, the legend says, when the senior boys first thought of football the sides of the ground were lined by the junior boys. Civilization advanced: the ends of the ground were still open (you scored a goal by kicking the ball over the wide terminal line) but it was flanked by 'Canvas', rope-netting stretched on iron supports about eight feet high. Then, I know not why, parallel to Canvas, and about three feet away, were 'Ropes', a stout rope stretched as taut as an iron bar, and passing through the heads of ten robust posts, just above stomach height. We had scrums, but called them 'Hots'. I was a swift and skilful 'hot-watcher', one of the three scrum-halves in a team of fifteen. When the ball came to rest between the rope and 'Canvas' it was generally a hot-watch who got there first and tried to get it 'out of Ropes'. But if you did not you were soon smothered by the forwards of both sides, all bashing and hacking wildly, your stomach frayed by the rope, your head perhaps against the Post. In my last three years I suffered water on both knees and sprained both ankles. I may have been unlucky: but I cannot imagine the Welfare State exposing the workers' young to such harsh exertions.

I loved 'Our Game', and I wish it could be 'Everyone's Game', for it has as many virtues as Rugger or Soccer but requires much less space. In the last month of the term we played six-a-side, and the three big matches *Houses* v. *Commoners*, *Houses* v. *College*, *Commoners* v. *College* provided some brilliant electric exhibitions. I can see the scene today, the worn saw-dusted arena, under the wintry sun, the old grey wall of Meads, the Chapel Tower, St Catherine's Hill, with its engaging clump of trees, the wild cheers of the supporters, for spectacular kicks or a strong, courageous run.

This gave me much more excitement and pleasure than soccer – or even cricket – but then I was good at it. I well understand the reluctance of those who found it rough and unrewarding. In my third year a man called Stafford Cripps, Captain of Houses Six, gave me my colours as one of Houses Fifteen. (This strange, good man was head of an adjacent house. I met him in the prefects' common room. I met him on the football field: later we were in the House of Commons together for I know not how many years – but I never got to know him. He seemed to live on a distant cloud.) In my last term I was Captain of Houses Six myself, but because of my injuries was unable to play, a sadness which in these days, I suppose, would cause a trauma.

I have said nothing about our mental enrichment. The academic name of Winchester is high and handsome and, I believe, well-merited, though we did not in my day take 'Science' very seriously. It was an old, bad joke that boys who failed to pass in to Winchester went on and got scholarships at Eton. I reject this. The Eton scholars I have known were as formidable as our own seventy gowned ones. These, I believe, get five years' teaching, food and lodging absolutely free, and thus was fulfilled the early promise of William of Wykeham that he would educate the poor. I could do no better than an Exhibition – £40 a year. 'Exhibitioners' went to 'houses' and wore no gown, but Commoners, we all thought, led a better life. College was a swot-house, and gowns were girlish.

Lover of Latin and Greek though I am, I have one complaint, both here and at Oxford, that I was given too much of them. I learned hardly any history and was taken away from mathematics just before I reached those fascinating logarithms, which I had to teach myself with great delight, during War Two. I learned them for the purpose of astronomy, but have used them since for endless everyday reasons, from greyhound racing to the authors' Public Libraries campaign.

Whatever was taught was finely taught, and the Senior Sixth, at the end of your time, was more of a forum than a class, where 'men' and masters discussed the wide world. Dr Burge, Headmaster, was always wise, but I cannot remember what he was wise about.

There was a lively Debating Society, where I remember supporting (or opposing) a motion: 'That in the opinion of this House Art is better than Science.'

The house library was pretty good, but I am hazy about our reading. I did not get much time for reading. My father had started me on Dickens, too soon, I think, but I enjoyed him. About one Thackeray and about one Walter Scott (to this day I have read only one of his works). I do not think I reached Shaw, Wells, Bennett, Galsworthy, Conrad, Hardy and Co. before Oxford: they had probably not reached the library. But Stevenson had; and the general favourites were that splendid row of second rankers, the men of action, Rider Haggard, Stanley Weyman, Marion Crawford, Seton Merriman, Anthony Hope, John Masefield. I wonder how much they are read to-day. They are not highly regarded by lofty literary men: but they told good stories and gave much pleasure. I have noticed that reviewers, who are seldom men of action themselves, seem to resent the action writers. That fine fellow Nevil Shute, Hammond Innes, Alistair Maclean, and others, do not get the marks they deserve from the pundits, however well they sell.

My musical career continued earnestly but not always with honour. In my very first year at the School Concert I was one half of a duet from Handel's *Israel in Egypt*. I stood terrified and tiny on the platform while the orchestra played two pages of preparatory black-note Handel. I then sang flutily:

Their land brought forth frogs

Another page of quavers:

Frogs – Frogs

More quavers, and then:

Even in their kings' places

I then had a rest while the other boy sang, at similar intervals:

Lice – Lice
Even in their kings' quarters.

So for several pages the sad narrative continued. Having read a good many school-stories, I quite expected after this exhibition to be beaten by the Captain of the Football team. It says much for the civilization of Cook's that I received nothing but praise for my fortitude during an inhuman ordeal.

There was a fine Music School with numerous sound-proof rooms, where all could practise, and none could hear if they practised the music of the Savoy. I was eager to learn Harmony, to be able to transpose a favourite tune to a key acceptable to the brothers. But the Harmony master was so unpleasant that I left him after one term: and I have regretted it ever since.

But the saddest thing was the 'Cello Episode. Dr E. T. Sweeting, the splendid organist, choir-master, and head of Music asked for volunteers to play the violoncello in the School Orchestra. I volunteered, I know not why: but I have always loved the velvet voice of a 'cello. The 'cello is an awkward companion. Mine had a great wooden case which porters and cabmen were reluctant to carry, and you had to have a ticket for it. My brothers nobly tried to accompany my erratic boomings in the drawing-room, but my father would ask what on earth Alan was up to. My technique never advanced very far, but I mastered the tremolo, and now and then the velvet voice was heard. But I loved being a member, however humble, of the orchestra. There you are – the team spirit, the social conscience again! I soon determined my policy; I would not be too ambitious, I would attempt nothing beyond me. After all, there were eight or nine other 'cellists. I should never, I feared, be capable of twiddly bits: so I let them pass, 'bowing' madly, of course, all the time. But I would select, far ahead, some nice round long note – a breve? – a semibreve? sometimes there were two or three together. On these I would come in with a splendid boom – the true voice of velvet. I enjoyed this: I was doing no harm, and I was making a modest contribution to the music. When Dr Sweeting tapped his desk and said "Cellos only, please,' I was hidden behind the other 'cellos and went through my usual routine. If there were any wrong notes they did not come from me. Can one, I thought, say more?

Unhappily, the main work in the School Concert was to be the Overture to Mozart's *Marriage of Figaro* and this we practised every Sunday morning throughout the Easter Term. The work, as you may know, begins with a deplorable procession of twiddly bits, played very fast – jigajigajig-jigajigajig diddle, diddle, diddle, diddle and so on. During this unfortunate passage the Herbert 'cello was always absolutely mute: but we had a satisfying boom fairly soon. All went well for some weeks, but then an epidemic of flu struck the school. It hit the 'cellos hardly. One Sunday there were only two 'cellos left: I hid behind a wide boy called Broadhurst and got through. The next Sunday, the faithful Broadhurst was gone. Almost at once Dr Sweeting said: "Cellos only please!' Not one sound emerged. Mozart might never have written the work. I was expelled from the orchestra, and never played in the School Concert.

I thought this was harsh. I was doing no harm. A rank ingratitude, I thought, to a volunteer.

But I have never regretted my innumerable hours of hammering the piano, and I wish that more boys hammered the piano today. I tried a fall or two with Chopin and Mendelssohn; my favourite piece is Handel's Largo, which I used to play on two grand pianos with Malcolm Sargent. It will be played, I hope, at my departure. But even if you cannot hit such heights it is a rewarding thing to be able to keep a simple sing-song going for two or three hours for club or family. What joy we generated at our family huddles round the piano! Many old songs, 'Shenandoah', 'Green Grow the Rushes O', 'Where'er you Walk', 'Who is Sylvia?', 'The Lass that Loved a Sailor', 'Silent Worship', 'She is Far From the Land', and a hundred others; then songs from modern shows, *Carousel* and *Oklahoma*, and some from my own, *Bless the Bride, Derby Day*, and Cochran Revues – the family singing 'God Bless the Family!' was a moving noise; and so, as a rule, to *The Beggar's Opera*, that mine of charming ditties. Michael Redgrave, a neighbour then, and Vanessa his daughter, were ardent choristers – Vanessa would sing full-voice all the evening though she was 'shooting' for a film next day. Odd strangers expressed amazement at these parties. Never before had they seen people making their own music, escaping from the tyranny of mechanical, dictated fun. All this was long before the 'skiffle group' and the Mersey Boys, but the same sort of instinct must have steered them too. My work at the piano was often unworthy, especially in the left hand, and how often I cursed the unpleasant man who frightened me away from Harmony, but I kept the company busy. I owe my modest powers, I feel, to those practising rooms at the Grange and Winchester, both boarding schools. In the Television Age it must be a brave boy who persists in practising the piano at home.

The beauties of Winchester abide with a Wykehamist for ever – the grey old College buildings, the long green stretch of playing fields, dotted with white boys, the water meadows beside them, St Catherine's little Hill beyond, looking down on it all with true Wykehamist modesty. I left the place in 1909 with sadness, grateful for many blessings. In my last year they crowded about me. In the summer term I was awarded the King's Gold Medal for English Verse and the King's Silver Medal for English Speech. There were only four Medals, as a rule monopolized by the scholars. It was unheard of for a mere Commoner to walk off with two of them. My verse was an execrable poem on the earthquake at Messina. The dons at that time were obsessed with earthquakes: the year before, I had won the Junior Maltby prize with a piece of Latin verse on the earthquake at San Francisco. Mr Asquith, then Prime Minister, who had sent two or three sons to the school, presented the Medals, and patiently listened to my spouting, first, Messina and then Macaulay. 'A very spirited oration,' he muttered, as he handed me the Silver Medal.

In the Christmas 'half', my last, I had all the cares of a 'Skipper of Houses Six', selecting and directing the teams, quite a job. I was also working hard for the New College Scholarships Exam. Once more I could do no better than an Exhibition: but I was surprised that I did as well. 'A life,' as Lady Bracknell said, 'full of incident.'

I hope that this rough and rambling account may please a few friends and even persuade some enemies. I am only one man, and I have known only one Public School; so my evidence may be discounted accordingly. But my own mind, at least, is clear. The Public School is like many of our strange English inventions; the pernickety may pick holes in it, but it stands, it works: not by accident but because in essence it is good. I make no sentimental nostalgic appeal for it: I do not merely say 'Why not leave it alone?' I assert that it holds much positive and fruitful merit, that the nation would be the poorer without it. When I say that, I do not care if the pupils be the sons of dukes or dustmen – it will benefit both: and if they could be there together so much the better. So far from abolishing the Public Schools I would, if I could, make more.

ξ 3 ξ

OXFORD – AND AFTER

'WE *know more*, and the more we know the more disillusionment, dissatisfaction, and frustration we feel. We are better placed to make informed judgements, and we are disregarded the more readily' ('A Student' – letter to *The Times*, 14 October 1969.)

'The first target for reform that was chosen by those of us who plotted some form of student protest three years ago was *representation in the decision-making structure* . . . our isolation *from decision-making . . .*'
(Mr Colin Crouch – a well-written and moderate article in the *New Statesman*, 31 October 1969. But what a title – 'The Role of Student Power!')

Who can say anything new about Oxford? I was at New College from 1910 to 1914, one of the fortunate survivors of the generation that went down in July and rushed into the Army in August. I can confirm the reports that many have made about the magic of the dreaming spires, the grey old quadrangles, the quiet lawns and flowered courts. It was in those far days a delight, a dream, merely to walk about the streets. The motor-bicycle had just appeared, hired out by a man called Morris in Holywell Street: but the horse-trams, like gondolas, ran down the High, and 'traffic problems' were not known. Inside the colleges the ancient charm and calm survive. New College with its great garden bounded by the City Wall, Worcester with its lake, Magdalen, Christ Church, Wadham and others are unforgettable corners of dignity and beauty. But I find it painful now to walk about the place. The busiest streets, even the sacred 'High', remind me of Hammersmith Broadway; the others with the parked regiments of cars make it, I say to myself, a city of dreaming tyres.

As an Exhibitioner (receiving £40 a year) I had to continue with the Classics and took Honour Moderations. I had had about enough of my beloved Classics by then and thought that five terms of them was too much. But I got a not very good Second, so I may be prejudiced.

Then I turned eagerly to the law, and finished with a very good First (11 alphas out of, I think, 13 papers) in the Honour School of Jurisprudence. I was still a 'swot', you see, but not a recluse. I played some soccer, a lot of lawn-tennis, and sometimes captained the 'Nomads' in village cricket matches. Now and then I ran with the Beagles (the Prince of Wales was in the same pack) but never saw a hare. I made reluctant speeches at the Union and was elected secretary (Harold Macmillan, I think, was Librarian the same term) but then I abandoned it to concentrate on 'Schools'. From first to last I enjoyed Oxford, and am grateful still.

I do my respectful best to understand the present discontents of 'students' (a word we did not know – we were 'undergraduates' or 'junior members of the University'). In two ways, I do believe, we were better off than many of them are today. One, the tutorial system. H. L. Henderson, for the Classics, and Professor de Zulueta, for the Law, were my personal 'tutors'. They were both Top Dons. I went to their rooms, I think, twice a week, I read them Essays and we discussed them. They would advise too on any points that puzzled me in the lectures I punctually attended – Carter at Christ Church, Cheshire at Brasenose, and dear little H. W. B. Joseph, New College, for Logic. On any personal problems they were ready to help as well. So one did not feel that one was a lone swimmer in a hostile ocean of books. 'One Man – One Tutor', is, I imagine, an impossible luxury in the swarming Universities today: but One Tutor – Four Men would be something. I am sure that the system is good.

Second, the physical conditions of existence. For three of my four years I fortunately lived in College – two in the part absurdly called New Buildings, New College, not far from the famous H. J. Laski – one year in the glorious Garden Quad, and one in 'digs' in Holywell Street with five friends from different colleges. I had to walk about a quarter of a mile in a dressing-gown to get a bath, but a friendly 'scout' brought breakfast to my rooms, a lordly benefit. You could lunch and dine in Hall, and if you were a home-bird need never go out of the College. This must give a man a sense of membership that he cannot get if he lives in lodgings, perhaps uncosy, and travels to his college as you travel to the office. If this is a London sore I sympathize but I am not surprised. I should not myself have started a university in the heart of London. (Nor, by the way, should I have expected a school devoted to economics and sociology to have a smooth existence. All adult economists must be mad, or the world would not be in such a mess. It seems a shame to expose the young to such upsetting studies.)

But I am still baffled by some of the other demands. The vocal students seem to want much more than we had. I cannot understand why they want, or why they deserve it. The conceit of their claims is shocking. 'The Role of Student Power!' It would be as sensible to talk about the Role of Tadpole Power. 'We *know* more . . .' they tell us arrogantly. We also hear that they care more. They care so much, some of them, that their studies become 'irrelevant'. 'The argument runs that in a world with problems like Vietnam there is no time or place for reflective study. Participation in the struggle is the only valid activity.' There must be 'involvement'.

Mr Crouch sensibly dismisses this as a pernicious doctrine. 'The main object of university life must remain the pursuit of academic excellence.' This, strangely enough, was our belief in the old-fashioned years of 1910–14. This was why I abandoned my activities at the Union just when I looked like getting somewhere. I preferred the chance of getting a First in Law to the chance of becoming President of the Union. But this does not mean that we spent our days up among the dreaming spires, or were indifferent to the world beyond them. I coldly deny that the boys and girls of today either know or care more than we did. Those were exciting times – Lloyd George's famous Budget, battles about poverty and wealth, about women's suffrage, about the House of Lords, about Irish Home Rule, about Ulster. I remember Lloyd George himself coming to address a tumultuous meeting at the Union, and saw those pheasants thrown over the wall, a political jest the point of which I forget. In one debate I spoke myself (very badly) just before the great F. E. Smith. (This was a disaster. 'F. E.' had a train to catch, I talked for too long, and the President passed notes down telling me to shut up and sit down. But I had prepared my speech, and lacked the experience to cut it short.) The theme, I think, was Tariff Reform, and that was then a debate as cosmic, as controversial, as the Common Market now. Also, in the background, there was always Germany, the Measurements of Fleets, the demand for eight Dreadnoughts – 'We Want Eight' – and so on. Among the five good fellows in my 'digs' were Gilbert Talbot, President of the Union, a natural statesman who, if he had not been killed in the war, would undoubtedly have been a Conservative leader, and Walter Monckton, also President of the Union. We never stopped talking politics: we talked politics at breakfast. We met many other statesmen, one Harold Macmillan, one Robin Barrington-Ward, afterwards editor of *The Times*, one Duff Cooper, one Philip Guedalla, a brilliant and biting Liberal, one Bobby Palmer, a Selborne, and another safe bet for the Conservative Front Bench. We sat on the floor with mulled claret at the Canning or Chatham Club and settled the future of the world: and when some London light came to address us we felt as 'involved' as they were. We knew, of course, that we were always right: but we were neither surprised nor pained if the London statesman 'disregarded' us, much less 'disillusioned and frustrated'. We did not think so much of ourselves.

I have just read an interview with the new Vice-Chancellor of Oxford, Dr Alan Bullock, in which he makes the same reply to the charge of monastic irrelevance (*The Times*, 1 November 1969): 'If you walk round you do not feel that you are in an effete, medieval cloistered backwater. Our links with public life are almost unique. Oxford has always been a very political university. It belongs to Britain in the twentieth century and it is just as full of contradictions as Britain in the twentieth century.'

Nor, so far as I can remember, did we ever make any demands or complaints for ourselves. At New College we chose (as a rule, without a vote) a Steward of the Junior Common Room, a sort of senior prefect, the undergraduates' voice, and if any small trouble arose within the College he would discuss it with the Dean, the Don for Discipline. We had to be back in College by twelve midnight; it was a pity if you were late, had to hammer on the gate and be reported, or climb in adventurously over the City Wall. But we thought the rule was perfectly reasonable, as I do still, remembering Mr Crouch's dictum that 'The main object of university life must remain the pursuit of academic excellence'. For the same good reason the presence of ladies in the College was not encouraged after dark. The College was *in loco parentis*, we were *in statu pupillari*, and did not resent it. Were we a meek and cowardly crowd? It did not seem so in 1914. When I walk through the Garden Quad today I cannot remember all the names that bounded out from the staircases or sat in the windows. But those that I do remember were all extinguished in the war. Were they a generation made feeble by 'paternalism' and unreasonable discipline? I think not.

Certainly there was never a thought of challenging the central authority of the University. We should as soon have thought of challenging the Equator. If the Proctors said you must wear a gown in the streets at night you knew that it was said for good reason and did not childishly rebel. If they had come to us and said: 'Look here! We want to give the undergraduates some "representation in the decision-making structure"' we should have said 'Good heavens, no! We have quite enough to do. "Decision-making"? That's the dons' job. Leave us alone!' I should have added myself: 'The undergraduate's existence on the average is for three years – sometimes four. In his first year, evidently, he can not know enough to "make decisions" about anything that matters; in his second year he has settled to his work but has embarked on other activities, speaking at the Union, acting in Shakespeare for the O.U.D.S., running, rowing, tennis, golf, and he has no spare time to sit on committees: in his third year he should be concentrating on a successful end to his academic career. Moreover, dear Dons, you can't tell me that you'll let the boys make any decisions that matter. If I come in will you on my motion reduce the period of Honour Mods from five months to three months? What a hope! So your committees will be a waste of more fleeting, precious, irreplaceable time at Oxford.'

Who knows? The students of today may be as they clearly believe, a sager, and a stouter breed. The idea of 'joint staff-student control' seems to be accepted in some staff circles too. If so good luck to them – and I look forward to Midshipman Power in the Royal Navy.

But with the greatest goodwill I still cannot discover what sort of 'decisions' the students hope to share and sometimes control. I pay them the compliment of supposing that they will not be merely 'Administrative' matters like the time they have to be back in college or the time the ladies have to leave their rooms. So does Mr Colin Crouch who speaks many thoughtful words on the subject of 'Content of Courses', and the various but vague reforms his colleagues advocate. They baffle him too. The charter of the National Union of Students, he tells us, asserts that: 'All academic courses must reflect the needs of society.' This, in the minds of some students, might well mean the institution of an Honour School of Journalism to replace the old-fashioned Greats' School: and such a 'decision', I feel, is best left to the dons. Courses must be 'relevant'. But relevant, he asks, to what? Then he speaks of the new demand 'for an ethical basis to education . . .', 'the complaint is that education leaves out the great ethical issues of life, and concerns itself merely with the acquisition of specialized techniques. It is held to be one-sided, leaving out man's emotions and moral sensibilities.' The Schools of Law, History and Philosophy, I should have thought, have a reasonable 'ethical content': and what about Sociology, the grand study of the London School of Economics?

Then there is 'the demand for commitment' . . . 'The disciplines of academic life are seen as a contrivance by which the biases of the capitalist world are impressed upon intellectuals; their intellectual discipline somehow alienates them from their "real" selves in much the same way as industrial routine affects a factory worker. Bizarre though their ideas seem they are influential in many areas of student dissidence. If the more one studies the more one becomes subject to the system's biases, runs the argument, then obviously the less one has studied in orthodox channels the more qualified one is to have "real" knowledge; *therefore students should have at least equal control over academic matters as academic staff.*'

I like 'therefore' and I love 'at least'.

Mr Crouch says well: 'There are dangerous implications in this, not least the insistence that men in universities should continuously make clear their moral commitments, and that academic work should be suffused with such expressions. There could be no surer way of undermining the freedoms of the University and its ability to contain within it a wide variety of people with different and conflicting commitments. This coexistence is only possible because of a general agreement not to saturate the whole atmosphere with lofty and passionate moral stances.'

Game – set – and match! Mr Crouch, a good friend of the student, and a father of student protest, can find so little good to say for all these 'bizarre ideas' that I feel absolved from trying. The poor students he quotes seem to be lost in a web of words.

But there must be some fire down below to have caused so much nonsensical smoke. I suspect that, like other things, the Universities are growing too big. The student population of Oxford was 10,700 in 1968; on present plans it will expand to 11,500 students by 1976–7 and to 13,000 by 1982 (*The Times* 1 November 1969). In my day it was more like 2–3,000. The bigger the ship the more lonely the passenger feels. New College, my Warden, Sir William Hayter, tells me, has climbed back to standards that had to lapse after the war. It is again One Tutor – One Man (according to subject): and most men have at least two out of three years in College. At London, I believe, it is more like One Tutor – Six Men, and the students are scattered in residential hotels and lodgings. I hear of little trouble at Oxford, but lots in London. Have the sage students, I wonder, any plans for making Oxford less big – for moving London into some nice place in the country?

I have myself a contribution to make to University affairs which no student body so far as I know, has mentioned. This is the introduction of the University Franchise, and the University Member in the House of Commons. I was for fifteen years (1935–50) one of the two 'Burgesses' for Oxford University. The undergraduates had no votes at the Election but the politically minded took great interest in the business, and the moment they took their degrees they became University electors. The tradition was 'No speeches' (likewise 'No posters' and 'No canvassing'). But in 1935 the young Conservatives invited all the candidates to make one speech. The great Lord Hugh Cecil loftily declined; Mr Stocks, the excellent Labour candidate accepted; I appeared at the last moment and they packed the Union Hall for me. The speech began outrageously:

'Mr Chairman – if all the innumerable sons of Oxford, fitted to so many tasks, equipped with so many weapons, were summoned home from the far corners of the earth and assembled in this historic Hall tonight, I suppose that the most searching scrutiny by the most scrupulous and exacting critic would fail to discover one who was so manifestly designed by Providence to be the Parliamentary representative of Oxford University as the shy and modest person who stands before you.'

I don't think there was a vote in the House: but they all had fathers, and uncles; and when they took their degrees they all became my constituents. I always felt that I represented the Young as well as their elders and worsers. In April 1939 Mr Hore-Belisha moved his motion in the House of Commons for the introduction of peace-time conscription. By a strange chance that evening the Oxford Union were debating the motion: 'That this House is in favour of conscription' – which meant that they themselves would be conscripted. I was then 'Senior Burgess', Lord Hugh Cecil having retired. I thought it my duty to hear what the young men had to say and, for once, I arranged a pair with the Government Whips. Liddell Hart (against the motion) and Randolph Churchill (in favour) spoke, and the young men duly carried the motion. I wish that this episode was as well remembered as the silly 'King and Country' affair.

There are many good reasons why the University representation should be restored. An immediately topical one is the link that it would provide between the great and growing world of students and Parliament. After the troubles of 1968 and 1969 the House of Commons lumberingly wound itself up and sent a Select Committee round the Universities to find out what was going on and report. If the University Members had still existed they would have been doing the job long before. There was one Member for London University. He would have gone to that nest of nonsense the School of Economics. He would have sought out the malcontents and talked to them. He might not have persuaded them to go slow but he would have formed a view about their sincerity and the weight of their grievances, and if they had any real message for Parliament he would have undertaken to deliver it. Then, more important, he would have met the contents and moderates. These, you will remember, were bullied by the Press for not standing up and showing that they were the majority, not jumping on the wild men. They replied, when they could, that their one desire was to get on with their work, and they did not want to waste good time on continual meetings, committees, and butt-ins. The Member would have said: 'You needn't do that. Hold one meeting. Let me have the terms of your resolution and the voting figures, and I will see that the House of Commons gets your message too.'

Thus, the aggrieved undergraduate, or 'student', would feel that he had a direct approach to the rulers, which he does not have today. There would be no point in his marching angrily to Downing Street:

he would have a right to walk quietly to Westminster and ask to see his Member – or Member to be. But he would have to talk sense or his Member would not listen for long.

But this is not the main reason for restoration. I did my best to state the case for James I's idea (it was he who first summoned advisers from the Universities) in my book *Independent Member** (1950). I also said a few words about our stupid and spiteful expulsion from Parliament.

But I have travelled too far from 1914. I enjoyed Oxford and am grateful still. I wish good fortune to the Open University, but it will not, I feel, put the other Universities out of business. For it must lack companionship, the great key to Oxford – and 'the other places'. Companionship even in work. A summer evening in the Garden Quad – I look out of my window at the quiet lighted windows across the quad: behind one of them, or two, is another Law-man, puzzled too perhaps by the judgement of the House of Lords reported in *The Times* today. I step across and we unravel together. (That, by the way, was one of the charms of the Law School, its topicality. Answers to ancient problems might emerge on the morning of 'Schools'. One, I remember, did.)

The lively talk at No. 8 Long Wall where I spent my last year was not all about politics, the Union or games. Gilbert Talbot was reading 'Greats', so was Jack Parr (afterwards a Winchester don), so was E. Besley (afterwards a judge in Cairo). Walter Monckton was reading History. Augustine, Justinian, Descartes, Disraeli, Lloyd George, and Asquith competed for attention at the breakfast table. It was, at a lower level, the tutorial system again, an exchange of information and understanding which the lonely fellow will not get from his television set.

Companionship in the learning of life. Men from Winchester swilling cocoa with men from Manchester. It was sometimes said that in a big place like New College old Wykehamists and Etonians tended to huddle together. This was not true, I know, of my lot of Wykehamists, or at least the scholars. There was a delightful Balliol don, 'Sligger' Urquhart, wise, witty, gentle and kind. To his rooms for light but luminous talk went the bright boys from all the colleges, and there they learned a lot. No Television University will provide a 'Sligger'. Then there was the companionship of the clubs, the running of them, the rows. I was myself, for a term I think, secretary of the New Tory Club.

The companionship of games, even for those that did not play them. One of the lasting pictures in my mind is Ronnie Poulton, the great three-quarter (or was he a half?) snaking through enemy forwards, the ball held well ahead of him, as if he were an invisible man. Even a

* Methuen.

Greek scholar, who had never kicked a ball, could scarce forbear to cheer. Ronnie was 'Oxford', so was the Greek scholar, thinking of Sparta. Television will never bring the twain so close together.

The wild 'Bump Supper' – New College Head of the River. Too much noise for the Greek scholar, perhaps, but he drank his glass of port and admired the great bonfire just under my rooms in the Garden Quad. I forget how it began but I sometimes made Tower Hill speeches from that window to the crowd round the fire – a character called 'Richard Price'. I also delivered mock sermons in the style that surprised London so much about fifty years later in *Beyond the Fringe* – my favourite text was 'And they cast off their clothes and threw dust in the air'.

Companionship in the beautiful chapel listening to the lofty music, companionship in the great dark hall, chattering, 'sconcing', and complaining about the food.

First, no doubt, for this smug fellow came work and the pursuit of knowledge. All else was a happy background, but, more than that, a vital inspiration. The chase could not have been so keen if I had sat at home with a television set. I have often been pleased with myself but never so pleased and puffed as I was when I heard that I had won a first in Law. I walked about like Hector or Ulysses. It seemed to me that this was the peak of human achievement. What else was there for a man to do?

Three or four weeks later I was an 'Ordinary Seaman' doing squad drill at H.M.S. *Crystal Palace*, and washing up on my 'cook' days in the steaming caverns of Lyons kitchens.

But in that elated month my young man's fancy lightly – lightly? no, damn it – turned to thoughts of love. On the top of Campden Hill, under Chesterton's Water Tower, there was a tennis club. Gwendolen Quilter was playing on one court and I on another. Her story is that she heard a magical voice call 'Forty-love!' (or it may have been 'Thirty-fifteen!') and that began it all. The truth is that I had had my eye on her for some time, for she had friends at New College and I had regarded her, respectfully, from a distance, here and there.

A close friend of mine at New College was another Wykehamist, Francis ('Cherry') Newbolt, the son of the poet, Sir Henry, who wrote 'Drake's Drum', 'Play Up' and other stirring songs. He had a modest but delightful house at Netherhampton, a mile or so from Salisbury. I stayed there, with others, through the last weekend in that pregnant July. There was much talk of 'War or Not?' Sir Henry was always optimistic, calm, and confident. If there was a war we should win it, of course. The others left early on the Monday, but I stayed for a mid-day train. It was a superb morning. When he had read *The Times* Sir Henry proposed a game of bowls. He was very good at this game but

I was not. At the first go he cunningly assembled his bowls (I forget how many) round the 'jack' – is it? – so that it could not be seen. The telephone rang in the house and he went in. I was left alone on the peaceful sunny lawn where nothing was to be heard but birds and bees, and I remember thinking 'That ring was about the war'. Out came Sir Henry, his lean face as calm as usual, 'War has been declared,' he said. 'Your turn.' I don't know whether he was thinking about Drake, but I was. I picked up the heavy bowl, and wondered what to do. What exactly, I wondered, did Drake do on a similar occasion? By cunning, I was sure, I should achieve nothing: I should probably get nowhere near the jack. My only hope was unskilled, immoral brutality: and would not this at the moment fittingly express our defiance of the enemy? I flung the great missile with an accuracy that astonished me, and all that circle of black shining mahogany was dispersed into beds and bushes all round the compass. Only the little white jack miraculously remained.

I rather feared that Sir Henry, a serious player, would disapprove of this disgraceful throw. All he said was 'But you missed the flagship'.

I went back to London, to the Oxford House Mission in Bethnal Green. I had promised to stay there for a year, doing what I could. When not bringing bliss to the East End I would learn some more law, do my Bar Exams, and perhaps go for a Doctor of Civil Law next summer. Jack Parr, my best Oxford friend, was there already.

But in a week or two all promises and plans were forgotten. I bicycled over to Lambeth and enlisted as an Ordinary Seaman in the Royal Naval Volunteer Reserve. When I got back to Bethnal Green Jack Parr said 'Why that?' I said 'Because I've got a brother in the Navy – we might meet.' This, at that moment, was not very practical, for Sidney was then in submarines: but blow me, only about ten months later he did come ashore from some great ship off the Gallipoli Peninsula. I took him up to the front line (in his whites, provoking the Turkish snipers) so my Lambeth reasoning was not so silly. In a day or two Jack Parr agreed to join me in the Navy. This was very good of him for he was an old Officers' Training Corps man and should have gone for a commission in the Army at once.

We just missed Antwerp and were sent with the first 200 to H.M.S. *Crystal Palace*. We were a mixed lot of volunteer novices like myself and tough Fleet Reservists, husky stokers, 'stripeys', and ex-petty officers. I shall never forget my first encounter with His Majesty's Armed Forces. There had been all summer a great Imperial Exhibition at the Palace. The public were still strolling about the sunny gardens and enjoying the sideshows. We were paraded before Commander Rupert Guinness who solemnly read to us (I think) the Articles of War. He was difficult to hear sometimes because of the merry-go-round airships whizzing just behind us. The Articles seemed to be a long list of offences for which 'the penalty is death, or such other punishment as may be etc. etc.' There were so many of these that the sense of solemnity gradually dwindled. I can't remember what I thought about. I am sure at least that I felt no self-pity or alarm, only a sort of content and some excitement. Jack Parr, standing beside us, had taken a First in Greats, a feat much loftier than my little First in Law. I am sure that neither of us felt that we were wasting our great intellects by enlisting. I have seen none of the versions of 'Oh What a Lovely War!' Its message, I gather, is that young men like Jack and myself were duped into the forces by damsels singing patriotic songs or bullied in by peremptory posters. I, at least, was not there because of Kitchener's pointing finger, and I don't think the recruiting ditties had then begun (those ditties, by the way, which seem so funny to the audiences today seemed funny to us at the time – and later we howled them with affectionate derision before we went up into the line). No, I was calmly persuaded that we had gone to war for a just cause, and that I ought to be in it, especially as both my brothers were in it already. I was very glad that I had joined the Navy, I would sooner be a sailor than a soldier, if I had to be either: and I hoped we should soon be learning seamanship on the Crystal Palace lake, signalling, knots and splices, and so on. I read in some young man's 'column' recently that the 1914 War was 'the most obscene and shameful episode in our history'. If anyone had told us that sunny afternoon that we had offered to take part in an obscene and shameful episode we should have been highly surprised: nor, four years later, though four years wiser, should we have agreed with the description. We had seen much that was obscene at Gallipoli, the Somme, and Passchendaele (which I was fortunate to miss) but nothing shameful. Would the war have been less obscene and shameful if we had lost it, if the British Fleet had steamed over to Heligoland to surrender or scuttle, if the people under British rule had been handed over to the gentle Germans? How I dislike these anaemic belittlers of our past!

The public stared; the airships whirred: the last of the offences for which 'the penalty is death' rolled over us, and we found ourselves carting hammocks full of blankets about, which is the principal employment in any naval barracks. We slept in hammocks in the vast 'Canada' building. Recruits poured in from the North and soon the hammocks were slung so close that you had to dress and undress underneath them, and when one man stirred in his sleep thirty hammocks on either side stirred like the leaves of the tree. An outbreak of 'spotted fever' (meningitis) had every encouragement.

All was pleasantly naval, the buglers, the flags, the ceremony, the language: we ate at mess-decks, and on leave we 'went ashore' into

Sydenham. But soon it emerged that we were not bound for the sea. The Benbow Battalion was to be part of the Royal Naval Division which Mr Churchill had created, on the lines of the Naval Brigade in the South African War. They taught us no seamanship. This was a severe disappointment. But at last the seaman's uniform arrived, and it was exciting to wriggle into the historic rig, that looks so simple but is so complicated. The adjustment of the black silk scarf and the blue tapes that secure it has to be studied, the collar is a separate garment, and no seaman can get it quite right without the assistance of another. But now we were really in the Navy. On the first day I proudly stepped 'ashore' in uniform and climbed a bus – I was going to show myself to Gwendolen Quilter – a man whispered to me: 'Is that right, Jack, the *Thunderer's* gone down?' I refused to tell him.

One day I took Gwendolen Quilter down to Bethnal Green to meet the Head of Oxford House, the Reverend F. A. Iremonger. He was the most compelling clergyman I ever met. As the sailors say (or did I invent it?) he could have charmed an anchor through the hawse-hole. No heathen could have withstood him for more than a few minutes. I always wondered why he never became a Bishop. I was not surprised to hear, a few days later, that Gwendolen Quilter was to be in charge of a Women's Club under the House.

We had not long learned our rifle-drill when I marched through the City, with fixed bayonet, in the Lord Mayor's Show. Still more alarming was Lord Roberts' funeral. Some of us were warned in our hammocks one night to turn out at 6 a.m. next morning for funeral drill. Whatever next? It was a cold and frosty morning. The rifle was not yet to any of us such a familiar friend as it was to become, and funeral drill is complex and difficult. One drill in a frosty dawn is really not enough. But we were to represent the Navy and march ahead of the Guards.

Too soon we were standing, in a bad dream, along one side of Northumberland Avenue. I can see the gravel that covered the road, the misty sun, the solemn people. On our right were the Guards. What, I wondered, will they think of us? How many of our caps, or even bayonets, will fall off. While we waited, we muttered anxiously about the contortions we had been taught at dawn, and tried to recall the sequence. 'On the command One . . .' 'What the hell do we do next?'

Then there happened a terrible thing. One of the Guards, to our right, dropped his rifle. 'Poor devil,' we thought. But worse was to come. A corporal with a file of men (two) approached the wretch and marched him away. I can see them now disappearing into the mist of Trafalgar Square.

Nobody will believe this story. Well, perhaps, it was a dream.

Then, suddenly, we were falling in, the bands began and away we went, the humble Guards astern of the Navy. I am proud to report that the Navy came through very well – not a cap lost, not a rifle dropped. As we trudged up Ludgate Hill, I caught the eye of two Guards Officers, New College men, with drawn swords, merely 'lining the streets'. We exchanged a discreet and delicate Oxford grin. I never saw them again. Winston Churchill inspected his infant force, and the Palace gardens, a mass of motionless sailors, must have been a pleasing sight.

They started a Scout section, and put me in charge of it. I am not sure why. I was made an Acting Leading Seaman, and wore a little red anchor on my left sleeve. This gave me as much pleasure as my First in Law. I took the appointment very seriously, learned semaphore and Morse, studied map-reading and military sketching, marched my scouts round Sydenham and Dulwich, and tried to pass my learning on to them. I saw Gwendolen Quilter rarely and briefly, mostly in cafés or restaurants, and she has since mildly complained that I spent too much of our courting time trying to teach her Morse, tapping with a spoon on cups or glasses.

But on 10 December we became engaged, without the aid of Morse; the parents conspired; and on 31 December we were married. The angelic Iremonger married us in the Red Church in Bethnal Green Road, Gwen in a fine conventional white dress, me in my bell-bottomed trousers and my little red anchor. All Gwen's good coster-women from the club were there, and as we walked down the aisle one of the lads from Oxford House played 'Every nice girl loves a sailor'. We had a honeymoon of four days in the Fulham Road, during which, I am told, I studied the stars and we practised semaphore; and Gwen learned cooking.

Back to H.M.S. *Crystal Palace*. Gwen took a room not far from the Palace: unhappily it was on the road to the cemetery. The 'spotted-fever' was raging, and almost every day a gun-carriage under the White Ensign carried the latest victim past my poor wife's window. What a time the young war wives had! Two – three – times a week I would get leave in the evening, and take one or two of my sailor friends for eggs and bacon, and songs round the piano. We sang songs like 'The Trumpeter' which must have given my musical wife much pain.

In the New Year I was hauled out of the ranks and ordered into the Officers' Training Class, under a wonderful Sergeant Major (after-wards Colonel) Levey of the Guards who made one realize why the Guards are so good. He was fierce but friendly, and the foundation, I believe, of the fame the Royal Naval Division won. By trying to imitate his 'word of command' I acquired quite a convincing bellow myself, and began to enjoy manœuvring a company. I passed the exam, with about thirty others. They made us sub-lieutenants, put me into khaki (which I resented) and sent me to a muddy camp in an amphitheatre at Blandford in Dorset.

I was sent to the Hawke Battalion. The breezy Leslie Wilson, its Colonel, once a Marine, had for some years been the Chief Government Whip, and he had a wonderful way with the General Staff, a bland mixture of courtesy and cajolery. His Adjutant was Douglas Jerrold, a descendant of the *Punch* pioneer. Vere Harmsworth, younger son of Lord Rothermere, commanded B Company. In the camp, too, were the famous, the truly 'fabulous', Freyberg and Ock (Herbert) Asquith, of the Hood Battalion, generally next to us in battles, Shaw-Stewart, and, I suppose, Rupert Brooke (but I never met him). Here too was Beak and others who were to win V.C's.

Gwen took rooms in a cottage at a charming village called Tarrant Monckton, and I got away when I could. I remember still one enchanting Sunday expedition to Shaftesbury, the little city on the hill. I was appointed Scout Officer, and had got seriously to work on the stars. I would madden Gwen by dashing outside on a cold night to identify Vega or Capella. You laugh? Then listen. One night in the line in France, when we were lying opposite Lens before we went down to the Somme, the Second-in-Command, Commander Fairfax, and the Adjutant came back to Battalion Headquarters with a great tale of a strange light they had seen over the enemy lines. It seemed to change from green to red and they thought it might be some devilish sort of signal to the artillery. I was then Assistant Adjutant and responsible for preparing the daily Intelligence Report. They gave me the map-reference and, with approval, I put this mysterious light into the report. It duly appeared in Brigade Intelligence, and Divisional Intelligence, and even Corps Intelligence Report. The next evening I got permission, as Scout Officer, to go up to the front line and study the alleged mystery. Jerrold went with me. The moment I saw the light I said: 'That's the star Capella. Look at it through the "glasses" and you'll see it does seem to change colour all the time. I believe it is two – or more – stars seen together.' But for my learned intervention the mysterious light, I am sure, would have made Army Intelligence, and possibly the headlines. So, as they say, there!

We all thought we should soon be on our way. I think, though I am not sure, that there were whispers about 'the Dardanelles' before we left Blandford for Plymouth. The very first landing, in which some of the Division, from the Anson Battalion, were engaged, was on 25 April. We landed at Cape Helles about the middle of May.

Another officer's wife, Mrs Farrow, was living anxiously like Gwen in Tarrant Monckton. They made friends somehow, so neither was totally alone. He was killed.

How grim such partings, many thousands of them, were – the last meal, the last embraces. Married three, four months, perhaps less: and then ripped asunder. If he went to France, it was bad enough: but France, after all, was just over there. A light wound might send him home safe in a day or two: later there might even be leave. But Gallipoli! Gallipoli was something like 3,000 miles away by sea, beyond the other end of the Mediterranean; and the other end of the Mediterranean might just as well be the other end of the world. There would be no easy coming back from there – wounded or well. Yet all must be obstinately cheerful. If we did take the Dardanelles the War would be over almost at once – and we should have done it. By Christmas it will all be over.

Early one morning the two wives came up to the Camp and saw us march away. 'Security' was not then such a tyrant as she is today. I suppose they waved their handkerchiefs and wept, but I don't suppose we saw them. Keen young officers, we should have our eyes to the front, an example to our platoons.

I forget why, but I did not meet my platoon – the 12th, I think, in C Company – till the day before we left. They were all Tynesiders, and most of them miners. At first I understood little of what they said, and they did not understand much of me: and there were two good fellows, from some Durham valley, whom *nobody* understood. They might have been foreigners. They were tough but friendly and we got along very well.

The troopship (the *Ivernia*, I think) was uncomfortable but the voyage was exciting, my first sight of Cape Spartel and Africa, and now and then the true blue velvet of the Mediterranean. I had made great friends with a young officer called Ker whose father was an eminent and learned Scot. He too had been a student of the classics, and one day we found that both of us had been thinking about Troy. We were bound the same way as Menelaus and Ulysses. If we were to land at Cape Helles, as we thought, and climb the big hill above it, Achi Baba, we should surely be able to look across the Straits and see the Plains of Troy. The thought pleased me. I even told my Tynesiders some of the story in one of my daily lectures to the platoon. They listened politely, they were interested, especially in the tale of Helen of Troy. It seemed to them a sensible thing to go to war if some something bastard kidnapped the Queen. Some of them had girls or wives called Helen and they too were going to war to get them back.

In fact, from the part of the line that we took over, on the left of the French, we could not see the Straits. But after two or three weeks, leave was given for small bathing parties, while we were 'resting' in our sandy holes, beset with dust and flies and the noise of guns. Ker and I led some of our men over the slope and down to the lovely water, and as we descended I could see at last the Plains of Troy. So, at least,

I told the platoon-sergeant, and so he told the men. 'Officer says that's the plain of Troy over there.' It was bliss unbelievable to our hot and dusty bodies to swim. An occasional shell came over from the gun called 'Asiatic Annie', but nobody paid much attention. Afterwards as we rested on the beach, democratically naked, it pleased me to think that I had been swimming in the Hellespont, in the blue channel the Greek ships had sailed in pursuit of Helen. They might have anchored over there. Across the Narrows to our left, Leander swam – and Byron too. I told the platoon-sergeant: he told the naked men, and one or two, as if inspired, again plunged into the sea. Thus did dear Winchester and Oxford accompany and fortify me in my first encounter with the foe.

But poor Ker was killed.

❧ 4 ❧

FIRST BOOK

I BEGAN writing verse with serious intent at the age of sixteen, or earlier.

I did not descend to prose till 1918, when I wrote *The Secret Battle*. Sitting in our little garden one sunny morning I suddenly said to myself: 'I will write a book about the war.' I was then working five days a week for Leslie Scott so I had to write the book in the evenings or at weekends, often in the drawing-room with the happy din of children playing about me, for I was not a 'writer' yet and did not qualify for a 'study'. This is not a complaint but a boast – and a bit of advice. God gave me good powers of concentration – but I believe that with practice and resolution such powers can be improved. I am not impressed by the writer who must lock himself in a top room, and not be disturbed till 1 p.m. For all we know he goes to sleep. Everyone bustles in and out of my study all the morning – wife, daughters, grandchildren, neighbours. As long as nobody talks to me I can work away as if nobody was there. The telephone can ring and ring as long as my secretary or somebody replies; the charming grandchildren from next door can watch 'Dr Who'. But if anyone addresses a remark to me the spell, the flow, is broken and that is a bore. On the other hand, if the flow is not strong and certain it may be a pleasant excuse to stop.

This book did flow, almost writing itself – much of it being personal experience. Soon after it came out I met the great H. A. L. Fisher walking down Bond Street. He had been Warden of New College during my last two years. He now thrilled me with compliments about the book; and at the end he said: 'A masterpiece of construction.' I nearly laughed aloud. I had no more notion of 'construction' than I had of cattle-breeding. When I felt 'This chapter's gone on long enough,' I started another. Today, when I do think I know something about construction I can sit for days trying to construct the framework of a novel and end with nothing fixed except that 'John loves Jane'.

But I go too fast. For the encouragement of the Young let me relate, without malice and with not much exaggeration, how my first book struggled into print. I had no agent, and sent the thing direct to Methuen's, who had published that year a book of war-poems called 'The Bomber Gipsy'. Here is another dose of advice: however obscure, however modest you may be, never send anything to a publisher (newspapers are another thing) except through an agent. Your work may be small, but – who knows? – in these days it may turn out to be the foundation of a colossal film in colour or a protracted television series. Do you remember those modest articles about 'Mrs Miniver' in *The Times* during War Two? I bet the authoress never guessed that they would emerge into the movies. Everything in this mechanical world requires a contract about half a mile long and an expert to draft it. Nowadays from the front rank of publishers even a young defenceless author can expect fair and friendly dealing, but there are always points for discussion which are better discussed by an agent. Remember too that a good literary agent does not charge you a fee unless through him you earn some money, and he may do a lot of work seeking money for you in vain. Lastly, let me shout this tribute, which has never, I believe, been shouted before. *He is the only man in the world who has not raised his price.* That is true, certainly, of my own venerable agents, A. P. Watt, and I believe, of the others. Fifty years ago they took 10 per cent of any earnings that they helped to secure – and 10 per cent it is today. What a glittering example? It used to be 10 per cent for waiters: but now it is fifteen.

I was invited to the dear old building in Essex Street, Strand, and pushed into the presence of the high Sir Algernon Methuen himself: there are no Methuens about today. My welcome did not strike me as warm, but this I did not expect: I felt as guilty as a bad boy summoned by the headmaster. Sir Algernon remained sitting at his desk and went on with his work. Presently he looked up and said: 'Oh? You're Mr Herbert? You've written a book, I believe.'

It sounded like 'You've robbed a safe,' but I admitted it.

'We've had a report about it,' he said and scrabbled among his papers. 'Ah, yes.'

(The 'reader's' report, I learned later, was by that fine writer E. V. Lucas, afterwards head of the firm, before that a colleague on the *Punch* table and a very dear friend.)

'It's not a bad report,' said Sir Algernon, 'not bad at all. Very promising . . . considerable literary merit . . .' and so on. 'But our reader does *not* suggest that your book is likely to be a commercial success.'

Then for the first time he looked straight at me and said: 'People like you, Mr Herbert – you bring your books to us, and think it's the simplest thing in the world for us to publish them. But, you know, it doesn't cost you any money to write a book, but it does cost us a lot of money to publish it. Books don't grow on trees – they have to be printed – they have to be bound – I wonder if you have the slightest idea what our bill for *paper* was last year?'

I indicated dumbly that I had not the slightest idea.

There was no internal telephone in those days – or at least, in that office. Believe it or not, Sir Algernon drew a whistle from the mouth of a speaking tube and blew it. After a little while there was a whistle in reply and Sir Algernon spoke into the tube. 'That you, Mr Thomas? Could you let me know what was our total bill for paper last year. Thank you.'

He replaced the whistle.

'And then, you know, books have to be *printed*, and printing costs money, not your money but ours. It's a highly skilled business, and the printers want more money every year. How much, do you suppose —?'

A shrill whistle interrupted him.

'X thousand pounds? Thank you Mr Thomas.' (I forget the figure but it seemed a lot of money to poor little me.) 'And Mr Thomas, while you're there, what about the printing bill? If you wouldn't mind?'

'So you see, Mr Herbert, it's not quite so simple a matter publishing your book as you thought.' The homily continued, broken by a whistle, and the ghastly figure of the printing bill. I think, in all, there were four whistle stops. Next was 'the binding bill'. 'Books have to be bound, you know, Mr Herbert.' Whistle. Mr Thomas? The binding bill shattered me.

Last, it was: 'And then there are our overheads, Mr Herbert. Can you guess what our overheads amount to?'

This finally broke my spirit, for I had never heard of 'overheads' before and had no notion what overheads were. I shambled out of that office almost ready to apologize for having written a book. I signed the contract that followed at once. It was not a generous contract: and when at last I had the sense to put myself in the hands of A. P. Watt they persuaded Sir Algernon to amend it,

I can assure the young that they need fear no such encounters today. A good publisher will make him feel that he is the hell of a fellow, and may even take him out to lunch. Methuen's have been my regular publishers ever since, and we have always been good friends. Alan White, Chairman for thirty-one years, but now retired, is a very good friend and has been a grand and selfless ally of the authors in the Battle about the Libraries.

I should not like to confess exactly how much I owe to Methuen's by way of 'advances' unearned. I mention the dismal fact only to throw a good word, which is not heard enough, to all the wicked publishers. Your agent persuades them to pay you a generous 'advance on account of royalties: but if the royalties earned by the author fall short, far short sometimes, of the 'advance' they do not expect you to return the difference. What other trade, I wonder, behaves so well?

I have had my laugh at the pessimistic Sir Algernon. But the big joke is that he was right. *The Secret Battle* was not – then, at least – a commercial success. It was what Noël Coward, I think, called a *flop d'estime*. It was too early, too close to the War. Years later inferior books (I judged) went better. But there was no doubt about the *esteem*. Arnold Bennett gave the whole of his two columns in the *Evening Standard* to its praise. Mr Lloyd George, I was told, read it all night. and recommended it to Mr Churchill who was Minister of War, and gave orders that court martial arrangements should be altered in some ways – I know not what. Later, he kindly wrote an Introduction to a new edition. 'It is a soldier's tale cut in stone to melt all hearts'.

Last year Field-Marshal Montgomery asked me if I could get him a copy – some beast borrower had not returned his own. 'It was one of the best tales I ever read.' It went out of print some years ago, but I bought the last 250 copies for one shilling each, so I was able to oblige. Monty, bless him, wrote again: 'It is the best story of front-line war I have read.' Now Ian Parsons, of Chatto and Windus has acquired the rights and published the book again. And so I thank Sir Algernon who, after all, in spite of overheads was first in the field.

I have not read the whole book myself for fifty years: but the other day I looked at Chapter III. It has little bearing on the story, but it gives, I felt, a veracious picture of daily life in the front-line on the Gallipoli Peninsula. I saw, I heard, I smelt it all again. The book moves to France, and the Somme, but I did not read any more.

{ 5 }

POETRY, LIGHT AND HEAVY

I SUPPOSE I have written more verse than any Briton alive. I have had the virus for sixty to seventy years, and am suffering still. But I recommend the practice. It clears and sharpens the mind, it increases your store of words, it makes truth and beauty memorable, it can pack wisdom or merriment into convenient vessels; it can be done in an armchair or up a tree, it gives the poet at least much pleasure and, who knows, may amuse the people or be the fount of music. I often wonder why the crossword puzzle addicts who spend so much time and toil fitting the right word into the right place do not write verse instead. The poet is always doing word puzzles too; but he can choose his own words and at the end has something to show. Years ago I tried to persuade *The Times* to start a regular *Times* Four-line Epigram contest. Many scholarly men would prefer this, I believe, to the fruitless conquest of 14 Across and 17 Down. Austen Chamberlain told me that he would certainly try. Thus a notable crop of topical wit might emerge.

I must have been born with this itch as well as hay-fever. I remember composing limericks in a sick room – I think it was measles – at the Grange. (This is the most difficult form of metrical art and I have not seriously tried again.) I was eleven or twelve when I won my first literary success on one of the family holidays at Bognor. The pierrots at the end of the pier offered a prize for a new refrain to one of their favourite songs. It had to begin: 'If I was Somebody or Other – I would – I would. . . .' My refrain began, 'If I was Winston Churchill —' I forget the rest, but I won the prize, that melting book *Black Beauty*.

My pursuit of Sullivan at the piano led me to W. S. Gilbert. A prefect at Winchester, as I have told, introduced me to C. S. Calverley, and that fixed my fate. From about the age of sixteen I began sending faulty verse to *Punch*. None of this, I agree, is of high historic interest but it may encourage some of the young and spur an Editor or two. I knew nobody at *Punch*, I did not even know the editor's name; I simply sent my humble stanzas in long-hand; and, to my astonishment, received a reply, in long-hand too.

Owen Seaman, a genial scholarly Cambridge man, must have been the most painstaking editor that any magazine has had. He was himself a master of 'light verse' of the more stately kind, and had a poem in *Punch* every week. If he sniffed promise anywhere, he was not content to send a printed rejection slip – he popped the useless offering into his week-end case. He was a bachelor and fond of country house week-ends. But most of Sunday he would work away at the unwanted 'contributions' in his case. With a stylograph pen, he would write careful pages of criticism and advice, 'I like the first two verses, but in your third don't you let down the logic of your argument. The last verse too ends rather weakly. I think you can do better.' Also, he was rightly firm about correctitude in rhyming. If I had put, say, 'corn' and 'dawn' together, he would write in the margin 'Do you say "dorn"?' For most Englishmen there is, in fact, small difference between our 'dawn' and our 'born', but there is for the Scots, and there should be for all of us in print. Seaman was right. His discipline has clung to me all my life – to my detriment. In lyrics for the stage the temptation to let a slack rhyme through is always arising. But I have always resolutely refused to commit rhymes like 'Malta' and 'falter'. W. S. Gilbert was also strict, but since his day I believe I have been the only purist on the stage. The great Noël Coward has never flinched from 'Malta' and 'falter', 'circus' and 'mazurkas', 'sailor' and 'Venezuela': and he has done much better than I have.

I wish I had written that superb song 'Mad Dogs and Englishmen' but it contains some rhymes which my cruel conscience would not have permitted me. I have often thought that my dear old editor owes me money. To most of the audience (unless they are Scots) 'sailor' and 'Venezuela' are natural and right – indeed, they may say the words that way; but if such writers publish their lyrics (not many dare) such points are visible and consolation comes to me.

Seaman's prompt attention to a schoolboy he had never heard of so much surprised and stirred me that I rushed at once into corrections. Sometimes I would send back two successive amended versions, still in vain. Two or three rejection slips might well have silenced me. But for three years in this way he nursed me along. My first appearance in *Punch* was in August 1910 just before I was twenty – a terrible 'set of verses', as Seaman called them, which I cannot understand. So I can boast that I have been writing for *Punch* for nearly sixty years. The paper was born in 1841, which makes it 129 years old – so I have written for the paper for nearly half its life.

A year before that, while still at Winchester, I published through P. and G. Wells, the School bookseller, a 'slim volume' of verse which included the dreadful prize poem about the earthquake at Messina. At Oxford I published another. I record these acts as an Awful Warning to the young. 'At the age of nineteen he published a book of verse' may look well in my obituary notice, but in my opinion it was showing-off, and there was not enough to show. Early indiscretions in a newspaper or magazine will not be remembered against you: but gather them together in a book and you are asking for trouble.

I am not ashamed, though, of my third slim volume 'Half-Hours at Helles' published by B. H. Blackwell in 1916. Some of the poems were actually written on the Gallipoli Peninsula and appeared in *Punch* not long after.

THE BATHE

Come friend and swim. We may be better then,
    But here the dust blows ever in the eyes
And wrangling round are weary fevered men,
    For ever mad with flies.
I cannot sleep, nor even long lie still,
    And you have read your April paper twice;
Tomorrow we must stagger up the hill
    To man a trench and live among the lice.

But yonder, where the Indians have their goats,
    There is a rock stands sheer above the blue,
Where one may sit and count the bustling boats
    And breathe the cool air through;
May find it still is good to be alive;
    May look across and see the Trojan shore
Twinkling and warm, may strip, and stretch, and dive,
    And for a space forget about the war.

Then will we sit and talk of happy things,
    Home and 'the High' and some far fighting friend,
And gather strength for what the morrow brings,
    For that may be the end.
It may be we shall never swim again,
    Never be clean and comely to the sight,
May rot untombed and stink with all the slain.
    Come, then and swim. Come and be clean tonight.

I have been using myself the expression 'light verse' but now I protest against it. That is, I protest against the distinction commonly made between 'light' verse and 'serious' poetry. A young man makes a vertical arrangement of words in short phrases (sometimes one word only) without metre, without rhyme, even without detectable rhythm, leaving a sense, if any, of vague depression – he is a modern *poet*. But the work of such giants as Hilaire Belloc and Chesterton, perfect in form, full of life and fun, is regarded as mere 'light verse'. Both these men were poets – even Belloc's alleged nursery verses are poetry. If such masters are dismissed as 'light' the other fellows should be known as 'heavy'. It is impossible to define 'poetry' and rather absurd to try. Macaulay did pretty well:

> By poetry we mean the art of employing words in such a manner as to produce illusion in the imagination – the art of doing with words what the painter does by means of colour.

I would go further (if I dared to move in this dangerous direction). There is poetry too where the words are employed to present *ideas* in a striking manner with more force and effect than can be rendered by prose – a Belloc epigram, for example:

ON A GENERAL ELECTION

The accursed power, which stands on Privilege
And goes with Women, and Champagne and Bridge,
Broke – and Democracy resumed its reign
Which goes with Bridge, and Women and Champagne.

For myself, I am for poetry that sings, that could, you feel, be set to music. Consider Oscar Hammerstein who wrote the songs in *Oklahoma* and *Carousel*. Any man who can extract such music from Richard Rodgers and such emotion from the audience as this writer does, by the songs in *Carousel* especially, is a poet – and in my view a better poet than Auden or Eliot.

I have written some faulty verse in my time, as everybody does, and mostly I have aimed to provide pleasure and even merriment; but my work as a rule does sing, and has been sung extensively, and I beg to move, as the statesmen say, that in my humble way I am a poet – though I do not run about shouting the claim.

Here is a piece I wrote more than thirty years ago. The theme is not profound or important, holiday golf by the sea in Cornwall; but it makes a picture, it speaks a mood, it has a hint of happiness, and, I submit, deserves the name of poetry as well as many heavier works.

MULLION

My ball is in a bunch of fern,
  A jolly place to be;
An angry man is close astern –
  He waves his club at me.
Well, let him wave – the sky is blue;
Go on, old ball, we are but two –
  We may be down in three,
Or nine – or ten – or twenty-five –
It matters not; to be alive
  Is good enough for me.

How like the happy sheep we pass
　　At random through the green,
For ever in the longest grass,
　　But never in between!
There is a madness in the air;
There is a damsel over there,
　　Her ball is in the brook.
Ah! what a shot – a dream, a dream!
You think it finished in the stream?
　　Well, well, we'll go and look.

Who is this hot and hasty man
　　That shouteth 'Fore!' and 'Fore!'?
We move as quickly as we can –
　　Can any one do more?
Cheer up, sweet sir, enjoy the view;
I'd take a seat if I were you,
　　And light your pipe again:
In quiet thought possess your soul,
For John is down a rabbit hole,
　　And I am down a drain.

The ocean is a lovely sight,
　　A brig is in the bay.
Was that a slice? You may be right –
　　But goodness, what a day!
Young men and maidens dot the down,
And they are beautiful and brown,
　　And just as mad as me.
Sing, men and maids, for I have done
The Tenth – the Tenth – in twenty-one,
　　And John was twenty-three.

Now will I take my newest ball,
　　And build a mighty tee,
And waggle once, or not at all,
　　And bang it out to sea,
And hire a boat and bring it back,
And give it one terrific whack,
　　And hole it out in three,
Or nine – or ten – or twenty-five –
It matters not; to be alive
At Mullion in the summer time,
At Mullion in the silly time,
　　Is good enough for me.

I am, thank God, a square (how odd, by the way, that the Young,
bless them, should use that good old word, which stands so often for
whatever is honest and brave, as a term of abuse). But I do my best to

circle the square, to ring it with a fringe of modernity and disorder. This is not to be in the fashion but to be in community with my friends. It is nice to like what they like; also, if I don't, there may, I feel, be something wrong with me, and I must be missing something.

As a good square, in music, I desire melody, or at least, agreeable sounds – I love both Puccini at his peaks and Wagner at his vaguest. Malcolm Sargent said to me once of a famous counter-tenor: 'I never heard him make a sound that pleased me yet.' I could almost say the same about Stravinsky and Shostakovich, though I have listened dutifully, hopefully, time and again. I like pictures and drawings which are done with reasonable care and resemble persons and things as I know them. I can enjoy a dashing 'abstract' very much, unless it is an evident impudence, a large white square with a small black square in the middle, or a canvas decorated with nails and an ash-tray. But as my Lord Harkaway said in *Tantivy Towers*: 'I don't like girls with triangular legs or one eye.' There is, I fear, a touch in me of the American who, when shown a Picasso, said: 'I wouldn't like it, even if it was good.' No, I am better than he, for I do try. I feel a fool, I feel a toad – but there it is.

I am distressed, by the way, by the modern style of comic artists, my natural brothers. With some exceptions, they can't (or they don't) draw a pretty girl. They can't (or they don't) draw more than one kind of nose. They seem to me to get worse every week.

In poetry and verse, where I have more title to speak, I want meaning, and metre, and, where appropriate, rhyme. Here, again, I have tried hard to understand and enjoy the free 'modern' poets, but with rare exceptions (John Pudney is one) they baffle me. I love John Betjeman's work, a fine craftsman, but him I regard as a fellow-square. He is guilty of meaning, metre, and rhyme, all three.

I do not insist on rhyme in serious poetry, though Shakespeare, Keats, Tennyson, Wordsworth and many other acknowledged poets did pretty well with it. Milton, I know, made a pompous and ill-reasoned attack on 'Rime' in his introduction to *Paradise Lost*.

> The measure is in English Heroic Verse without Rime, as that of Homer in Greek, and of Virgil in Latin; Rime being no necessary Adjunct or true Ornament of Poem or good Verse, in longer Works especially, but the Invention of a barbarous Age, to set off wretched matter and lame Meeter; grac't indeed since by the use of some famous modern Poets, carried away by Custom, but much to their own vexation, hindrance, and constraint to express many things otherwise, and for the most part worse then else they would have exprest them. . . . This neglect then of Rime so little is to be taken for a defect, though it may seem so perhaps to vulgar Readers, that it rather is to be esteem'd an example set, the

first in English, of ancient liberty recover'd to Heroic Poem from the troublesom and modern bondage of Rimeing.

Yes, but who wrote *l'Allegro* and *Il Penseroso*, and *Lycidas*, all in rhyme. Who wrote:

> Who would not sing for Lycidas? he knew
> Himself to sing, and build the lofty rhyme.

The joke is that this great man came back to 'troublesome Rime' in his last important work *Samson Agonistes* – but how poorly, how spasmodically! The last fourteen lines, given to Chorus, are rhymed, and the last words are the famous 'all passion spent' which rhyme with 'intent' and 'invent'.

Much of Milton's rhyming looks tired and lazy. He was blind, and sight has much to do with rhyme. No wonder he abandoned it 'in longer works especially' with relief. He may be forgiven for that, but not for his incompetent return to it. Long ago I lectured our present heavy poets for this fault. 'If you announce in the first of many stanzas that you propose to follow a certain rhyming scheme, you must stick to it, not abandon it when you find it difficult.' Is this not the age of efficiency and thoroughness and precise attention to 'technology'? What should we say of the boxer who having engaged to fight with his fists let out with his boot when that became too difficult, or of the steeplechaser who ran round the most formidable obstacles and said that jumping was after all a troublesome antique (or modern) invention? For many generations the English have had light poets who obeyed their own rules – Gay, Sheridan, Gilbert, Chesterton and Belloc – perhaps the best of them all. Dear Milton, do you really find that Hilaire Belloc is 'constrained by Rime' to express many things otherwise, and for the most part worse than else he would have expressed them? Everything these poets want to say is said: but every word and every rhyme is as precisely fitted into its place as the stones of an arch.

When they do descend to regular rhyme you would think the serious poets would be more severe than the mere light-hearted singer for the stage. Not a bit of it! I pick up one of the works of Mr W. H. Auden, who once at least was the prince of the 'new poets' and indeed Professor of Poetry at Oxford University. In the first page my finger touches I see:

> The shutting of a door
> The tightening jaw. . . .

Another poem begins:

> On Sunday walks
> Past the shut gates of works
> The conquerors come
> And are handsome. . . .

and lower down I see:

> Pursued by eaters
> They clutch at gaiters. . . .

Here is another pair of couplets, most of which rhyme in orthodox fashion: 'fires – wires', 'doors – floors', 'girl-whirl', 'cramp – damp', 'bad – cad', also by the way 'canals' and 'rails'. But suddenly, with a shock, remembering my dear Owen Seaman, I see: 'afford – abroad'.

Do you say 'abrord?'

You and I may, for our diction is deplorable. But surely the sensitive and scholarly Mr Auden does not? If I had ever been tempted to use such a rhyme in a stage lyric, nothing could have induced me to put it in a book.

If you really despise rhyme, my boy, don't put 'eaters' next to 'gaiters', 'walks' next to 'works', or 'door' next to 'jaw' in a poem the rest of which is composed of correct rhymes like 'night' and 'fright' and 'date' and 'gate'. If you don't want a rhyme you can put 'gate' instead of 'door' or 'leggings' instead of 'gaiters'. This will be honest and give no offence.

(I now see that in the Foreword to his Collected Shorter Poems 1927–57 Mr Auden handsomely comes my way:

'Re-reading my poems, I find that in the nineteen-thirties I fell into some very slovenly habits. . . . It makes me wince when I see how ready I was to treat – or and – aw as homophones. It is true that in the Oxonian dialect I speak they are, but that isn't really an adequate excuse. I also find that my ear will no longer tolerate rhyming a voiced S with an unvoiced. I have had to leave a few such rhymes because I cannot at the moment see a way to get rid of them, but I promise not to do it again.' I salute Mr Auden.)

Mr C. Day Lewis, now the Poet Laureate, should repent also. In a Birthday Song for a Royal Child (music by the Master of the Queen's Music):

> Touched with a primrose blow of dawn
> For every child that's born . . .

I do not think that the great Mr T. S. Eliot was often guilty of such rhymes (though I note with sadness in 'The Waste Land' these three lines:

O the moon shone bright on Mrs Porter
And on her daughter
They wash their feet in soda water . . .)

but he treats rhyme in the casual manner that distresses me. He will
start a poem (take 'The Love Song of J. Alfred Prufrock') with a
stanza rich in rhyme: but as he goes on the rhymes grow fewer and
the reader is disappointed. Or he would start a long poem that looked
like being utterly rhymeless. Very well, we know what to expect. But we
don't. Suddenly the spell is broken by two or three lines that rhyme,
like Mrs Porter. Half-way through 'Ash Wednesday' there is a startling
clot of three double rhymes – 'slender' – 'offend her ' and 'surrender'.
It is a shock.

As I have graciously admitted, I do not insist on rhyme. I can read
good blank verse by the mile – with pleasure. (I can also write it – see
page 87 – 'Two Gentlemen of Soho'). I can recite most of Tennyson's
fine poem *Ulysses*, and I love it. But poetry, for me, must, like music,
have form. One of the 'formal' elements is metre, another is rhyme.
If you offer neither metre nor rhyme you are not offering poetry, but
prose. True, your lines may have rhythm, and you may use fanciful,
'poetical' language: but prose should have rhythm and you may use,
within reason, 'poetical' language in prose. Consider the following
quotation:

'April is the cruellest month, breeding lilacs out of the dead land,
mixing memory and desire, stirring dull roots with spring rain. Winter
kept us warm, covering Earth in forgetful snow, feeding a little life
with dried tubers. Summer surprised us, coming over the Starnbergersee
with a shower of rain; we stopped in the colonnade, and went on in
sunlight into the Hofgarten, and drank coffee, and talked for an hour.'

A blameless piece of prose. But the author wants to be known as a
poet, so he breaks up his sentences, and sets the same words before
you thus:

April is the cruellest month, breeding
Lilacs out of the dead land, mixing
Memory and desire, stirring
Dull roots, with spring rain.
Winter kept us warm, covering
Earth in forgetful snow, feeding
A little life with dried tubers.
Summer surprised us, coming over the Starnbergersee
With a shower of rain; we stopped in the colonnade,
And went on in sunlight, into the Hofgarten,
And drank coffee and talked for an hour.

Those are the opening lines of that famous poem 'The Waste Land' by T. S. Eliot. I must, and do, approach Mr Eliot respectfully, for all my friends say that he is good, and he received the Order of Merit, which is not lightly bestowed. So it is with due respect that I confess myself baffled – try as I may, I cannot see what it is that entitles this passage to the name of poetry.

It is difficult to explain exactly the purpose and effect of rhyme. But one thing I am sure about: it is not a mere 'ornament', as some high persons say. Where rhyme is fitting, and well done, it is a positive part of the poetic process, adding force to the poet's message. When you start a rhymed poem you create an expectation, you make a promise: and every time you fulfil that promise (unless the rhyme is forced or faulty, from repetition or any other reason) you give the same sort of satisfaction as a composer correctly resolving a chord in the key that he has chosen. If you suddenly decide that you cannot think of a good rhyme, and go ahead without one, you are letting expectation down, as a composer would who finished in the wrong key.

Belloc took a couplet of Goldsmith's and added a wondrous couplet of his own:

> Ill fares the land to hastening *ills** a prey
> Where wealth accumulates and men decay.(G)
> But, how much more unfortunate are those
> Where wealth declines and population grows! (B)

Put 'expands' for 'grows', and you will see what I mean.

I like work which cries aloud that the maker is a master of his material and in command of his craft. I get this sense from a well-fitted cupboard door. I get it from the drawings of some of the old comic artists. I do not get it from some of the moderns who give exactly the same nose to nine or ten figures in the same picture.

I wrote long ago a poem called 'Breakfast' which began:

> Give me a little ham and egg
> And let me be alone, I beg.
> Give me my tea, hot, sweet and weak,
> Bring me *The Times* and do not speak. . . .

You may not like it, but here is a sharp, compelling picture. Indeed the first two couplets, thirty words only and all monosyllables but one, give you most of the scene. But suppose you cut out the despised rhymes – 'pray' instead of 'beg', 'strong' instead of 'weak' or 'talk' instead of 'speak'. The thought is the same, but the force and the fun have gone. It is like playing the same tune on a second piano, where

* 'an execrable line' as Belloc remarked.

the last note is cracked or out of tune. It is as if the last boom of Big Ben's chimes suddenly went sharp. I cannot explain this but I know it is true.

Or take a famous couplet of that master Hilaire Belloc:

> Whatever happens we have got
> The Maxim gun – and they have not

Suppose it was:

> Whatever happens, we possess
> The Maxim gun and they do not.

Milton in his erroneous lecture said that Rime was 'the Invention of a barbarous Age, to set off wretched matter and lame Meeter'. Today, as we have seen, those who avoid rhyme have no Meeter at all. It would be truer to say that a man who takes the trouble to begin and carry out a full rhyming scheme is more likely to be strict about Meeter. Moreover a good practitioner of rhyme is more likely to end his lines strongly, than the 'free verse' writer. It is possible to end one line with a weak word, or phrase – 'they say', 'it seems to me' – in order to provide a rhyme for an important word at the end of the next line. I may have done this myself, here and there: but one is always ashamed. The 'free' modern poet does not care how weakly he ends a line – with words like 'and', 'or', and 'as', words which no despised rhymester would think of putting at the end of a line.

Nevertheless, it is, I agree, great fun to write free verse, and I have done much of it in my poems 'From the Chinese' and 'From the Russian', some of which you will find in *Look Back and Laugh*.

CONFESSIONAL

> Judges of the People's Court,
>   Do not forgive me.
> I confess
>   My grievous aberrations,
> I kneel, I grovel,
>   I crawl about
> On all fours.
>   In my commodious cell
> For two years
>   I have been well-treated.
> I have had the best
>   Of everything
> Oysters
>   (When in season)
> Were brought to me daily
>   From the Bay of Lenin.
> Heartening extracts
>   From the speeches

Of Joseph Stalin,
  The Wise, the Good,
Who discovered
  The Laws of Gravity,
Were played to me
  On the gramophone.
No man ill-used me,
  No drug was administered.
My conscience,
  The eyes of my comrades,
The teachings of Stalin,
  Have illuminated
The dark abysses
  Of my disgusting soul.
I told Comrade Ratovsky
  That I was surprised to hear
That Joseph Vissarionovich Stalin
  Had split the first atom
With his own hands,
  Well knowing
That this was a Party decision.
  I questioned the assertion
Of Comrade Larinski
  That Soviet submarines
Are able to fly. . . .

August 2, 1950

Some young folk of today believe that they invented the protest song. Here is part of one I made for the Germans about the time of 'Munich', about the Führer:

THE ROARER

Our Roarer is a simple soul, his heart is always bleeding:
He's kind to his old mother, he is fond of flowers, and reading:
But he has cowed the Continent from Russia to the Riff
By roaring into microphones and boring people stiff.
    Oh, rally round the Roarer!
    Our Roarer beats the band;
    We have a ruder Roarer
    Than any other land!
    He'll roar and rant and rage
    Like something in a cage;
    He rages, roars and rants
    And no one kicks his pants.
    The world may sigh and stop its ear,
    But everybody has to hear,

And it's so very boring
That all the frantic nations say
'Oh, let the Roarer have his way,
And stop the Roarer roaring.'

Oh, rally round the Roarer! etc.
September 28, 1938

And here's another:

THE SPRINGBOKS' TOUR

It may be bad, I grant you that,
If blacks are barred from ball and bat.
But how much worse if we should fall
To government by brawl and bawl!
December 1969

From February 1940, for nearly twenty-five years, I sent short topical poems every week to Lord Kemsley's *Sunday Graphic* – both, alas, no more – designed to cheer, comfort or chide my fellow citizens. Many Londoners have cause to remember Sunday 15 September 1940, and all the nation celebrates it now as Battle of Britain Day. It was on that day that the R.A.F. shot down fifty-six German machines. That morning I also did my best to repel the enemy with some verse in the *Sunday Graphic*:

INVASION

Napoleon tried. The Dutch were on their way,
A Norman did it – and a Dane or two.
Some sailor King may follow one fine day:
But not, I think, a low land-rat like you.

That was written two days earlier at Hole Haven, Canvey Island, where invasion was very much in every mind (the *Water Gipsy* had been provided with two cutlasses). Two days later, on the seventeenth, I have read, Hitler called off his invasion plans and orders – no doubt, he read the *Sunday Graphic*.

Throughout the War (except for those months when Mr Attlee sent me to Newfoundland) I never missed a Sunday. Sometimes, late on a Friday night, after patrolling Sea Reach, I would sit up in my blankets with my beneficent tot of rum and manfully attack the Muse. But then, how to get it to Gray's Inn Road? There was one telephone at the Lobster Smack in a dark corner by the kitchen. A big raid in the night perhaps – lines down. Sailors eager to ring their wives. Tug-men, barge-skippers seeking orders. How patient they were with the agitated Petty Officer holding them up with yells of 'How is the old

Top Wop today?' 'TOP – T-O-P – WOP – William – Orange – Patrick!' and so on. Somehow the stuff always got through.

On 23 March 1943 my slender Muse (through no fault of mine) was hauled before the House of Commons. In October 1942, when enthusiastic idiots were scrawling on walls 'Second Front Now' I wrote a poem called 'Less Nonsense', an answer to the excessive adulators of Joseph Stalin. It was published in *Truth* by my bold and brilliant friend Collin Brooks. The full text is in *Independent Member*.

Some may think the lines unfair to dear Russia; but I am still not quite sure.

> Let's have less nonsense from the friends of Joe;
> We laud, we love him, but the nonsense – NO!
> In 1940, when we bore the brunt,
> WE could have done, boys, with a second front.
> A continent went down a cataract,
> But Russia did not think it right to act, etc.

Whatever their merits they seemed to 'fill a need', caused comfort, I am told, at No. 10, and had a wide private circulation. Indeed, they quietly went round the world. In Newfoundland that autumn I met a Canadian who showed me a copy which had just been sent to him by a friend in Australia.

Unfortunately some keen poetry-lovers who were also leaders of men distributed copies of the work among their men for the purpose of 'ameliorating morale'. At Short's works at Rochester, I was told, the shop-stewards threatened a strike and sent an angry telegram to Sir Stafford Cripps, the Minister for Aircraft Production. On 23 March 1943 Mr D. N. Pritt, M.P. (another Wykehamist) put down a solemn question and produced a comical column of Hansard:*

VERSES, 'LESS NONSENSE'

3. Mr Pritt asked the Secretary of State for War whether he is aware that Lieut-Colonel Parkinson ordered to be distributed on 24 February 1943, to units under his command, over 200 copies of a piece of verse entitled 'Less Nonsense', which is offensive to the Soviet Union and calculated to injure our friendship towards that country; that these copies were to be distributed on the scale of three copies for every unit down to batteries and companies, one copy for the officers' mess, one for the sergeants' mess, and one where it could be seen by the men; and whether he will take immediate steps to put a stop to this political activity and arrange that lectures on the Soviet Union be given to the units involved to counteract the effects of this propaganda?

* Vol. 387, col. 1445.

SIR J. GRIGG: I am making inquiries into this matter. On the facts as stated, I do not think the action of the Divisional Commander was at all suitable. The troops in the area in question are already getting lectures on Soviet Russia from both military and non-military sources besides a good deal of other material on the subject, and I doubt if any special steps are necessary.

MAJOR-GENERAL SIR ALFRED KNOX: Is it not true that this poem contains nothing offensive to Soviet Russia, and is it not British patriotism from a British point of view?

SIR J. GRIGG: I have been careful to express no opinion on the merits of the verses.

COMMANDER LOCKER-LAMPSON: Can they be circulated as a White Paper?

PETTY-OFFICER HERBERT: Is the Right Hon. Gentleman aware that these verses, whatever their merits, were not directed against Russia at all, but against certain British citizens who are never happy unless they are running down their own country and the efforts of their own countrymen in the war?

Mr Pritt did not say a word.

Sir Winston Churchill was a lover of verse and carried much in his capacious head. Early in the war it was decided that the church bells should be rung as a warning of invasion. So they had to be silent on other occasions. I never thought that this was a very sensible arrangement; and how, while it lasted, could we blame the enemy for bombing church towers? On 7 November 1941 I wrote some verses about it in the *Sunday Graphic*:

> Bring back the bells. The bells are dumb
> Until the parachuters come;
> And even Huns may be excused
> For bombing belfries so abused. . . .

I cannot claim that the lines had an instantaneous effect, but perhaps they sank in. It was sixteen months later (20 April 1943) that Mr Churchill brought back the bells. He replied to a question from Sir Thomas Moore:

> We have come to the conclusion that this particular method of warning was redundant, and not in itself well adapted to the present conditions of war.

Then came a true Churchillian shaft in reply to a 'supplementary' question:

SIR T. MOORE: Will my Right Hon. Friend say what alternative arrangements have been made?

THE PRIME MINISTER: Replacement does not arise. For myself, I cannot help thinking that anything like a serious invasion would be bound to leak out.

By a strange chance I had sent him that morning a little book entitled *Bring Back the Bells*. Three pages away from the bells poem were some simple lines I had written for his sixty-seventh birthday:

To W.S.C.

Many happy returns of the day
   To the father of purpose and plan,
To the one who was first in the fray,
   Never doubted, or rested, or ran,
To the Voice of old Britain at bay,
   To the Voice of young men in the van,
To the Voice of new worlds on the way –
   To 'We must – and we will – and we can!'
May he live to hear History say,
   'This was their finest man'!

This was not, then, such a safe bet as it may seem today: for this was 30 November 1941, things were not going well, and the 'Churchill Must Go' movement of 1942 was still to come.

He went off on one of his long voyages. At Washington he addressed the assembled legislators of the United States. 'Then I thought it well to go to North Africa', and he flew to Gibraltar and Algeria with General Marshall. He came home and on 8 June gave us a long speech about all this. At the end we all trooped out for lunch. In the Smoking Room, when he came in, the only vacant seat, by chance, was next to mine and he sat down. We stood the great man a sherry, and he talked about Roosevelt and de Gaulle, and Africa, and this and that. Then, suddenly, he said to me: 'Those verses you were kind enough to write for my birthday – where did you get the metre?' I said: 'I don't know. It started "Many happy returns of the day" and then it seemed to run on.' 'I thought I recognized it,' he said. 'I went to a shelf and found it.'

Then he began to recite. I do not know now what the piece was. It was some kind of a *ballade*, with some French in it. There were three or four stanzas. He began a little haltingly: but the last verses flowed as smoothly as a Head Boy's recitation on Speech Day. We listened in astonishment, wondering how in the midst of his mighty cares he had been able – he should wish – to get all that graceful verse into his mind, and keep it there.

We offered him another sherry. But he said: 'No. I am going to lunch at Buckingham Palace; and it would not look well if I were to s-slither under the Royal table.'

Later that year we had another strange verse affair, this time in mid-Atlantic. With Derrick Gunston, M.P., one of Mr Attlee's three-man Goodwill Commission, I had the good fortune to come home in a new destroyer the *Orwell*, Lieutenant-Commander J. M. Hodges, D.S.O., R.N. On the second day we had a rendezvous with the *Renown*, in which great ship was Mr Churchill, his wife and his daughter Mary, returning from Canada. It was an exciting encounter – late on a dark and ugly afternoon, low, purple clouds, not a gleam of sun, driving rain, and a dirty sea. Our sister destroyer looked very small and lonely, plunging along in a flurry of spray. Suddenly, converging through the rain, we saw a small fleet, two cruisers, whose names I forget, and the *Renown* with four destroyers about her. All were steaming at twenty-six knots: all were winking morse at a fantastic rate. Perhaps I am a sentimental old thing, but I must say it stirred my soul to see that punctual meeting of the ships, the British Fleet defying the enemy in mid-Atlantic and carrying the great leader safely home. The speed of the evolution was astonishing. Almost immediately, it seemed, we had taken station on the starboard bow of the *Renown* and the destroyer we relieved had gone.

Derrick Gunston and I felt it our duty to salute the Prime Minister, and to let him know that he had a House of Commons as well as a naval escort. Our Commander was all in favour: and he agreed that it should be in verse, for like so many naval officers he was no mean poet himself, and had shyly showed me some of his work. The sailor – I have noticed it in bargemen too – seems to have a finer feeling for words than his brothers in arms: and in the long lone watches he finds time to think of things he wants to say. So the slower sailor runs to poetry and the speeding airman to slang.

'Security', in that high moment, I am glad to say, restrained the Muse. I thought 'Who knows what periscope may read our salute? Nothing about Churchill.' But what about Ulysses returning to his island after many doubts and dangers? Trouble at once. We did not know then (though we guessed) that Mrs Churchill and Mary were aboard. I could not remember if Ulysses had a daughter: I could not even at first remember the name of his son. But soon I composed, and the Commander passed, the following signal. Long after, the Signals Officer of the *Renown* sent me the original copy.

NAVAL MESSAGE

To *Renown*   From *Orwell*

From Derrick Gunston and A. P. Herbert. Respectful salutes and greetings. Return Ulysses soon to show the secrets of your splendid bow.

Return and make all riddles plain to anxious Ithaca again. And you
Penelope the true who have begun to wander too we're glad to meet
you on the foam and hope to see you safely home.
Light P/L T.O.R. 1526 K. Dist. Cdr. Thompson 1520
                                 Cdr. Dawnor N.O.

The last couplet was to have been better:

> Resist the tendency to roam
> And keep your mighty man at home.

But in committee we decided against it.

I remember vividly how that unusual signal was dispatched. Morse
signals, by day, are sent by a sort of searchlight, with shutters, which
make a great clatter, rather like a milk-cart. Our little ship was rolling
largely, and, the wind being on the starboard bow, our smoke kept
hiding the *Renown*. But nothing, not even verse about Ulysses, disturbed the Yeoman of Signals, a regular, and very keen on sending
any message to Mr Churchill. He stood behind the bewildered young
signalman and dictated. 'Uncle – (clatta-clatta-clat) – Lizzie (clatta-
clat-clatta – clatter) – Yellow – Sugar – Easter – Sugar – (clatta-clatta-
clatter).'

Then we all peered through the smoke, looking for the long light
('T') which means 'Word understood'. I imagined the Yeoman in the
Renown muttering angrily 'What the so-and-so is Ulysses?' But, after
a slight pause, a light glowed steadily in the big dark shape astern:
and how excited I was! The *Renown*, of course, was equal to 'Ulysses'
(though, in fact, she spelt him wrong). The Yeoman went merrily ahead;
and in all that message only one word – I think it was 'Ithaca' – had
to be repeated.

All next day there was no reply from the great ship. Derrick Gunston
and I said anxiously, 'Perhaps we have done the wrong thing. Perhaps
the old man does not think it seemly for Members of Parliament to
send the Prime Minister signals in rough verse, in mid-Atlantic, in
time of war. Or if not the Prime Minister, perhaps the Admiral has
frowned.' Even our Commander, I think, was worried.

In fact, I heard later, our salute was circulated and half the ship's
company were at work on a reply. A little before dark a sailor told us
that a signal was coming through. I rushed up to the signal-bridge and
enjoyed the flashing and clattering again. Alas, I cannot find the
signal. It was no longer than ours and ended with the charming
couplet:

> TO CHIDE THESE SIMPLE RHYMES BE CHARY
> THEY ARE THE FIRST ATTEMPT OF MARY.

By now all aboard *Orwell* were eager parties to the correspondence, and two or three sailors said, 'Send Miss Mary a message from us'. Rolling about the captain's bunk the night before I had at last remembered the name of Telemachus; and, very rapidly, I did my best. It began:

TELEMACHA, THE SAILORS SEND
THEIR GREETINGS TO A FIGHTING FRIEND

and ended:

WHY NOT, WHEN MISTER MASEFIELD'S PASSED,
A LADY LAUREATE AT LAST?

Some months later, I happened to meet Mrs Churchill and her daughter getting out of a car. I again congratulated the young poetess on her 'first attempt', and asked, ungallantly, perhaps: 'Did you do it all yourself?' 'Yes,' she said. 'All except the last two lines. *Those were Daddy's.*'

So I can claim to have goaded the Prime Minister to poesy in mid-Atlantic and, who knows, the presence of U-boats. What a mad – but what an English – occasion! Not, I suppose, the kind of thing that would have happened during an Atlantic passage of serious men like Adolf Hitler or Joseph Stalin.

And note, dear Milton, that it was the rhymes that set the scene.

I am told that some of the pop-song lyrics are good: but I have never been able to hear enough of them to judge. Certainly, the authors have a gift for repetition.

Denis Norden, reviewing last year a solemn book about Dirty Jokes, said: 'The book contains some mind-boggling assertions.' The first he quoted was: 'Modern erotic poetry is generally attributed to A. P. Herbert. . . .' There is something in this. I have seen one or two gay pieces not merely attributed to me but circulated in typescript with my name or initials at the bottom – verses with which I had nothing whatever to do. I have heard of many others which I have not even seen. One, I believe, about four-letter words, has been 'attributed', and this annoys me for I dislike the blatant use of these words, and have rarely used any of them. One man told me for certain that I had written 'Eskimo Nell', but this I have never seen or heard. During War Two, one night at Hole Haven, I was talking to an R.N.V.R. officer who spent the war there waiting to touch off a string of mines under Hitler's fleet when it arrived. He shyly showed me some verses he said he had written about some things that Mussolini had done to the Abyssinians, and asked for my professional advice. I said I should not wish to alter a word. They were clever and decently abusive, and, given the theme, I should by no means have been ashamed of them. A few days later, at the House of Commons, my friend Dingle Foot came up and said: 'You must give me a copy of your wonderful verses about Mussolini.' Even when I told him that in this case I had actually met the poet he would not believe me. 'Everybody knows,' he said, 'you wrote them.'

I am rather tired of this erroneous reputation. So I will relate for the first time the story of the one work which started the legend. The subtitle of the story should be 'How Homer Got About' and here is its only important interest.

In, I suppose, 1927 or 1928 I was coming home from Ceylon in an Orient liner, I think, the old *Otranto*, and I was working hard at my light opera (as we used to call 'musicals' then). Sooner or later on sea-voyages I become convinced that I have cancer on the tongue from too much smoking. This time we were in the Red Sea. I went down to my friend the surgeon's room to inform him of my condition: but he was inconsiderately attending to sufferers elsewhere. While waiting I dipped into some of his learned books. There was one which seemed to be the medical version of What Every Married Man Ought to Know. I had been married for nearly twenty-five years, and was amazed to find how little I knew about the female form divine. So I 'borrowed' the book and returned to the promenade deck. It was painfully hot, the *Derby Day* dialogue was flagging, and chiefly, I think, as an excuse for stopping work I committed these lines before lunch:

LINES ON A BOOK BORROWED FROM THE SHIP'S DOCTOR

> The portions of a woman which appeal to man's depravity
> Are constructed with considerable care,
> And what appears to you to be a simple little cavity
> Is really an elaborate affair:
>
> And doctors who have troubled to examine the phenomena
> In numbers of experimental dames
> Have made a list of all the things in feminine abdomina
> And given them delightful Latin names.
>
> There's the *vulva*, the *vagina*, and the jolly *perineum*,
> The *hymen* (in the case of many brides),
> The sort of thing they show you in a medical museum,*
> The *clitoris*, and God knows what besides.

* The original line was 'And a lot of little gadgets you would like if you could see 'em'. But I did not know then that the work was destined to go round the world – both ways.

> What a pity then it is that, when we common fellows chatter
> Of the mysteries to which I have referred,
> We should use for such a delicate and complicated matter
> Such a very short and unattractive word!

Generally, before lunch, I had a noonday gin with the Purser, Mr Watts, and the Chief Officer, Mr Nicholls. 'Watty,' I knew, kept a portfolio of literary curiosities, parodies of Kipling and so on. Today I offered him the 'Lines' for his collection, and later he sent me a typed copy. Later still, in the English Channel I was clearing the decks for packing, tearing up the ship's information on Pompeii, Gibraltar, the programme for Gala Night, etc., and I thought so little of the lines that I tore up the one typed copy I had. My steward asked me if he could have a copy of the piece of poitry I had done for the Pusser, and I told him to apply to 'the Pusser'. I believe he did.

A few days after we landed I met 'Watty' in the Strand and took him, just before lunch, into the Savage Club, then in its old home in Adelphi Terrace, a hundred yards from the flats of Barrie and Bernard Shaw. I introduced him to that dear, amusing man Morris Harvey of the Follies. While I was fighting for drinks the Purser told Morris about the lines, and Morris said he would like a copy. Watty gave him one, saying that it was the only copy, but he had the words in his head – and I think he must have had the manuscript.

From these beginnings the damned composition went, first all round London, and then all round the world. I met it often myself. Dear old E. V. Lucas, I remember, at about the fish stage in some public banquet, pulled a crumpled document from his pocket and said 'Have you seen *this*?' as one who is offering you a big surprise. I said 'Very amusing' and handed it back. I do not quite know why, but for about six months I did not let on that I had ever seen the thing before. I was not ashamed of it but I was not strongly proud of it. I heard it attributed to Noël Coward, and even to Belloc (most unlikely) but I never said, 'You're wrong. That's mine'.

Then I met men who had come across the work in America, others who had brought back a copy from Australia. Next came the reply from the Australian doctor, whose name has never been revealed. It was a precise piece of work, four stanzas again, and the same metre. It ended neatly, something like this:

> And though the word is lamentably lacking in Latinity
> It seems to fit the object it describes.

There is one more chapter to this long story. One Saturday morning during War Two I was walking happily along the south side of Jermyn

Street. The *Water Gipsy* had made a good passage that morning from Canvey Island to Westminster Pier. I had week-end leave, I was wearing my Number Ones – my proud Petty Officer's badge in gold – and my new second Good Conduct stripe. Some way ahead I saw a Captain in the Royal Navy approaching. I was always punctilious about salutes, I wound myself up and gave him a 'smashing' one. He stopped and said:

'You're Herbert, aren't you?'

'Yes, sir.'

'You wrote those verses about the Portions of a Woman?'

'Yes, sir.'

'Before the War, I was on the China Station. We wrote a reply from the point of view of "the experimental dames". Care to hear it, Herbert?'

Yes, sir.' And I think I saluted.

So there we stood on the narrow pavement, taxis hooting by, mere civilians struggling past us, myself standing severely to attention, while the Captain in his deep voice recited the four stanzas of the China Station. They were good. It was, I suppose, the strangest literary episode in the history of Jermyn Street. At the end, with one more salute, I asked the Captain for a copy and he sent me one, but it has disappeared.

Today, at least forty-two years since they were lazily written in the Red Sea, I meet the Lines often: and it is extraordinary how few errors or amendments the furtive circulators have made. I have a shrewd fear that if any of my works survive me long it will be this blasted work.

But let us close with an instructional chord. The thought behind the Lines may not shake or save the world: but it would not have survived for forty-two years if it had been expressed in prose – or in verse without metre or rhyme.

⧼ 6 ⧽

PUNCH

I HAVE had five editors of *Punch* shot over me, and am still hanging about the premises, so it would not be seemly for me to say much more than 'Thank you'. But to anyone who is interested in the story of this great paper I commend *A History of Punch* by R. G. G. Price (a fellow-member of the Round Table), published by Collins in 1957. Like so many splendid books it is out of print, but no doubt you will find it in the libraries.

If I survive till August 1970 I hope that the present editor of *Punch*, the lively William Davis, will graciously allow me to contribute some small piece or poem, however square or senile, to *Punch* of 12 August so that I can say proudly: 'I have written for *Punch* for sixty years.' (I am not far off now, I have been in the paper twice this year.)

From 1917 I was allowed to sign my work with my initials, then a rare privilege, and after the war I became a regular contributor. My first prose contribution was on 7 March 1920.

In January 1924, fourteen years after my first queer contribution, Sir Owen Seaman sent me 'a formal invitation from the Proprietors and myself, to join the Staff of *Punch* and attend the dinner here on Wednesday February 6 at 7.0 p.m. . . . I shall look to you, then and always, to come armed with two or more ideas for the cartoons. . . .' He invited also any suggestions 'in addition to your regular weekly article', but being 'on the Staff' did not mean doing any duty at the office beyond dining once a week. The position then carried one extraordinary privilege: it was assumed that anything written by anyone 'on the Table' was sure to be good and acceptable. For very many years I did not even send my offerings to the editor. They went in long-hand (pencil) direct to the printer, Mr Goeby, and the editor saw them for the first time in proof. I have often wished that such Contributor Power existed everywhere. The printers soon read my writing miraculously, and there were very few mistakes. Years later, when we condescended to a typewriter, the printing folk were far from grateful. I was told at a Christmas party that they missed the fun of interpreting my scribbles.

It was exciting to sit down at the famous Table in the pleasant old room at No. 10 Bouverie Street. Round the walls were the faces (mostly bearded) of our ancestors right back to 1841. Under the table-cloth, I knew, were the carved initials of Thackeray, Leech, Mark Lemon, Jerrold, J. S. Tenniel, Burnand, Charles Keene, Phil May and the rest. Every new arrival had to make his mark. I practised long before I dared to mutilate the sacred board. At my first dinners there were long clay pipes on the table. I tried one, but I don't think any others went into action. My arrival made the number thirteen, but nobody seemed to mind. Twenty years later, though, the old superstition asserted itself, and if we were thirteen some mere non-Table fellow was invited to avert disaster. Owen Seaman sat at one end with Raven Hill the cartoonist on his right and my humble self on his left. At the other end was Philip Agnew, of the proprietors, Bradbury and Agnew, between Bernard Partridge, the senior cartoonist and E. V. Lucas. There was also Charles Graves, elderly and sage, who was Seaman's lieutenant. Between them these two ran the paper. I don't believe there was a female secretary in the building. Frank Reynolds was the Art Editor. That dear talented droll George Morrow joined the Table just before me: he was intensely shy and no one except the man next to him ever heard him say a thing. Next to me was young Ewan Agnew who should have worked up to the proprietor's chair, but died untimely. I never saw a Bradbury at the Table: and A. A. Milne had left it after the war. But Ernest Shepard was there.

Thackeray wrote a gay song for his colleagues called 'The Mahogany Tree' – a pity, because the Table is deal. The song began:

> Here let us sport,
> Boys as we sit,
> Laughter and wit
> Flashing so free.
> Life is but short –
> When we are gone
> Let them sing on
> Round the old tree.

We sit on – 130 years later – but in my time we have never sung. There was laughter and wit at those agreeable meals – there is still: and for those who work at home it is a good thing to meet those who are practically engaged on the common purpose, to hear the 'shop' (I always like hearing other people's 'shop'). But it was not an orgy with intent to hilarity. After lunch we settled down to our serious business, the selection of subjects for two political or social cartoons – yes *two* – the treatment of the selected subjects, the details of the drawings, and the title (if any), the caption, or 'cackle', below the pictures.

'Serious business'? So it was – 'solemn', almost. No one ever said so, but I felt myself that I was one of a sort of unofficial Imperial Cabinet. (I don't think the 'Shadow' Cabinet had been invented then.) These cartoons we were preparing were intended not for Aldershot and Chelsea only but for Australia and Canada, South Africa, New Zealand, all the Dominions, all the corners of the Empire. In all these parts the people would understand what we meant if we put Britannia or John Bull into a cartoon; and they would expect Britannia and John Bull to act and speak with appropriate pride and dignity. John Bull could deliver a lofty rebuke but never a jest. I forget when the great fellow departed; for some time before that he was used with reluctance.

The sense of responsibility lengthened our labours. Later, when the dinners became lunches, we might be debating still at five o'clock. The editor might arrive with a firm design for a cartoon about This: but it was a democratic gathering and bright ideas would pop up all round the Table. Presently the popular subject was That, closely followed by The Other. But how was That to be treated? How did the cartoonist see it? Sometimes the docile Bernard Partridge did not see it at all – if this was the choice could not Raven do it? Well, what about The Other? The trouble about that was that something might happen over the weekend which would make the 'cut' look very silly next Wednesday. So the talk bounced back and forth for an hour or so: and suddenly the patient editor would steer us back to This, and we began again. We graciously left the details of the drawing to the cartoonist, but we gave orders about some of them, and dictated the general plan – the expression on the Kaiser's face, how Lloyd George should be dressed. You may say that no work of art can emerge from such a committee. But I have seen many a fine cartoon built up from an unpromising start by this process of miscellaneous suggestion. All the famous cartoons, including the great Tenniel's, were made in this way. 'Tenniel himself,' says Richard Price, 'scarcely ever suggested a cartoon idea or requested any but visual alterations.' I can't remember that Sir Bernard Partridge (he was knighted in 1925) had much to say at the Table. In 1939 he wrote: 'I have no illusions about my work, which I know to be really very second-rate stuff. The subject matter is not often of my own conceiving, and as to the execution it resolves itself into a strenuous stand-up fight against a rigid time-table . . .' But Richard Price records also that 'as he grew older he simplified his style and showed brilliant ingenuity in edging discussion away from any cartoon that involved more than two figures . . .'

Seaman would then carefully write down : 'Senior cartoon. Lloyd George as Ajax defying the lightning . . .' and all the rest. But the picture was only half the task: now the words. Generally in those days there was a brief piece of dialogue ('the cackle') under the cartoon and over that a title that summed up the whole work.

Kaiser: 'So now, you see, you've lost everything.' *King of the Belgians:* 'Not my soul.' So ran 'the cackle' of Partridge's famous and effective cartoon in 1914. I have often wondered how long it took the Table to settle for those particular words.

Sometimes, at our end of the Table, politics took charge and tempers flared. Raven Hill was a strong and voluble Conservative, E. V. Knox, next to him, was Liberally inclined, and now and then there were hot words, real rows.

Half-past three, perhaps. 'Well, now the second cartoon. There are two or three possible subjects . . .' In the 'senior' cartoons (Partridge's) we put the World or the Empire right: the second (Raven Hill's) was generally 'domestic' and did not take so long. But the long business began again – with, perhaps, another row. After the stickiest discussion E. V. Lucas and I would go out exhausted and have a glass of milk at a Fleet Street Milk Bar. 'Alan,' I remember him saying, 'can you remember what the first cartoon was about?' And, blow me, for a minute or two I could not.

Owen Seaman seemed to rule the artists as well as the writers. I remember a sad scene at the end of one of the long afternoons. Dear shy, small, George Morrow, beloved of all, put a picture before O.S., one of his fantastic Tudor conceits, not a rough sketch, not a suggestion, but a fully finished piece of work. Seaman examined it carefully and long, said at last, 'Do you think that's funny?' and handed it back. Poor George did not argue or explain, but retired, I imagine, hurt. I was sorry for George but I sometimes wish that editors kept so close an eye on their comic artists today.

Seaman reigned for twenty-six years (1906–32). 'He retired,' says Richard Price, 'only under presence of ill-health. Various attempts had been made to indicate that the time was ripe, including a very elaborate placing of dinner guests at one of the out-of-town *Punch* dinners, which was supposed to hint that proprietors wished him to consider the matter. Seaman was not the man to take hints of this subtlety, and the Chairman of the Company [then Lawrence Bradbury] was deputed to approach him privately. During lunch he talked about the need for the old to take their rest and for the young to have their opportunity. After a good deal of this, Seaman suddenly leaned nearer to the table and said in an agonized tone "Lawrence, surely you're not thinking of retiring!" His colleagues believed that he genuinely could not imagine *Punch*'s continuing without him. Even on his holidays in the South of France he had never stopped discussing what the office would be doing at that particular moment. However, he was too sick a man to carry on. His friends, and one can never understand his complex, infuriating, and fascinating character unless one realizes the qualities of his friendships, were glad to see him returning to the idea of working on a full-dress study of Browning: but a recurrence of illness cut his retirement short.'

I shall always remember him with affection and gratitude, for did he not start me, professionally, along the way of words? More important, did he not discover, and deploy, A. A. Milne?

E. V. Knox succeeded Seaman. In 1949 came Kenneth Bird, the first artist editor: in 1953 Malcolm Muggeridge, in 1958 Bernard Hollowood, and in 1969 William Davis. It is not for me to trace, as Richard Price has so ably done, the changes of course, the different styles of command. One great change has been the decline of the political cartoon. The protracted births I have described are no more. First it was one cartoon not two. Then the cartoon was expelled from the Table, and we met at 12 noon to settle the matter before meat. Now, I believe, the whole thing is done in a private huddle by the editor and artists. But the lunches go on; I do not often attend now, but I find them jolly. 'Bill' Davis – a good innovation – began inviting distinguished strangers to the lunch: one week I sat next to my old House of Commons friend Mr Callaghan, and another next to another, George Brown. In the old days an outsider at the sacred Table was as rare as a seal in London River. I can remember two only, Prince Philip, who was made an honorary member and carved his P on the Table, and the venerated James Thurber. After eating there is some general topical talk in which the Guests take part and may well put ideas into our heads. Richard Mallett is, I think, the only man there who sat under Seaman too. He has been described (by an American) as 'the best film critic in the world'. Basil Boothroyd is an inexhaustible fund of fun: he has been selected by Prince Philip to do his biography. Alan Coren is a very bright new (comparatively) spark. Then there are David Langdon, and Norman Mansbridge, funny artists, and W. A. Hewison, Art Editor. The man I miss, since 1966 began, is Humphrey (H. F.) Ellis, one of the funniest writers, and, what is more, the best writers of 'fun', with a pregnant polished style, that I remember.

At the other end of the Table I have seen three hosts – Philip, Alan and Peter Agnew. We shall see no more. Last year too the old firm of Bradbury and Agnew, which took over in 1872, sold *Punch* to United Newspapers and so just missed a reign of 100 years. We have found a hospitable and sturdy home just round the corner in Tudor Street: but it was sad to see 'the old guv'nors' go. No more will the lofty staff of the *News of the World* look down at the solemn funny men the other side of Bouverie Street. Each Agnew, each editor, has been different and left a little of himself behind, but the ship rides on still much the same, and I at least am proud to have been so long a member of the crew. As this is a work of record, and the *History of Punch* is out of print, I feel it my duty to repeat Richard Price's account of my part in that history, far too generous here and there but justly severe elsewhere:

A. P. Herbert, long established as a direct and forceful poet, especially during the war (1914), and a writer of most kinds of article, was the other main star of the Twenties [he had been discussing E. V. Knox]. It is a point strongly in Seaman's favour that just as he published the drawings of W. Bird, who seems now to have been everything he disliked, he published A.P.H., who said in print the kind of things that people said in private. As we look through the issues of the period, A.P.H's stature grows. The decline of his reputation [this was 1957] seems a temporary thing, based too much on one bad patch in a life of sustained quality. He was quite unlike any other *Punch* man of the Burnand, Seaman, or Evoe (E. V. Knox) regimes.

A good deal of A.P.H. can be dismissed as routine. He tried to write the typical *Punch* article, and, like most men who have tried it, apart from its inventors, he failed. He had little talent for making bricks from the straw of suburban life and he lacked the kind of comic invention with which Evoe rearranged reality into wildly funny patterns. Much of modern life he simply did not understand. No *Punch* man was more likely to burst into an attack on modern art, long-haired yellow-bellies and the rest of it. Where he disliked he attacked and, as with all extroverts, his attacks sometimes embarrassed admirers by their ignorance, frivolity, and narrowness; but, unlike some of the men whose timorous hates weakened the paper, he was a man of genius and he is entitled to have his weaknesses disregarded. A.P.H. was the greatest journalist of our time [O, come! Richard]. He wrote magnificent plain prose in argument or comment and sometimes in description. He belonged to the same line as Swift, Hazlitt, Cobbett, Shaw and Orwell. He was one of the very few *Punch* men of this century to have created a personal style. A Herbert article nearly always had an individual voice, persuasive, infuriating but as sharp and recognizable as Shaw.

A.P.H. lived in the present; he was one of the few humorists who rarely used the past as material. He lived with enormous energy, wrote as easily and straightforwardly as he lived and was always readable, direct, and relevant. At a time when the paper was turning its back on the world it lived in, he almost alone represented the greater sanity of fighting back. Whether or not he was wrong is, for this purpose, irrelevant. What is important is that he regarded right and wrong as worth fighting about. To many readers *Punch* was A.P.H. He was genuinely a satirist unlike many of the *Punch* men who are given this title by people who do not understand what satire is. When his indignation was aroused by some abuse he might denounce it in admirably-written invective, but more often he picked out its weaknesses and laughed at them. Very often he used the *reductio ad absurdum*. Nearly always the evils he attacked were capable of improvement and in and out of *Punch* he has improved them.

He has fought more reforms through than any living man; he is, indeed, a survival of an obsolescent type, the Reformer. His miscellaneous journalism, his chairmanship of committees, his active social life, even his Membership of the House of Commons as Junior Burgess for Oxford University have all helped, but it was primarily through *Punch* that he aroused opinions and got things done.

A.P.H. fought whatever party was in power. He fought against the maintenance of wartime regulations, against the Licensing Laws, against resorts that interfered with bathing, against policemen who acted as *agents provocateurs*, against the survival of obsolete laws like the one that said you could not get married after 3 p.m., and the neglect of the Thames as a highway. His most important reform -- though the total effect of his libertarian campaigns should not be under-rated -- was the big change in Matrimonial Law. This was actually brought into effect by one of the most remarkable Private Member's campaigns in history, but the ground-work had been laid by persistent fighting in *Punch*. It says something in Seaman's favour that he published articles which must have aroused frenzied complaints from many readers.

A.P.H. was successful with a number of series built round characters like Honeybubble or Poker. The Topsy articles, written in a breathless rush, were tremendously popular. The most original and successful form that he invented was the mock law Report. The *Misleading Cases** were sometimes fantastic odd bits of law logically extended until the result was absurd; sometimes they were aimed at amending the law by ridicule. The variety of basic ideas, the scholarship, the magnificent judicial English, far clearer and finer than the real thing, the incidental fun and the directness of purpose behind them made them one of the great *Punch* series.

In verse, he soon left behind him the mock ode and classical allusions and moved towards the verse-epistles which really suited him. He always had something to say, and this made for verse that swung on instead of lagging about in the same spot. He was always trying new forms and he mastered nearly every one he tried, with a mastery unspoiled by ostentatious effort. [Richard, how sweet you are!] As his work for the theatre widened, his rhythms became influenced by music. This inspiration from musical comedy and revue was the first big new influence on light verse since the adaptation of Aristophanic metres. You could not sing Seaman, but you could sing Herbert. Here is a typical chorus from *Ballads for Broadbrows*, a late-Twenties attack on busybodies, the members of Town Councils and Prosecuting Societies:

> Let's stop somebody from doing something!
>> Everybody does too much.
> People seem to think they've a right to eat and drink,
> Talk and walk and respirate and rink,
>> Bicycle and bathe and such.

* Began 9 July 1924 – the same year as my first assault on the stage.

So let's have lots of little regulations,
Let's make laws and jobs for our relations,
There's too much kissing at the railway-stations,
Let's find out what everyone is doing,
    And then stop everyone from doing it.

A.P.H. has been rather unfairly neglected of late. Some ill-judged attempts to lecture the Left without any clear alternative doctrine, a few grumbling Blimpish verses, eccentric references to a world in which dancing at night-clubs seemed to be the full expression of the human personality, a certain ingenuous liking for the limelight and some thumping errors of judgement have distracted attention from the range and brilliance of his work as a whole. If his views have sometimes been silly, so were Shaw's, and, like Shaw, he is entitled to be judged by his best.

Well, well – thank you, Richard. But one day you must tell me about those 'thumping errors of judgement'. It is my modest opinion that I am nearly always – in the end – right.

I was glad that he mentioned my character Topsy. She made three books, *The Trials of Topsy*, *Topsy, M.P.*, and *Topsy Turvy*, which are – or were – presented in a single *Topsy Omnibus*.* She was fun to write, but a great labour – it took me three days to write 1,200 words of her. She made some lasting additions to the language – one of them was 'It's the done thing'.

I enjoyed too my Mr Mafferty. I have, I fear, been an absentee Irishman. I have made one visit to Dublin to lecture some high Society and I came down in the Shannon in a seaplane on my way to Newfoundland; these have been my only contacts with my native land, and I feel guilty. But in my youth I was a warm student of J. M. Synge, and in Oxford days I never missed a chance to see the Irish Players. Arthur Sinclair was my favourite man, and I developed a respectful imitation of him.

Some years ago I was the 'guest celebrity' on the B.B.C. Television show *What's My Line?* Before his appearance the 'panel' were blindfolded and had to guess his identity by his answers to questions. One or two theatrical victims I had seen confined themselves to grunts and squeaks. I thought this feeble, one should say something, but in what voice? I knew Gilbert Harding and two others quite well. I decided to try my bogus Irishman: and that morning, for the first time, I looked at the map and learned that Muckross, my father's home, was in County Kerry.

Gilbert Harding asked the first question – a common one:
'Are you anything to do with the entertainment world?'

* Ernest Benn.

10, Downing Street,
Whitehall.

April 17, 1943.

My dear A.P.

I must say that I think "Punch", in the cartoon
this week, pays the Eighth Army a very back-handed compliment by representing it as a squirming little ferret.
Considering that the intention was to do them honour, the
shot was a very poor one.   Nor is the proportion of
Montgomery and his Army that between a man and a ferret,
and he would be the first to resent it.

As a constant reader of "Punch" over so many
years, I think I must tell you that this is the biggest
flop since the cartoon of John Bull waking from his wartime
nightmare on the very day the Germans marched on Prague.

I am sure your colleagues will welcome criticism
from their readers.

Yours sincerely

Winston S. Churchill

A.P. Herbert, Esq., M.P.

'Sure,' I said, 'at one time I did be thinkin' so, but if you'd see what the critics would be sayin' about me, you'd not be thinkin' the like of that at all, at all.'

There was a solemn hush. The panel was baffled. Even the agile Gilbert could think of nothing to say and 'passed'. To my surprise I kept them baffled for about two minutes. At last one of them said:

'Would you please say something in your ordinary, natural voice?'

'Natural, is it?' I replied with great contempt. 'Isn't it the tongue me father taught me, an' he climbin' the hills of Kerry man an' boy, an' huntin' the wild craytures in the bogs of Kilbay? Sure it's the only voice the good God gave me, an' why would I tell you a lie?'

In the end the wizard Lady Barnett got me. The joke was that two days later I received two letters from Irish folk (one said she was 'Topsy' Herbert) which said:

'What a treat it was to hear the true Kerry accent you had on you last night!'

Mr Mafferty, fake though he was, was intended as a salute to my (nearly) native land.

Here begins one of his many discourses:

MR MAFFERTY HAS A HAIRCUT

'The hair's a little thin, is it?' said Mr Mafferty, taking his head out of the basin. 'Well, maybe it is thin, Mr Barber. An' what way would it not be thin, an' you diggin' in the roots of it with your sharp fingers, an' tearin' it out with your fierce machines, an' frettin' it with your rough towels, an' washin' it away with your cascades of water, like a Chinaman tormentin' the sands of the river for a few grains of gold? It's the wonder of the world, I'm thinkin', if there's one hair clingin' to the poor crown of me head, an' it swollen and sore with the great buffetin' it's had this day. It's not thin the hair is at all, Mr Barber, but sensitive itself. It isn't a doormat you have in front of you, or a frayed rug, or a piece of a carpet is hung in the backyard on a Saturday mornin' to be beaten by an old woman, an' she chokin' with the dust. It's a human head, an' tender as a little child's. But maybe it's in the stable you worked as a boy, Mr Barber, an' you mistakin' the top of me skull for the back of a horse' . . .

It all began with *Punch* sixty years ago: and to that great paper I offer my salutes and thanks. The old ship rides on, with a new rig but the same stout hull. Good luck to her!

{7}

'CREATIVE JOY'

'IT seemed to him that the only solution was to go into the form that has shown the greatest creative vitality in the past ten or fifteen years – musical comedy. I am an admirer of musical comedy and I agree that it is, at present, the only theatrical style exhibiting signs of spontaneous growth . . .

'We might pause for a moment over musical comedy, though. It is interesting to note that, of all the forms of our time, musical comedy is the only one to make use of: free, unrealistic backgrounds, rapid leaps through time and space; bold colour; heightened language (in its lyrics); rhythm (in its music); dynamic movement (not only in its dance, but everywhere); direct address to the audience. Musical comedy is the form that makes the most extensive use of theatrical convention in our time, and something of its theatrical vitality must stem from the feat. The form is eager to please its audience, and to explore the theater as theater – two things that the serious drama has not thought of doing in quite a long while. We generally regard the popularity of musicals as a sign of public illiteracy; it may actually be a response to creative joy.' From *How Not to Write a Play* (1956, Max Reinhardt, London) by Walter Kerr, Dramatic Critic of the *New York Herald Tribune*.

I read with relish this pronouncement by a much respected man of the theatre. I remember so many sniffy remarks from lofty fellows in the opposite sense – the musical comedy is illogical, unnatural and so on – how absurd to have your characters talking prose one minute, singing in verse or dancing, or both, the next! I read it with comfort now, for in all, I reckon, I have made nineteen efforts at 'creative joy' – that is, I have written the words for fifteen full-length musical revues and plays, and four short ones. It is an expensive perilous 'form', and not all these ventures made money, but all, I like to think, mainly through my composers, made some joy. The total output is greater than Gilbert's, and nine or ten of the works, in my humble opinion, deserve to endure like his. But I have no D'Oyle Carte. At least, Mr Walter Kerr assures me that I was not, artistically, wasting my time. When I first cast ambitious eyes at the theatre my addiction to verse naturally inclined me towards the stage that wanted songs. My first effort was in 1924, a Christmas play called *King of the Castle*, commissioned and directed by that fine, hilarious fellow, William Armstrong for his Repertory Theatre, the Playhouse, at Liverpool. Dennis Arundell did the music, tuneful but elegant. Angela Baddeley, who had won affection and renown already as Jenny Diver in *The Beggar's Opera*, played 'The King'; but she was the only importation. All the other parts were played by regular members of the repertory company, and serious 'straight' actors found themselves for the first time singing. Some of them later were to make good names in London and 'the pictures', Cecil Parker, Tam Williams (the playwright), Angela Baddeley, James Harcourt, Herbert Lomas (who later played 'Lincoln' in Drinkwater's play).

William Armstrong, very properly knighted later, was a great man of the theatre and rich company, one of the funniest talkers I have met. I wish I could remember all his stories about Mrs Patrick Campbell. The play went well enough. It began prophetically with a display of Child Power: the children took over an office – Blunderbuss and Cheese, stockbrokers – by force in the first Act and ruled the grownups in the last. It was highly praised and well attended. 'One leading London paper's critique went so far as to suggest that if a possible successor to *Peter Pan* in universal popular favour were needed "perhaps it is here" (meaning *King of the Castle*). The artistes excel both in the libretto and the music.' 'Hilarious success ...' 'Lyrics delicious...' But it was not quite right. Billy Armstrong and I talked for years about revising it for London, but we never did.

Cheese (Mr James Harcourt) has a very fruity number, sung in piratical rig after an arduous sea voyage, in which he defines the limits of patriotism:

> I've always been extremely keen
> On anything at all marine:
>   I used to rave
>   About the wave
>   And with no small emotion
> I used to sing the sort of thing
> That sailors are supposed to sing
>   Explaining what
>   A pleasant spot
>   They find the raging ocean.
> But Ah, how short a step is there
> From high romance to *mal de mer*!

The nation, Sir, that lifts a hand
Against our well-beloved land,
That race must reckon first with me,
But anyone can have the sea. . . .

Riverside Nights

All through the great Nigel Playfair's reign at the little Lyric Theatre, Hammersmith, I was a faithful courtier. I can't think how often I saw his adorable *Beggar's Opera* (1920–4) – and I have been unable to listen without rage to one or two modern productions. The points they miss! Frederic Austin's delicate arrangement of the music won from me at least the rare word perfect. I would as soon tamper with Handel's Largo. It shocks me that anyone should dare to do 'The Beggar' without him. I shall never forget Edith Evans playing Millamant in *The Way of the World*. I loved too Sheridan's *Duenna*. There was an elegant lyric writer!

It was, I really believe, my earliest ambition to have a play performed at the Lyric, but I never nursed it seriously. Then Playfair became a neighbour, and I was thrilled by an invitation to River House, near the Dove, with the great magnolia tree. I was not merely thrilled but incredulous when he asked me to write an 'Entertainment' with him. For my beloved Lyric. Such excitements are the true wine of youth. Later in life you sip the tempting glass, and say you will think it over. Will it pay? Is it really what you want to do? But now I swallowed eagerly, and began five happy years in harness at the Lyric.

They were not money-making years. Nobody made money at the Lyric. I was not in the secrets, except about my own plays, but my guess is that only *The Beggar's Opera*, which ran for four years, showed a good profit. For the rest, however well things went, it was always scrape and pray. Nigel liked to do things well – and get West End stars to perform in a suburb. Frederic Austin rightly insisted on a worthy orchestra for the musical pieces, and there was one long good-humoured quarrel about 'Freddie's band' – 'Now he wants a bassoon'. At the prices of those days the house held about £1,200, filled to capacity, and with Freddie's band, a chorus, a costly singer or two and a 'getting-out' figure of nearly £1,000, long runs and large gains were impossible. We opened my *Derby Day*, I remember, on a capital sum of £1,000, of which the author contributed £100. We had a 'successful' run of about seven months but the author did not see his £100 again. It was a miracle that Playfair and his board (of which Arnold Bennett was a member) kept the Lyric flag flying so bravely for fourteen years.

He was fine company, round and comfortable in person, forthright and witty in speech, with a strong, surprisingly high voice. His mind was keen and cultivated, and always pursued perfection. It was a joy, and an education, to work with him, though there were interludes of obstinate error (or so we thought) governed, as a rule, by money worries. In the actual production of a play he had the flame and the forgivable faults of genius. Brilliant improvisations would suddenly be sounded from the dark stalls or dress circle, and I, at least, never wanted to quarrel with them. One example. In the Third Act of *Tantivy Towers*, the hero – or rather, the tenor – shoots a fox which being hunted chances to pass a shooting party during the lunch interval. On this I wrote the following comment, to which Thomas Dunhill gave some admirably solemn music:

There are some things which are not done:
To shoot a fox of course is one.
But the offence is fouler still
If hounds are just about to kill:
For this is nothing, we conclude,
But robbing hungry dogs of food:
And persons who torment a pet
Deserve whatever they may get.

We gave this to the chorus, and it is marked in the score CHORUS (Tenors and Basses). But Nigel, in rehearsal, had one of his inspirations. He made the sportsmen turn their backs on the painful scene, and he gave the words to the three 'flunkeys' – butler and footmen, who were serving the picnic lunch. He set them in a small grim group in the right-hand corner near the footlights; they looked, and sounded, like implacable judges. Done like this the commination had a strong dramatic effect, not merely satirical but solemn. One felt the full horror of the hero's deed.

But he did, we thought, rely too much on the spur of the moment and rather lazily refuse to make plans, where plans are necessary, for example, the handling of Chorus movements. The second Act finale of my *La Vie Parisienne* (Offenbach) was the usual complicated comic opera affair. A French restaurant, husbands and wives at different tables not recognizing each other, some of the chorus in rings round their tables, others moving about, all singing madly and now and then dancing. A. Davies Adams (the musical adaptor) and I had all the manœuvres carefully planned and elaborately described in stage directions. A producer like Wendy Toye would have come to the rehearsal with sketch-maps showing where every actor was to be at any minute all the way through. Dear Nigel had not, I think, so much as glanced at my poor stage directions: by lunch-time he had the company in utter confusion, and he cried: 'Alan, this finale is wrongly constructed. Thomas, I'm going to play golf now.' Ultimately the finale was played exactly as we had planned it.

Stephen Thomas was his faithful stage-manager, and 'Thomas, I'm going to play golf now' often ended a difficult morning. Miss X, the leading lady of another play of mine, was near to tantrums one day: she didn't like her dresses, her dressing-room, and hated everything she was asked to do on the stage. She was a delightful girl, and had a big success, but I thought that morning she might easily flounce out altogether. Sooner than usual there was a bellow from the Dress Circle: 'Thomas! I'm going to play golf now. You and Alan must talk to Miss X.' And so we did. Miss X was pacified: perhaps Nigel was right.

But C. B. Cochran, my other dear master, would never have done such a thing. He kept everything in his hands, and himself chased every trouble, especially actor trouble, to the kill. Many years after, to my alarm and embarrassment, he made me read my script for *Helen* (*La Belle Hélène* – Offenbach again) to the distinguished company he had engaged in the bar of the St James's Theatre on a cold and frosty morning. There were the famous Evelyn Laye (*Helen of Troy*), George Robey (*Menelaus*) and W. H. Berry (the High Priest *Calchas*). There were also clouds of Cochran's Young Ladies, few of whom, I imagined, were classical scholars. This was my first appearance in such company, and I felt as out of place as a Hammersmith mouse in a Royal kitchen. George Robey was keen and loyal from the first: he knew all about the classical legends. But Bill Berry did not, and till the end of the run he could never pronounce Ulysses correctly. His red-covered part was three times the thickness of Robey's and had the best jokes. But at the end of the reading he came up to me and made the classic comedian's remark: 'Sounds all right, old chap, but, you know, there's nothing in this for me.'

I did not repeat this to anyone, but Bill Berry must have muttered to others. For next day Cochran summoned him to the same bar and gave the old star a stately dressing down. 'How dare you,' he said, 'say such things about the play in which you have been engaged to play! It is to be produced by the great Professor Reinhardt. The music is by Offenbach. You have with you Miss Evelyn Laye and Mr Robey. The book is by A. P. Herbert and' (I'm told he added) 'Homer.' Poor Bill Berry left that bar like a jelly.

Riverside Nights was an odd but attractive medley. John Galsworthy, who kindly wrote a foreword to the published version called it 'a delicious entertainment'. 'It's the only revue I've been able to sit through entirely without grief. They tell me it's a new departure. But why? It appears to be an ordinary revue, so far as my limited knowledge of the article goes. There is singing and there is dancing; there are playlet skits, and the other devices peculiar to this form of entertainment; and there is no connecting link between them. *Riverside Nights* has in fact a most engaging inconsequence. Where, then, does it depart from revues as we know them? Only in quality. *Riverside Nights* happens to be really witty and to lack vulgarity. Its manufacturers are a cut – and more than a cut – above the ordinary; and there you are! This entertainment has the beauty of inspired amateurism.'

There was, in fact, a tenuous 'connecting link'. It was all a family theatrical party prepared by the seven daughters of Mr Jolly of Hammersmith (Nigel Playfair). To please literary Papa there were two exotic items, a poem by Wordsworth, and one of Landor's Imaginary Conversations which no critic raved about. There was an operetta by *Arne, Thomas* and *Sally*, and a more successful one, *The Policeman's Serenade*, by Alfred Reynolds and me. There was an 'engaging play' called *Lambert Simnel and Perkin Warbeck in the reign of Henry VII*, written in the nursery by young Lyon Playfair. Here are some extracts from his manuscript:

Warb: This no earthly king we have upon our English throne, doth do no good to his people whatsoever, we must try and rise another in his stead.

Simn (after thinking for a long time): I have got a wonderful idea.

Warb: What is it?

Simn: Why, I will pretend to be the Duke that's shut up in the tower, I'll pretend to have escaped, I will go North and stir up a rebellion against the King, then march with troops I have gathered to London and overtake the King, and put myself on the throne.

Warb: Yes that is a very good plan, when are you going to set about it.

Simn: Tomorrow.

Warb: Well I shall not join in your plans, as I have been thinking of a plan to do if yours does not come off, would you like to know what it is?

Simn: Yes very much but it isn't much use thinking about, as my plan is sure to come off.

Warb (Leaning forward): You know the bones of the princes in the tower were never found, well I shall pretend to be one of the princes and get up a rebellion, nobody can say I am not one of the princes as they cannot find the bones to prove both princes were smothered, then I shall march against the King and put myself on the throne.

Simn: Not half as good as my plan.

Warb: It is better than your plan in a way. . . . Remember it is easy to talk but not so easy to do a thing. So you are starting to Yorkshire tomorrow are you?

Simn: Yes. Tomorrow.

Curtain

And I like the end:

Simn: Now we have lost all hope of turning (pointing to the king) off the
throne a blackguard and wicked criminal.
King: Now Perkin Warbeck you will be tried and executed.
Warb: What did I tell you.

Curtain.

The End

Elsa Lanchester, known only at a night-club called *The Cave of
Harmony* now made her name (with Harold Scott) for their Victorian
songs – 'Please Sell No More Drink To My Father', 'The Ratcatcher's
Daughter', and so on.

I supplied three or four songs. 'It May Be Life . . .' was brilliantly
set to music by Dennis Arundell, and sung with huge success by Dorice
Fordred. Many critics put this ditty top of the bill. '. . . a romantic maid
of all work laments over the dullness of her existence and sighs for
the adventure and glories of the world of films, a good song, an amusing song, a song full of human understanding and uncommonly well
sung by Miss Dorice Fordred, who has a comic style that is in the
line of genius.'

She sits on her pathetic little iron bed:

> I wish I hadn't broke that cup,
> I wish I was a movie star.
> I wish there weren't no washing up,
> And life was like the movies are.

So, you see, I may claim to have started the Kitchen Sink School,
generally attributed to the brave boys of the 50's, in 1926.

> I wish I wore a wicked hat;
>   I got the face for it, I know.
> I'm tired of scrubbing floors and that,
>   It may be life – but ain't it slow?
>
> For I don't have no adventures in the street:
> Men don't register emotion when we meet.
> Jack don't register jealousy and such,
> Jack don't register nothing very much.
>   But Jack says 'Evenin''
>   And I says 'Evenin'',
> And we both stand there at the corner of the square,
> Me like a statue and 'im like a bear.
> He don't look lovin' like the movie men,

He just holds tight till the clock strikes ten.
Then Jack says: 'Friday?' and I say 'Right',
Jack says: 'Happy?' and I say: 'Quite'.
Jack just whispers, and I can hardly speak,
And that's the most exciting thing that happens in the week.

In rehearsal Dorice became confused and forgot her words. Her song was nearly cut. But I took her home and played the song till we were both nearly mad, and this seemed to give her confidence. But such work should not be left to a mere author.

The highest praise went to my parody of a Chekhov play, *Love Lies Bleeding* (Chekhov had been cropping up everywhere, even in Barnes, across the river). 'It is not only amazingly funny, but has the true quality of parody in that it is also a just criticism, especially of translation from the Russian' (*The Times*). 'A Russian burlesque supremely and sardonically funny' (*The Scotsman*). 'An unbelievably perfect parody which even the illustrious Russian author would have been forced to laugh at' (*Punch*). 'Magnificently funny throughout and supremely true to the master' (*Sunday Times*). 'Not only good fun but good criticism, and very neatly devised' (St. John Ervine in *The Observer*). I repeat these verdicts for practical reasons: the piece is quite undated and somebody, I hope, will do it again.

It began thus:

EBENEZER STEPHEN STEPHENSON (a lunatic, deep in income-tax forms)
What is the time, Thomas William Love?
T. W. LOVE (after a pause – and with a shrug of utter disillusionment):
What does it matter?

T. W. Love was played by the late James Whale, a Chekhovian actor who was then Playfair's stage-manager. On the First Night, as he said this line, he turned his head toward the wings: and in the wings he saw his assistant stage-manager engaged in a fist-fight with the stage carpenter – a fitting Chekhovian scene.

Thomas Love was dressed in football-clothes. Henrietta Jolly, played by Marie Dainton, gave a brilliant imitation of Mrs Patrick Campbell:

But, excuse me, why are you not playing in the cup-tie, Thomas William Love?
LOVE: To be perfectly accurate, I am. Or rather, shall we say, I was. I will tell you what happened. I was standing in goal. The score, as we say, was five goals each, and half the game to go. Five times the ball had passed me and entered the net. (*Bitterly*) That is the sort of man I am. The centre-forward of the other side was running straight for me with the ball. He had passed the backs – there was nothing between

him and me. Suddenly, at that moment, I realized the utter futility of my whole existence. What in the world, I reflected, does it matter whether a goal is scored or not, by one side or the other? Will anybody be wiser, more beautiful, have more elevated ideals? Some of the cheering crowd will cheer louder, and some will utter blasphemy and threats. But what, after all, is the crowd? What are they for?

STEPHENSON (*muttering*): Retirement, bankruptcy, death, et cetera.

LOVE: Well, you will understand, Henrietta Jolly, that having reached that conclusion, there was only one thing for me to do. Without so much as another glance at the advancing centre-forward, I turned on my heel, walked away from the goal, and came to this house.

STEPHENSON: Did he score a goal?

LOVE: I did not notice.

HENRIETTA: This is a very peculiar house.

J. JOLLY: Ha! I tell you what it is. I believe I am the most extraordinary character alive. I have absolutely no influence over a single human being, I say to one 'Come!' and he goes, 'Do this' and he does exactly the opposite. But when it comes to horses I have the power of an arch-angel. Put me on the back of a horse and it becomes possessed of a devil, flies over mountains, jumps hedges, plunges into ponds. Put my money on a horse and it stops dead. I do not believe that in all the world there is an animal so mild and swift that I cannot turn it into a wild beast by sitting on its back or convert it into a lumbering cart-horse by putting half-a-crown on the creature. I have only to draw a horse in a sweepstake and it bursts out coughing or swells at the knees. Ha! Truly a remarkable power!

(Nigel's 'Ha's!' were significant utterances)

That clever, lovable performer (and playwright) Miles Malleson played an old newspaper-seller, drunk. He halted outside the house, crying:

Paper! Paper! All the losers! (highly amused) He, He! The trouble about me is that half the time I yearn after beauty and the other half I drink gin. Paper!

The end is terrible:

THE BRIDE: What are you doing, Thomas William Love?

(The others also slowly begin to take things in)

T. W. LOVE (with an eloquent gesture towards the dead man): Well, at any rate you will admit that we can now be married, and live happily ever after.

THE BRIDE: But that is not my husband. That is the best man.

T. W. LOVE (throwing down his revolver, with a shrug): Now that is just the sort of thing that happens to me.

CURTAIN

Nonsense, no doubt: but it went so well that I can claim a fair 'sense of the stage'.

I am proud of my *Two Gentlemen of Soho*. This was a one-acter, done first at Liverpool by William Armstrong in 1927. Then Playfair put it into a double bill with Sheridan, no less (*The Critic*), first at the Lyric on 24 October 1928 and later at the Royal Court, Sloane Square.

'It is now accepted,' said the programme, 'that Shakespeare loses nothing by a performance in modern dress' (there had been a lot of this, and it was thought to be terribly clever): 'and this is a shameless attempt to uplift a modern theme by clothing it in Shakespearean language. Some may think the play wordy, but then there are brutes who think Shakespeare wordy.'

The scene was a night-club in Soho. The principal character was Plum, a police officer in disguise, seeking evidence of offences against the licensing laws (there was much of this then).

PLUM: I am an officer from Scotland Yard,
             Dressed in the likeness of an English lord,
             And night by night, while seven weeks swung by,
             Have I to this lewd haunt made pilgrimage
             In search of some irregularity,
             Sometimes disguised as a gentleman,
             And sometimes in the costume of a virgin,
             But nothing happens. I have offered bribes,
             I have been suppliant for sweet wine or opium
             After the hours by Parliament provided,
             But like the fabulous Mongolian drop
             Of water, on strong rock forever falling,
             I have made no impression. I believe
             There is no falsehood practised here but mine,
             There is no jot nor tittle of the law
             By these respectable impostors broken . . .
             So, gentle sleep, upon my eyelids press (sits)
             And let me wake to catch some wickedness . .

He wakes to see Lord WITHERS ordering a cocktail

WITHERS: But let me have a nice Martini. Ho!

PLUM: This is a viscount, and I never saw
             A lord that did not love to break the law.
                      (The waiter kneels)

WITHERS: Pluck me ten berries from the juniper
             And in a beaker of strong barley spirit
             The kindly juices of the fruit compress.
             This is our Alpha. Next clap on your wings,
             Fly south for Italy, nor come you back
             Till in the cup you have made prisoner
             Two little thimblefuls of that sweet syrup

The Romans call Martini. Pause o'er Paris
And fill two eggshells with the French vermouth.*
Then home incontinent, and in one vessel
Cage your three captives, but in nice proportions,
So that no one is master, and the whole
Sweeter than France, but not so sweet as Italy.
Wring from an orange two bright tears, and shake,
Shake a long time the harmonious trinity.
Then in two cups like angels' ears present them,
And see there swims an olive in the bowl,
Which when the draught is finished shall remain
Like some sad emblem of a perished love.
This is our Omega. Go, fellow!

WAITER (rising from knees): Sir. It is too late. I cannot serve you.

PLUM: Damn.

WITHERS: Oh, that in England might be born a man,
Sprung from the loins of English liberty,
To rise and sweep, twice daily, like old Thames,
In a strong tide 'gainst petty tyrannies,
And though at evening he be beaten back,
Flood in at morning to clean the channel again
Of busy women, and suck out to sea
Bans, prohibitions, interferences,
Movements, Societies, Government Departments,
Such as curtail, diminish, and cut down
The antique privilege of true-born Englishmen
To take their pleasure in what way they please,
When, how, which, where, whatever, and with whom!
Was it for this I joined the Infantry
And took up arms against a Continent?

I like, too, this reflective exchange:

TOPSY: Life is a most extraordinary thing.
HUBERT: Man, like a pebble on a glacier.
Moves imperceptibly, but always down.

All the eight characters are dead, for one reason or another, when the curtain falls, and all in a neat heap in the centre of the stage. On the first night at Hammersmith Marie Ney, who died fairly early, said she felt a mouse running up her leg but nobly endured it.

Plum dies last of suicide. He took four stabs and fifty lines of blank verse to die.

* In these days no gentleman would drink a 'gin and mixed', but we did in those days.

(*Stabs self*)
This is the gate and portal of my ending,
I think there doth not any word remain,
But silence and still quiet touch my lips
With the mute harmony of things unspoken.
I never was of that loud company
Which seek their harvest in a waste of words;
'Do' was my dictionary. And my sword
Leaped from the sheath ere I could mention it.
   (*Stabs self, and falls. Sits up perkily*)
As you may see in some great orchestra,
A little lonely fellow at the end
Sits by the cymbals, and the instruments
Thunder around him their tempestuous din,
Flutes, horns, and oboes, harp and clarinet,
And the wild fiddles like the forest swaying
On Swedish mountains when the storm is high.
But he, that could with one most royal clash
Startle the city, and make all that music
Like the small twittering of birds appear,
Sits with his brasses, but doth make no sound
Till the conductor shall command him so;
And leaves his cymbals and goes home at last,
Still with no sound, nor kindly thanks, nor notice,
For the conductor hath forgotten him –
So sit I here, and die without a word.
   (*Stabs self. Sits up and looks about*)
Well, this will puzzle them at Scotland Yard.
   (*Stabs self. Dies*)
   CURTAIN*

Anyone can achieve a spasm of this sort. In *Beyond the Fringe* they had a brief and feeble Shakespearean effort. But five hundred lines – with a plot – takes some doing. I applaud modestly when I think that I got away with sustained parodies of Chekhov, Shakespeare, and W. S. Gilbert.

Next came on 18 April 1929 an alleged 'adaptation' of *La Vie Parisienne* by Offenbach, and, I *think*, his famous librettists Meilhac and Halévy. The late A. Davies Adams, composer, a keen student of Offenbach, had begun to do an adaptation, book and all, himself, but had got stuck about half-way through the first Act. He brought what he had done to Playfair who asked me to take it over, characters and all, continue and complete, which I did. Playfair, I am not clear why, would not let me look at the original play, so I had to invent my own 'story', and to this day I have not the slightest idea what happened

* An acting edition of *Two Gentlemen* can be obtained from Samuel French. The full text is in *Ballads for Broadbrows*.

in the piece which I 'adapted'. Our version was all about a Victorian English family in Paris with a good deal of disguising and so on. There was some good singing from the charming Kathlyn Hilliard and Kathleen Burgis, and a lusty good baritone from grand opera, Herbert Langley. Davies Adams produced some jolly music which he protested was pure Offenbach, though I suspected that he had done some inventing too. I enjoyed writing some (alleged) French verse:

> Paris, c'est l'amour,
>   Et l'alimentation,
> Manger toujours
>   Et toujours la passion
> Meals and misses,
> Bocks and blisses,
> Cooking and kisses
>   Ça c'est Paris.

Later I put the same thought (for which I have found much support among the French) into more stately verse:

> Paris se divise en trois parts –
> L'Alimentation – l'Amour – et l'Art:
> Mais ni la peinture ni la passion
> A l'importance de l'alimentation.

'La Vie' is not my favourite work: but it went well, and the amateurs liked doing it.*

Next was one of my pet works *Tantivy Towers*.† This was done at the Lyric, Hammersmith on 16 January 1931. The music was by Thomas F. Dunhill, a scholarly musician, who was no Puccini but had a good sense of the stage and wrote some good tunes. It was 'A Light Opera' in three Acts, and for once was justly described for it was true 'opera' without a word of spoken dialogue, and with hardly any 'recitative'. This not only helps the sense of continuity and illusion. Good singers, professional or amateur, are not always good actors, often they are pretty bad. A pretty girl, a lusty tenor, may thrill you with a song, but let you down with a bad bump when you hear the speaking voice and dull delivery. But continuous music covers a multitude of sins.

The theme has not been touched, I believe, in any other musical work – the Counties *v*. Chelsea, Bloodsports against Bohemia. The first Act is at a Chelsea party to which the Earl and Countess of Tantivy have been lured. The second Act is in the Great Hall of The

---

* Leslie Boosey.
† Published by Methuen. Full score by Kramer.

Towers, the Third in a Glade where both fox-hunting and pheasant-shooting are going on. Except for one reference to Augustus John it is, after forty years, as 'contemporary' as ever.

Playfair produced it beautifully. It went off with a bang and was the talk of the town. Percy Cudlipp, over three days, printed the entire libretto in the *Evening Standard* (he was a verse-writer himself). The piece, probably for the first time, lured the hunters out to Hammersmith, and it excited them both ways. I was impartial (I thought): I put as much into the hearty hunting stuff as I did into my satiricals. Indeed, at the end, the Counties won, I thought. Hercules won; and Orpheus, the intruding artist, was told to go home to Chelsea. One night in the crowded little bar, during the first interval, I met Anthony Eden and his lady. He introduced me to a hunting party of four who were very kind and enthusiastic about Act One. They liked, for example, young Lord Harkaway's comments on the modern pictures he saw about him:

> Was Sheba the Queen, who made
>   Solomon gape,
> A collection of parallel lines?
> Was Juliet just an elliptical shape
> With a few geometrical signs?
> Paint peonies green
> And I see what you mean,
> Paint eyes like an ostrich's eggs,
> But *is* it the case
> That the girls of our race
> Have such very triangular legs?

They were not so keen on Hugh's Toast to 'the Arts' (which, damn it, might have been written for a Student-Beatle gathering today):

> We are the makers of tunes,
>   We are the singers of songs,
> We are the dreamers of dreams,
>   And we are the righters of wrongs:
> We are the minters of mirth,
>   We are the salt of the earth,
> So, monarch and marquis and merchant, take care,
> For it's up with the Muses and down with Mayfair!

> We are the wizards who weave
>   Laughter and love for you all,
> Leave you our griefs in a song,
>   Or paint our poor hearts on a wall:

We are the children who see
Earth as God meant it to be.
We are the fearless, the tender, the true,
So it's up with the Poet, and down, Sir, with *you*!

(This was 1929. But the young things of today think they invented 'protest' songs, about Society and so on.)

My friends in the bar had enjoyed, too, the Earl's statesmanlike assault on the Arts (this was in a favourite metre of Gilbert's):

It is a very curious fact
That those who write or paint or act,
  Compose or etch,
  Or sculp or sketch,
    Or practise things like pottery,
Have not got consciences like us,
Are frankly not monogamous;
  Their moral tone
  Is all their own,
    Their love-affairs a lottery.
It's hard to say why writing verse
Should terminate in drink, or worse,
  Why flutes and harps
  And flats and sharps
    Should lead to indiscretions.
But if you read the Poets' Lives
You'll find the number of their wives
  In fact exceeds
  The normal needs
    Of almost all professions.

Not these the kind of people who
Were prominent at Waterloo,
  Not this the stock
  Which stood the shock
    When Kaiser picked his quarrel:
Let Dagoes paint and write and sing
But Art is not an English thing:
  Better be pure
  And die obscure
    Than famous but immoral.

As my poor father used to say
  In 1863,
Once people start on all this Art
  Good-bye, Monogamee!
And what my father used to say,
  Is good enough for me.

In the second interval I saw the Edens again and said: 'Where are our friends? Their drinks are here.' Anthony said: 'They're not coming up. You should have heard some of the things they were saying, "Not drinking with that feller" and so on. I *think* I heard something about a horsewhip.'

I could not understand why. Act Two opened with a brilliant little scene which should have warmed the heart of any fox-hunter. Playfair had set the dinner table up right over the footlights. Every man was in his pink, the port was passing, the small stage seemed enormous.

Then to an electrical galloping tune the young folk give the Earl an account of the day's hunt's ending:

> That fox was a fellow, no touch of the yellow,
>   As bold as a bellow for Yaffle he ran.
> But we tumbled him over in Farmer Joe's clover,
>   And the first of the field was our galloping Ann.
> ALL (astride of chairs): A-larrup – a-larrup – a-larrup, etc.

Not a word, not a thought of satire. I loved it.

The foolish Lady Ann has gone and fallen in love with the intruding tenor, the Chelsea host, Hugh, who has come to the Towers as a 'hired musician'.

> BAREBACK: Lord Tantivy, I must insist
>   On horse-whipping this vocalist!

Persuaded to calm down he asks Hugh for a song and chooses John Peel. Hugh sings it through with tremendous effect. The company are thrilled. Hugh is a hero. But it is a trap. Bareback invites the stout fellow to come out hunting tomorrow. Hugh refuses – even to Ann's request. Horror – 'the yellow streak'! Hugh then sings his reasons to the red-coats (this must be the longest 'protest song' in the British light opera). At first they listen quietly: but as their indignation rises, they begin to interject mocking scraps of 'John Peel'. The scraps grow longer, and as he approaches his end they are singing the full song full-throated and Hugh can hardly make himself heard as the red-coats gallop eagerly round him.

> HUGH: Listen! I will go riding where you will!
>   I love the horse – though I have not your skill.
>   But do not ask me to enjoy
>   This pretty sport, for, as a boy,
>   I've seen your butcher's work, and had my fill.
>   You fouled the charming country's breath
>   With scent of blood and boast of death,

While every spinney blushed for shame
To be a partner in the game!
　　One day a fox,
　　A beaten fox,
A sinking, slinking, shrinking fox
　　Crept through the hedge
　　And refuge took
In our great chimney,
　　And his look –
His hunted, haunted, human look,
　　Said, 'I have run bravely –
　　More I cannot give –
And now, kind gentlemen,
　　Have mercy – let me live!
　　Kind Gentlemen!'
They tore him out,
They wore him out,
With mighty fires they smoked him out,
With jolly jests they joked him out,
And, brick by brick, they poked him out,
　　And flung him to the pack:
I was a child and saw the sport.
　　Then with his bloody pad
　　In crimson streaks
　　They stained my cheeks –
To make a plucky lad.
And so, kind gentlemen,
These are, kind gentlemen,
The reasons, gentlemen,
I will not hunt the fox with you tomorrow!
CURTAIN

Dunhill did the music of all this with superb skill and power. It was, I think, the best finale I have ever designed. For once, there was a real clash of thought and feeling on the stage which through the music – and, if I may modestly say so – the 'dramaturgy' – took hold of the audience and truly split them too. But, after all, it was John Peel that won, drowned and downed the sensitive Hugh: and I still wonder why my hunting friends did not come up to enjoy the drinks that I had bought for them. I wish I could see that finale again.

If this piece does survive, as it deserves, for hundreds of years, high marks must be given to Mr Dunhill, the King of Pipes, who put up some money to secure for his brother a libretto and a production. The lot fell on me.

Previous works had caused some embarrassing talk about 'Here comes another Gilbert'; and *Tantivy Towers* caused more. I modestly

{ 94 }

shook my head but secretly I wanted someone to say 'He's much better than Gilbert'. In 1930 a kind Australian writer did. 'He is in the tradition of W. S. Gilbert, but altogether he is a bigger man than Gilbert, more professional, more subtle, more versatile. He is also a master of his craft: in his light verse he stands alone. Calverley, Gilbert, J. K. Stephen, and Seaman, but Herbert transcends them. His prose, too, is at all times impeccable.' With the best will in the world I cannot go all the way with this good friend: but I go some of the way about Gilbert. I could write as good light verse any day. Some said that I had not the same capacity for 'ingenious' rhymes but this trick I have generally avoided, especially those tiresome rows of three syllable rhymes – 'Pinafore – din afore', 'strategy' – 'sat a gee'. I prefer my lines to have a natural sound, unforced, and these are much easier to set to music – and sing.

My serious songs, I think, are superior. Gilbert, so far as I remember, never created any real dramatic excitement or emotion, as I did in *Tantivy Towers, Derby Day, Big Ben, The Water Gipsies* and elsewhere. In *Bless the Bride* I set out to make the people cry, and bless them, they are crying still. I cannot recall a single lump that the great Gilbert ever raised in this old throat. I detested, too, some of his persistent habits, his eternal elderly spinster for example. I was never keen on the 'patter-song'. So I did not want to be 'another Gilbert' and resented it when people said I wasn't.

For the struggling dramatist 1932 was a big year. On 30 January I made my first appearance under the great C. B. Cochran – *Helen* at the Adelphi – and, on 24 February, my last at the Lyric with *Derby Day*, and all that year I rode with pride these two very different steeds. *Helen* was the richest, grandest, most beautiful show I ever was in. *Derby Day*, with a capital, as I have said, of £1,000 behind it, was perhaps the humblest, but I loved it. I wrote much of it on an ocean voyage, by Orient Line, to Melbourne and back, *Otranto* (Captain Matheson) out, *Orford* (Captain Owens) home. The music was written by my good friend Alfred Reynolds, who died last year. He was then musical director at the Lyric. He was a true musician but had a gift of melody (which does not always follow) and he did a wonderful job.

Derby Day was humble in theme and character as well. *Helen* was all about Gods and Kings: but at the other end of London, as my Prologue boasted:

> We have defied the canons of the age
> And put the British people on the stage.
> Prepare your shoulders with the rough to rub:
> Most of the action centres in a pub.
> Our heroine is not as others are,
> But works those engines just behind the bar:

And you may nominate for leading man
Either a tipster or a publican.
Bookmakers, gipsies, coster-mongers, what
A very raffish and plebeian lot!

Reynolds's great feat was to please the high-minded 'musicians' and
his low librettist as well. He produced apt little tunes for every section
of the plebeian lot whether it was costermongers, jockeys, or cockneys
playing darts, a love-sick tipster or a broken-hearted bar-girl, the
crowd in the bar, or the crowd in the paddock, or the entry of the
Licensing Justices on mischief bound at The Old Black Horse. He got
both humour and feeling into his music.

That was the strangest of my many 'first nights', for my own voice
was the first to be heard. Sweating home from Ceylon, I had written a
lengthy Prologue in rhymed couplets, more than 200 lines. Nigel's
original plan was to deliver a cut version of this, about seventy lines,
himself. Then he accepted a part in a West End play, and so could not
be present. But to my horror he said: 'Alan, you must recite your
Prologue yourself.' At first I spluttered 'No!' I had never in my life
uttered a word on any stage: and to add such an ordeal to the author's
normal first night agonies seemed barbarous to me. But – 'try anything
once' – I consented; and quite incredulous, I saw the friendly curtain
rise, found myself facing the horrid wall of light, and faltering:

> Bold is the poet, and his fate unsure,
> Who makes an opera about the poor:
> But he twice over will invite disgrace
> Who sings a pauper of the English race.
> Music, it seems, is not quite music which
> Deals not with royalty, or else the rich: . . .

Looking back over the whole history of human entertainment I think
that this must have been one of the bravest things an amateur has ever
done before the assembled critics of London and swarms of professional
performers. After a few lines the sound of my slender voice frightened
me so much that I felt like walking off the stage. But I held on – and,
I believe, warmed up.

At least, I remembered my words – seventy lines or so. I cannot
find any cuttings, but the critics, I think, were charitable about my
performance.

They must have been, for Nigel asked me to repeat it on the *second*
night – 'There'll be some more Press – the weeklies and so on.' I obeyed
again: and this was interesting. On the second night I was a seasoned,
relaxed, blasé old actor, no longer worrying about my words: they
seemed to emerge automatically. I had time to peer through the curtain

of light seeking the face of a friend I knew to be there, and hearing some noise or another I casually looked into the wings. I don't know whether I spoke the lines any better, but I was as bold as brass. There must be some 'lesson' here, but I cannot say what it is.

Derby Day was, alas, the last production at the Lyric under Nigel Playfair's management. The battle of the Lyric had become too much for him at last and he announced during the run that he was going to end it. He died, prematurely, on 19 August 1934. He had seemed depressed for a long time and I have a feeling that he had lost the will to live. One hot afternoon Lady Playfair (May) telephoned and asked me to go along and see Nigel. They were then on Chiswick Mall at Said House – he had put in that enormous bow window which miraculously survives today (we were all in fear of small boys with stones). Nigel, said May, was being naughty: the doctor wanted him to have an operation, but he wanted to sign a contract for a play in the West End. I went up. The operation was for the prostate gland. It was then a much more alarming affair than it is today – a double operation. But Owen Seaman, my editor at *Punch*, had recently had the thing, so had Lloyd George: they had sailed in the same ship on their convalescent voyage, and they were both as right as rain, whatever that means. 'You're much younger than both of them,' I remember telling Nigel, cheerily, 'and abstemious too.' I hope I was not the only cheery optimist. The next thing I heard from his son Giles was that he was dead.

Helen. C. B. Cochran, in one of his books, said that *Helen* 'more nearly realized my idea of theatrical perfection than any other play I have presented'.

Some time in 1930 or 1931 I had a summons from the great man – and I mean great. So great was he, and so small did I think myself, in spite of my suburban successes, that this was like a summons from the Pope. I knew nothing about *La Belle Helène* (Offenbach and those skilled and mischievous librettists Meilhac and Halévy). C.B. was then in a house in Montagu Street. That was the day, I think, when he showed me his beloved Toulouse-Lautrecs, and other pictures on the staircase, and said: 'They're going tomorrow – most of them.' He was selling them, he explained, to help finance the new show. He did not even know which pictures were going. 'I told the dealer how much money I wanted, and to pick out the pictures he wanted.' This sounded like a man who was keen on his work. On the first night of *Helen* I knew why he had sold his pictures.

He played some records, and I was at once charmed by the music, especially the song 'L'Amour Divin' ('O God of Love', in our version). It was sung by one of those magnetic French sopranos who seem to snuggle into your soul so much more often than the English do. I took the French libretto home and read it, much assisted by my studies at old-fashioned Winchester College. It struck me at once that the play stopped at the wrong place. Paris and Helen are approaching an affair, and the unpopular husband Menelaus is chivvied off to Cnossos. But what happened then? The point of Helen's story was that she went off to Troy and caused the Trojan War: but the original play ignores this event. But it had been famous for something like seventy years, and perhaps it was not for an upstart from Hammersmith to start messing about with it now.

This revival of *La Belle Helène* was not a sudden whim but a dream that had been maturing for years. C.B. could tell you about all the revivals there had ever been. That year the famous Max Reinhardt had one running in Berlin, and we made a pilgrimage to Berlin to see it. Also went with us young Oliver Messel who was to design our scenery and costumes and make a tremendous name. It was not his first encounter with the grand 'West End', but I think he was as much in awe as I was. I took with me an old book 'Tales from Homer' and in the train, with some trepidation, I mentioned my audacious plan to add a new Third Act, ending before the Walls of Troy. 'With trepidation' for I did not know C.B. as well as I knew him later. I had very small claims to consideration as a playwright, and but for Nigel Playfair's persevering efforts I should not have had so much. This great popular entertainer, I thought, the man of circuses and boxing-rings and rodeos, might well reply kindly: 'My boy, we have got to make large audiences laugh. You keep Homer for high-brow Hammersmith. In any case, this opera is a "classic" of its kind, and we mustn't talk about adding new Third Acts to classics.'

C.B. said no such thing. He listened attentively and read the book for the rest of the journey. We saw the play in Berlin, and I met again the charming Rudolf Kommer, Reinhardt's lieutenant who was always in and out of London, and spoke English better than the English. In the bar I muttered something to him about my Third Act, which, by now, had been taking shape in my mind. We travelled on to Salzburg, and up the hill to the famous *Schloss Leopoldskron*. It was a dark and thunderous Sunday afternoon. We sat in a circle of deep armchairs, the deepest I remember, with long cigars, the thunder rolling, myself and, I dare say, Messel, in some alarm. This was the illustrious Reinhardt, quiet and courteous, but daunting in his own dark castle: and this was Cochran – two kings and veterans of the European theatre. I expected my little plan, if it obtained notice at all, to be brushed aside like the feeble joke of a new Court jester: or, at least, if I were bold enough, to provoke a lengthy argument. But Cochran was an artist, always open to new notions. I think he had swallowed this one already, and was merely waiting for Reinhardt's verdict. I spluttered; Kommer translated and supported: there were a few questions in English and German, a few nods and comments; and within three minutes I had permission to go ahead. I was never so warmly surprised in my life.

Reinhardt was to produce, and his E. W. Korngold was to contribute his musical arrangements: but, granting all that was due to them, *Helen* was the artistic creation of C.B. and nobody else. It was he who discovered Oliver Messel, he who plucked this small flower from the suburbs, he who cast Evelyn Laye for Helen and George Robey as Menelaus, he who chose Massine, the master of ballet, to arrange the Bacchanale or Orgy. What a jigsaw puzzle of a job he had given himself! A French play to be 'adapted' into English, in part from a German adaptation – French, German, English – and ancient Greek – humour all claiming a hearing. An Austrian producer and musical 'arranger' – and a 'Buy British' campaign raging. Two celebrated 'broad' comedians and an author suspected of 'literary' tendencies. A show designed for large modern audiences, but founded on ancient Greek mythology and accompanied by 'old-fashioned' music. How to reconcile Homer and 'show-girls': and how to please both those who would expect the sly old jokes about Leda and the Swan, and those, fairly numerous in our land, who had never heard of Leda. Reinhardt, Evelyn Laye, Offenbach, Homer, W. H. Berry – other men might have collected this thoroughbred, but miscellaneous team: only C.B., I swear, could have kept them running in harness and harmony. Some said that the pot would boil over from sheer excess of personality, but it never did. It was better mixed than the outsider knew: and it was watched by a master. Trouble and temper there must be in every theatrical brewing but C.B. had his own secret for melting them down.

His motto, I think, was: 'Choose your man, believe in him, give him a free hand – but watch him.' He kept a distant finger on every detail in every department, from the words of the songs to the size of the shoes. Messel and I were watched, paternally, all through, always with encouragement, never vexatiously. C.B. read through the first draft of my lyrics (the one department of which I did claim to know something), praised them and within a few days could sing (or perhaps hum) them all by heart: but he put his unerring finger on two particular couplets, and gently asked if I could not do better there (a kind and stimulating formula). There was nothing much wrong with them; they would have passed muster with most men, but I had to confess that there, at least, I should try to do better than that, and I believe I did. It was the same with the dialogue, a long labour of drafting and re-drafting, pruning and grafting. Every line and every word was scrutinized with the eye of a hawk but a hand both considerate and careful. There were letters and telephone conversations, two or three times a week, about this scene or that. One would have thought that C. B. had nothing else in the world to do but get the dialogue of this one play right. I do not say that we always agreed. I can be as stubborn as most men: but I gratefully acknowledge that his advice was generally proved to be right and was always constructive and helpful.

Massine, a genius at his job – to watch him at work was a continual feast – wanted nothing better than to spend day and night filling the stage with an orderly maze of lovely dancers. But in his mazes he had little use for the singing members of the chorus who did not dance; and the musical and the author's departments used to rage humorously together while we watched him tucking the poor singers away in remote corners up-stage and off-stage, behind bits of scenery or on platforms in the wings, anywhere but near the footlights where their words, or at least their voices, might be heard. Then C.B. would have to hold the scale and decide just how many singers could be allowed within earshot of the audience without ruining the dance: how much pageant and how much opera – problems for Solomon.

At a rehearsal I never heard him raise his voice beyond what was strictly necessary to carry his words from the stalls to the stage: I think the crisis was not conceivable that could induce him to utter the notorious yell of the agitated producer which, oft repeated, can shatter the nerves of overworked actors. I saw him make strong and drastic decisions in a crisis but never an impulsive or hysterical one. I saw him dominate but never bully the unruly. I saw him angry but never without control. He studied the minds of his flock, and, as the awful night drew near, was ready with the right technique to deal with every explosion that fatigue or temper or nerves provoked: infinitely serene himself, he made uncommon allowances for those not so serene under stress. I have forgotten them now, but I remembered reluctantly for a long time some very hot and foolish things I said at four o'clock in the morning at a rehearsal in Manchester and how C.B. moved quietly away as if he had not heard them. Nor did he ever refer to them.

Indeed, in one of his books (*I Had Almost Forgotten*) he gives me good marks for calm:

> . . . In a musical production there is almost invariably some part that causes trouble and which has to be written and rewritten over again. The second-act finale of *Helen* was the troublesome spot during rehearsals. . . .
>
> The story was carried on in matchless lyrics by A.P.H. (all written to music, exactly as it stood in the original score) but it did not in the opinion of Max Reinhardt, the producer, allow for the ending on a big musical note which he believed to be necessary. Each side made compromises, and I tried to hold the balance fairly. The following was submitted to me, by A.P.H. at a time when he was getting dangerously near to being fed up.

In order that the reader may appreciate the joke, I must point out that the 14th edition of Act II was to accompany *several pages of music*!

FINALE – ACT II (Fourteenth Edition)

Instead of 'The fault was yours – you married her!'
ALL (to Paris): But that is no excuse for you!
                    To war, to war!
                    A dirty trick to play us!
                    The man's a bore,
                    But we want war,
                    So to war for Menelaus!
(2nd time): So we all go to war for Menelaus!
(Meanwhile, when in doubt, everyone sings *'Hurry, hurry, hurry!'*
HELEN holds the centre of the stage throughout, but adequate opportunities are given to MENELAUS, ORESTES, CALCHAS and the other principals; and the thirty-two dancers are dancing an expressive ballet which *clearly brings out the plot of the play*)
    HELEN *and* PARIS *sing 'Farewell' and go. The others sing 'Though everyone the fact deplores etc.'*

CURTAIN

Readers of A.P.H.'s brilliant satires (bless him!) 'will appreciate the irony of that delightful stage direction concerning 'the expressive ballet which clearly brings out the plot of the play'! It suggests that for once in his energetic life A.P.H. had had enough.

Yes, I had my problems too. In the end, so far as I remember the Finale was done exactly as Meilhac and Halévy, Offenbach – and Herbert – had designed it, and almost as the illustrious Reinhardt *had performed it in Berlin.* Long before Reinhardt arrived on the scene I had been through every note of the music with his Herr Korngold. At some point in the same Finale, I remember, I had transferred a phrase of five or six words from Helen to Paris, I forget why. Korngold, at my piano, screamed in horror: 'But vy? For sixty years Helena has sung those words!' Let all this be a warning to 'adaptors' of foreign classics. It is one thing to write a new verse for a single song, it is quite another to reshape a great set-piece of a finale, write and rehearse new words, interfere with the composer's procession of keys, let the dancers loose when the singers should be telling the story – and all this two days before production. The Herr Professor was rather naughty – and C.B. knew better.

I have written many a lyric for foreign music – Offenbach, Oscar Strauss, Johann Strauss, Lehar – and enjoyed it. Having got the general sense of their songs I try to make my words sound as natural as if they had been written first – I sometimes wish that I had been given a go at Grand Opera. But to do this and please the musicians as well, words easy to sing, the right vowels on the high notes, is not easy.

I was pleased with my treatment of the famous point-song in Act Two. Helen, looking up at Leda and the Swan, her father and mother, sings to Venus:

> Ah, Venus, nobody could wonder
>   If now and then a woman fell;
> Man is enough to make us blunder,
>   And we must fight the gods as well; . . .
>
> For instance, there was my poor mother
>   Who met a most attractive swan;
> They fell in love with one another
>   (Though I don't know quite what went on):
> It seemed in need of some protection,
>   For trembling to her breast it came,
> And if she showed it some affection
> I think I might have done the same –
> I'm sure I should have done the same . . .
>   Poor little waif!
>   Do you wonder she erred?
>   If it's not safe
>   To be nice to a bird,
> No wonder some of us struggle and struggle in vain!

Evelyn Laye sang it beautifully. But I was worried about one word in the second refrain – the key-word 'bird', which was a nice singable sound on a high note. I thought she held it too long and blurred it. But who was I to pick holes in our leading lady? I plucked up my courage and shyly put the point: 'I wonder if you could possible clip off "bird" a bit? This is a point-song, and that word, I feel, ought to come out clearly.' Helen was not at all offended, but she said: 'But darling, that would spoil my vocal line.' I think I said feebly: 'Oh, I see, darling.' But, bless her, she did what I asked.

We opened for four weeks, with two or three days intensive rehearsal by Reinhardt, at Manchester in that fine barn the Opera House. What fun those expeditions were! Action in sight at last after the months of troublesome gestation. Cochran's special train, Cochran's gay Young Ladies (I had made friends with many of them) seen at last in their best, the whole Cochran regiment. A hundred souls, at least – there were seventy-one performers – alight with expectation and the hope of triumph – and for a humble author the rich comforts of the Adelphi. How exciting to slip down to the Opera House next day and see them fumbling with the scenery, Helen's wonderful Bed and the Walls of Troy. I always loved the first 'band-call'. After four or five weeks of that tinkling piano on the stage it was thrilling to hear real fiddles, clarinets and the rest playing the familiar tunes and the singers coming up in turn to sing their numbers – to sing my humble words! With all the agonies of the theatre there is this advantage for the writing fellow that it stops him scratching alone in his den, digs him out of his hole and sets him to work among all sorts and conditions of men.

But Manchester was hard work. Reinhardt and his German lieutenant liked rehearsing all night – and this had the advantage that the scenery and lighting fellows had the stage to play with all day. We would start about seven in the evening, work through the whole play and finish about seven or eight in the morning. The Herr Professor was a wonder to watch. He had a great admiration for our robust comedians, and George Robey at least returned it. Over Evelyn Laye he seemed to have the power of a Svengali, drawing new splendours from her. In every important scene he was a tireless hunter of detail. Just before George Robey's big comic scene comes the famous duet 'Is It a Dream?' in which Paris comes to Helen's chamber and Helen thinks (or seems to think) that she is dreaming. It is a charming episode and plays for about seven minutes. Reinhardt, early one morning, rehearsed it for about two hours. (Paris, by the way (Bruce Carfax), to satisfy the Censor, was fully clothed throughout, with some elegant long boots. I heard my favourite bar-maid tell a customer solemnly: 'Oh, yes, that was the custom in those days.')

George Robey's big comic scene (where Menelaus returns unexpected and discovers the stranger), followed 'Is It a Dream?'. About six in the morning I was in the wings watching Reinhardt's clinical work on the duet. George Robey was there too; he had been dutifully waiting for his cue for two hours. There was a ring of tired Young Ladies round him whom, in whispers (so far as he could whisper) he was keeping cheerful. He was a battery of cheerfulness and loyalty for the whole company. If anyone flagged George would have a word with him; if anyone was mystified George would patiently explain the appropriate point of Greek mythology. He never flagged himself; he was tremendously fit and strong; he had not missed a performance, he boasted, for I forget how many years. He was very proud of his stomach muscles. 'Hit me there!' he would say, giving himself a great bang in the abdomen. 'It's like timber, it's like iron! Hit me there!' Tom Webster, the cartoonist, told me that George had once overdone it, and knocked himself over backwards. This I doubt, but his blows were certainly brutal. Another of his secrets was instant sleep. During one full dress rehearsal I saw him fast asleep in the front row of the stalls, just behind the conductor, while the band was booming and banging fortissimo a few feet away.

Now, at about 6.30 a.m., he was beginning to be impatient, not because he wanted his bed, he wanted to work: 'Why don't they get on with it?' he grumbled, regarding with a grin the lovers on the stage: 'All this love-stuff. Women! They don't want love. They want to laugh. They want me! Hit me there!' Then he turned from the giggling girls to me. 'Have you heard this? What is it that comes out of cow(e)s all hot and steaming – and goes plonk-plonk?' The girls giggled still, and I said: 'Really, George,' or something. 'A PADDLE-STEAMER,' he boomed, and got a big 'S'sh!' from the stage-manager. Then he moved off a little and lightly did a 'cartwheel', a sideways somersault. The wit was not distinguished, but the vitality was astounding! So was his fidelity to the new style of job we had given him. The King of Gags did no gagging. He stuck to his lines. New lines and 'business' crept in during rehearsal, but by general consent: and he did the same thing every performance.

Cochran wrote in *I Had Almost Forgotten*: 'I had never worked with George Robey but . . . I soon discovered that there were very few artists with whom it was such a joy to work as him. Robey is a truly great artist inasmuch as he does not think only of himself but of his colleagues in the show. He is a remarkable force in maintaining the morale of the theatre in which he is working . . . His performance in *Helen* became a classic creation.'

Manchester gave *Helen* a warm welcome, and happy were the supper-parties, truly happy; too often they are no more than bravely gay. The critics have still to play their part and someone has always heard somebody say something in a bar.

My new Third Act went well and pleased my fine masters. It was written long before Korngold turned up, so I had to plan most of the music myself, using *reprises* of tunes already heard.

The Act opens, in the tenth year of the Trojan War, with a sad little bedroom scene. Helen, still in love with Paris, sings fondly 'Sleep on' to a beautiful tune: but the valiant Hector thinks it is time that Paris, still on the staff, went out and did some fighting. Down on the plains Menelaus who is 'Duty King' challenges Mercury and Juno who tell him that he is to fight Paris for Helen. 'But not Hector,' says Menelaus. 'Life is sweet, however disgusting' (a line which Sir Winston Churchill used to quote with satisfaction).

Paris is goaded out by Hector, and a truce is called for the battle of champions.

But then Helen appears, with Priam, on the high Walls of Troy – both armies are hushed in wonder at her beauty and raise their spears in salute. This was a magnificent spectacle.

AGAMEMNON: Yes, there is Helen. And now she has come all else seems to be in shadow

Is that the face that launched a thousand ships,
The fatal grace, the killing eyes and lips?
No wonder, Helen, the fleets put out to sea,
No wonder nations fight and die for thee!
Beauty is magical and knows no laws,
And men have fought for many a meaner cause.
For who wants life if Beauty liveth not?
What worth has gold where Beauty can't be got?
No wonder, Helen, the fleets put out to sea,
No wonder nations fight and die for thee.

My Marlovian effort was ready for Korngold when he arrived. To my relief, he pounced upon it eagerly, and produced a grand tune which he assured me was genuine Offenbach. It was his 'first English composition' and I could hardly stop him playing it. He would sit at my piano singing over and over again:

No vunder, Helena, ze fleets put oot to zay,
No vunder ze nations feet and dee fur zay.

On the stage not many of the deathless words were heard, for all the warriors had their backs to the audience, looking up at Helen: but the sound was fine and the scene superb.

Then the great duet began, but when Menelaus had Paris at his mercy the gods, as usual, cheated.

'(VENUS appears carrying a silvery shroud (representing a magical mist). She descends close to Paris, wraps the mist round him, and carries him off, now invisible, towards Troy.)'

But Menelaus has won. Helen comes forth from the gates to surrender. 'Come home' he says, having failed to destroy her, as he had promised, and royally she moves up-stage to his ship. From the deck she sings – I put these words to my favourite tune 'L'Amour divin' – O God of Love! and no man said me nay:

There's no life without love, and no love without pain.
I have lived, I have loved – and I will not complain,
I have opened my heart like a rose in the rain
I have played a great part – I would play it again.

'. . . The kings and warriors stand, as if transfixed, gazing at HELEN, the portent, the peerless and undefeatable; and HELEN proudly returns their gaze. But just before she disappears she looks up and sees the handsome young captain and they exchange a glance which suggests that the troubles of poor MENELAUS are not yet over. THE END.'

So back to London, and the familiar agonies of beginning again.

The structure that seemed so solid in Manchester has to be built again, brick by brick. The scenery, the lights – all that fuss again. How about the sound – with a different band in a different building – all to be tested and talked about *again*.

And Venus gave trouble again. Poor C.B. had had trouble about Venus from the beginning. Venus had to unveil at the Judgement of Paris scene – the Golden Apple – and in my Third Act she had to whisk away Paris, in godly costume. But she did not have to say a word or do any difficult acting, and every female in London thought they were fit for Venus. C.B. was badgered, politely, by a very high legal officer, and kindly told him to call. 'It's my wife,' said the official, 'Venus. I can tell you at once it's quite absurd, but you must see her. If you don't, I can tell you my married life is over.' So C.B. said Yes.

I shall never forget the final Venus audition – God knows how many others there had been. It was at Drury Lane, a vast open space, pitch dark. One tiny light at the prompt corner, two or three people about C.B., and two or three cleaners fumbling about at the back of the stalls. There was a hush like a cathedral's. Even Frank Collins as he announced the names of the aspirants spoke low and reverently. They were all in swimming-suits, they moved across the stage under a spotlight, then back, and off again. At last came a lady who made me say to myself: 'This is the lady' C.B. turned his head, and nodded. The charladies gave their only titter, a tiny one. It was very sad. But C.B., with his good heart, had saved a marriage.

When Frank Collins, hard-faced but friendly, read in my Third Act the bit about Venus descending and flying off with Paris, he said: 'Wires, eh? Ever had anything to do with wires, Alan? Not a hope.' 'Well, it's Homer,' I said, 'so I put it down. But I'm not expecting anything.' 'Homer?' said Frank. 'Not a hope, old boy.' So at Manchester Venus simply walked through the warriors under a spot, spread her mist over Paris and walked off with him. Not very exciting, but I thought no more about it.

Then one afternoon in that last week in London I dropped in at the Adelphi – a wonderful thing, that, to be able to drop in at a great theatre as if you owned it – and there were the whole company on the stage and all the orchestra in the pit. By the conductor stood C.B. and Frank Collins in earnest talk with Venus, who stood over the footlights, clad only in a very light mist, and with an evident wire attached to her shapely back. 'My God!' I said to myself. 'Flying!' Nobody had said a word to me – perhaps they wanted it to be a surprise – but I was immensely pleased that at the last moment they were toying with the childish notions of Homer – and Hammersmith. It was C.B., I am sure. I can imagine him saying to Frank: 'Frank, are we really going to be beat by Peter Pan?'

Then followed a diverting hour, or more. It was a matter of timing. There was a deafening clap of thunder, huge chords on the band, and all the lights went out. Then Venus, with a light on her, floated off the high stepladder on the prompt side, alighted beside Paris, nicked a hook into a ring on his back, and flew off into the wings on the O-P side. The lights came on, Menelaus turned with his spear raised, ready to cast at Paris. But Paris was not there. The play continued.

It sounds simple: but the things that could go wrong were numerous. All the lights would come on again after the clap of thunder, or else Venus would descend in total darkness. Once Venus failed to attach the wire to Paris and flew away leaving him standing in his invisible mist, in broad daylight, an easy mark for Menelaus. Sometimes the pair flew off correctly but the company had to continue the play in pitch darkness.

But at last all went well, the lights went on, the play was continuing, and the management were smiling at each other. Frank was saying: 'What about that, Alan?' when Venus slowly floated across the stage stark naked. 'I'm awfully sorry, Mr Cochran,' said Venus. 'I slipped off the ladder.'

So they began again. But that was the last time, I do believe, that anything went wrong. Throughout the run, Homer won.

They don't have such fun, you know, in straight plays.

The end of *Helen* was a little sad, and I tell it in Cochran's own words:

That *Helen* did not run longer at the Adelphi was another disappointment. It had an almost unanimously enthusiastic Press and played to capacity houses nights and matinées for about twelve weeks, but then the receipts dropped.

This production pleased me more than any with which I have been associated. It seemed to me the perfection of theatrical art combined harmoniously with the happiest inventions of musicians and painters. As for A. P. Herbert's adaptation of the French original, this was a brilliant and genuinely creative work, and I strongly recommend those who missed the performance to buy the book and revel in its wit.

For the drop in the receipts after a magnificent start I blame the players – not all of them, but I am afraid the law of libel restrains me from citing individual cases. After the first few weeks I was compelled constantly to complain of the slackness of the performances, not only of some members of the chorus but also of some of the more prominent artists. Those who saw it in the first weeks at the Adelphi could scarcely recognize it towards the end of the run. All its spirit had departed. It is a curious phase of theatrical enterprise that occasionally one runs up against a company which does not invariably give its best. With such a company the manager is powerless, for, though performances may be watched and rehearsals called, if the team spirit is not on the stage nothing can be accomplished.

On more than one occasion I called the company together on the stage and told them that their engagements were being thrown away. Then there would be an improvement – but for a few days only.

And Heaven knows what *Helen* cost! There were seventy-one names, as I have said, on the actors' page of the programme.

I wrote in my Introduction to *I Had Almost Forgotten*: 'I can truthfully say,' as I did say to C.B. at the time, 'that if the production had been a failure I should have been glad to have played my part in it.' I feel still as C.B. felt then, that though I have earned more praise and more money from others, this was my finest show. It was an assembly of arts and talents presented by a master of taste and understanding: it had a grandeur and a grace that I have not met elsewhere; and like Helen, if I had the chance, I would play the part again.

Next was an odd, but amusing affair, *Mother of Pearl*, which opened at the old Gaiety on 27 January 1933, not long after the demise of *Helen*. This was not a full musical with chorus and so on, but a straight play with a few songs added, by Oscar Straus. So here I was writing words to foreign music again. The main excuse for the piece was to provide a 'vehicle' for the incomparable Alice Delysia, an old friend of Cochran's: and that was a very good purpose indeed, for she was a wonder. The original name of the piece was *The Woman Who Knew What She Wanted*, but I called it *Mother of Pearl*, because Pearl was the name I gave to her daughter, Sepha Treble, a 'Helen' Young Lady.

It was all rather nonsense, but it served its purpose well. You should have heard Alice sing:

> Every woman thinks she wants to wander
>   And turns her money when the moon is new:
> Happiness is hiding just beyond her,
>   And perfect love is farther down the queue;
> Round the corner gentlemen are fonder,
>   Over there the sea's a brighter blue.
> Ev'ry woman thinks she wants to wander
>   And be a naughty girl with someone new.

The way she sang the word 'naughty'!

In the Third Act (which, once more, I think was an invention of my own) she had made a telephone call in a crisis. The automatic 'dialling' system had just started in London, and we told her about this. Accordingly she dialled FLA 1234, or whatever it was, with the grace and a sweep of an artist. She had never done this thing before, but she might have been practising for years. It was like ballet dialling. At the end she gave a sweet little sigh, as if she had gone through a long labour (as indeed one has). I had an inspiration and suggested timidly:

'Suppose, after that, Alice, you say, "And they call that *automatique*!"'
She did, and it got a loud laugh every night.

But another morning I ventured rashly to murmur from the stalls
the correct pronunciation of some word she had not got quite right.
At lunch-time, Cochran called gently from the stage: 'Alan! Come
up here. You've made Alice cry.' I duly apologized, astonished that
so small a pebble could strike tears from such a rock.

The last thing an author in his senses does is to go near his leading
lady just before a First Night. She is fairly sure to say: 'I feel terrible.
I have forgotten all my lines, and I *think* I am going to be sick.' But
C.B. gave me some message to deliver to Alice, and through the
pass-door I went. I knocked at her door and heard a hearty 'Come
in!' 'How are you feeling, Alice?' I said. She smote her bosom, rather
in the George Robey style, and said: 'I am feeling fine. I am going out
there to show them what I can do.' And so she did. This utterance
must be a theatrical record.

In 1944 Delysia did a brave job entertaining the troops at the wrong
end, the shelled end, of the Cherbourg Peninsula.

Then she married a French consul. There was nothing shocking in
Mother of Pearl. 'La Pavani' was simply a lady who had had many
lovers in the past. After the war I met Alice in an American chemist's
in the Strand. She said: 'Alan, I want a play.' I said: 'Why don't you do
Mother of Pearl again?' 'Ah no,' she said almost primly. 'Now I am
consul's wife.'

In September 1934, at the lovely Palace Theatre, Cochran put on his
Twenty-First Revue, *Streamline*. Ronald Jeans did two or three
sketches and a song, but I wrote the bulk of it, and here began my
long and happy collaboration with Vivian Ellis.

I remember vividly the good old-fashioned opening of *Streamline*.
The curtain rose and there at the back in a brilliant light were two
rows of pretty girls – twenty, I suppose, or more. All were dressed
exactly alike and all danced down the stage, making exactly the same
movements, till their shiny stockinged legs were waving uniformly
over the footlights. They also sang a lyric called 'Alive and Kicking'.
There was life and beauty in them and I wish this kind of thing would
come back. I weary soon of the modern style, what I call street-dancing,
the young things bounding about in jeans and sweaters, their movements carefully drilled, I know, but merely athletic.

We had a strong cast, George Heslop, Florence Desmond, and
Naunton Wayne for comedy, Nora Howard and Esmond Knight:
Tilly Losch danced, and C.B. imported a charming Austrian dancer
'La Jana'. Most of us had never seen the female navel exposed on the
stage, and I here record that La Jana's navel made a great hit in 1934.

Nora Howard made a great hit too as a Nanny in *Other People's Babies*, some old *Punch* verses of mine dug out of a book and superbly set by Vivian Ellis. This is still sung now and then.

I liked too our pathetic duet for a couple of lovers on a park seat – 'Kiss Me, Dear, before they move us on'.

> I dunno!
> Life's difficult, ain't it?
> Being in love and nowhere to go.
>
> Kiss me, dear, before they chuck us out:
> Not so loud – you don't know who's about.
>   Say you love me – but say it low
>   I love you ever so – but don't you let Lord Trenchard know.
> Kiss me, dear, but don't let no one see
> Hold me close – but watch the referee.
> There may be bishops up that tree –
>   Kiss me, dear, before they move us on.

Things are easier, I gather, in the Park today.

Then there were two elaborate musical scenes.

'I Will' was a registry wedding, all sung. Naunton Wayne, as the Registrar, sang:

> O will you take this wife to wed
> And promise not to read in bed,
>   Till you are five-and-fifty,
> Will you renounce the primrose path,
> Leave no tobacco in the bath,
>   Be thoughtful, true and thrifty?
>   O will you cherish, feed and bless,
>   And will you always, more or less,
>   Be lovingly connected
>   Till death do part, or shall we say,
>   As long as at the present day
>   Can fairly be expected?
> *We will! we will! we certainly will! Hooray!*

> That's very nice, but understand
> It is your duty to expand
>   The British population.
> The State expects, I can't say why,
> That you'll increase and multiply
>   This overcrowded nation.

Flowers and fairies concluded the usually grim ceremony.

In 'Speech Day' Florence Desmond was a perfect head-boy in Eton's. The prize-giving General (Naunton Wayne) sang, as they generally did:

I was always at the bottom of my class
   When I was a boy at school
Examinations I could never pass
   When I was a boy at school:
      And now I'm a General
      And earn large amounts.
But where are all the clever boys who used to do my sums?
They're hidden in the Church, the Civil Service, or the slums.
      In the face of savage foes
      What's the use of Latin Prose?
   Brains don't matter – it's character that counts

There was a sad exhibition of Pupil-power, the two senior boys inserting improper lines into the School Song.

But our masterpiece, we thought, was *Perseverance*. This, though I say it myself, is a first-class parody of Gilbert and Sullivan.* It packs all the Master's inevitable tricks into a small space. There is an idiotic female chorus who open the piece on the Terrace of the House of Commons:

Fifty fisher-girls are we,
Selling fishes from the sea *etc.*

There is the arch soprano song, the unaccompanied quartette, the patter-song, the elderly spinster who puts all right in a contralto number. The plot is vintage Gilbert.

PERSEVERANCE: Lord Rudolph! will you purchase a plaice?
LILY: Lord Robert, may I sell you a sole?
RUDOLPH (who has a very high fruity speaking voice – brushes them aside): Pray observe the decencies of etiquette, young ladies. There is no Lord Rudolph –
ROBERT (gloomily): Lord Robert does not exist.
RUDOLPH: There is only the Viscount Bunion.
PERSEVERANCE: Yes, but which is he?
RUD. and ROB. (linking arms): *WE* are the Viscount Bunion.
LILY: What, both of you?
CHORUS: Singular coincidence.
PERSEVERANCE: Will you not explain this curious circumstance?
RUDOLPH: Certainly, my dear Perseverance. (Comes down stage,)
   On the death of our father, the Earl, one of us will succeed to the title.
CHORUS: O rapture!
            (PERSEVERANCE clings to RUDOLPH)
RUDOLPH: Yes, but we do not know which.
CHORUS: O disappointment!
* Score published by Chappell.

(PERSEVERANCE, with the other hand, clings to ROBERT as well)

LILY: But surely, Lord Robert, the eldest son must succeed to the title?

ROBERT (gloomily): Ah, but we are twins.

RUDOLPH: And therefore are the same age.

PERSEVERANCE (coy): But though you are the same age it seems to me that one of you must be the elder.

CHORUS: Strange paradox!

RUDOLPH: True, my dear Perseverance. Even among twins there is generally, I believe, some trifling element of seniority.

ROBERT: Unfortunately our father has refused to reveal the true facts until his death.

RUDOLPH: For he feared that the heir, secure of his future, would spend his youth in profligate enjoyment.

CHORUS: Ingenious precaution!

PERSEVERANCE: But were not both of you present on the occasion you have mentioned? Surely it was a little careless of you not to notice the order of your arrival?*

RUDOLPH: The reproach is just.

PERSEVERANCE: Is there *nobody* who can tell you which of you is which?

ROBERT: Our mother – a good Conservative – perished in a One-Way street.

PERSEVERANCE: But unless we know which of you is to be the Earl how are we to know which of you we love the best?

RUDOLPH: That is easily adjusted (RUDOLPH and ROBERT both kneel). Provisionally you must love both of us.

Next comes the sort of song which made me determined *not* to be 'another Gilbert':

PERSEVERANCE: Though I am loth to plight my troth
    With exact particularity
Yet I might part with hand and heart
    On terms of honest parity.
I will not kiss the one (like this)
    Unless I kiss the other.
Pray hold my hand, but understand,
    You share it with your brother.

CHORUS: Arrangement unromantical!
With equity pedantical
She will not kiss the one (like this)
    Unless she hugs the other.
This proposition frantical
Is almost transatlantical:
    Half a loaf is not much fun
    But half a lady's worse than none.

* I can *see* old Gilbert writing that line.

(Isn't it horrible? It makes me sick. But isn't it 'Gilbertian').

Next comes the Official Receiver in Bankruptcy who sings an admirable patter-song:

> When your furniture swarms with income-tax forms
>> Or Notices Final in red,
> With magistrates' warrants arriving in torrents
>> And bailiffs asleep in your bed:
> If shares go to nought the moment you've bought
>> And soar to the skies when you sell,
> If insurance collectors and taxing inspectors
>> Are constantly ringing the bell . . .
>> Etcetera

He brings bad news : 'The Earl has passed away. He has, in short, kicked the bucket. In point of fact he is deceased.'

CHORUS: O horror!

Then, of course, the Unaccompanied Quartette:

> Death is the terminus of all our travel,
>> Whether in firsts or thirds our lot is cast:
> Some live on clay and some reside on gravel,
>> But all must hand their tickets in at last.
> Death is a riddle man can not unravel
>> Fal – lal – di – did – di – ly ay!
>> Fol – lol – di – did – di – ly O! etc.
> Death is the terminus to which we go.

But who is to inherit?

RUDOLPH: And in his will does he disclose the name of his eldest son?

OFF. REC.: That trifling detail is not so much as mentioned.

RUDOLPH: Technically, therefore, we are both the Earl of Billingsgate?

OFF. REC.: That seems to be the position. I congratulate each half of your lordship.

ROBERT: In that case we shall have to take the same seat in the House of Lords —

RUDOLPH: Make the same speeches —

ROBERT: Wear the same coronet —

PERSEVERANCE (curtesying): And marry the same Countess.

LILY: Agreeable dilemma!

RUDOLPH: But stay, here comes an elderly female who may be able to disentangle us.

OFF. REC.: What should this antiquated ruin know of the matter?

ROBERT: It is our Nurse.

RUDOLPH: Nanny!

OFF. REC.: On the contrary, I now perceive, it is the Lady Chancellor.

(Enter the LADY CHANCELLOR – an immensely tall Contralto, in her robes of office, with full-bottomed wig. An attendant carries her Great Seal.)

> I am the Lady Chancellor, I am:
> But once I was a nurse – and drove a pram.

> Two lovely twins they trusted to my care.
> Alike in size, in features, form and hair.
> No marks, no moles, but I knew which was what,
> For one was musical – the other not.

CHORUS: Ah, one was musical, the other not.

> The elder babe would crow and croon all day,
> And cry for mamma in the key of A:
> The other seldom sang, and, if he did,
> Was out of tune – Ah, how I loved that kid!

CHORUS: Though out of tune she dearly loved that kid

> What if my age is rather more than middle?
> For his sweet sake I now resolve the riddle.
> If one can sing the rightful Earl is he –
> The other, still more blest, shall marry ME.

OFF. REC.: A highly diverting narrative. But, so far as is known, neither half of this nobleman can sing a note.

LADY C: That is easily ascertained. Let them try.

OFF. REC.: May I warn your Ladyship that at the moment each half of this individual is an undischarged bankrupt?

LADY C: No matter. My miserable honorarium will suffice for two.

OFF. REC.: But not, I take it, for four?

PERSEVERANCE (taking an oyster from her basket): It is of no consequence. This oyster has just opened its doors and expelled a pearl of reassuring dimensions (holds up an enormous pearl).

CHORUS: O rapture!

OFF. REC.: Intelligent bivalve! Satisfactory pearl! Devoted girl! But still no Earl.

LADY C: Sing, Viscount!

(ROBERT opens his mouth but fails. RUDOLPH succeeds, so all is well.)

So now you know (a) how it is done, and (b) why I have never done it.

Streamline was one of the rare theatrical enterprises I had a hand in that actually made money. If they revived revues there is much of this one, I believe, that would still stand up.

It was in *Streamline*, too, that Florence Desmond did her famous talk by the First Mother to fly the North Pole (with affectionate reference to Amy Johnson). I wrote most of this during rehearsals, in the stalls.

I note with surprise how busy we were in the early 30's!

In 1931 *Tantivy Towers* was produced, in 1932 *Helen* and *Derby Day*, in 1933 *Mother of Pearl*, and in 1934 Cochran's *Streamline*. In the same five years my two most successful books were published, *The Water Gipsies* in 1930 and *Holy Deadlock* in 1934. In 1934 I prosecuted the House of Commons, and in 1935 was elected to it: but in 1937 I scored one revue, *Home and Beauty*, one play, *Paganini*, and one Act of Parliament, and one book *The Ayes Have It*, the story of the Marriage Bill. Total 7 shows, 1 vast election address, 1 general election, 1 prosecution and 1 statute.

Not bad for seven years.

The next thing was another Cochran revue, *Home and Beauty*, which, after a preliminary canter at Manchester, opened at the Adelphi on 2 February 1937. This was to have been Cochran's Coronation Revue, but the sad Abdication of Edward VIII put an end to that. Another sad thing for me was that the rehearsal stage of Cochran's revue (in which for the first time I was responsible for every word, songs and sketches and all) coincided with the Committee Stage of my Marriage Bill (which was to become the Matrimonial Causes Act 1937). Standing Committee A met for the first time on 3 December 1936. Its eighth meeting was on 2 February 1937, the day of the Adelphi opening. That morning, I see, my mind full of the usual First Night worries – How is Binnie Hale's throat? Will Nelson Keys forget his lines again? – I moved six amendments, and was on my feet ten times – 'New Grounds for Nullity' – 'Presumption of Death' – 'Abolition of the Decree Nisi' and Heaven knows what. You may say that I should never have got myself into such a position. But, of course, far back, when I had made my contract with C.B. and begun the work, I had not the slightest hope or notion that my Bill would get a Second Reading in my second Parliamentary year. It was one of what I call 'God's strange arrangements'. It is a wonder the amateur legislator-librettist did not go mad that winter. I wrote, I see, nearer to the event (in *The Ayes Have It*, page 117):

After lunch every day I would rush away across the river to a barn-like building near the Elephant and Castle and endeavour to switch my mind to the manifold problems of Mr Cochran's *Coronation Revue* (one of which was now 'Will there be a Coronation?'). Then, with appeals in my ear from a Hungarian composer, an American producer, and an English comedian to write more words or better words, I would hurry to the Treasury Solicitor to get the text of the new amendments and to the House to confer with De la Bere and the team. Then I would find an odd assembly of telephone messages. 'From Mr Kent, insanity amendment on the way' – 'From Mr Collins, please send second verse of *Twilight Sonata*' – 'Please ring Treasury Solicitor' – 'Please ring Miss Binnie Hale' – 'Please ring Mr Cochran'. Mr Cochran, who had always been accustomed to get a whole mind from me, nobly forbore to complain of my distraction. Twice I woke up from a fitful sleep and found myself trying to set divorce words to one of M. Brodszky's tunes. A weird and worrying time.

That day was the grim day when Mr Baldwin made his famous speech announcing the abdication of King Edward. Having heard that, I went off to Walworth and found the company strenuously rehearsing, by chance, the Coronation number. I amended the words of the song (how did I do that, I wonder) and went back to the King's Proctor.

Mr Brodszky had some pleasant tunes: but the song that has survived is my 'I like a nice cup of tea in the morning', set by an American, Mr Hank Sullivan. This was sung with great effect by Binnie Hale as a housemaid:

> I like a nice cup of tea in the morning,
>   For to start the day, you see,
>   And at half-past eleven
>   Well, my idea of Heaven
>   Is a nice cup of tea:
> I like a nice cup of tea with me dinner
>   And a nice cup of tea with me tea,
>   And when it's time for bed
>   There's a lot to be said
>   For a nice cup of tea.
>
> Some folks put much reliance
> On politics and Science –
>   There's only one hero for me:
> His praise we should be roaring,
> The man who thought of pouring
>   The first boiling water on to tea:
>
> I like a nice, *etc.*

Recently this ditty swam back into our ken. It was used many times as a 'commercial' by the Tea Council (no less) on Independent Television. This brought to Herbert and Sullivan an acceptable windfall and showed once more the beauty of Performing Right.

No rest for the wicked. On 20 May 1937 Cochran presented *Paganini* at the Lyceum. On 28 May was the Report and Third Reading of the Marriage Bill, its last day, for the present, in the Commons.

Paganini was a not wholly satisfactory piece with music by the great Lehar. I got mixed up with it through my friend Reginald Arkell, the writer, who was to collaborate but did not write a word. The big thing was that Richard Tauber was to play Paganini, and Cochran captured Evelyn Laye again for the Princess Elisa, one of Napoleon's sisters. There were some good tunes naturally, which I enjoyed 'adapting'. The song I called 'Girls were made to love and kiss' which Tauber loved, and sang beautifully, is still a favourite. This song, like 'A Nice Cup of Tea', has been about for thirty-three years: but I never meet anyone who knows I wrote the words, for the B.B.C. give the names of composers only, even if the author is a Newbolt or a Gilbert. Lehar sent over the manuscript of a vigorous new tune he specially wanted to be added to the play. It was Whitsun, I took the family up the River Lee in the *Water Gipsy*, and I wrote the song – 'Fear Nothing' at the wheel. Tauber liked that too and sang it well. He was great company, always full of life and fun.

The trouble was that the 'book', in my opinion, was poor. The structure of this kind of piece is so much governed by the music that amendment is difficult. But the third Act was puerile, I thought, and if I could have a free hand with that I could do a lot for the whole. But if I suggested the slightest amendment dear Tauber would rush off and telegraph or telephone to Lehar: and he always came back with a stern, 'No, no! Lehar will not allow it!'

For some reason I missed the First Night for once – perhaps it was divorce: but C.B. said it was one of the brightest and best he had ever had. But *Paganini* did not last very long: no play would long survive that Third Act. Not being allowed to help I lost interest. At the end, by the prompt copy it looked as if all the stage-hands had been having a go at the Third Act. A year or two ago Messrs Weinberger invited me to do a new version for amateurs, and at last we did what I wanted. There it is, all ready – more logical, moving, I think, and funny.

During the War, except for weekly verse in the *Sunday Graphic*, my Muses were dumb. So were Cochran's. But on 17 July 1946, he made his 'comeback' with *Big Ben*, at the Adelphi again – the excellent music by Vivian Ellis. The sad thing was that C.B. was too ill to attend the first night, which was a swell occasion – Royalty, the Prime Minister, Mr Churchill (rather sleepy), Lord Montgomery, and a cloud of my fellow-Members. For once, when writing this play I had slight apprehensions about the Censor – not for the usual reasons. Feeble old Gilbert, in *Iolanthe*, never got beyond the sentry-box outside 'that House'. I boldly penetrated the Palace. There was one scene on the Terrace, which some of my characters invaded from the river: there was another in the Chamber and a second reading debate, on a Prohibition Bill, all sung. The Speaker was not seen, but his voice was heard, and at the end of the scene my villains invaded the Chamber, kidnapped a Member and forcibly resisted the Serjeant-at-Arms. Nothing disrespectful to the House was said, but I wondered whether the action might be thought to trespass across the bounds of privilege. Towards the end of the long (I think, two days') dress rehearsal, I was sitting on the stage next to C.B. He was keeping his usual patient watch on every item of costume that appeared, listening to every complaint from the girls, making the decision in every dispute. During a lull I said: 'Did the Lord Chamberlain have anything to say?' C.B. looked at me with horror in his eyes. '*My God!*' he said, '*I never sent it to him!*' My heart, as the song says, stood still. This was three or four days before production, no more. The Lord Chamberlain might send the thing to the Speaker. Objections might be too massive to meet in the time. We might have to postpone. We were both dismayed.

But the script came back in two days, objection taken to one line only. There was an old Parliamentary story about Nancy Astor and Jack Jones, the Member for Woolwich, who had a proper respect for the Englishman's beer. Nancy, in a speech, had said something about the damage men did to their stomachs with this and other liquids. Some time later Jack Jones, who had a very well-developed stomach, intervened in the debate; and said: 'I heard what the honourable and noble lady had to say about our stomachs. I tell the noble lady that I'll lay my stomach against hers any day.' A picture which drew long laughter from the imaginative legislators. Mentioning no names I gave one of my characters the line, but, though Parliament had approved, the Lord Chamberlain wouldn't have it. But he and his officers (who then included the genial Tim Nugent) were never content to condemn: they did their best to help, and often gave much thought to it. They now suggested that the line should be: 'I'll *bet* my stomach against yours any day.' I did not think myself that this would burst many bellies, but I was so touched by the kindly care of the Censor that we put it in – and, I still don't know why, it got a laugh every night.

Trefor Jones, again, played my hero, Henry, and Carole Lynne, wife of that big theatre man, Mr Delfont, was a charming heroine. W. A. Darlington, the much respected critic of the *Daily Telegraph*, in a kindly notice, said that I had made the mistake of letting Boy get Girl too soon (early in Act Two). I have had much advice, good and bad, from critics: but this was the only time I have shouted to myself: 'Of *course* he's right! I won't make that mistake again.'

Big Ben was something different. It was like no 'musical' that had gone before, and I do not know of anything like it since. It plunged into politics more boldly and deeply than Gilbert ever dared. The First Act contained a General Election and ended with an election meeting for all the candidates. The heroine became a Labour Member, but married a Tory, and was locked up in the Tower with him for obstructing the Serjeant-at-Arms. Henry, the tenor, was red-hot. Grace's only electoral weapon was to sing, to one of Ellis's liveliest tunes, 'I want to see the people happy'.

HENRY: Now that's enough of that! . . . It's no good ambling about telling people you want them to be happy. You've got to tell them what's your policy. And anyhow they're not going to be happy. So don't put ideas into their heads.

GRACE: Not going to be happy?

HENRY: Well, not for five or ten years.

That got a big laugh from the Members on the first night. This was 1946.

But at the meeting he sang a song which Labour should have adopted – 'Wheels of the World'.

> March, brothers, march – ever freer and faster!
>   We are the bridge, and the ship, and the plough!
> We are the engine, the gun and the steeple,
> We are the voice and the might of the People –
>   Left, Right, Left – the bully must bow.
> We are the makers. We must be master,
>   For we are the Wheels of the World.
> Wheels of the World, roll on to glory,
>   Carry mankind to a nobler day.
> Wheels of the World, roar a new story –
>   Carry us all on the one good way.
> Over the frontiers, over the seas,
>   When the bad old flags have gone,
> The Banner of Man shall ride on the breeze!
>   Wheels of the World, roll on!

The play ended patriotically in Parliament Square.

> Big Ben! Big Ben!
> The clock all people know,
> The King of Time in every clime
> Where ships and sailors go. . . .
> Big Ben! Big Ben!
>
>   The clock they could not kill,
> Chime out again, and tell all men
>   That England's England still.

In the Second Act all parties unite against Mrs. Busy's Prohibition Bill. I enjoyed writing the Second Reading speeches; all in verse.

> MRS BUSY: One drop of spirit such as men are fond of swilling down
>   Will kill a healthy rat or burn a hole in half-a-crown.
>   One bottleful of brandy is enough to drive a train;
>   Imagine the effect upon the kidneys and the brain! . . .
>   Meanwhile, the victim's habits very naturally fail,
>   And now the question is – will it be hospital or jail?

And happy are the tipplers who in agonies have died
Of cirrhosis or a stroke, but were not hanged for homicide.

GRACE: I disagree; for Nature's laws
    Are generally sound,
And everywhere, for some good cause
    Some alcohol is found.
There's alcohol in plant and trees:
    It must be Nature's plan
That there should be, in fair degree,
    Some alcohol in Man.

Grace, the heroine, then burst, as she did on the slightest excuse, into 'I want to see the people happy . . .'

Eric Fort, as Lord Lavender, made a hit with five verses in praise of the House of Lords.

While the Commons must bray like an ass every day
    To appease their electoral hordes,
We don't say a thing till we've something to say –
    There's a lot to be said for the Lords.

Big Ben did not get stentorian praise from the Press, though the public said they liked it very much. Cochran suffered for success. Every hill he climbed was expected to be another Everest. After the opening he had to go into hospital for an operation. Vivian Ellis and I went to see him. Physically he was feeble, but the old spirit was strong. Almost the first thing he said was: 'I want you two to write another play for me.' I began work at once. That play was *Bless the Bride*, which ran for two and a quarter years.

I can find no 'notices', but there was a heartening letter from Leslie Bloom, leader of the Gallery First Nighters' Club:

Thank you very much for giving me a treat last night. 'Big Ben' is grand and the enormous reception at the end must have convinced you that the audience were of the same opinion as myself – that the play is one of the most brilliant productions seen for many a long day.

I felt too that I was proud of being of English birth and throughout the evening I was thrilled.

Please go on writing. The Theatre needs you.

Leslie Bloom

C.B. wanted a Victorian period play. This was his only request. I went at once to some old volumes of *Punch* on my shelves, all about the '60's. My first aim was to avoid the crinoline, which had been such a nuisance in *La Vie Parisienne*. *Punch* in those days was a real mirror of the scene, and there in the '60's, as if in slow motion, one saw the crinoline going out and the bustle coming in. There, in 1869, were the bustled beauties playing croquet with the Archdeacon. And so naturally to 1870 and the Franco–Prussian War, never treated, so far as I knew, in opera, grand or light.

So to my story – and here, if I may, a brief lecture. There are always a few inexperienced scribes who complain that the story of a musical play is 'slight', 'thin', or 'non-existent'. It should be obvious that where two-thirds of your time must be devoted to singing and dancing there will not be so much room for an elaborate plot as there is in a straight play. Indeed, the complaint is often that there is 'too much plot, with tiresome sub-plots'. My story, I maintain, and events have proved it, was just about right. We spent a good deal of time in the First Act on the atmosphere of a Victorian country house, the indomitable institution of the Family, the Golden Wedding of Grandpa, the compulsory wedding of Lucy; but it was not time wasted. This fortress is invaded by a fascinating young Frenchman who spirits the Bride away while the Family are awaiting her in Church. Grandpa dies of grief and shame. You can't tell me that that's an uneventful First Act – not to mention about four 'hit' songs in it.

In the Second Act the Family pursue and finally catch their fugitive in France, but she refuses to go home with them. Then war breaks out, her lover, Pierre, has to put on his uniform and go, so she has to go home. She is told that he has been killed but – I won't weary you with all the complications, but Boy did get Girl in the end, in the very last minute; there was feeling, there were tears (there are tears today though the actors are amateurs) and the audience wanted to know what was going to happen – a fair test – not to mention three or four more hit songs and a lot of laughter. I don't say it would have made a three-volume novel; that was not my purpose at the time. But the scribes who went on about 'slightness' saddened me. Agate began his pronouncement from Olympus with the words: *Ex nihilo magnum fit*: but Harold Hobson praised the piece many times.

Bless the Bride opened at the Adelphi on 26 April 1947. Four days later at Drury Lane, *Oklahoma* opened, which, so far as I remember, has no story at all. It did not worry me, for it was a beautiful show, and I enjoyed it. (I wish I had written the song 'I Cain't Say No' and one or two more.) The funny thing was that not one scribe said a word about the 'slightness' of the Oklahoma story. It was American, so it was good.

Six weeks later *Annie Get Your Gun* opened at the Coliseum. *Bless the Bride* ran successfully alongside these two formidable invaders for two and a quarter years. It came off still running 'to capacity' and could have run much longer but Cochran, bless him, was itching, as he often did, to get on with the next show.

I am a warm admirer of the American work in this field. I love Richard Rodgers' music (*Carousel* was my favourite) and Hammerstein's lyrics, and *My Fair Lady* – 'I Could Have Danced All Night' is about the best song of them all. But I resent the rot that is talked. Some awe-struck scribes will tell you still that *Oklahoma* began a new era, a new style and method of writing. This is utter nonsense. It might

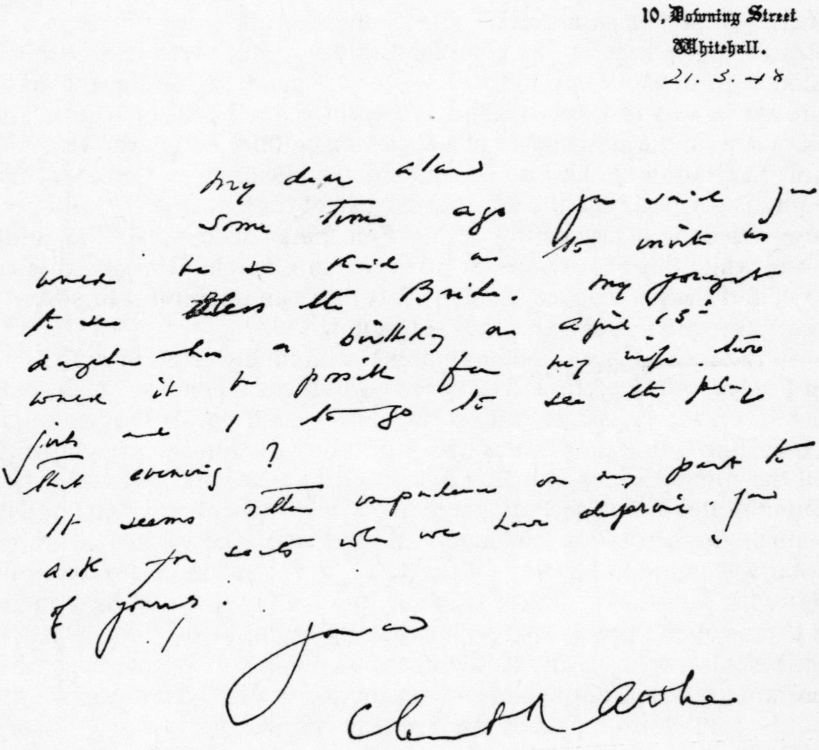

10, Downing Street
Whitehall.
21. 5. 48

[handwritten letter]

as well be said that *Bless the Bride* – all in all, a worthier work – began a new era. Neither did. They were both very healthy infants from the same good family, that is all. I have seen it solemnly said that the Americans of those days were the first to make the musical numbers natural offspring of the action. This again is utter rubbish. Never in my life has this humble person inserted a song that was not relevant to what preceded it, or followed it, or both. More important, this has been the way of all the English practitioners from Gay and Sheridan to Gilbert and after. 'How happy could I be with either' was not an irrelevant interjection: nor was 'Three little maids from school are we'.

After all, the English have been playing this game for a very long time and know something about it. Where the Americans score, perhaps, is in the vigour of their production, their orchestrations, and, I dare say, the dancing – but that is not the author's department. If I was to start a libretto tomorrow I should not give the slightest thought to any American model. But I should try to write even better lyrics.

We 'opened cold' in London, that is, without a trial run in Manchester, but I do not think we added or altered a word. The piece was beautifully produced by Wendy Toye who had done the same for *Big Ben*: we were fortunate in our principals, pretty Lizbeth Webb with her schoolgirl air and angelic voice, Georges Guétary, who really looked like a Frenchman in love, poor Brian Reece (now dead) as Thomas Trout, the funny part, Betty Paul, the French girl, and Anona Winn, the Nanny, and others.

We had some notable visitors – Royalty twice. The first party took two adjacent boxes – the King and Queen, a young couple called Elizabeth and Philip, with General Eisenhower and his lady.

One hot matinée Queen Mary came by herself. In the interval the principals were invited up to the Royal box, and Cochran being away, I had to introduce them. Conversation flagged, and at last, after a pause, Queen Mary said: 'There are a lot of very high notes in this play. How do you all do it?' There was no rush to answer this difficult question, indeed there was an ugly pause. At last Liz Webb bravely slipped into the breach: 'Well, Ma'am,' she said. 'We all take a very deep breath.' Considering that five or six of those present had no high notes to sing I thought that 'all' was a nobly chosen word.

Then, another hot summer matinée, C.B. asked me to meet a very high American theatre man in the interval. I think he was one of the Schubert brothers. He did not impress me. He said: 'You should give the comedian some more robust humour.' I said firmly, 'No. This is a Victorian costume piece, and we've been very careful to keep the whole thing in character, from first to last. Give anyone "a lot of robust humour" and you'll spoil the picture.' (I think it was that shrewd critic Mr J. C. Trewin who said that this was the secret of our success.) 'Then,' I said, 'Mr Reece is not a "comedian", he's an actor playing a part, which has some funny bits in it. But at the end of the play, as you'll see if you stay, his character develops, he's no longer a "silly ass", he behaves nobly and hands over the heroine to the Frenchman. He's the key of the drama – which is a very delicate structure. If he's been doing "robust humour", whatever that means, all the evening, the audience won't take the change at the end.' I may not have used all these words, but that is what I tried to say. I don't know whether Mr What's-his-name stayed till the end, but we heard no more of him.

My collaborations with Vivian Ellis have always been happy, but this was a special one; and some account of it may interest not only the up-coming young artist but the elderly audience. The old question is still heard (it maddened, I imagine, Gilbert and Sullivan): 'Which comes first – the words or the music?' The only answer is something ridiculous like, 'Yes and No.' Vivian is no mean lyric-writer himself, but he has always paid me the compliment of setting as much of my stuff as he can, just as it is, Finales, minor songs, connecting bits, and so on. Even here there will be long conferences round the piano. The third line in the second verse does not quite fit the tune, and must be altered: another line is not singable enough. Then he may hit on a tune that both of us like but it will mean taking two lines off a verse or chorus, or perhaps adding two: and this may take long thought to get right. Or there may be musical variations. Where there is friendly liking and understanding all this labour is fun. Only once have I found it wearisome and wearing – never with Vivian.

It is the only way. What a pity that James Thomson and Arne did not take the same trouble with *Rule, Britannia!* The fine tune was written, evidently, for the first verse, which it fits perfectly. But they left the other verses, which it does not fit so well, as Thomson wrote them. Take the third line: '*This was* the charter – the charter of the land' – the strong, emphatic notes do not go so well with: '*As the* loud blast – loud blast,' etc. The lyric (excepting the absurd verse about the oak) is excellent: but, however well we liked it, Vivian and I would have worked at it till every word was suitably wedded to the music.

I had many arguments with dear Malcolm Sargent about that famous song. For one thing I begged him not to give it to those stately but woolly contraltoes who made so few words audible. In the original 'masque' *Alfred* it was sung by King Alfred himself. Why not a baritone with good diction? But Malcolm would not have it. Then I quarrelled with his choice of verses. He would not have the second verse which he called the Jingo verse:

> The nations not so blest as thee
>   Shall in their turn to tyrants fall –
>   (*And so they did, every one of them*)
> While thou shalt flourish, great and free,
>   The dread and envy of them all.

Make it 'hope' instead of 'dread', I said, and it's not Jingo, but jolly – and true. What a wonder, by the way, that James Thomson should have written such a verse, such a song, at such a time. The first performance of the Masque was in 1740 at Cliveden, in honour of the birthday of the Prince of Wales who had the great house then. We were at war with France, Spain, and a few more – and, very nearly,

Scotland as well. But James Thomson sat down by the river at Hammersmith (I like to believe), next to the Dove Inn – or in it – and wrote these valiant verses about the inferior nations doomed to go under – as they did.

But Malcolm, instead, would have the deplorable 'oak' verse (which is something like this):

> Still more majestic shalt thou rise
> More dreadful from each foreign stroke
> As the loud [rude]? blast that tears the skies
> Serves but to root thy native oak.

This is unsingable, agriculturally unsound (I believe) and, I should have said, fairly Jingo: but I could not persuade the Maestro.

How splendid too is the last verse (which he did use):

> The Muses each with freedom found
> Shall to thy happy coasts repair,
> Blest isle, with matchless beauty crowned
> And manly hearts to guard the fair.

'The Muses each with freedom found'! The Star Chamber, I believe was still alive. What a man!

But look at that second line: 'Shall to-oo-oo-oo-oo-oo-oo thy happy coasts repair.' The music was written for the second line of the first verse: 'Aro-o-o-o-o-o-o-oo-ose from out the azure main.' For 'arose' it is fine – you can hear, you can *see* Britain arising. But the same musical exaggeration of a mere preposition, 'to', is all wrong. Some stronger word is needed. Vivian and I would cheerfully have spent two days huddled over the piano to get that one song right. He wrote four or five different tunes for the simple, but very successful, number 'I Was Never Kissed Before'. 'Or do you like this one?' he would say. 'Or this?' By the end of the day I would feel as muddled as one does when the oculist slips yet one more lens before your right eye and says: 'Is *that* better?' I myself wrote three different sets of verses for 'Ma Belle Marguerite', which was one of the hits of the show. This was a song to be sung by the Frenchman, Pierre, at the Willows' Golden Wedding Party. The first set was about a girl who, for some reason, was walking about the hills with a donkey. The donkey had bells on it, so Vivian put a lot of 'Ting-a-lings' into the refrain. Long after Cochran rang up and said: 'Alan, somebody was saying that there have been too many songs about donkeys.' I said: 'I can only remember "Dear little donkey" in that French piece, I've forgotten the name. I think it began with M – Massenet? but that was ages ago.' 'I remember,' he said, 'but they say there was a donkey song at the beginning of the war.' 'I didn't see anything during the war,' I said. 'Nor did I,' he said. 'But do you think you could try again?' 'Aye, aye, sir,' I said, and I did.

The next set was the song of a weary *poilu* on the march, who was always imploring his Capitaine to halt and give him a rest; the refrain was:

Mon brave Capitaine–e
Arretez s'il-vous-plait —

But he would not stop, even when Madelein-e was at the window. This version caused no great excitement and one day somebody asked for another. I said: 'Very well. But I've had enough of this tune. If this effort doesn't do that's the end.' And so I wrote 'Ma Belle-e Marguerit-e', the song about the wine, with which Georges Guétary 'stopped the show' on the first night. We were stuck of course with those 'Ting-a-lings', which started with the donkey on the hill: but nobody seems to mind. 'Stopped the show.' One of the unkindest, but funniest things a critic ever said was about Liz Webb in another show. 'Lizbeth Webb stopped the show with the singing of ——. Unfortunately it started again.'

Then Vivian would come up with brand-new tunes, demanding words. I always enjoyed the challenge and often these numbers became 'the hits'. I wanted a touching duet at a certain point in the Café scene, just before the elopers were cruelly torn asunder by the war. Vivian then was doing a lot of work at the piano at Chappell's, with a telephone beside him. One day he rang up and said: 'I've got a wonderful tune. Listen.' Over the telephone came the beautiful tune, tinkling, like the donkey's bells. 'Now,' he said, 'I want a title, a phrase to repeat.' 'Play it again,' I said. He did, and I said: 'This is my lovely day.' 'Fine,' he said – and it was so – the prime song of the piece. They are singing it still; and they will be singing it, I predict, long after the last Beatles number is dead.

In those days the top price of a stall was 16s. and on that there was entertainment tax. This was deducted from 'the gross' before the author's royalties were calculated, which seemed queer but was never questioned. I have here the 'Return' from the last (886th) performance of *The Bride* (11 June 1949) – Receipts £642, Entertainment Tax £116. I must say I feel a tiny touch of envy for the authors of successful plays today, with stalls at perhaps 24s. and *no* entertainment tax. (The play at present at the Savoy has been taking £1,200 on Saturday night – no orchestra, and no tax.) I fought that wicked imposition for twenty-five years. It was abolished just after my last play *The Water Gipsies* came off. Never mind. It's off.

I have no quarrel with the critics. How, without them, should I have got so far as I did? And, having for six months attempted the grim task myself, for the old green *Westminster Gazette* (with Aldous Huxley and Naomi Royde-Smith), I sympathize with them. They are like everyone else in the theatre, the victims of a world in which 'you never can tell'. They praise a play unanimously and it flops: they nag in unison, and it runs for two years. '*Bless the Bride* will not vie with those wonderful productions at the old Empire (he means 'Pavilion') when Cochran was a great showman and not, as now, a great legend.' *Later*: 'This, said C.B., has already made a bigger profit than his great success Noël Coward's *Bitter Sweet* . . .' '*Bless the Bride* which *began a little uncertainly* has become C. B. Cochran's biggest success for many years . . .' '700th performance, being the longest run of any musical play since Sir Charles Cochran has presented . . .' – '*Bless the Bride*, now in its third year, is still playing to capacity.'

Yet: 'A. P. Herbert has given it just about as much plot as would go on the back of a cupronickel sixpence . . .' – 'He hardly troubles to find his play a plot . . .' – 'Musically sugary and undistinguished.' 'Sir Alan Herbert has not had to exert himself unduly in the matter of wit . . .' – 'The piece shimmers with wit' – 'Wit, music, setting, performance – all admirable. What is missing? . . . I feel, robust comedy.' 'A lack of robust humour.' But later: 'The chief reason (for the second anniversary) is that all concerned . . . boldly trusted their own sense of the subject . . . Neither the librettist nor Mr Vivian Ellis was ever betrayed into a discordant idea or a discordant note. . . .'

What a job! I am glad I gave it up. But I am duly grateful to that much-maligned craft.

Tough At The Top (which opened 15 July) was not such a happy affair. It was about a heavy-weight boxer and a sort of Ruritanian Princess, whose country was badly treated by a bullying neighbour. (In the background there was supposed to be a subtle satirical reference to Russia's way with small countries, but it was so subtle that nobody seemed to spot it.)

Critics and theatre-folk are often heard to say, when a play does not go well, that they cannot understand how experienced men can ever have put it on with hope of success. This, with great respect, is to forget that the theatre is about the most incalculable of human enterprises. It is like wondering why Eisenhower chose rough weather for D-Day. Not even Monty, I believe, could command success on the stage. How barbarous to put a tax on turnover – *receipts* – on so precarious an enterprise! Anything can put a favourite among the also rans.

Cochran, Lord Vivian (his very helpful partner), Vivian Ellis and I all thought it was (or would be) a better show than *The Bride*, and one or two critics said the same. Ellis's music, though not perhaps so 'popular', had a new maturity and distinction: and my book, I still believe, was a worthier work. We had that brilliant (but expensive) designer Oliver Messel, and the same electric producer, Wendy Toye. The singing and the band were fine: and there was sufficient fun, especially from that brilliant comedian, the late Brian Reece. True, it opened in July and suffered twelve weeks of unprecedented summer: true, it was far too expensive. True, it was my thirteenth musical production. Also, it was the first time I 'had my name in lights', and when I saw them, crossing the Strand, I said to a friend: 'This will be fatal.' I was right. The great new ship sank after five months, and lost I know not how much money. You can see the same sort of thing in the House of Commons. A Minister opens a debate, brings in a new Bill, calm and complacent. Something wholly unforeseen is said or done, and the day ends in uproar.

For once (privately) I found fault with C.B's casting. I had deliberately written the part of the Princess for Lizbeth Webb, who was by now a high favourite of public and Press. The dialogue was in the simple girlish style which had suited her so well in *The Bride*. But dear C.B., without a word of warning, engaged a foreign lady – from Puerto Rico. She sang like an angel (rather better), her voice was thrilling: but it was very difficult to hear her words, singing or speaking. For the boxer C.B. engaged a husky American, who sang well too. My *Punch* character Topsy used to describe some people as 'quite definitely unmagnetic'. I would not go as far as that: but it is desirable that the principals of a musical should, apart from their technical skill, be reasonably magnetic to the audience. If none of them would care to get either Boy or Girl themselves they cannot be wildly interested in Boy getting Girl on the stage: and, of course, we had lost the positive goodwill that Liz Webb could have brought with her. Still, this less fortunate piece has left one thing behind. The title, *Tough at the Top*, which I invented, was criticized, I forget why: but I wish that I had a pound for every time these words have been used by the papers, especially in sporting headlines. My Princess, by the way, made the boxer her Minister of Sport. This was thought to be very absurd: but behold, we have had one for years.

Vivian Ellis wrote some fine music for the last scene where the bully won and the Princess had to abdicate:

> This is not the end: this is but a beginning:
> When the fight is lost, there's a fight worth winning.
> Nothing is wasted, nothing is in vain:
> The seas roll over but the rocks remain.
> They can break man's happiness but not man's will:

Little lamps of liberty will smoulder still,
Till the trumpet sounds and we break the chain
And the wings of the spirit ride the free air again.

A song for Czechoslovakia today – written in 1949.

It was the end of my long partnership with Cochran – eighteen years – eight shows. That was the last 'musical' he did. He died terribly in 1951. For long he had had severe arthritis of the hip, which he endured with uncomplaining courage. It became so bad that he could not get up to the Dress Circle for a rehearsal – or sometimes even on to the stage. He was caught in a bath with a tap running too hot which he could not reach: he could not get out of the bath without aid, and his wife could not hear his cries for the noise of traffic.

I was on a ship, on my way home from Australia. I cabled home a sad farewell:

Dear master, this blue sea is dark today,
That Fate should finish you in such a way!
But I will think of all the joy you made,
Of gallant fighting in a fearful trade.
I think how many famous folk there are
You found and fostered – and behold a star!
Of brilliant memories you leave behind,
Of one courageous, courteous and kind.
No more we'll put our harassed heads together,
About the plot, the critics, or the weather.
Unless in heaven there's an angel cast
The Prince of Showmen is at rest at last;
Though few of us will be surprised, I swear,
If you devise new fun and beauty there.
Farewell, dear friend and master, could we all
See with such pride the final curtain fall!

In 1950, I suppose, on holiday in Cornwall, I suddenly began to write a musical version of my book *The Water Gipsies*, all about the canal folk. Vivian Ellis, though not consulted, nobly consented: and away we went. It was not the ordinary West End manager's meat – 'Too earthy,' said one. But Peter Saunders (*The Mousetrap* man), who had never done a 'musical', is an enterprising fellow and bravely gave us a welcome first at Nottingham and then at the old *Winter Garden*, the wrong end of Drury Lane – 31 August 1951. Charles Hicks directed very well, Pamela Charles (who later played the lead in *My Fair Lady* in New York) was Jane; and Dora Bryan her naughty sister Lily. Dora is a natural fount of fun: I gave her some good material, I think, with some of my best lyrics, and here she really made her name. I remember Peter saying to me after the first night: 'We must put Dora in lights.' But, alas, for a long time she had been longing to be a mother, and after about seven months we heard the ghastly news that she *was* going to become a mother. Peter Saunders was just about to renew the contract for the theatre: but now he didn't, and the play came prematurely off. Still more ghastly, poor Dora did *not* become a mother– so we might be running still. Dora had a very good under-study, Vivienne Martin, who had been on two or three times and got better applause for 'You never know with men' than Dora did. She could well have kept the flag flying if we had known, or guessed that the baby was a false alarm. I felt like the character in my Chekhov play – 'Now that's *just* the sort of thing that happens to me.'

In the Budget, a few weeks later, Mr Peter Thorneycroft abolished the Entertainment Tax. I had been paying it for twenty-seven years.

That was Number 14. Number 15 has long been ready, but has never been performed. A year or two before War Two I was asked to do into English the lyrics of Johann Strauss's *Die Fledermaus*. Some firm (I forget who) wanted to make a film: I saw some of the shooting but I'm not sure that the picture ever met the public. The producers were a large and commanding German called Fellner, and a meek little Austrian (I *think*) called Thiele. They were always having fierce, rather one-sided rows. I came at last to the famous Champagne Song in the finale of Act Two – 'The Ball' – where almost everybody is masked and slightly tight. Each verse ends with a hearty salute to 'His Majesty King Champagne!' Personally, I detest champagne: but I wrote a dutiful verse (two, I think) for Rosalinda (Evelyn Laye) – 'bubble' and 'trouble' – 'life' and 'strife' and so on. Then I thought 'Eisenstein, the hero, is a low suburban fellow like me and probably dislikes champagne as much as I do. Also, he is more than slightly tight. Let's have a little variety.' I gave him these deathless words:

> This wine is full of gases,
>   Which are to me offensive,
> It pleases all you asses
>   Because it is expensive.

(the truest quatrain, I think, I ever wrote)

> But not a chimney-sweeper
> Would touch it if 'twas cheaper,
> Let's pour it down the sewers
> And stick to honest brewers.
>   It's only fit for women,
>   To wash in or to swim in –
>   It's only fit for weddings
>   And rather nasty then –

{ 130 }

ending with

'Give me a glass of Rain!'

Fellner and Thiele came out to Hammersmith on one or two hot afternoons in August. The family were away on holiday and I was sweating away, alone, at *Fledermaus*. One afternoon they had a deadly row. Fellner won, as usual, and I remember the frustrated little Thiele tearing a document into very small pieces and flinging them out of the window. They floated down into my aquarium. Then we got back to the piano and I played the Champagne Song. Little Thiele was enthusiastic: '"*Ser Komisch!*" Very witty,' and so on. But then there was a slight moan behind me, the big boy, I think, must have dug the little one in the ribs: and Fellner said: 'But no! ze hero cannot speak so of Champagne. Out! coupé! cut!'

'Very well,' I said, and it was so.

Not till long later did I realize that Ribbentrop, the Champagne King, was then the German Ambassador in London, and it would probably be fatal for Herr Fellner to countenance an irreverent word about champagne.

I heard with a shock, about a month after the film was finished, that Herr Fellner had hanged himself. I do hope it was nothing to do with my verses.

Then, in 1950, I think, my friend Reginald Arkell came to me with a tale that Max Reinhardt wanted to come over to England and produce a new version of *Fledermaus*, and would like me to do it. Since I had done so much work on the lyrics it seemed reasonable that I should finish the job. I should, of course, have asked for a contract, an 'advance' etc., but with my usual impetuosity I charged ahead and hoped for the best. Then Reinhardt went to America to make films, he never came to England again and we heard no more of him.

Never mind. There is the play, called *Come to the Ball* (by A. P. Herbert and Reginald Arkell – but Reggie didn't write a word) prettily published by Ernest Benn Limited. It is out of print, but I could lend a serious impresario a lot of copies. The Vienna folk approved of it. Sir David Webster said long ago that if ever Covent Garden did the work again they would use my version. Challenged later he said that the right kind of tenor was in short supply: and now he has left the Garden.

Veracity compels me to say that it is the best of the many versions I have seen.

'Knowing something of the difficulties of comic opera composition, we should be very far from laying wanton hands on the work of the original authors or later adaptors. We have not altered for the sake of alteration: nor have we attempted any elaborate modernization (which would not be in tune with the music). But we have imagined Johann Strauss saying to his authors in 1950, "Look here, this work of ours goes very well at Covent Garden and enchants the musical folk. But can't you do a little more work on the book? It's bound to be 'old-fashioned', but need it be *quite* so old-fashioned?"' –

So, Mr Impresario, here you are, old wine in a better bottle.

After a good deal of boasting in the musical world, I must confess that my contributions to the 'legitimate' stage (an offensive expression) have not caused overcrowding anywhere. I have mentioned *The White Witch* at the Haymarket. I have now forgotten the story, but the main point was, I think, that a couple who had the opportunity and inclination did not commit adultery. This is often protested, but hardly ever believed in the courts. Arnold Bennett liked it; John Galsworthy who read it, came to the first night, and said 'It *might* do': but it didn't. I still feel there must have been something more in the play than got across the footlights: or why did the great Haymarket put it on?

Then, in 1925, there was the play which Nigel Playfair ruined with a Charity Matinée, a laughable but sad experience. It was called *At the Same Time* and was all about dirty work at a General Election. (I had helped Sir Leslie Scott at two elections in Liverpool). I think it was quite good, and some of it was certainly funny. Dear Nigel had promised to arrange a matinée for the Victoria Dock Children's Country Camp, and thought it would send my play soaring into a long West End run. We had some good performers, Athene Seyler, Angela Baddeley, Claude Rains. Every seat at the Aldwych was sold, chiefly to Countesses. Unfortunately, the date kept being postponed, and the matinée at last was given on a hot day in July. Few Countesses came, though many sent their maids. The brief rehearsals were on the small stage of the Lyric, Hammersmith, and the company had only two hours that morning in which to adjust themselves to the wide open space at the Aldwych. The funny man, whose name I forget, deliberately, had had a good lunch and was far from remembering all his lines. Angela Baddeley and others prompted him efficiently, but this did tend to take the edge, if any, off the dialogue. The matinée did not begin till after three, and there were three Acts. After the second Act someone came on to the stage and made a protracted speech – about twenty minutes, or so it seemed – about the Victoria Dock Children's Country Camp, and what fun they had, besides, of course, warm thanks to all concerned, the pretty programme-sellers, and even the playwright. Then the play began again, and by this time even I had forgotten what it was all about. The matinée did not end till after six, and before that many of the maids had had to depart to their evening duties.

There was no ugly rush for the play by West End managers next morning. My advice to a struggling dramatist is, on the whole, not to have a play done at a 'charity matinée' on a hot afternoon in July: and, if he does, allow no speeches about the charity.

During the war I saw a good deal, now and then, of that ball of fire, Robert Newton, and his wife, when the *Water Gipsy* spent the night at Chelsea. Somehow – I can't imagine when – I dashed off a play for him. It was all about a patrol boat like mine, down in Sea Reach, a sailing barge, and some German prisoners from a fallen bomber. Bob liked it, Cochran liked it: he got someone to design a set, and started to 'pencil in' some 'dates' in the country. This was highly exciting. To put Bob 'in the picture', give him the atmosphere, I took him down to Hole Haven one day and he spent a night with us on patrol in Sea Reach. There was a terrific air-raid that night, and all the bombers roared over us, going there and back, the great Reach like a luminous plain under the searchlights. Bob was thrilled. In a few days Cochran rang up and said ruefully: 'Alan, you've overdone it. Bob's joined the Navy.'

That was the plain fact. Fired by my example, he had 'joined up' and spent the weeks before D-Day on harbour duties at Portsmouth and Spithead. After the War Bob was snapped up by the films, so the play was off, and now I do not even remember its name. There is a theory (which I dispute) that all humour is founded on misfortune. Certainly there is a funny side to all my theatrical misfortunes: but this was the funniest of the lot – and I am glad to say that we said so at the time.

Then – I had almost forgotten – I made a play, called *Better Dead*, of my book *Made for Man*. This was done at the charming Richmond Theatre and by B.B.C. radio, but set nothing alight. I always thought the book might make a good film. The heroine, after all, does plunge off Lambeth Bridge.

Altogether, then, I have written nineteen full-length dramas, fifteen of them musical. Only one of these has earned much more than bread-and-butter money. Only the rare beings, if any, like Noël Coward can expect long luck in the theatre, and even he has had some bangs. I have had as much good fortune as I deserve. How fortunate I was to serve for so long two such masters as Nigel Playfair and Charles Cochran – to work in happy harness with gifted and agreeable composers like Dennis Arundell, Alfred Reynolds, Tom Dunhill, Dickie Austin and especially Vivian Ellis!

But I distinguish between fortune and luck. Good fortune gives you a game: luck controls the bounce of the ball. Looking back, I sometimes feel that I have had more bad bounces than I deserved. One leading lady lost to baby-duty may reasonably be expected, but three seems excessive: and two in one play must be a good cause for complaint.

But I do not complain: and if I was asked 'Would you like to do it all again, making no more money than you did before?' I should cry heartily 'Yes'. However the ball bounced, I loved belonging to the theatre, I loved the work, and the brave, merry people.

The theatre is a fascinating but fatiguing mistress. You sigh for her when you are not with her: but she is an endless worry when you are, even if she smiles. If you write a book the critics may like it or not, the public may buy it or not. But you do not see the public *not* buying it. You do not see or hear them disliking it. Nobody can boo or go out ostentatiously in the middle of it. I did hear Sinclair Lewis tell this story long ago. Crossing the Atlantic he saw a lady on deck reading his latest book, about which there had been some hot discussion. By the place of her finger in the book he judged that she was approaching the passage which had earned most trouble, and he thought he would keep an eye on her. Presently the old lady rose up, walked firmly to the rail and flung the book far into the ocean. But such public verdicts are rare.

Nor, if a book fails, are you likely to ruin your publisher, and several supporters, or throw a great many people out of employment. A book is not, like a play, the prey of chance and circumstances outside your control – bad weather, bad casting, laryngitis, babies: it stands or falls by itself. How often have I sat in the stalls during rehearsals, thinking: 'Everything seems to be going wrong. Fifteen or twenty thousand pounds* have been spent already on the production: and it will have to run "to capacity" for six months before it begins to show a profit. Sixty good people are employed upon the stage, twenty or thirty behind it, twenty-five in the band. Fortunes, reputations, livelihoods, depend upon this affair. There are many others engaged in it, and all that goes wrong cannot be put down to me. But still, it all began far back when I sat down in Cornwall and wrote upon some fair white paper: "Act One, Scene One". What a responsibility!'

If you write an unsuccessful book it is a pity: but by the time you know its fate you may be busy on another. If a play is harshly received or even has a faint aroma of doubt about it, you go about London feeling like a suspected person. Even if it looks like a success it is always jogging at your elbow, and saying 'Quite sure?' You have survived the prenatal agonies ('All seems pretty well, but what would happen if the tenor fell under a bus, or the soprano's throat continued?'), the emotional ordeal of the First Night (I always sat through every second), the un-Christian insults (as you think) of one or two jealous and ignorant scribes. 'Business' is pretty good. You stroll into the theatre, to see how things go: or simply, let us confess, to enjoy yourself. It may be a vanity; but it is a pleasing thing to make perfect

* Heaven knows what the figures would be today.

strangers laugh, and a thing more pleasing still to hear them laughing.
I never tired of listening to Dora Bryan and Pamela Charles, the two
sisters in *The Water Gipsies*, in their comic passages. You think a line
is funny when you scribble it down in your den. It makes the company
laugh when they hear it at the first rehearsal: but when it has been
said ten or twenty times nobody laughs any more and you begin to
wonder if it is funny after all. Then, on the first night, if all those
strangers open their friendly faces and throats in a loud, long laugh
it is for the author a moment of triumph: 'I was right! I was right!'
you say to your little self: and if all the other nights more thousands
roar their irresistible laughter at exactly the same point of time the
pleasure, the sense of power, does not diminish. This may be thought,
I suppose, a rather shameful confession, but I make it gaily. Did not
my song say: 'I want to see the people happy'?

Nor did I ever weary of hearing my composer's music, especially a
song that the public seemed to like as well as we did. I used to lurk in
'Harty's Bar', near the orchestra, at the Adelphi, dart out and peep
through the curtain to hear 'This is our lovely day', or Guétary singing
'Give Me A Table For Two'. The best of your books will never give
you such pleasure. But still, your mistress nags. The house is full.
But the leading lady, or the comedian, is 'off'. The valiant understudy
does well, but not well enough for you: and you go back to the bar
for comfort. A strange man totters in from the stalls, panting as if
he had just escaped from the Gestapo. 'Give me a brandy,' he says.
'This is the lousiest show I ever saw.' He is only one of two thousand,
perhaps, but he is discouraging.

At the end you go round 'behind', to show the company you have
not forgotten them – and to enjoy perhaps a friendly word with the
stage-staff, waiting to 'strike' the Library or roll the Palace on. I
always tried hard to understand their mysterious and indispensable
arts. Twice, at the old Lyric, I climbed up into the lofty 'flies', over the
stage, during a performance, and heard all the secrets proudly explained. The second time, as I climbed down, a box of Swan matches
took fire in my trouser pocket and I descended smoking. I was not
allowed up there again.

But tonight the leading lady is in tears, mixed with make-up: her
throat is worse and the 'Income Tax' has upset her. The baritone is
reproachful: he should have had a better song. The comedian still
thinks he should have a funnier exit-line in Scene Three; you still
think he says it wrong. Someone else has had a searing row with the
stage-manager, and you hear both sides.

Then, one day, there are gaps in the stalls. Receipts are 'down' on
last week. It is not really very serious. Last Thursday the public paid
£600: this Thursday they have paid only £580. We are '£20 down on

last week'. If it was the other way – £620 today – we should be '£20 up' and all would be smiling. But we are '£20 down' and there are grave debates. Is it the fog, the snow, or the sunshine? Is it Christmas shopping, or the General Election? Or is it the actors, getting slack? Or, ghastly thought, is it the public getting tired? The only time I met Gertrude Lawrence she told a delightful tale about Lillian Braithwaite. The Dame had a long run in a play called *Arsenic and Old Lace*. They kept going even when the doodle-bugs appeared, though this I found it difficult to believe – to go on acting when those terrifying falterers and stoppers were about. The Dame lived in some penthouse in Mayfair, and used to spend the noisy night in the bathroom. One morning – it may have been the night that I myself, on duty on the river, counted eighty-five of the obscene machines – the secretary, maid or someone found the Dame cold and half-asleep in her dressing-gown, woke her up and said: 'O Dame, did you have a terrible night?' The old lady drew herself up and said: 'No, indeed. We were £30 up.'

'Nag, nag!' Every breakfast-time a 'return' of last night's receipts arrives by post, to be anxiously compared with the week before. Every day somebody writes to say that he loved the show but could not hear a *word* of the songs – and *can't* you do something about it? That damned band! Nag, nag! A book keeps quiet.

Against all this, you have some respectable pleasures not enjoyed by the novelist, high and dry and undisturbed in his den – the pleasure, for example, of communal effort, of working with a team. This is very good for you. In no other industry, I suppose, are the different levels and departments so close together. The stage-hand, the electrician, who are never seen, the chorus-singer and small-part players are as keen upon the common business as the manager, stars, author, composer or conductor. The property-man or linesman is no less proud of success and even more resentful of unjust (as they think) criticism. It is their show too. When the fortnight's 'notices' go up at last, and the play is under sentence of death, we are moved by more than loss of money or employment. It is like the breaking up of a happy family or regiment. We have shared many toils and trials and emotions. The painted scenery has become a common home. The costumes and characters have taken on a kind of reality. There is no cause for tragical thought – except, perhaps, for the bold men who have risked and lost their money. In a few weeks, with luck, the golden girls will be pattering and chattering up the stairs of another theatre, as merry as ever. But there is much food for honest sentiment. The living unity that we built up together is to die, and tomorrow we shall be sixty or seventy separate individuals again, sharing nothing but memories. So we are inclined to weep a little. But there are still the songs and the music; and we can gather round the family piano, and croak the tunes again and wistfully revive the old days, the glorious Lucy, the handsome Georges, and the clapping crowds. This is something. I do not think that any novelist sits down and sentimentally reads his forgotten books.

Happy the writer, I think, who can bite a bit – if it is only a little bit – from both these worlds. For my part, I do not regret at all my humble contributions to 'creative joy'. 'I would play the part again.'

POSTSCRIPT – Here was a refreshing letter from Arthur Christiansen, then Editor of the *Daily Express*, who went to the first night of *Big Ben* 'quite by accident'.

'Sometimes,' the Editor wrote, 'the newspapers drive me crazy. I read with astonishment and distress the cynical and hard-boiled reception *Big Ben* received in one or two places this morning . . . (July 18, 1946).

'I confessed my inexperience as a First Nighter to my friends, and asked them if this was not one of the most emotional and moving occasions in the theatre in the last twenty-five years. I found that the non-professional audience and one or two of the professional audience – including, I am happy to say, our own Ernest Betts – were in agreement with me. Therefore I looked forward to a unanimous Press that would praise you and that wonderful composer Vivian Ellis (whom I do not know) as well as C. B. Cochran . . . the wit of your lyrics, the astonishing beauty of the music and the wonderful patriotic pageant – and the deep love which everybody concerned with the production showed for our country . . .'

Christiansen sadly concluded: 'I can only believe that cynicism is an occupational disease that comes to Dramatic Critics, and that having attended First Nights year in year out their judgement becomes warped and their enthusiasms cold.'

I cannot go all the way with the Editor. The 'real' critics, men like W. A. Darlington, Harold Hobson, J. C. Trewin, B. A. Young and others, retain their keenness, and kindness, amazingly over the years. The lesser breeds may make the theatre folk sad – and even 'cynical'. But for comfort they should study *Punch*'s notices of the Savoy operas – *Iolanthe* – 'the dialogue is not worthy of the author' – *The Gondoliers* – 'there is nothing in the music that catches the ear on a first hearing'.

{ 8 }

THE LAW

D R JOHNSON said: 'No man but a blockhead ever wrote except for money.' Some lesser fellow said recently that no man writes for pleasure. As President of the Society of Authors I must rebuke them both. If they were right there would not be so many splendid letters in *The Times*, the *Daily Telegraph* and many other papers. We may tend to hope, more and more, for some material reward, but in most persons the original urge or itch came from worthy purpose or pure pleasure. One is not paid for writing to the papers, which is, I think, a great injustice. If they did pay for letters, I should be wealthy. You would think that at my age a man would be sensible enough not to spend precious time in this way: but no, if I am bursting with something to say, something that will solve the problem, something that will save the nation, something that all the other fools have missed, away I go – 'Sir' — So Dr Johnson can stand down.

Nobody, I think, has said that nobody writes *with* pleasure. Certainly for forty-six years it has given me pleasure to concoct and plan and polish my *Misleading Cases*, and if you gave me a good idea, I would start one more with pleasure today. It is a wonder how they have multiplied and endured – and this may be some encouragement for the Young. The first Case – I think it was *The Reasonable Man* – Fardell *v.* Potts – appeared in *Punch* in 1924. 'Just journalism.' But see how it has bred – there was one in the first *Punch* of this year. They have been promoted into books, *Misleading Cases in the Common Law* (1927), *More Misleading Cases* (1930), and *Still More Misleading Cases* (1933). Three great judges, Lord Hewart, Lord Chief Justice, Lord Buckmaster and Lord Atkin kindly wrote introductions to the little books. Then there was *Uncommon Law* (1935 – in an 'omnibus' volume, reprinted eleven times and in a new edition this year), *Codd's Last Case* (1952), *Bardot M.P.* (1964), and *Wigs at Work* (a Penguin paper-back – 1966). The Cases have been quoted on the Bench of the Supreme Court of the United States, in our own High Court and in the House of Lords. They have been good exports. Canada has been kind for many years. I had this warming letter from

Ontario: 'Lawyers throughout the English-speaking world and assuredly this one have been delighted and refreshed over the years by the cool and pleasant breezes you have brought to the consideration of legal problems. For myself, I have not hesitated to quote you in our Courts and in other gatherings on more than one occasion and your words have never failed to receive due appreciation and to illuminate the subject under discussion.' In 1966 the bold and brilliant Frank Muir, then of the B.B.C., presented six or seven cases on television; and in 1967 some more were done, and seven more are now being prepared. Sir Robert Menzies told me that he had viewed them regularly in Australia. Last year Zambia bought the television rights of some of them, which delighted me. The sum my agent sent me was only £4 but never mind. I like to think of Mr Haddock brightening life on the banks of the Zambesi.

All this, dear Young, is not mere boasting (though, if a man is not to give himself a kind word in his autobiography, where shall he?): it is to illustrate that ancient truth 'You never know'. A tiny seed may yield a respectable beanstalk, therefore hope on; therefore, too, take great pains with every little thing.

As I wrote in an introduction to *Wigs at Work*:

'Mr Bumble's famous saying on the law is nearly always quoted as a general condemnation. In fact, it was applied to a particular point on which he had particular information:

'You were present,' said Mr Brownlow, 'and indeed are the more guilty of the two, in the eye of the law; for the law supposes that your wife acts under your direction.'

'If the law supposes that,' said Mr Bumble, 'the law is a ass – a idiot. If that's the eye of the law, the law is a bachelor; and the worst I wish the law is, that his eye may be opened by experience.'

'If I had ever thought that our law was generally an ass I should not have been called to the Bar more than fifty years ago, nor should I have given so much time and toil to the sincerest form of flattery. I have in fact a warm admiration for those who wear the wig, for their lucid language, delicate reasoning, and – don't laugh – their pride in the pursuit of justice and order. "Lucid?" you may say with surprise. Certainly, when they are roaming free the plains of the Common Law where so many splendid crops of principle and practice were sown by former gentlemen in wigs. They tend and improve them still, making new law, now and then, if you will, grafting and pruning, but the fruit is well bred and the process is clear. Here and there an ancient plant should be dug up and allowed to die: but it is too deeply rooted in history for the judges to touch. Then you must blame not "the law" but Parliament which has failed to use a spade.

'Again, when you hear the gentlemen in wigs talking, it seems,

Double Dutch, and reeling round in conflicting circles, put it down to Parliament, not the fraternity of the law. They are struggling, stifled, in a labyrinth of modern legislation, constructed brilliantly by Parliamentary draughtsmen, who are not allowed to explain what they meant, even if they know . . .

'The law is not always an ass though it is often an enigma. So I hope that whatever you think of the laws, made in Westminster or tinkered by the Temple, you will find nothing in my pages to make you think less of "the law", meaning the gentlemen in wigs. If I laugh at some of them I laugh with affection and respect.'

'These frolics in jurisprudence,' I wrote somewhere else, 'are sometimes essays in reform as well and are shyly intended not only to amuse but amend.' Some, certainly, have been prophets, if not prompters of reform. One of my favourites is *Board of Inland Revenue v. Haddock* – 'Why is the House of Lords?' This appeared in *Punch* on 9 August 1933. The Court of Appeal declined to consider the case. 'It will go to the House of Lords in any event,' said the Master of the Rolls, 'so let it go at once.' But he made 'a few general observations upon our appellate system.'

'The human mind is admittedly fallible and in most professions the possibility of occasional error is admitted and even guarded against. But the legal profession is the only one in which the chances of error are admitted to be so high that an elaborate machinery has been provided for the correction of error – and not a single error, but a succession of errors. In other trades to be wrong is regarded as a matter for regret; in the law alone it is regarded as a matter of course . . .

'The institution of one Court of Appeal may be considered a reasonable precaution; but two suggest panic. To take a fair parallel, our great doctors, I think, would not claim to be more respected or more advanced in their own science than our greatest jurists. But our surprise would be great if, after the removal of our appendix by a distinguished surgeon, we were taken before three other distinguished surgeons, who ordered our appendix to be replaced: and our surprise would give place to stupefaction if we were then referred to a tribunal of seven distinguished surgeons who directed that our appendix should be extracted again. Yet such operations, or successions of operations, are an everyday experience in the practice of the law . . .

'When a man keeps two clocks which tell the time differently his fellows will receive with suspicion his weightiest pronouncements upon the hour of the day, even if one of them happens to be right . . .

'For all these reasons we recommend that either this Court or the House of Lords (as a Court of Appeal) be abolished; or, in the alternative, that the House of Lords retain its appellate functions as a specialist body for the settlement of questions of exceptional difficulty, *such cases to be referred to them upon the order of a High Court judge.'*

That was 1933. Twenty years later, in 1953, an imposing Committee on Supreme Court Practice, on which that fine judge Lord Evershed, and other judges, worked for *seven years* (I gave up after two) made roughly the same recommendation – 'leapfrogging' the Court of Appeal 'in certain circumstances'. In 1968 the Administration of Justice Bill contained a similar 'leapfrog' clause; which was carried: and, my goodness, *it came into force on 1 January this year 1970.*

Thirty-seven years. Well done, Haddock.

Another favourite of mine (and, I believe, the profession) was the Reasonable Man case. The Master of the Rolls said:

'The Common Law of England has been laboriously built about a mythical figure – the figure of "The Reasonable Man". . .

'This noble creature stands in singular contrast to his kinsman the Economic Man, whose every action is prompted by the single spur of selfish advantage and directed to the single end of monetary gain. The Reasonable Man is always thinking of others, prudence is his guide, and "Safety First", if I may borrow a contemporary catchword, is his rule of life. All solid virtues are his, save only that peculiar quality by which the affection of other men is won. For it will not be pretended that socially he is much less objectionable than the Economic Man. Though any given example of his behaviour must command our admiration, when taken in the mass his acts create a very different set of impressions. He is one who invariably looks where he is going, and is careful to examine the immediate foreground before he executes a leap or bound; who neither star-gazes nor is lost in meditation when approaching trap-doors or the margin of a dock; who records in every case upon the counterfoils of cheques such ample details as are desirable, scrupulously substitutes the word "Order" for the word "Bearer", crosses the instrument "a/c Payee only", and registers the package in which it is despatched; who never mounts a moving omnibus, and does not alight from any car while the train is in motion; who investigates exhaustively the *bona fides* of every mendicant before distributing alms, and will inform himself of the history and habits of a dog before administering a caress; who believes no gossip, nor repeats it, without firm basis for believing it to be true; who never drives his ball till those in front of him have definitely vacated the putting-green which is his own objective; who never from one year's end to another makes an excessive demand upon his wife, his neighbour, his servants, his ox or his ass, who in the way of business looks only for that narrow margin of profit which twelve men such as himself would reckon to be "fair", and contemplates his fellow-merchants, their agents, and their goods, with that degree of suspicion and distrust which the law deems admirable; who never swears, gambles, or loses his temper; who uses nothing except in moderation, and even while he flogs his child is meditating only on the golden mean. Devoid, in short, of any human weakness, with not one single saving vice, *sans* prejudice, procrastination, ill-nature, avarice, and absence of mind, as careful for his own safety as he is for that of others, this excellent but odious character stands like a monument in our Courts of Justice, vainly appealing to his fellow-citizens to order their lives after his own example . . .'

This elaborate kind of parody will not do for television, though parts of the reasonable man were used in one of the cases. I always said – and so for a long time did the B.B.C. – that they were too 'literary' for the domestic screen. But some of them contained opportunities for comic action before the court-scene, and Frank Muir feared nothing. Alan Melville and Henry Cecil, the judge, both old hands, did the 'adapting' very well: and Michael Mills, in charge of the production, won a deserved award. But, in my view, Frank's superb casting was the thing. Roy Dotrice is a young man with a genius for playing old ones and he is a perfect Haddock. Alistair Sim as Mr Justice Swallow, with his sly glances and eloquent intonations, is fascinating: his face seems to be able to say two or three things at the same time.

However well done, they were not likely to challenge 'Coronation Street' or 'The Avengers'; but among those who did 'view' them they had a surprisingly wide appeal. The simple folk in Hammersmith shops were as enthusiastic as 'my learned friends': indeed, they enjoyed one or two cases in the second series more than we did. I am myself collaborating in a third series with Michael Gilbert, solicitor and author, and John Howard Davies, producer: and we hope that Zambia will come again.

The Cases have had some comic international adventures. I can't remember how Albert Haddock was born, but his initials are the same as mine (his middle name is Percival, I *think*), and I do maintain that I invented him. After the first television case, in which Haddock paid his income tax with a cheque made out on a cow, I received a spacious cutting from an American newspaper (the Memphis Press – *Scimitar*) headed:

A CHECK CAN BE WRITTEN ON A COW

The article made not the slightest reference to me, my works, or the B.B.C., but used as *news* all Haddock's arguments and opinions on unconventional cheques. Halfway through it suddenly claimed the authority of the Chase Manhattan Bank for the particular case of the cow: 'In the nineteenth century' – 19th century! – 'an Englishman named Albert Haddock got mad at the local tax-collector over his bill and conceived a most ingenious idea for getting even.' Then followed the whole story. I suppose I should have chased the *Scimitar* for libel as well as copyright.

Then there was the mini-skirt case. My beloved *Punch* rejected this one because they had recently made a resolution to have no more jokes about the mini-skirt (as one might say 'Never again will we mention the Equator'). I sent it to the *Evening Standard* who printed it without the usual heading 'Misleading Cases'. In three foreign lands, America, France and Italy, to my knowledge and, I expect, a good many more, the story was reprinted as straight news. The American reprint gave the absurd proceedings almost in full. The French report (in, I think, *Paris Libre*) was headed:

LES MINI-JUPES
ET
LA LOI BRITANNIQUE

Poor Mr Haddock had found himself in an Underground train opposite to three pretty young things in minimal minis: and he was unjustly accused (and convicted) of conduct likely to cause a breach of the peace. Counsel for the Crown, towards the end of the appeal, asked the Court to say that it was the duty of a gentleman in Mr Haddock's position to close his eyes, and keep them closed until he heard his destination announced. But the judge thought that this would be an intolerable invasion of individual liberty, and he ruled, on the contrary, that it was the duty of any female who entered a railway train in a non- or minimum-skirt to remain standing till her journey was terminated. All this was solemnly repeated on both sides of the Atlantic. I wonder how many Parisians who read it have refused to use our perilous Underground.

Then there was a case called *Is It a Free Country?* which went very well on television and by chance was repeated while we were waiting for Armstrong and his companion to descend from the Lunar Module on to the Moon. Haddock, with as good reason, jumped off Hammersmith Bridge into the Thames. The police arrested him and, not quite certain what he had done wrong, made various charges.

My Lord Chief Justice said: 'It may be said at once that in any case no blame attaches to the persons responsible for the framing of those charges, who were placed in a most difficult position by the appellant's unfortunate act. It is a principle of English law that a person who appears in a police court has done something undesirable, and citizens who take it upon themselves to do unusual actions which attract the attention of the police should be careful to bring those actions into one of the recognized categories of crimes and offences, for it is intolerable that the police should be put to the pains of inventing reasons for finding them undesirable.'

This nonsense crossed the Atlantic with dire effect. Two kind friends – one of them a British Lord of Appeal – have sent me a page from a serious American work called *The Lawyers*. On page 167 the author writes (to my astonishment): 'In Britain . . . despite the general maxim that people cannot be punished for violating laws that have not been announced and defined, the British courts probably retain some marginal power to create new crimes. In 1927 a London magistrate was confronted with a man who had jumped off Westminster Bridge on a bet, whose defence was that there was no law against it. The magistrate convicted and fined him anyway and the conviction was upheld on appeal.'

> It is a principle of English law, said the Court of Criminal Appeal, 'that a person who appears in a police court has done something undesirable and citizens who take it upon themselves etc etc. [exactly as above] . . . It is not for me to say what offence has been committed but I am satisfied that he has committed some offence for which he has been most properly punished.'
>
> 'No such opinion,' says the author with pride, 'could be written by an American court.'

'The index of references,' my friend tells me, 'includes p. 167 *Rex v. Haddock* C.C.A., miscellaneous law, Criminal Law (31) 1927.'

Dear, dear! I have never set out to be really misleading, and such episodes disturb me. Yet I take them as compliments, for they seem to show that my judges' conclusions are at least plausibly expressed. This has always been my ambitious aim. It is easy enough to make spasmodic fun of the law, with the Latin expressions, for example: sustained parody, correct in logic and language, is another thing. I am a devoted admirer of Beachcomber, J. B. Morton of the *Daily Express* (why on earth, by the way, has he had no Honour from the Crown?) but his admired Mr Justice Cocklecarrot will never, I fear, be quoted on the bench of the Supreme Court of the United States.

I was called to the Bar in 1919 by the Inner Temple, with Walter Monckton and Harry Strauss, now Lord Conesford. I often wish that I had answered the call if only for a spell. If I had 'practised', or tried, I say to myself, just a year in Chambers I would have written a legal novel that would have knocked the lot of them. But you must, I feel, know the life from the larva upwards. Besides, I like being with lawyers, that much-maligned but beneficent body of men, I like their language, their stories, and their ways. To dine at one of the Inns on Grand Night is a grand experience. There are no speeches, but every custom, every moment in the ordered march of the evening, every panel, every picture, every stately decanter of port makes quiet speeches, saying how old, how indestructible, are the traditions of the law, how proud and faithful are the brotherhood who serve the laws of England. I am sorry that I was never truly one of them; but at least for fifty years I have saluted them as a loyal guerrilla, prancing in the woods, salutes the regular troops. I am in debt to those who have generously advised me, and grateful to those who have read and recommended me.

{ 9 }

WATER

WATER has been the big thing in my life (though wine has played a part), water, that gentle, soft, beautiful companion, that tough, terrifying, ugly villain. The charm, the power, the cunning of water are wonders. We often think it unjust that God gave the Arabs so much of the oil. But let us be truly grateful that he gave us so much water. Water all round us, washing the shores, smoothing the golden sands, water running, roaring, trickling and gleaming everywhere, in lakes and streams and rivers, water refreshing and decorating the land.

One of the great virtues of water is that its pleasures do not depend upon size. A mountain, to attract our praise, has to be big. The true motorist must have a monster car and a three-lane road. But the infant paddling and splashing in six inches of sea, the old lady trailing her fingers over the side of a punt, the small boy peering into the mysteries of a rock-pool or a tiny pond on the downs, the busy stickleback, the water-spider, the caddis-flies and beetles; all these are in love with water as warmly as the tough mariner at the helm of an ocean-racer beating into a hostile sea.

Thus it is with our rivers. Our dear Thames, and our other dear rivers, set against the great rivers of the world, are tiny ditches. The Mississippi flows 2,560 miles from source to sea, the Thames a little more than 200. At the mouth of the Thames each side of the estuary can clearly see the other, which to the world's great rivers must seem absurd. Our rivers are as rock-pools beside the ocean: but they have the charm of miniatures.

Then there is our still worthy network of canals. Again, beside the sprawling systems of Europe these waterways, and the craft and equipment, are modest, but it would take you a long time to navigate them all, and they would lead you into magical corners and quiet beauties unknown to most of us. You can still, I believe, take a boat from the West of England over the Pennines to the Humber; and you may meet a narrow boat towed by a horse. This is a rare sight, I believe, for all is being 'improved'. In March 1939 I introduced a Bill under the Ten Minutes' Rule about the London Water

Bus. It was accepted by 174 votes to 132. In a waspish oration, I said:

> It is a singular and saddening thing that in this great maritime country whose greatness has been built upon the water, and even in this House which stands beside the mighty Thames, anyone who suggests that our waterways should be more efficiently equipped and more fully utilized is regarded as queer and cranky.

That is no longer true. The water has become respectable and popular – almost too popular. The Inland Waterways Association, of which I am the humble President, and in recent years the British Waterways Board (a Government body) have done great things on the canals. On the tideway of the Thames – because of the tide – things are not much better: but on the Upper Thames it is difficult to get a permanent mooring, and the coasts are becoming crowded too. The boat is booming. When history sums up the present age, an age of noise and speed and poisonous fumes and murder and maiming on the roads; an age when men were the slaves of machines and had forgotten how to walk; they will give us two great good marks – in all this mechanical and ugly fury we preserved the horse and were mad about the boat.

The horse, we must admit, is practically useless; he does not even pull the plough: but he is beautiful and splendid and we love to have him about. The policeman's horse is now one of the rare attractions of the London streets.

The boat, like the horse, is an old-fashioned form of transport, but like the horse it is a thing of beauty – and it is very far from useless. If those bombs do come down one day and wreck our mechanical world, it may be the boat, and its arts and crafts, that make the cosmic answer.

But mostly we love the boat because it is an escape from the roar, the risks, the rudeness of the roads. The young boy or girl at the tiller of a dinghy has a thrilling sense of freedom. They can sail where they will, turn this way or that on the tiniest whim, without concern for traffic-lights, speed limits, large lorries or policemen.

The young man in his motor-car spends most of his time obeying rules and restraining his machine: the boy in the boat can let her go, considering nothing but wind and water, and revelling in his artful mastery of both.

Best for escape, of course, is the cruiser, under sail or engine, the boat that is a second home and takes the family away. I have no boat now, and I watch with envy at holiday times the procession of smart white craft trooping down from Teddington to the sea. Some of them look small on the tideway, but they are tough, well found and well handled. They rarely come to grief. They are bound for France, perhaps, or up the East Coast. Tonight they may be at anchor in the creek at Hole Haven, Canvey Island. Supper in the small cabin under the hurricane lamps – sausage and mash and a bottle of wine. Rolling now and then in the wash of the big steamers going down they feel themselves at sea, and a million miles from London, though, in fact, it is only thirty-six.

Heroic it may be, but this sailing round the world, alone, without a stop, is a strange, unnatural performance. Boats need company, and the whole point of cruising is to find a nice new place and call a halt. The great Captain Slocum was alone, but he took his time. He bought tallow in one port and sold it in the next, and he enjoyed good company at all of them. I have never risen to the heights of ocean racing, but if I had, I should never have gone for the races that take the brave boys across the Channel, round a buoy and back, without a word of French or a glass of wine. I think of many a happy halt up the Thames or on the canals, moored to a meadow within sound of a tumbling lock. Alas, those days are done for me!

I have lived by the water, in the same house, for fifty-four years, and, I feel, I could not be content away from the water: I have worked for the water, thirty years a Thames Conservator – long President of the Inland Waterways Association; I have fought on the water – or, shall I say, been present during many hostile proceedings; I have twice enlisted in the Navy. I was married in bell-bottom trousers. I have two Good Conduct badges; for six months I was a mounted officer in the Navy (as Adjutant to the Hawke Battalion 63rd Royal Naval Division); I spent the whole of War Two on the water, flying the White Ensign on my own small boat. Then I commanded a vessel (a little larger) up the North Sea for the Admiralty. I have served as Third Hand in sailing barges out of the London Docks and up to the East Coast rivers; I have travelled round the world (in liners) and yachted round the Mediterranean and the Isles of Greece; I have sailed in Belloc's famous *Nona* up the Channel (and put her on the Hamble Spit). I have sailed up the rugged coast of Labrador among the icebergs and the whales as far as Goose Bay. I have been towed by horses on the Grand Union Canal, which is the poetry of motion, and steered my own ship through a lengthy tunnel. I am always sad to leave a ship, always glad to leave an aeroplane: in the stage version of the *Water Gipsies* I had a song with a refrain beginning 'Put me on the water and I'm happy', and that is true, though I do not relish real, rough weather.

Yet it was Accident not Ancestry that led me to the water, and so I salute the charmer Chance. It is an interesting, a literary story.

During my five years at Oxford (1910–14) I had nothing to do with the water. I admired the rowing men and envied the mighty fellows.

When I am near enough I can still be thrilled by the power and precision of a racing eight. But their sport seemed to me to be not far from the slavery of the trireme, and unsuited to an Exhibitioner who was expected to stick to his books. I did not even sail on Port Meadow. Yet the rowing men had a large effect on my life.

In my life Oxford always won the Boat Race, and New College was always Head of the River. This was largely due to one man, the celebrated R. C. Bourne, the stroke of both boats. He stroked Oxford to victory four years running. (Later Bob Bourne was Deputy-Speaker of the House of Commons, and, often, when I was trying to 'catch his eye' I wondered whether a New College man had a better chance of doing that. I don't think he had.)

Though a landlubber I was a loyal New College man. I used to trot along the tow-path crying 'Well rowed, New College! You're going up,' and similar assurances. Also on Boat Race Day I would journey out to Duke's Meadows, below Barnes Bridge on the Middlesex side, and bellow: 'Oxford! Ox*ford*.' One year – it must have been 1913 – I was introduced on the bank to a little old man who was the famous F. Anstey (Anstey Guthrie) author of *Voces Populi, Vice Versa* and other amusing works. He was still, I think, writing for *Punch*. I suppose I boasted that I had had two or three things in *Punch* and he was very kind to this aspiring youth. After the race I was going to take a bus back to Kensington, but the great man said: 'No. Come with me. I will show you a nice walk.' I went with him eagerly and he walked me along the water-fronts of Chiswick and Hammersmith, the best part of two miles. He told me about Hogarth, buried in Chiswick churchyard, and de Loutherbourg, the scenic artist. I saw Chiswick Mall for the first time with its trees and river-gardens and gracious old houses (some of them), Walpole House, which, he said, was supposed to be the original of Miss Pinkerton's Academy in *Vanity Fair*, great Bedford House (where, till recently, the Redgraves lived), Strawberry House, Swan House – in front of them the island, Chiswick Eyot and the high tide lapping the road. Then past a tall terrace of narrow houses called Hammersmith Terrace, about which he had some literary stories. I think he said that Carlisle and Dickens used to come here. He stopped and showed me a favourite curiosity of his – Number 13. This, like the other houses, is only ten yards wide, but it has two front doors, and over each is the number 13. We wondered about the two front doors. One was an ordinary front door like the others: but one was a grand double door with a fine fanlight over it and an imposing porch. Anstey thought it must have been made for one of the Georges, wide enough for a sedan chair to take him in to his mistress. De Loutherbourg, the artist, he said, had lived in this house and, not content with art, had practised as a faith-healer. His patients had waited on the pavement where we were, and later, losing faith, had gathered in anger. 'Two 13's,' said Anstey. 'That might be unlucky.' 'I little thought', as they say, that I should have my first 'study' in that house, and work there for many years.

Then we went on past the Black Lion Inn (which has been my 'local' for fifty years) and the robust and elegant buildings of the Metropolitan Water Board. (They have been knocking some of them down, and found it a job. They are merely bricks but they might be rocks – we knew how to build in Queen Victoria's days.)

Then on past the Ship and we stopped to admire the beautiful Linden Lodge, standing back from the river. Little did I think that one day this would be the home of the London Corinthian Sailing Club, and its President the young undergraduate who was sucking up to the great F. Anstey.

'Now look back,' he said. We looked West, upstream, and saw one of the best views in London. (True, our eyes took us out of London, but we were standing well inside the old London County Council area – about half a mile from the boundary with Chiswick.) From Chiswick Church to Hammersmith Bridge – two miles – all this coast is set in a graceful curve to northward. From almost any point on the curve the roving eye can see the whole of the coast, one way or the other. The tide was flowing, rising still – in those days they started the Boat Race just two hours before High Water – and Chiswick Eyot was almost under water. Beyond it the gentlemanly skyline of Chiswick Mall. In spring there is a blaze of blossom between the houses and the river, and the green curve ends in Chiswick Church. Here, you would say, is a waterside village far out in the country.

On again, past Kelmscott House, once the home of William Morris, the Dove Inn – where, Anstey said, James Thomson wrote 'The Seasons' – and the distinguished Doves Press. (Long later I learned that James Thomson also wrote the great song 'Rule Britannia'. I like to think that it may have been written on the shores of Hammersmith Mall, at the Dove, or next door.) Over the creek on which the ancient fishing village of Hammersmith was born – they were salmon fishers too. Past the Hampshire Hog, the haunt of Fabians, past the Sims' boat-yard where the brothers had built the Oxford boat, and Hammersmith Bridge, the elegant suspension affair, which has always been too low for navigation and is now too narrow for traffic but stands defiantly still. From here there was another fine view to the West of the wide stream, still swelling, and the charming curve of the coast, and the Richmond Hills beyond.

I must have thought often of that walk with the kind old humorist, whom I never saw again. But it leaped back to me at the beginning of 1916. I was out of hospital after the Dardanelles, and had a spell of light duty under Admiralty Intelligence. (Not exciting. I attended at the Wallace Collection and prepared a report on, of all things, the Methods of Agriculture in Egypt.) My father had died while I was away, and my wife and I were looking for a home more suitable than the great Kensington barn. Suddenly I thought of the little old man. We took a bus to Hammersmith and walked westward from the Bridge. We looked longingly at Kelmscott House, with its spacious garden. We could then have bought it, I believe, for £2,000: but we had not got £2,000 to spare. Today, I suppose, it would fetch £50,000. We walked on, excited by the scene; and lo, over the door of No. 12 Hammersmith Terrace (next to the double-doored 13) was an estate agent's TO LET board. I do not think such a thing has been seen in the Terrace from that day to this. With the help of some kind folk at No. 11 we burgled the house at once, and took it next day, at a rent of £55 per annum. In February we moved in, and I went back to the Division in France. See, then, how much I owe to the rowing men who lured me to the Duke's Meadow, and to Accident that led me to Anstey.

All the seventeen houses of the Terrace have gardens at the back which run down about thirty yards to the river. It must always be a blessing to have a river at the bottom of your garden, rather than a road. But here, after the War, safe home at last, I found a great artery, the mighty Thames, the tideway, at the bottom of our garden.

But I was not content, like most of my neighbours, to enjoy the river with my eyes. I said to myself: 'Sometime I must make myself a friend of the great artery. I must become a part of it. I must marry the river. One day I must go down the mighty Thames, sixty miles to the sea. But I have no vessel, no knowledge, no skill, not even a step-ladder. Indeed, unless I jump off the garden wall I have no way of reaching the river.'

I went about all this, I thrust myself at the river, with that tenacity which is often accounted a virtue but may, I think, develop into a vice. First, the ladder.

Then the vessel. I went to Gamage's who had advertised some clinker-built dinghies. I bought an almost invisible dinghy, 7 ft long. The price was three guineas a foot. The brothers Cole, who afterwards built my *Water Gipsy*, fitted *Seven Feet* with a sort of Peter Pan mast and lugsail.

Then the skill. I knew no more about the arts and crafts of sailing than I had learned from my little boat on the Round Pond; and I had then no navigator friends. I bought Knight's *Small Boat Sailing*, and I hope it is still in print, for I have met no better book.

Then, one hot summer day, I said: 'I will sail down to Westminster.' I forget why, but *Seven Feet* had no rudder: perhaps it was to come. But a detail like that was not enough to deter me, such was my itch to challenge the tideway. I would steer with an oar over the stern. It was an afternoon tide. I waited impatiently, but sensibly, till an hour after High Water, to let the tugs and lighters go by before me, and then with a light south-westerly breeze behind me, and some dubious glances from my wife, I sailed away on the ebb.

Fairly foolish, all this, no doubt, but how magical a moment it was, to be alone in my own boat, a companion of the Thames at last! Thus must the Chichesters feel as they steal away from Plymouth Hoe.

The voyage was uncomfortable but eventless. Approaching Putney I ran over Mr Knight's instructions, and with high excitement performed my first 'jibe' just before the bridge. I met some pleasure-steamers who looked like battleships to my little egg-shell, and I remembered a splendid story of Captain Slocum, the first man to sail round the world alone in the '90's (there's a good book for you*). In his third year, on his last leg, he met an American cruiser who signalled in flags: '*Have you seen any enemy warships?*' Slocum, having no radio, had not heard of the Spanish-American War, and was mystified. But he was a man of humour and he hoisted the signals: 'NO – LET US KEEP TOGETHER FOR MUTUAL PROTECTION.'

I gave the battleships no trouble. I 'hit the bridge holes' safely, and after about two hours – it is eight miles – we proudly sailed past Parliament, and the Members enjoying their strawberries. We must have been the first ship under sail to be seen in those waters for a very long time. I had some trouble with the fearsome eddies below Westminster Bridge, but somehow survived them, and, stiff and sore, but triumphant, made the Pier.

Now, how to get home? There were people coming to dinner. It was not long to Low Water, and the kindly Pier Master said he would get one of 'the early craft' to give me a 'pluck'.

At last a tug, one of Cory's, with a long tow of lighters, came slowly up through Hungerford Bridge, bound up for Brentford or beyond. There was some unintelligible but effective yelling. I got my small oars out and rowed through the bridge to intercept the tug beyond it. I worked up beside her but the bow-wave kept thrusting me away. At last one of her crew leaned out, took hold of the top of my mast and pulled us in. The boat filled with water, away went a cushion and Knight's *Small Boat Sailing*, but I saved the oars and scrambled into the tug, feeling less triumphant. The strong waterman then picked the boat up as if it had been a bucket, upended and emptied it as if it were a bucket, and dumped it on the tug's deck. We were now abreast of the Terrace of the House of Commons – cocktail time – I looked across and saw a row of grinning faces – grinning, I guessed, at my indignities. 'You wait,' I said to myself. 'One day I'll be there and I'll

* *Sailing Alone Around the World.*

tell you all about my Great Sail.' One day, twenty years later, I did, but I forget who the happy Member was. That, I believe, was the first time I ever gave a personal thought to Parliament: so perhaps one Anstey may be blamed again.

This was my first encounter with that splendid breed the watermen and lightermen of London River. They are professionals with the due conceit of their craft. But they readily accept the amateur as one of the brotherhood of the water, interested as they are in the handling of vessels, in the making of knots and splices, in the mysterious ways of the tides. They will be always kind and helpful, as long as you are ready to learn, do not put on airs, defy good customs or advice, or make a nuisance of yourself. I got no lectures that evening for wrong or rash behaviour. My little boat, which they examined, was sound and sea-worthy, my seamanship, so far as they knew, was sufficient; and knowing how rough the tideway can be they thought that *Seven Feet*'s voyage was a worthy achievement. I purred again, and had made some good friends before they put us over the side at Hammersmith. But if I had pretended to know more than I did, if I had complained about my picking up, it might have been a different story.

I often think it strange that in the first chapter of Genesis, in the great list of God's gifts to Man, there is no mention of rivers or waterways. 'Let there be light . . . Let the waters be gathered together, unto one place' – the Seas. 'Let the dry land appear' – the Earth. Yet how much more happiness have rivers brought to Man than the savage seas and too extensive oceans! 'Let there be Rivers,' the Book should say, 'threading the Land like silver ribbons, watering the fields, making beautiful the cities, safe highways for men, peaceful homes for the birds and fishes and the flowers and green things that love the water.'

A man beside a river has calm company always. The water you see from your window is alive. It has come from the hills and is making for the sea. The fish jump, the waterfowl cry or quack, the owl and the heron are heard at night. Small boats glide by, perhaps with blue sails, or a Dutch barge slowly thudding up with good things from Amsterdam. You are seldom alone. But there is none of the rush and roar of the road. The road looks always the same; but the river changes as often as a young girl's face. This morning, while you shave, it is a smooth and placid plain sliding past. But, as you feel your chin, the sudden breath of a breeze brings little ruffled islands that scurry here and there. A strong wind going the stream's way makes the whole surface shiver, no more, but blowing against it throws up a pattern of waves or ripples. The river is one colour under a fine sky, another under clouds: many an afternoon I have seen the muddy Thames above the bridge at Hammersmith a true sea-blue under the sinking sun. The racing sailing-dinghies have a blossom of white under their bows and along their sides, but a different white under the stern. The cunning of water – it can take on as many colours as a flame.

On your road you will not see swans flying, cormorants diving, ducks mating, herons like statues watching for fish. The birds come and go like Members of Parliament. Today it is calm and fair and most of the seagulls have gone back to their constituencies by the sea. Only the faithful mallards and swans remain. But with the first of the winter storms a regiment of seabirds will come squawking home to our waters, as the Members crowd to Westminster at the first cloud of a crisis. The Black Backs (Lesser) always clean, with their proud spread of wing, the little Black Headeds, their heads still white, huge young Herring Gulls on their first visit to town, the tufted duck, the coot, the moorhen and now and then the cormorant, or Paradise Shelducks, or some superior Canadian Geese. And how comforting the river at night, with the moon's trail across the water, and the lights of Hammersmith like the lights of Como!

If I lived by the Upper Thames I should like my home to be near a lock with a good weir, for here you have most vividly exhibited the power, the wizardry of water. Stand on the bridge over a modest weir, only ten yards wide, and look upstream. The grey smooth water – sadly grey it is true, but clean enough – approaches gently, innocently, as if incapable of harm or violence. But turn the other way and what a change is seen. The innocent grey water is tumbling, a few feet only, in a white fury, and making an expanse of many-coloured roaring turbulence below. It has gathered from the forces of gravity not only brutality but beauty. And in the middle one of the heavy 'paddles' has been 'drawn', that is, lifted out, and this small cascade is whiter than the rest. But look now at one of the great wide weirs, at Goring, or Benson, or Marlow, where the music of the water is so triumphant you can hardly hear what your neighbour is saying. At one end there may be a long 'overfall', a simple wall over which the river thunders without control, and the noisy cataract in colour and volume is governed only by the level of the water above. Next to that there may be four or five different sets of sluices, the common or garden paddles and rymers, the new radial gates, concave segments of iron which the lock-keeper handles with chains, great sluice-gates lifted with chains and a windlass handle, perhaps a simple 'lasher', long, low boards pressed, in summer-time, against a row of pins. At Benson Lock you can see six different cascades, different in the colour and the quantity of the water and the angle of its descending. Here, I believe, you will find more variety than you will at Niagara. It is a wonder that you do not see artists gazing at the great weirs all day, but I suppose they find the subject too exacting.

Then, as a water worshipper I am fascinated by the locks, the locks that enable boats to climb hills, and can convert a torrent into an orderly stream. The 'pound lock', as we wrongly call it, the ordinary lock that everybody knows, Boulter's lock, for example, was an invention almost as important as the wheel. It was not, I think, one of the inventions claimed by the Russians in Stalin's days, but I have heard it attributed to the Chinese. The first pound lock in this country, it seems, was built upon the Exeter Canal in 1563, but some say that there were locks still earlier in Lombardy, and I read without surprise that that wondrous fellow Leonardo da Vinci had a hand in such work. That good writer Roger Pilkington, in *Small Boat Through France*, says:

'The pound lock with a gate at either end had been in use for more than two centuries on certain waterways of the Low Countries (i.e. this might make it as early as 1300) and Italian engineers had already built others along the canals of Milan, Padua, and Bologna, but when Leonardo was appointed private engineer to the Duke of Milan he turned his attention to improving the operation of the locks. It was he who invented the mitre gates still in use throughout the world, even on such large waterways as the Kiel Canal and Panama Canal.'

And, may I add, the mighty Thames.

But the extraordinary thing is that the pound lock did not reach the mighty Thames till about 1630. Before that, and after, primitive 'flash locks' dominated the river. This was a mere single fence of brushwood and stone, which first of all provided a good head of water for the mills and conveniently assembled fish behind it. Then when navigation asserted itself, a central span of the fence, or weir, from ten to twenty feet wide, was fitted with movable paddles and rymers; and this opening was the original 'lock'. 'Flash' or 'flush' meant the rush of water released by the removal of the tackle. A barge waiting to pass up river had then to be hauled up through the gap, up an inclined plane of water, by horses, by gangs of men, or by winch and rope. Going down, it merely shot the rapids.

This arrangement wasted much water and caused much friction between the navigator and the rapacious miller. But in 1605 the good James I appointed the Oxford-Burcot Commission, four men from the University and four from the City of Oxford, and by a later Act of 1624 they were empowered to make 'weirs, locks, and turnpikes', and the first three-pound locks were made at Iffley, Sandford, and Swift Ditch.

'Pound lock' is defined in the Oxford English Dictionary as 'A lock on a river for pounding up the water'. But the early fences kept up 'pounds' or 'ponds' of water above them. The stretch of water above a lock or a canal is called the 'pound'. The virtue of the new design was that it had a *chamber*, with a gate at each end, in which boats could be confined and the level of the water changed, for their convenience, up or down, without lowering the level of the 'pound' and so losing water. The device seems obvious today, but it was a wonder, and we do not owe it to those clever Roman invaders. Another odd thing was that after the 1630 batch no other pound locks were built for 150 years, and the first of those was the famous Boulter's lock.

To me it is a wonder still. Today every lock from Teddington to Iffley is worked by electricity or, more often, hydraulic power, and no lock keeper has to march up and down the lock and lean and heave against the great oak beams. We go down the river, lock after lock, 'turnpikes', as our fathers called them, of order and calm. Leonardo's gates close themselves as if by magic. Water enters at one end with musical and gentle trickles: at the other end it goes out unseen and silent. The boats rise and fall almost imperceptibly, like the sea near the top of the tide. The whole operation seems so tranquil, inevitable, that you might think it was one of the works of Nature, no more unusual than the fall of rain or the opening of a rose. It is hard to imagine that behind this cool quiet picture are six, seven, or eight centuries of trouble and tumult, of simple bargemen shouting obscene complaints and arrogant millers sneering from the weirs, of boats and barges climbing up steep slopes of water with men and horses sweating on the ropes, of protests and reports and well-meaning statutes and monarchical commands and stubborn resistance, and rarely anything done. But it is true. So I should be very content to live by a lock and see the obedient water at work for men.

If it is a tideway at the bottom of your garden the power, the versatility of water will be endlessly on view. Twice in every twenty-four hours the sea, or rather the tidal stream that surges up from the sea, rolls right through our capital and passes our house which is ten miles west of London Bridge. This is absurd, and full of mischief. There have been floods; there will be more. In 1928 we had six feet of water in our basement dining-room. They wisely raised the flood-works – the garden wall – by eighteen inches (we are paying for it still). But in 1953 the water was only two inches from the top of the new wall. More than that, for eight hours out of every twelve London is separated from London's River, except where the few piers stand out into deep water. For eight hours out of every twelve no vessel can approach the shore, enter a dock or make fast to a wharf. Sir Winston Churchill made his last voyage from Tower Pier to the Festival Pier. By God's grace High Water was at 1 p.m. that day. The Saturday before, and the Saturday after, it would have been Low Water, and the landing could not have been done. The angle of the 'brow' would have been so steep that even those gallant Guardsmen would not have got the coffin up it. In Paris the glorious remains could have been landed at any place at any time.

For more than thirty years I have been among those who want to see the tides excluded from London, by a fixed barrage or dam at Woolwich or elsewhere. (I am the last surviving Vice-President of the Thames Barrage Association of 1934.) I share the great Lord Desborough's dream: in a Lords debate in 1937 he said: 'We have been told that our old men should dream dreams and our young men should see visions. My visions and dreams for some time past have been to stand on the Terrace of the House of Commons and see a river flowing one way, clean and full, worthy of the capital of the Empire through which it flows'. I have told the whole story of our battles in *The Thames*.* The new Greater London Council, under Mr Desmond Plummer, has been hot on the trail for a year or two, and in January 1970, the principle of a tide-control 'barrier', perhaps in the end a 'barrage', was accepted by the Government. Hooray!

But the artists, my own wife among them, don't agree. They like the varying view, the curves on the naked foreshore, the light on the mudbank, black or green, the rare layers of sand or gravel, the water washing the pebbles, the crooked boats and barges lying helpless on the river-bed.

I must recognize too the appeal of the ever-changing scenes. All day long, all night long, the tide is going out – the ebb, or the tide is coming in – the flood. The river never rests, the scene is never quite still. The sea-birds like Low Water too. They have the freedom of the foreshore. They man the water's edge like the crew of a man o' war, and natter amicably like Members in the Lobby. But they can hunt for dead eels in the shallows, or *tubifex* – the tiny 'blood worms' – or tasty, sniffy morsels from the homes of man, on the wide muddy slopes. When the river is full they can only soar and swoop over the murky river, from which, they know well, they will rarely snatch a fish. At night they must retire to the island or sleep adrift on the water. No, the sea birds of London will vote against the Dam.

At Hammersmith the ebb runs out for seven hours, and the flood runs in for five – lower down it is about six and six. So a dead cat which leaves Hammersmith at noon will travel, if not obstructed, at 3 m.p.h. as far as Barking and come back as far as Battersea at, roughly, midnight, and so, by slow degrees, proceed to sea.

I have described the tricks of London River tides, especially at the turn, in *The Thames* and the *Singing Swan*.

Few of us have the time and patience to watch the whole process. But – we are so clever now – someone should photograph it all, from

* Weidenfeld and Nicolson.

one Low Water to another, and show it in *quick* motion, in shall we say one hour. It would be a fascinating film.

I did not sail the *Seven Feet* again. My appetite and ambition had grown. I bought an old fifteen footer with a good beam, the *Winnie*, fit to carry the family. I joined the London Corinthian Sailing Club, and, whenever I could, taught myself to sail. Soon I passed myself out as an expert, though fresh learning came each day. What excellent arts are these! What superb sensations! What a sense of mastery is in that light hand on the tiller as you fill your sails and dance away over the water. What a wonder it is that with two stretches of cotton, some rope, and some wood you can make wind and water your slaves, force your way against an enemy wind or turn and move like a bird in its embrace! Those engineers have invented nothing better. There is something like the riding of a horse in your delicate handling of the helm; but then the horse, if need be, can do very well without you: your boat is a dead thing without your artful fingers, knowing plans, instant response to peril. A great yacht gives great excitements to many but one man in a small boat is as independent, as lordly, as a conjurer.

But practice is the thing, however good you think you are. I devised a game called Hunting Wood. The driftwood on the Tideway was even more of a mischief than it is now. Some days you might think that the Sargasso Sea, carpeted with wood not weed, was advancing from Hammersmith Bridge. Much of it was old tarry stuff, and, properly dried, fine firewood (in those barbarous times we still had 'a nice red fire'). I used to take the *Winnie* out and sail up and down the Sargasso, picking up fire fuel. It was a rule that I must never stop, and never give two hands to the timber. I held both mainsheet and tiller in my left hand, selected my prey well ahead, and steered so that I could pluck the prey with my right hand. This was good practice: but they made us a Smokeless Zone and that was the end of that.

To keep a boat going is one thing, to stop her dead is another. I taught myself, and I always teach young ladies in the Mediterranean, with constant Man Overboard drill. When a pupil is happily bowling along suddenly throw your hat or handkerchief or a lifebuoy (if any) into the water and cry: 'Man overboard! Can't swim!' You have warned her ahead that she is to find her own way to the drowning man and lay her boat's head against his without bashing out his brains or running past him so fast that she cannot go forward and grab him. At first she will be all a-fluster, how soon should she turn, and which way, shall she jibe or not, and how far away shall she turn into the wind so that the way on her boat carries her far enough but no farther. She will do involuntary jibes and get herself tangled with the tiller, set her foot firmly on the mainsheet, forget about the tide, turn into the wind too soon and never reach the drowner. But presently, when her nerve returns, you must make her do it again – and again – and again, till she knows quickly what to do and how to do it. At last you may trust her to 'come alongside' the gangway of the yacht. This is a tricky business, and exciting if you have been caught by a strong breeze, a sudden mistral. Then I would trust no woman in the world. You race through the bumpy water straight for the yacht's hull, the Captain fearful for his paint, his boat and his gangway; but at just the right distance you swing the boat into the wind, letting everything go, so that, the sails empty, her way carries her five or six feet, and gently she lays her nose against the ladder. This is the most magical feat of the small sailing-boat, from high speed to halt in a second or two – and she has no brakes or parachutes to help her. It is also, if all goes well, a fine show-off for the sailor. Therefore, boys and girls, throw something unsinkable and cry 'Man Overboard!'.

Man is a strange being. Whenever he finds a nice, calm, simple thing to do, he must make a race out of it, and it becomes complicated, argumentative, and often noisy. I entered the Club weekend races for a year or two, but the *Winnie* was not a sprinter, and I preferred taking the family for picnics. I did win one race. There was not then the order and organization of today. We were always meeting rowing races and heard complaints about our 'zigzagging up and down the river' – 'Why can't they sail straight?' One day I was vainly beating upstream behind my great rival Mr Byles, said to be chauffeur to the Editor of *The Times*. A sculling race came down the opposite way, and as Mr Byles 'went about' a sculler rammed him, stem to stem. The sculler's sharp bow was so firmly embedded that both craft had to be towed to the bank, where the sculler was extracted like a bad tooth with a motor boat. I sailed on heartlessly and won my only race.

All is more grand and decorous today. The small boat, like other things, has leapt up the ladder of dignity. Then there were no 'classes' of boats, now we have four – international 14-footers, K class, Enterprise, with blue sails, Fireflies, and the nimble one-manned O.K's, which capsize, are righted and away again, sometimes in a minute or two. We have Open races in which the 'Aces' of this world attend, Stewart Morris, and others, 'trailing' their boats long distances by road. It is a stirring sight at the start, thirty or forty white boats – or maybe there are thirty great coloured spinnakers – sweeping across the line together as close and urgent as the starters in the Derby; and it is a strange sight for the metropolitan area of London. Each boat is a thoroughbred in her own family, her measurements exactly to order, each rope and shackle and pin has been lovingly checked and tended. On our open reaches, with plenty of room for a rough sou'-wester or easterlies, there are special eddies and tricks of the tide: but often young men come down from quiet waters above the tide, even from flooded gravel-pits, and defeat the local veterans who know the ways of our waters so well. This shows how general is the growth of the sailing art. Our own boys and girls race every weekend all through the year. With astonished admiration I watch them 'planing' before a wicked gale, capsizing in icy January waters, righting their boats, refusing all aid, baling out a boatful of water, and often continuing the race. Their President is proud of them, but they do not get such publicity as the hippies. Whenever I read about the Saturday doings of those wild creatures I try to remember what the London Corinthian boys and girls were doing, and say to myself 'All's well'. They have won glory too in other waters. The President is proud too to have an Ace in the family – a grandson, Jeremy Pudney (son of John Pudney, poet). He has a magical touch, they say, and has been runner-up for the Prince of Wales' Cup. Last year a team of six Britons, Jeremy among them, went over to Canada, and defeated Canada, Eastern America, and Western America too. They won every race. Four of the six were London Corinthians. Next week Jeremy won the Canadian Championship. Only in the *Daily Telegraph* were these deeds recorded: yet, all the papers are always loud about our one racing catamaran, an unnatural craft which ought not to be allowed about. Britain may not be Top Nation now, but a country so good at handling boats and horses can not be far down the list. I was delighted by Max Aitken's and Edward Heath's victories in the Sydney-Hobart race.

In the '20's we invaded the Grand Junction Canal which runs from Brentford to Birmingham and elsewhere. We passed through Dr Johnson's Lock into a new beautiful, friendly, delightful world.

Through an old friend, Patrick Hobart, afterwards one of Monty's main Generals, we were given a strange craft which had been built for pleasure on the canal. She was flat-bottomed, drew very little water, had a cockpit forward, and was 43 ft long. She looked like a Noah's Ark and she soon named herself the *Ark*.

In the *Ark* we had much fun and many adventures, and I gathered most of the experience that inspired my book *The Water Gipsies*. She must, I think, have had a tired and disloyal engine, for I remember, very early, dragooning some weekend guests, including Gerald Barry (now dead), and a girl or two, on to a tow-rope, having despaired of the engine. I remember too getting a tow from a narrow-boatman, who had a horse and one boat only. (There are generally two; the second, the 'butty-boat', slides into the lock besides the leading boat. We became the 'butty'.) This, we thought, was the perfect motion – no clattering engine, no smell of petrol, nothing to be heard except the steady clip-clop of the horse's hoofs. Yet we moved as fast as anyone should wish to move through such fair surroundings.

Like Jane, my heroine, we enjoyed our first days 'up the Cut':

The passengers look down from the flying train and think it a meagre and a murky stream and wonder idly whither it flows. But the boatman at his tiller looks up and sees the railway tiny and the canal large, a river of adventure and hardships and toil, with a people of its own and a hundred years of custom and tradition which were old before the railway was imagined. Every boatman feels this and is proud of the 'Cut', and jealous for it. And this affection takes hold of those who live beside or go upon it. It is in the public houses and the row of cottages and the children playing on its banks . . .

There are no lock-keepers on the Cut, you do your own lockwork: it was hard work for novices, could be worrying, and blistering, but, when you got the hang of it, fun. As on the tideway, the boatmen, if you behaved yourselves, were friendly and helpful. We loved, as every-body did, their 'narrow boats', the traditional decorations, Hearts and Roses and Castles, the long curved tillers, the polished brass ornaments at the doors of the tiny cabins, the great watercans on top, a blaze of Roses. We watched with awe the skill and speed of their work. Where we strained and struggled with our 'windlass', lifting the 'paddles' at the head of a lock, for these professionals, even the dark-eyed young women, it seemed to come as easy as winding a watch. 'It's a knack,' they'd say. But what a knack!

I was rebuked by someone for giving the boatmen an 'insulting' label. I got it from them. One year, unthinkably, there was a strike on the peaceful canal. We were lying astern of the *Adventure*, and Mr Green was painting a biscuit-tin for me. Hearts and roses and 'A Present from H. Green'. While he painted the bright roses he talked, splendid tales of the 'Cut'; and presently he said: 'D'you know what they call us, Mr Herbert? They call us The Water Gipsies, because we carry our house wherever we go.'

My wife had a strange adventure on the Grand Junction one summer when I was away in Australia. The Nigel Playfairs the year before had borrowed the boat and tried to take her to Stratford. They got stuck in a lock and left her on the Stratford branch. Gwen wanted to give three of the children a holiday on the Cut, but she could not manage the engine: so she hired a horse and a man to look after it. Neither horse nor man were trained to the canal. Even the work of a canal horse is not so simple as it looks. This horse kept stepping, sometimes falling, into the canal, or it would step through a gap into the field and have a feed. All went well otherwise, but not far from Birmingham the man took my wife's purse and departed. She was left with three children, a large boat, no money, and an unreliable horse. Somehow, though, she got to Birmingham and so, by land, to London. How she got rid of the horse I never heard.

The two of us had one mad exciting voyage in the *Ark*. By this time, I think, I had saved up and given her a new engine, a Thornycroft 'Handy Billy', 8-brake horse power, an excellent machine which I mastered thoroughly and loved a lot. We had tickets for Covent Garden that night, a rare treat. Something had held us up and in the afternoon we were still well up the canal Uxbridge or Cowley way. But we thought we could get back to Hammersmith in time. The distance was not far, a dozen miles or so: but there were more than a dozen locks, including the series of six outside the Hanwell lunatic asylum, and these, because of the steep fall, have side-ponds which must be filled and emptied too.

There is a lot of luck in canal travel. If a lock is 'with' you, ready, that is, full (when you are going downhill) with the top gate open, you sail straight in, shut the top gates, empty the lock, open the bottom gates, and sail out – five minutes, perhaps. But if it is 'against' you, that is, empty with the top gates closed, you have much more to do. You must make your boat fast outside the top gates, run to the bottom gates and close them (a different person on either side, or a long walk round for one), run back to the top gates, wind up two – no, I think three – sets of 'paddles', let the water in, squeezing musically through the sluices, till the lock is full and the top gates can be opened (unless the pressure is equal on both sides they can't be opened). Then you must bring your ship into the lock, make her fast – and this needs care, for she is going to drop – shut the top gates, drop the 'paddles', to close the sluices and keep the main stream out of the lock, then run to the bottom gates, wind up the paddles to let the water out, wait till the lock has emptied, open the lower gates (in our case one would give us space enough) and sail away – perhaps fifteen minutes.

Normally, on a waterway one does not worry about time, enjoyment is the thing. But today we had made time important, and, as luck would have it, *every single lock was against us*. To a well-manned professional pair of boats this would not have mattered. They send a scout (male or female) far ahead on a bicycle: and if the scout finds the next lock in the wrong condition, he works hard, as I have described and has the lock ready by the time his boats come round the corner. But my wife and I were two amateur mortals – we had no scout to send ahead – *and we had no bicycle*. Sometimes, in a situation like this, there is a boat coming the other way, which makes all the locks 'ready' for you. But this afternoon, I know not why, there was no other traffic – it may have been just after the strike. So, at every lock, my wife and I had to go through the full drill as described. How we divided the work I cannot remember. I suppose we both abandoned the boat and bounded up and down the lock. I know that we were exhausted, sweaty, but jubilant when at last we reached the Thames. Then there was four or five more miles to go, but I had cleverly arranged for the ebb to be running so the rest of the passage was easy. Then there was the business of mooring, washing and dressing. But I report with pride that we were in our seats at Covent Garden just before the band began.

The Water Gipsies was the first novel of the canals and I modestly believe that it did something to restore respect and interest. But there are better 'documentary' books with a wider range – I have known personally the one canal only. In 1946 Robert Aickman founded the Inland Waterways Association which with him, and his successor, Captain Lionel Munk, has done great work. It is a vigorous, vigilant body with branches all over England, ready to leap to the defence of any threatened or neglected waterway. Nor are they content to denounce and argue. Here and there the young folk have roared into real action themselves, restoring derelict locks, embanking, dredging and clearing. The Stratford Avon was a triumphant example. At first the battles were all with the State which looked at the canals through purely economic glasses, and found them discouraging. But that battle has been won. Amenity, boating, fishing have been admitted into the values of Whitehall. The Transport Act 1968 included some triumphs for our Association. It is recognized that Trade and Amenity together (and even Amenity alone) may justify the preservation and development of a waterway. The British Waterways Board was given leaders who loved the water too and even had boats of their own. Barbara Castle, as Minister for Transport, won medals from the waterfolk. As President I do little more than preside now and then. Years ago I had to handle some tempestuous and swollen meetings, with venomous attacks on the Government misdeeds and bitter internal disputes about our dealing with them. At the last two dinners I have happily found myself between purring waterways men and welcome Government men, apparently harmonious. Those who know the great European systems dream of bigger things still, bigger canals and bigger craft, but such dreams, I fancy, are far away. At least it is no longer considered 'queer and cranky' at Westminster to be a friend of the waterways.

Now we took the flat-bottomed *Ark* down the tideway into Dockland – once, greatly daring, we made Gravesend. There was nothing to show the stranger that she was flat. One evening I was lying at a buoy near the Millwall Dock when a Customs boat came alongside. The officers were suspicious, and at first unfriendly: they searched the ship thoroughly, for they thought that I had 'been foreign' and was full of French brandy. I took this as a compliment and filled them with Scotch whisky.

It was from the *Ark* that I did my Big Swim. Today to swim in the London Thames is considered suicidal, not for its currents so much as its contents. This shows what Technology has done for us. When I came to Hammersmith, and for many years after, swimming was common. There were boys and men swimming every summer Sunday. Nigel Playfair used to stump down the foreshore before breakfast for a dip. Now and then we gave cocktail-bathing-parties. We chose a spring tide high water at about 6 p.m. The boys and girls dived in from the garden wall, clambered up my 'proposed works', took a cocktail and dived again. It was all very merry, and more than one marriage began at those parties. But now they say if you fall in you must be stomach-pumped.

My big swim was in 1934. I was alone in the *Ark* just above the old Waterloo Bridge. It was a hot Sunday afternoon. I had been enjoying a talk with my old friend, Captain Beadle of the Waterloo Bridge Tug. He was a fine fellow with a deep magnetic voice, he had been a sailing-barge skipper, and knew all the stories in the river. When the flood began to run he had to go through the Bridge for it was his job to take care of any craft that looked like falling foul of the bridge. There was not enough tide for me to start home, but I thought that I might have a swim. It is impossible (for me at least) to swim against the tide, so my custom was to let my dinghy drift (I think it was dear old *Seven Feet*), and when I was tired of swimming climb into her and row back over the tide which was easy. So I cast her off and plunged in after her. I did not expect to go far, for I am not a strong swimmer, even in the salty velvet Mediterranean. But half-way to Hungerford Bridge I made a mad resolve. I would do a literary 'record', I would be the first writer to swim from Waterloo Bridge to Westminster Bridge. As I passed under the hideous Hungerford Bridge a small boy spat on me, not knowing what a heroic enterprise he was insulting. (How odd boys can be! What sort of satisfaction can it be to spit on an unknown swimmer? During War Two there was worse. Many times, approaching or leaving a bridge, wearing the White Ensign – and spectacles – I received handfuls of gravel from valiant boys above.) I was tired already, for the water did not assist the swimmer like the sea, though the authorities insist that there is salt in it. This varies enormously, they say, with the state of the tide, and other things. The L.C.C. weekly sample for 1962–5 ranged from ·1 per cent to 20 per cent. During the drought of 1921 some trees of Kew Gardens were said to be damaged by water taken from the river. During War Two, for three days, a small pale seal sat on the eastern end of Chiswick Eyot, watched indignantly by the swans who made way for him,

1914 July. Oxford – a First in Law

1914 September. Crystal
Palace – Ordinary Seaman

1915 Sub-lieutenant, Hawke Battalion, R.N.D.

1940 Petty Officer – Royal Naval (Thames) Patrol. One 'Good Conduct' badge – another to come!

1930 The garden and family, 12 Hammersmith Terrace – river beyond

1932 'Is that the face . . . ?' – C. B. Cochran's *Helen!* Evelyn Laye as Helen on the Walls of Troy

1933 Alice Delysia as Madame Pavani in *Mother of Pearl* at the Gaiety. All her past lovers were invited to come in their best clothes.

1929 Hilaire Belloc steering his *Nona* up the English Channel. On his left J. C. Squire, on his right a son, Peter

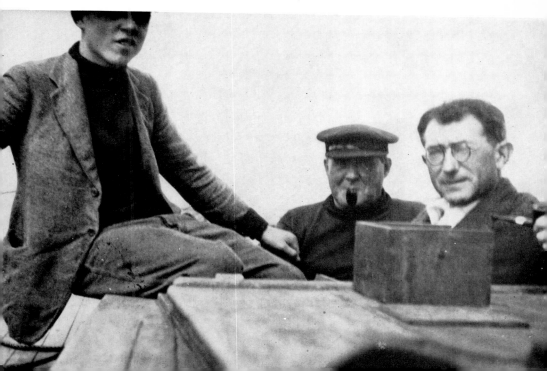

1925 Beginner's luck. I ride my first wave at Waikiki Beach, Honolulu. Note the 'University Costume', then the regulation wear

1935 A prophetic cartoon by Mr Middleton – see 'Fifteen Years Hard'

1946–8 *Bless the Bride* at the Adelphi. Downstage Lizbeth Webb, Georges Guetary, and Betty Paul

Sunset. Chiswick from the foreshore off Hammersmith Terrace

1946 Preparing for *Big Ben*. Carole Lynne (who sang 'I want to see the people happy'), C. B. Cochran and Vivian Ellis. Why the librettist and not the composer is at the piano I cannot explain

The sailing barge *Pretoria* 'going about' under Tower Bridge. Probably the first time the bascules have been raised for a sailing barge under sail – they used to lower their 'gear' before passing under the bridge. On her right is a hover-craft 'in flight'. I am on the barge, but that morning had the honour to steer the hover-craft down Limehouse Reach, flying

Violet Attlee, Arthur Salter, and the Prime Minister see the Boat Race from No. 12

The 'Study'

1937 Passage of the Matrimonial Causes Act

1965 Bob Boothby and Malcolm Sargent – television party for Sir
Malcolm's 70th birthday
A Charity cricket match – with soft ball. The batsman is (I think)
Miss Ursula Jeans. The fieldsman, with pipe, is J. B. Priestley

On the bridge of the *Water Gipsy* – with 'Gaby'

'A lovely cheese' at the Black Lion skittle alley

1939 River Emergency Service – *Water Gipsy* at Westminster Pier

1969 The Town Hall, Hammersmith – the Mayor, Alderman Seton Forbes Cockell, the Town Clerk, Mr Carey Randall, beyond him. I have been appointed an Honorary Freeman of the Borough and am humbly replying. Left, the Mayoress, and my wife who is wearing her now illegal Golden Wedding necklace, seven 1914 sovereigns

My Sundial table at the Black Lion, a Watney house, my 'local' for 50 years. On my left Crystal, the first-born, with John, and Arthur Lambert, landlord for many years. Solemn arguments about the time at this table could be a great help to the dallying customer

Washing-up in *Water Gipsy*, with John Herbert

Speech at a 'Lord's Taverners' lunch

1958 Encaenia (Commemoration) at Oxford. The Honorands, who are to be
made Honorary Doctors of Law, Literature, Music, wear their new robes in
the procession – Mr Harold Macmillan and Lord Beveridge, Mr Gaitskell
and the Chief Justice of Australia, myself and (unseen) M Poulenc, and,
astern of me, in white, Shostakovich

1964 Golden Wedding. (*Si monumentum requiris* . . . We laid every
stone of the Crazy Paving together.)

protectively by a policeman posted on Chiswick Mall. Another – or was it a dolphin? – was reported romping below Teddington Weir a few years back. In April 1965 a third got as far as Kingston – that is, it must have passed over Teddington Weir at the top of a high spring tide. After two or three weeks in the warm water from Kingston Power Station it made a dignified departure through the lock. Later that year a shoal of dolphins was reported as high as Woolwich. None of these was heard of again, so presumably they safely reached the sea: and even the tideway water cannot be as bad as they say, even in the London reaches. In Sea Reach, ten miles below Gravesend, they catch shrimps and fish, seaweed grows on the piles of the jetties, and barnacles on your boat, if you stay there long enough: at Hole Haven, Canvey Island, in 1940, the water flashed sometimes with phosphorus.

But I need more than 20 per cent of salt; I was strongly tempted to climb into the dinghy, but, bent on my record, I held on. Now, coming down from Westminster Pier, I saw one of the pleasure steamers, crowded with passengers. I said to myself: 'No publicity today.' For some time the friendly crews, as they passed our house, had been including me among the objects of interest they distributed to their passengers through rather loud loud-hailers: 'On the right is the residence of Mr A. P. Herbert, the well-known novelist . . .' and so on. Once, after some complimentary extracts from my past, I heard the great voice boom: 'HE'S A VERY FAMOUS MAN – OR WAS'. An old lady said to me – and I don't think she can have invented it: 'We passed your house – and do you know what the captain said: "On the right is the residence of the well-known novelist Sir Edgar Allan Poe, who wrote *The Water Babies*".' All this was a nuisance to my neighbours, and I pretended that it embarrassed me. Some of my stories, I fear, must have got back to my good friends, and there are no more passing biographies. I rather miss them; they were a link with the working world of the river, and I am not often described as 'the well-known novelist' by anybody else.

Now I said 'No publicity today', for when swimming I am almost invisible. One feeble flailing arm appears. But as the steamer bore down on me I heard – spoken without a pause – 'RIGHT AHEAD IS THE HUNGERFORD BRIDGE AND CHARING CROSS STATION BEYOND IS RENNIE'S WATERLOO BRIDGE ABOUT TO BE PULLED DOWN AND REBUILT BY MR HERBERT MORRISON ON THE LEFT IS THE SAVOY HOTEL AND CLEOPATRA'S NEEDLE THE GENTLEMAN SWIMMING IN THE WATER IS MR A. P. HERBERT THE WELL-KNOWN NOVELIST'.

'I had to laugh' as they say. Whenever I laugh in the water I have a tendency to sink. Now I feebly waved an arm and sank. I sank twice, but by a stout effort of will I avoided number three and struggled on. The episode had taken a lot out of me and I was very tired indeed.

My main locomotive force was the tide. But I passed the Air Force Memorial and Westminster Bridge was near. Then through the bridge came a canoe driven by two young men with double paddles. They altered course towards me, brought up and told their tale. They had come from Devizes or somewhere in a race (which they had won). Where could they go now? By now I could hardly tread water with confidence, but I advised them to make for Charing Cross Pier and ask the pier-masters. They thanked me and paddled away; but after a few strokes they stopped and one of them called back: 'Are you A. P. Herbert the novelist?' I sank again.

But I did it. I floundered through the bridge, captured the dinghy, and safely regained the *Ark*. The record was mine. But Harold Nicolson told me that that damned fellow Byron had swum from Lambeth to Southwark. I have seen no written evidence of this. I did mean to do better than that one day, but never did. At all events I can say that I am the only President of the Society of Authors who has swum from Waterloo Bridge to Westminster Bridge.

It was at the Waterloo Bridge buoy that I first met and fell in love with the London River Sailing Barge, that beautiful unique and dying vessel, which I saluted in my book *The Singing Swan*. They would lie there for a night or two waiting to go into a draw-dock on the South bank and unload the sand they had brought from St Osyth. To come up through the bridges they had had to lower their 'gear', the great mast and sprit. Before they could unload, the gear had to be lifted again, to clear the hold. In this laborious task anyone was welcome at the windlass, and with members of the tug's crew, I lent a hand when I could. I loved the talk of these men as the great mast slowly rose, the bargemen's stories of the sea, the tugmen's learned lore of suicide and the behaviour of 'stiffs' in the water. Captain Beadle could remember his father steering a barge in a top hat, he could name first, second and third in all the famous Barge Races. He had sailed in the old *Favourite* which was built two years before the battle of Trafalgar (and died, a sad accident, at Chiswick in 1966). He had yarns about rough characters like Robert the Devil and Bill the Baron, of the mad Bank holiday when they towed Johnny the Nutman across the river at Erith to get the beer out of him. It was Johnny the Nutman who would go up to a perfect stranger in the street and say: 'Pardon me, sir, but could you oblige me with a latch-lifter?' A latch-lifter was enough pennies to admit him to a pub and buy him a beer.

But under all the merry talk was depression and foreboding. The bargemen were wretchedly paid, freights were harder and harder to get, the Dutch motor-barges, and their English imitators, were eating into the trade, they were building no more sailing barges. A fine old breed of craft and men, they felt in their bones, was doomed. All this was just under the windows of the Savoy Hotel but the bargemen neither knew nor cared which building was the Savoy. In this part of London they never went ashore unless on Sunday the mate would go for the *News of the World*. Here was a strange world of which they wanted nothing. In those days I met no barge skipper who ever went to the cinema. So they spoke simple vivid English, undefiled. They never said O.K. You would hear many good unexpected words from the man behind the wheel. 'If you look past the starboard rigging you will discern the Jenkins buoy . . .' 'That breeze is paltry . . .' 'I don't much like the appearance of things . . .' (a dubious verdict on the weather) 'That torps'ls audacious old . . .' 'That's a pretty bit of wood' (a barge), 'That's the handiest bit of wood afloat . . .' When they had done their business at Waterloo they lowered their masts again and went down through the bridges to Godstone Buoy – 'Starvation' Buoy – to wait for a freight. This was opposite to the Surrey Commercial Docks. I called on them there in the *Ark* now and then.

Sometimes at Starvation Buoy, or Waterloo, one of the bargemen would have time to teach me a little about the rigging and running of the barge, the cunning mysteries of sprit and brails that enable two men – or one man and a boy – to sail 100 tons of wheat safely across the sea. One day, with not much hope, I asked if it would be possible to take a trip in a barge, and got an instant invitation. So with Captain Bob Eves of Colchester I made my first voyage as Third Hand in the *Paglesham*. We sailed from the Surrey Docks at dawn on a summer morning with a load of wheat for Colchester, which we delivered in four days. This, for me, was a thrilling experience, though some of it was tough for an amateur seaman, hoisting the torps'l, winching up the lee-boards. I made many other voyages, in the *Paglesham*, again to the Crouch, in the H.K.D. to Whitstable (she was mined and sunk in War Two), in the *Saltcote Belle* and the *Plinlimmon*. So when I watched the annual Sailing Barge Match, as I often did, I knew what was going on in those swift and lovely vessels, with their brown sails reeling, their bow-waves foaming across Sea Reach. I filled five small note-books with notes on the voyages, the handling of the sails, the bargemen's talk. So, thirty years later, when I wrote *The Singing Swan* the language was as true as any layman could make it. The book was a labour of love. I did not think it would make a wide appeal, but I loved the craft and the men, and it was a last salute to a noble breed. Men of the water, in my experience, tend to be good men, men of sound sense and generous instinct. I think of my sailing barge friends as gentlemen of the water.

The last Thames Sailing Barge Race was in 1963, and I sailed as a passenger in the *Venta*, a thing never permitted in the old days. (Only the five crewmen, all skippers themselves, could be aboard.) There are still, I believe, about thirty alive (mostly with auxiliary engines) and till recently the *Cambria*, and the famous Captain Roberts, were trading, under sail. They still have races on the Stour River. If I were Dictator of this land I would breed the sailing barge as we breed the horse, also economically dead – not for mere spectacle and speculation, but for a better purpose. My hero in *The Singing Swan* put forward, I believe, a good scheme. The Sail Training Association with their cruises for boys in their two big square-rigged ships do splendid work. The discipline, all that hanging on the yards and so on, is wholesome. But there are only two ships and the boys are not likely to meet square sails again. Before the cunning arts of barge building (see pages 184–7 of *The Singing Swan*) are quite forgotten, before all the old skippers and builders are dead, I would set two or three of the old yards to work, at the State's expense, so that there were never less than fifty barges in active being. They would be posted all round the coast, used for training in the winters and cruises in the summers. Twelve or fifteen boys could sleep in hammocks in the ample holds. The fore-and-aft rig will never die and so the study of it is practical. The breed of the barge should not be allowed to disappear. Beautiful, efficient, enduring, she is one of the finest things that Britain ever made.

The next great event in my water life was the building of my beloved *Water Gipsy*. She has been dead many years, but I dream about her still. These are some of the few dreams I wish were true when I wake up. We do long exciting voyages with good company aboard. She is bigger than she was in life, and sometimes acquires the qualities of a 'Duck'. We load up on the foreshore, I start the engine and steer her down into the water. Once I steered her round Piccadilly Circus.

She came into being at the speed of an elephant. She was built at the yard of the Cole Brothers at Hammersmith, next to 'The Seasons', where James Thomson lived. They were good craftsmen but leisurely. Her protracted birth became a local joke, but at last I insisted that she must be ready for the Coronation of 1936 and she was, at about 11 p.m. the night before. She followed the plan of the *Ark*, with the wheel right aft and a cockpit forward, but had a good keel and much stouter construction. The unconventional forward cockpit I recommend to anyone who has not got ocean ambitions. It is ideal for river, canal and even tideway work, especially for handling the anchor or picking up a buoy. On the usual foredeck the sailor is precariously perched, with awkward guard-rails in the way, and a lot of tiresome stooping to do. I stood erect in my cockpit on a level with the great buoys of the tideway and could comfortably pass a line. In the war, for the stormy seas of Sea Reach, which can be formidable, I fitted a removable foredeck which kept the worst of the waves away. She had two cabins, with four bunks, good headroom which is essential. I transferred the 'Handy Billy' engine from the *Ark* and bought another to keep it company. So she had 18 brake horse power (whatever that means) and in slack water, I reckoned, could do 5 knots or 5¾ land miles an hour – say 8 knots with a good tide.

The elephant's time had not been wasted. Her long cabin walls gave her a tender look, but she was robust enough. One misty night during the war I rammed the unlighted Ovens Buoy below Tilbury. This was not through error but an excess of accuracy. My orders were to drop one of our imaginary 'mines' (which we did by illuminating a balloon) 'close to the Ovens'. I had to approach the buoy across the tide steering by compass, in darkness, so the collision was creditable, I thought. But she did take a big bang on the starboard bow. At the yard where she was repaired they remarked on the toughness of her timbers.

About six months after War Two began there was a survey of the small cruisers – about 100 – which had volunteered in 1938. *The Water Gipsy* was put on the condemned list – too soft and slow. But she was reprieved. During the war she steamed 20,000 miles, fair tide and foul, took a terrible hammering against wharves, piers and other vessels, and survived a bomb close on her starboard bow. At the end of it all her engines were weary but her hull was sound, a credit to the ship-builders of Hammersmith.

Now, in many bright coats of Oxford blue, she steamed down early on Coronation morning to Westminster and made fast to the Speaker's Stairs, for I was now a Member. My brother Sidney, in full Commander's uniform, duly saluted the quarterdeck of Parliament as we went ashore. We stayed to see the fireworks in the evening, and nearly had some of our own, for one of Cole's men had put petrol in the hurricane lamps.

In *The Water Gipsy* I did much 'commuting' (absurd expression) between Hammersmith and the House. It gave me a grand feeling to drop my anchor off the Houses of Parliament. A mere citizen, I think, would have been asked to pick it up again by my friends the river police. But my favourite berth at night was in the Savoy Reach, just above Cleopatra's Needle. In the early part of 1937 I would sleep there most of the week. The Divorce Bill was in Standing Committee and Cochran's Revue (*Home and Beauty*) was in rehearsal, and I was nearly dotty between them. I would row out after the worrying day, climb aboard and light the lanterns and feel safe at last. No one could ring me up about amendments to the Bill or Binnie Hale's songs. Above me the trams swam through the lighted trees along the Embankment. Above them was the clock on my mantelpiece, the great Shell-Mex Clock to which some wag gave the name of 'Big Benzine'. I could see Big Ben too, the lighthouse of London, and the other way, St Paul's. Green and red lights decorated Waterloo Bridge. A few trains rumbled slowly into Charing Cross. But *The Water Gipsy* lay aloof from the great world, tugging at her anchor or sidling round it on the turn of the tide, gently tossing now and then in the wash of a police boat. I was the lord of London, the only man alone.

At the end of one of these weeks, on my way home to Hammersmith I passed a tug with a tow of lighters, just above the bridge. It was a quiet evening, I could see my house, and I was thinking 'Thank God, no more divorce till Tuesday'. Then I heard a voice from the tug: 'Yes, there he is,' and then another, deep, accusing, but friendly: 'You're doing no good. Bill wants to get rid of his old woman now.'

In the *Water Gipsy* the family and I slowly discovered London River. Greenwich, that glorious corner, the best thing in London,* Greenhithe, where Everard's built their famous sailing barges, Gravesend and Tilbury, the real gateway of the river, Hole Haven, Canvey Island, the sheltering Creek and the welcoming Lobster Smack. We ventured as far as the Nore and handed newspapers to the tossing lightship. We made Whitstable and were hit and nearly sunk by a steamer in the Swale. We explored the charming Medway as far as Maidstone and beyond. I taught myself to steer by compass to a degree: and I studied all the tricks of the tide, the eddies and strips of slack water, knowledge that with only sixteen horses under me, I needed during the war. Nelson, too, at the age of eighteen, learned his seamanship in the lower reaches of London River. 'In this way,' he wrote, 'I became a good pilot for small vessels from Chatham to the Tower of London, down Swin and the North Foreland, and confident of myself in rocks and sands, which has many times since been a great comfort to me.' As the humble captain of a tiny vessel which, proudly flying the White Ensign, plied up and down the Thames between Southend and the Tower for six years of the War Two, I know what he meant. Yachtsmen, with but a weekend for their voyages, may yearn for the nearly tideless Mediterranean, with deep water always and everywhere, but there is no doubt that the ruthless complicated tides of this island, with all their peculiarities and perils, are a searching school for seamen. They add, as it were, a third dimension to the business of navigation. Southey speaks of the 'intuitive genius' with which Nelson seized the situation before the Battle of the Nile, when he found the French fleet in their narrow anchorage. He saw at once that where there was room for an enemy ship to swing at her anchor there was room for an English ship to enter. But he saw it, I feel, with a mind and eye that had been trained in the channels and shallows of the Thames and Medway. Tug masters are making similar judgements every day.

World War Two gave me my longest, most intimate encounter with

* See *The Thames* (Weidenfeld and Nicolson, 1966) by the author, and Frank Carr's *Maritime Greenwich* – a Pride of Britain Book – Pitkin's Pictorials.

the water. Late on the last night the House of Commons met before the war, as the last Members were leaving, I said to Mr Churchill: 'Do you think there will be war, sir?' 'Yes', he answered without hesitation. Then he added, without a cue from anyone: 'I think we shall have to abandon the Thames.' I was highly surprised by the great man's remark, and I remember protesting shyly: 'I belong to a service which means to see that we don't.' A puny and pompous pronouncement, you may think, but it was true. Very many months before the Port of London Authority, in concert with the Navy, had determined that we should *not* abandon the Thames. Rear-Admiral R. W. Oldham had been appointed Air Raid Precautions Officer as far back as *May* 1938, well *before* Munich. It was about the same time, I think, that the late Mr. W. L. Wrightson, the Chairman of the Port of London Authority River Committee, said, 'The Port, however fiercely attacked, is indestructible. We are ready, we are prepared to carry on, whatever may happen . . .' War was declared on 3 September; but it was on 25 August that the Navy took over that popular joke Southend Pier, from which those 3,367 convoys were directed, not to mention the ships for Normandy. 'Abandon the Thames'?

In my book, *The Thames*, in the chapter called 'The Port at War' I have given a full account of the fine feats of the Navy, and the Port, and all concerned with London River, both in the Blitz and the long build-up for revenge.

Not long after Munich the little *Water Gipsy* put the defences of the Thames on a firm foundation. At some City Dinner I met my splendid friend Captain Coleman, for many years Chief Harbourmaster and River Superintendent, and we were at once enrolled in his River Emergency Service, a fleet of private motor-boats. All that uncertain 1939 summer we were organized and exercised and instructed in the gases. We lifted dead men out of lighters and dashingly delivered them to ambulance boats under way, which came in useful later when wounded steamers in Sea Reach wanted oil or other aid. The fleet mobilized punctually on 1 September from Lambeth (our first station) to Southend. On 3 September we opened the war hilariously. War had been declared, and I was walkng across New Palace Yard on my way to the Chamber to hear the Prime Minister, when for the first time 'the sirens went'. 'How like Hitler!' I thought. 'Striking at once!' But how clever was I – for I had left the *Water Gipsy* anchored off the Speaker's Stairs. I ran to the Stairs, one of my crew came off in the dinghy, the anchor came aboard just as I did, and there we were steaming nobly back to our station, ready to save the nation. What a cheer (ironical) we got, I remember, from some fellow Members on the Terrace!

We began as Civil Defence, two days on, two days off: but after

Dunkirk (to which they would not let us go) officers came at dead of night to Hole Haven and asked us all to join the Navy. None of my crew, professional men mostly, could oblige, but I said, 'Aye, aye, sir' and for the second time enlisted in the Navy, as a Petty Officer. I never thought that the White Ensign would fly on my little ship. For two days, in patrol orders, she was addressed as H.M.S. *Water Gipsy*.

So for the best part of six years I worked and lived and slept on the water, two or three feet from the water. We had some alarming times, and some dull times, but we were nearly always busy. We had two jobs which took us from top to bottom of the river, one from Tower to Hole Haven, another from Teddington to Southend. So we had a grandstand view of the Battle of the Thames. I am one of the very few men who have seen Charing Cross Bridge and Waterloo Bridge on fire at the same time, and now and then with our tiny flags we ordered destroyers to alter course. Thrilling.

One day in 1940 – or 1941 – my wife and I were invited to lunch at No. 10. I sat next to Mr Churchill. Suddenly, but casually, he asked me if I would like a job. I said 'Thank you, sir, I am very happy where I am.' He did not say, as a few did, 'But should you not be doing something more useful and, (some said) more comfortable?' He left me to be the judge of that. And perhaps he remembered that old thought about abandoning the Thames.

In 1944, I think, one of the Sea Lords genially badgered me to take a commission. I said, 'If you'll send me to sea as a navigator's assistant, I will.' In any spare time I could find I had been studying 'celestial navigation'. The widow of a master-mariner had sent me his sextant, saying 'I shall be glad to know that it is in the hands of a real sailor'. I blushed hotly at this, for I had not seen a sextant before. I must, I felt, make myself able to make use of the gift. I bought many books and began. At school I had been weaned from mathematics just before logarithms (what a mistake!). I now found them fascinating and passed on bravely to trigonometry and the spherical triangle. In Sea Reach, and sometimes elsewhere, I could use my sextant, and at last I fancied myself as a navigator. But the Admiral wanted me to edit a magazine for the air-boys of the Navy, and be a lieutenant-commander. At that I jibbed: but to humour my friend I consented to an officer's medical. They rated my eyes C3. They had been rated A1 at my Petty Officer's Exam in 1940, and I had been safely steering my ship in a river without lights for five years: but that was the end of my navigational ambitions. I was not going to dwindle into an editor, however highly ranked, and I happily remained a Petty Officer afloat, with two machine-guns, rifles, revolvers, two cutlasses and God knows what else. What editor was so heavily armed?

'Afloat' is the word. Even when the enemy was quiet, there were always the problems, the demands of the water to be met. A small vessel on the tideway is on active service all the time. Your car can simply go to sleep in its stable, but every night the boat must be artfully moored, one line balancing another, so that whichever way the tide runs, she will hold her position, stand off a little from the pier or the lighter to which she is attached, and not be too rudely knocked about by the wash of passing tugs or police-boats. But the wind may change, the lighters shift, and for all your art you are never sure of a quiet night. One night in Gallions Reach, a whole 'road' of lighters broke loose from the next buoy above us and bore down on us on the ebb. I was awake, fortunately, and we got away with no worse than a crushed dinghy, but I had a Cabinet Minister on board, Arthur Greenwood, and I was worried.

We learned a lot that night. One learned something every day. When we were 'Mail Boat', we did our daily run (Canvey Island to London – or back) fog or fine, fair tide or foul. This meant about forty-one (statute) miles if we penetrated as far as Chelsea: and with only eighteen horses at our command it meant some elaborate exercises in 'cheating the tide' when the tide was foul. We learned laboriously all the helpful inshore eddies, and stretches of slack water, the best points for crossing the river, the best arches of the bridges: we crept along as close inshore as we could without going aground. In this way I reckoned to do about 5 m.p.h. but it needed constant vigilance and care. Without 'cheating' we should not have done more than four. This, with calling at four or five stations to deliver ammunition, weapons, recruits or stores, made a long day. I enjoyed more fighting the fog. From the first I had noted the compass course of every reach in the river. When dense fog sent the tugs and lighters to the buoys and all the ships dropped anchor, the *Water Gipsy* crawled on alone, provided she was travelling *against* the tide, and at her slow speed could spot an anchored ship or dredger in good time. I should not have been so foolish as to go ahead in fog with the tide under me.

Down at the bottom of the river, in the wide open spaces of Sea Reach and the Lower Hope, I had compass bearings from buoy to buoy – Mid Blyth, West Blyth, the Muckings, the Ovens, Tilbury Buoy and so on. More than once we left Hole Haven about 7 a.m. or earlier and steamed safely over the tide for two hours without once seeing the shore or any other moving vessel. That took us nearly to Gravesend. These were exhilarating passages, though my crew and I were sneezing and coughing in our Duffel coats. How exciting to hear Connolly or Tom Cheesman cry from the bows: 'Buoy ahead, skipper!' Especially if we had crossed Sea Reach and had had to make an allowance for the tide. What seamanship! I would mutter modestly to myself And how exciting was the silence! Nothing to be heard but an

occasional steamer moaning every two minutes away below Southend
and the obstinate clatter of our eighteen horses. The *Water Gipsy* had the
silent invisible river to herself. The grey clammy fog was a protective
friend. Where were all those great steamers? Prisoners. But the little
Water Gipsy, a free thing, strode on. Her bow-wave was the only white
water in the river, her White Ensign the one flag in the fog.

All day, whatever our particular duties, we were 'going alongside'
something or other, a pier, a lighter, a tug, a ship, a fat bouncing iron
buoy, a long ladder, a causeway in shallow water. Again, this was not
like stopping a car beside a stationary pavement. Both the boat and
her pavement might be heaving up and down, with a strong tide and
wind to counter and a small space only to enter. Every time it was a
different problem, a challenge and a satisfaction to do the thing well,
without ramming or bumping other craft or damaging your own. I
always approached the high Tilbury Pier with apprehension, so fierce
would be the wash from fast tugs and ferries.

At Cadogan Pier, Chelsea, where we sometimes spent the night after
the long plug from Hole Haven, there was a particular challenge, and
when I drive past the pier in a taxi today I often look down and recall
the excitement and professional pride – or, if you will, conceit – with
which I used to meet it. We had to lie inside the pier, to be out of the
way of bigger craft. The flood tide would be running, and in the narrow
gap, raging. I had to drop astern, both engines going gently ahead, or
idling, into a blind alley: a dangerous, blind alley – for behind me was
the 'brow', or bridge that connected the floating 'pier' to the Embankment. The water was malignant, swirls and cross-currents, bent on
getting us broadside on, and if we dropped broadside on to the brow
Her Majesty's Patrol Vessel might be a total wreck, for the hull would
go under it and the brow would take the topsides off. Playing one
propeller against the other I had to keep her straight, stop her just
above the brow, and then edge her sideways into her narrow berth. I
contrived to look calm but inwardly I was quaking. Even the pier-
master used to applaud. But I thanked God, my stoker and the faithful
engines, which had been running non-stop perhaps for eleven hours.

Then, there was the continual care of the ship, her engines and armament. I detested her armament, but, though no engineer, I knew a lot
about her engines, and if my stoker was sick I sucked at a blocked
petrol-pipe with a will and cleaned the plugs with an air.

If you would know how we dealt with the enemy you must read
Independent Member and *The Thames*. This is merely a chapter about
Water, and its fascinations. For me at least the company of water
was a high compensation for the fears and fatigues of war. After the
All Clear had gone I would sit up in my blankets, sip my tot of rum,
drink one toast to my lonely wife at home and another to the water

slapping, swirling, and chuckling by my bed. Gwen, throughout the war, was a gallant ambulance driver, and had some terrible jobs. She had two incendiaries on the roof, one in her bedroom, and hardly a window in the house.

I did, though, in spite of the Admiralty doctors, finish the war with a command – yes, a command – at sea, doing Admiralty work. I have told the story in *Independent Member* (Up The North Sea – But Why?) but I insist on a brief boast here: for this absurd voyage I regard as the crown of my efforts to serve the Navy at sea, which had begun at Lambeth R.N.V.R. headquarters thirty-one years earlier in 1914. (True, I did finish War One physically at sea but only as bottle-washer to the Commodore of a Convoy on an exciting voyage to Port Said, on which we lost two ships.)

During War Two at the Royal Ocean Racing Club and elsewhere I had met often and admired much the good fellows who worked for the Admiralty Small Vessels Pool (sometimes called the Ferry Service). These were civilian amateur yachtsmen of all ages – but mostly more than middle. Their job (voluntary) was to take over new 'small vessels' of any sort and shape from the builders and deliver them to the port where the Navy wanted them. They did many fine uncomfortable feats, these civilian sailors: some were sent to the States and brought their small charges, not in convoy, across the Atlantic. One of the regulars, named Holland, had promised to sign me on if ever I were free. The *Water Gipsy* was 'paid off' in March 1945, and in April, still a Petty Officer, I signed on as Mate in one of the 45 ft M.F.V's (Motor Fishing Vessel) to be taken from Brightlingsea to the Forth. (She was to be taken through the Caledonian Canal from Grangemouth to the Clyde, and shipped to the Far East for harbour service). Unhappily a day or two later, I received another invitation to visit Field-Marshal Montgomery ('I suggest you pay me another visit: and see Germany. I will send my aeroplane for you if you can come' – 14 April 1945.) I had a feeling that this was an invitation to see the end of the German war, and so it was. If I had gone I should have seen the surrender of the German generals: and, afterwards, the personal staff told me they wished they could have had some 'outsider' to witness those tremendous days. Any sensible man, I suppose, would have asked to be excused from the job for which I had, quite unnecessarily, volunteered. But 'Duty!' I said, poor fool, and away we went to Brightlingsea. This will show you my attachment to the water.

The M.F.V. was a fine sea-boat and, I expect, is doing good work somewhere still. But just then she needed caulking, was full of water, had hardly any ballast and an almost invisible propeller. In an area of strong tides and winds she was almost incapable of transfer from one place to another. We took so long to get to Lowestoft and have her caulked, degaussed etc. that my captain, a solicitor, had to go to London and handed her over to me. Two of my crew, including the gallant Colonel Blewitt, were seventy. I got her as far as Yarmouth and conducted an unofficial speed-trial, which gave her about four knots in slack water. Our next objective was the Humber via little Wells, if possible, but that is rarely possible. We made three attempts. Twice, with north winds, we never got round the Cromer Corner. The third time we did and were plunging doggedly into the teeth of a nor'-wester towards the Wash, when Cromer lighthouse signalled RETURN TO YARMOUTH (I was glad of my Morse).

I was almost fond of the ridiculous vessel by now. Off Cromer she had stood on her head, she stood on her tail, and we were flung about the wheel-house like elderly peas. But always she rode the great waves with an air, as contemptuous as a cork. After six years of the muddy Thames it was nice to have clean sea come aboard and salt spray on the face. But all the time I kept thinking, 'Why the hell am I doing this? Why am I not with Monty?'

I surrendered then and accepted a tow from one of His Majesty's mine-sweepers bound for Scapa Flow. Towed indeed – for 300 miles? It may sound a lazy way to finish a journey. Try it. The first day was fine. Our astonished cork found itself bounding through the sea at more than ten knots (a thing, I swear, it has never done again) and the man at the wheel had to watch everything like two or three cats. But the waters which we had three times attempted so painfully and vainly were now smooth and blue, and even the fearsome Wash was gracious. We made Bridlington before dusk, 120 miles, and anchored south of Flamborough Head. I never thought I should be able to say, 'Let go the anchor' south of Flamborough Head. I washed in beautiful clean sea water.

The second day was northerly, rough, and anxious, the third was very tiresome indeed. Five times the tow-rope parted, and in the end we pulled one of the mine-sweeper's strong bollards clean out of the deck. When the line went, the cork without way on her rolled and wallowed, wildly, intolerably. In these conditions my two septuagenarians forward had to haul in seventy or eight feet of heavy, wet, new, intractable rope. It would not coil easily like old rope. As it came in it piled and twisted itself into enormous insoluble 'snarls' on the fo'c'sle head. I could only slip out and lend an occasional hand for I must watch the wheel, signal to the engine-room, and now and then semaphore to the mine-sweeper, reeling precariously on the see-saw deck. My magnificent septuagenarians bore the brunt and did heroic work. At last the patient Navy hauled us into the Forth, and next day under her own steam I proudly steered my cork past the Fleet to Grangemouth. But I refused to take her through the Caledonian

Canal till she had been given a propeller more suitable for Bangkok, Rangoon or Singapore. Besides, something was in the air. I caught a night train from Edinburgh and arrived in London at dawn on VE Day – 8 May 1945. I was in my place in the House in time to hear Mr Churchill tell his tale. But, of course, I should have been at Luneberg, seeing Victory itself.

Never mind, I had commanded one of His Majesty's ships at sea.

To this day I have no clear idea why in 1945 I became a Knight Bachelor – Mr Churchill's last list. The reason given was 'For political and public services'. So no fellow author need resent me as a 'literary' knight. I did not feel that my miscellaneous ten years in Parliament had earned an honour. My first instinct was to say 'No'. But the letter came from Winston Churchill, and I thought, 'If Winston Churchill, at the end of the war, thinks I deserve to be knighted he must have some good reason for it, and who am I to say "No"?' Should not any man be proud to be one of Winston's knights?

'Public services'? I had, at his request, reluctantly done four or five of those difficult Sunday radio Epilogues in the wake of J. B. Priestley. But one of his Ministers, with a stray remark, gave me a better idea. Perhaps the Prime Minister had recalled those few words we exchanged just before the War, and this was a reward for my long refusal to 'abandon the Thames'. So I have a fond private fancy that I am a part-knight of London River: and I hope an old man is entitled to his fond private fancies.

The actual 'dubbing' was odd. I was sitting in the Chamber of the House of Commons quietly waiting to make a speech (if I could) on I forget what subject. Suddenly a message came from the Chief Government Whip requiring my instant presence at the Palace. I rushed off in a taxi, was quickly sworded by His Majesty, returned, rather dizzy, to the Chamber, and made my speech after all. Never a dull moment!

⸙ 10 ⸙

FIFTEEN YEARS HARD

IN May 1934, on a cold Monday morning, I laid an information against the Kitchen Committee of the House of Commons for selling 'liquor' without a licence. In December, Lord Hewart the Lord Chief Justice and Mr Justice Avory decided that I was wrong – but I had to pay no costs. Moreover, by my failure I established for ever the rights and privileges of Parliament in this department of life. They had been dubious. The following year I became a Member of the House of Commons and enjoyed those privileges. So did my counsel, Harry Strauss. I have told the whole story in *Independent Member*.

I have given a full account of my fifteen years in Parliament in the same book; in *The Ayes Have It* I related, blow by blow, how my Marriage Bill 1936 became the Matrimonial Causes Act 1937: and in *The Point of Parliament* I tried some simple instruction for the Young about the working of the place (Herbert Morrison said that this little work, which first appeared in *Punch*, should be used by the schools).

But a brief salute would be fitting here. It is not every literary man who has had a kindly welcome and a long stay in that critical place. The great Edward Gibbon, it is said, sat there for eight years without once opening his mouth. 'It is more tremendous than I imagined,' he said. 'The great speakers fill me with despair; the bad ones with terror,' so he sat quietly in his place, thinking, no doubt, about the Decline and Fall of the Roman Empire. Sheridan did well, and stayed, but after his 'maiden' a reporter said: 'You had much better have stuck to your former pursuits.' Macaulay became a Minister too, but he said: 'There is not a more terrible audience in the world.' Addison, the famous essayist, failed and made but one attempt to speak. Steele was howled down by the Tories with cries of '*The Tatler!*' because he had made fun of them. John Buchan did well for eight years, but my dear Belloc, that master of words, was not a success. I count myself fortunate to have survived so long with reasonable repute.

The strangest thing was the way in which I got there. Chance, as I have told you, led my wife and me to a house by the river, and myself into a lifelong 'affair' with the water. Chance, I also maintain, led me to the House of Commons. In both cases, no doubt, I had some hidden little bug in me, but without some provocative event it would have stayed inert and harmless.

Three weeks before the General Election of 1935 I had no more idea of standing for Parliament than I had of swimming the Channel. But by chance a friend of mine, one Sidney Rogerson, of Imperial Chemical Industries, invited me, I know not why, to go up to Billingham in Durham, and see Mr Ramsay Macdonald open their new plant for converting coal into oil. I was scribbling away at something or other, and coal-into-oil was not an obvious cup-of-tea of mine, but by chance I accepted. Lord Melchett invited me to his table on the special train. After lunch an old Oxford man passing down the train, paused at Lord Melchett's table. I did not know him; we were not introduced: but I happened to hear his name. That chain of chances changed the course of my life.

In those days I spent much time (and raised a little money) abusing 'the politicians' in the papers about my pet grievances and reforms, divorce laws, licensing laws, betting laws and so on. But I often felt that articles, however powerful and unanswerable they may seem to your friends, beat in vain on the walls of Whitehall like the great waves on the beach at Brighton. The right thing, the only thing, was to speak your stuff in Parliament. But how? Good friends in the House said now and then: 'Why don't you come in here, old boy?' One answer was: 'I can't afford it.' Another was: 'I'm not a party man.' The friendly Mr Baldwin said it. I remember saying: 'All right, sir. Give me a seat at Oxford University' – and how he laughed. The distinguished Lord Hugh Cecil and Professor Oman were there impregnable.

On this fateful day Gilbert Frankau, the novelist, was also a guest of Lord Melchett's. He spent the morning lecturing me on the good old theme of 'Stick to your last'. I was wasting too much time writing articles on odd corners of politics. I was a novelist not a politician. I had written two very successful novels, *The Water Gipsies*, and *Holy Deadlock* (the latter in 1934). I should get on with another, and let someone else deal with divorce law reform, betting tax and so on. By lunch-time I was admitting that he was right: I would mend my ways, I assured him.

But after lunch Fate struck at once. A man 'in transit' paused near our table and somebody said: 'Hullo Lindemann.' At that name I pricked up my little ears. It was in the news. Professor Oman was not going to stand again for Oxford University. Professor Lindemann (later Lord Cherwell) had offered himself instead, but had been rejected by the Conservative 'Caucus' in favour of Professor C. R. M.

Cruttwell, the Principal of Hertford. There had been some unpleasantness.

I commiserated with the Professor now and we talked a little about the election. 'Would there be any chance for an Independent?' I asked him. 'Must you have taken your degree?' (I had never taken mine) and so on. 'There's very little time,' he said, 'and you'd have to get the addresses of the electors.' He raised no hopes and I said no more.

But black Chance stepped in again. On the way home, at St Pancras, I ran into the Professor on the platform, and said madly: 'If any young man would like to help would he let me know.'

I forgot all about it and began to think about a new novel. But, rather to my dismay, young men turned up at Hammersmith, Frank Pakenham (now Lord Longford) a great friend of the Professor's, Eric Linklater, Peter Fleming. They invited action on my rash words at St Pancras. I said I was no good and wrote a huge election address to prove it. It was deplorable, I thought, and I was delighted. I should be let off: but no – they liked it. Now I was in real trouble. Lindemann's box-file of the names and addresses of the constituents was smuggled up from Oxford by taxi in the dark of night (it was death, among the dons, they said, to be 'a Lindemann man'). The family and friends addressed the 22,000 envelopes on every floor of the house. My official agent was Frank Pakenham. My active agent, who arranged all things, was a good friend and neighbour named Frank Bluff. When this leaked out some of the dons thought it was one more unworthy attempt at fun by the Independent candidate.

So, about ten days after I promised Gilbert Frankau to cast politics aside I was standing for the House of Commons. What an ass!

My Address, the longest in history, was an innovation. Neither of the official Conservative candidates expressed himself at all: a stately 'statement' was issued for them both. Neither of them turned up for the Nominations or for the Counting of the Votes. Two junior dons attended, and one of them had to take to poor Mr Cruttwell the grim news (1) that he had been defeated by the Hammersmith humorist and (2) that he had 'lost his deposit'. I was very sorry about (2), though I had heard that there were some reasonable bets at All Souls that I should lose mine. It was through an undetected flaw in the law. In *The Ayes Have It* I gave a blow-by-blow account of the voting which was under the Single Transferable Vote System, and anyone who has the slightest interest in Proportional Representation should read it. I believe in the system, and should like to see more of it. But the point is that no vote is wasted, surplus votes are transferred; and a man can have more votes on the last count than he did on the first, as Cruttwell did. But the said 'flaw in the law' decreed that to retain that ridiculous 'deposit' he had to win one-eighth of the votes on the *first* count instead of the last. I record with pleasure that the first card of congratulation I received came from poor Mr Cruttwell.

The procession of votes, briefly, went thus:

1st Count (1st Choice)	Cecil (C)	7,365	
	Herbert (Ind.)	3,390	
	Stocks (Lab.)	2,683	
	Cruttwell (C.)	1,803	
1st Redistribution	Cecil	7,365	Elected
	Herbert	3,864	
	Cruttwell	3,674	
	Stocks	2,776	
2nd Redistribution	Cecil	7,365	
	Herbert	5,206	Elected
	Cruttwell	3,697	
	Stocks	2,776	

So I was second all the way – and was not, as some said, sneaked in by Proportional Representation.

Note that none of this would have happened if I had not improbably accepted an invitation to go to Billingham to see coal converted into oil.

I wrote to congratulate Lord Hugh Cecil, and asked for advice. That man of principle replied, with characteristic frankness:

Dear Herbert,
Thank you for your very kind congratulations. I wish I could reciprocate them, but sincerity obliges me to say that I deeply and keenly regret, on public grounds, your election to the University seat.

Rather a slap, but I liked it. Then followed two pages of good advice: and always in the House, he treated me like a favourite son.

In 1937 the great Lord Hugh resigned. That fine public servant, Sir Arthur Salter, succeeded him, and I became 'the Senior Burgess', which made me smile. It made others smile too. 'Oxford University,' said a certain divine, 'is now represented by a boat-builder and a buffoon.'

But the dons, may I add, forgave and used me very kindly.

However bold, or impudent, I may sometimes have sounded, I was always humbly conscious of the might and dignity of Parliament. I had a true sense of awe as I walked through St Stephen's Hall past the huge figures of Burke, Pitt and the others, to think that they were once mere new Members too. The very stones, the arches, the panelling, the pictures, the churchy smell of the place, breed reverence. I did all my audacious deeds in a state of trepidation. I carefully studied the Standing Orders, or, at least, the Manual of Procedure and was always asking questions of the friendly Dennis Herbert, Deputy-Speaker. Party Members in those days rather neglected this branch of learning, and when in doubt or trouble were content to run to Nanny – the Whips. The thing is – especially for an Independent – to know the rules so well that you can seize with propriety the sudden opportunity for action.*

My maiden speech was well within the rules though not the customs. William Cobbett opened fire on his first evening in the House. Having listened to a debate in which all the swells had taken part he rose and said: 'Mr. Speaker, it appears to me that since I have been sitting here I have heard a great deal of vain and unprofitable conversation.' (He was an old man and did not do much after that early promise.) I was not rude, but it was only the second day of the Parliament, and I cannot imagine now how I had the hardihood to do it. A Prime Minister's Motion, the opening of the Session, the house packed – I can see today the dazzle of nameless faces on the terraced benches. Against the advice of old hands, the entreaties of my friend and counsellor William Mabane, even a kindly message from the Speaker, some demon drove me 'over the top'. Churchill afterwards praised my 'composure and aplomb': but it was the composure of a man in a dream, of a madman who knows that he is mad but does not mind. At least I did better than Mr Gladstone and was heard: his first speech was thus reported: 'Mr Gladstone made a few remarks which were not audible in the Gallery.'

I got some laughs, some sought, some not (the whole oration is in *Independent Member*†). How they laughed at my impious vow! Mr Baldwin had justified, quite reasonably, the filching of a private Members' Friday, on the ground that we should not yet be ready with our Bills. I waved Mr Holford Knight's Divorce Bill, which had long been banging at the door, and declared:

I have in my hand a Bill which I am ready to introduce next Friday, or on the Friday after, or on all the Fridays, until it is passed into law; and I swear that it shall be passed before this Parliament is over. [Laughter.] Hon. Members laugh. But I must remind them that all the serious politic-

* This paid. 'The capital part of the situation is that Mr Herbert has completely mastered Parliamentary procedure in an incredibly short space of time – a thing which old-timers have always maintained was a matter of years and years – and has got the wits to make short-cuts through that procedure and the personality to make those short-cuts acceptable. He has brought off some audacious coups during this Session, and has gained the warm respect of the whole House. It is not easy to do both.' (A. G. Macdonell.)

† Hansard 4 December 1935: Vol. 307 Col. 134.

ians laughed when I disclosed my obscene designs on my almost virgin University. They said that with my extraordinary opinions I ought to go to Hoxton, to the taverns, to the race-courses of our land, and hope perhaps to scramble together a discreditable vote or two; but that to go to Oxford, the citadel of Christian enlightenment and the stronghold of orthodoxy, a constituency with more parsons to the square vote than any other constituency – this was lunacy. However, I went on, and the walls of Jericho fell down. Therefore, I would ask hon. Members in the north-east corner of the House to consider again before they laugh at my intentions!

My last words, I am glad to see, were these:

Whatever may be said on this matter, and whatever may happen, I should like to say that I am proud indeed to be standing in this place among the faithful Commons of His Majesty the King.

By the grace of God, and the goodwill and energy of my companions, notably Rupert de la Bere, the Member for Evesham, the impious vow was fulfilled in less than twenty months, and eight years before the Parliament was over. Sir Archibald Sinclair said some nice things: so did James Maxton, and his Independent Labour Party divided the House. With Eleanor Rathbone there were five of us in the No Lobby against 232 for the Government – a strange opening to the career of a Member for Oxford University.

A remark of Mr Churchill's has often been quoted as a rebuke. It was in fact part of a pleasant compliment. Alone among the swells he sought me out and comforted the naughty boy: 'Great composure, great aplomb.' It was right, he said, for a young Member to take advantage of the rules of Procedure, to say what he had in him. Then he made that famous sound, half-grunt, half-chuckle: 'Call that a maiden speech? It was a brazen hussy of a speech. Never did such a painted lady of a speech parade itself before a modest Parliament.'

I won a small, but special, leading article in *The Times* (which was more than Mr Gladstone did); but its purpose was rebuke, more in sorrow than in anger:

A PREMATURE CRUSADER

. . . It may be hoped that his mistake yesterday will not prejudice the chance of a discussion of his Bill . . . The success of a private member depends upon securing the sympathy of other private members, who prefer that even the most attractive speeches should be reserved for the right occasion.

Quite right: but others were more encouraging, especially Mr Stephen Gwynn (in 1937):

no means willing to accept without question the assurance that everything is being done which could be safely done to develop our resources, and employ our people, by utilizing that credit which by such sacrifices we have established. I shall press, for example, for the restoration of our inland waterways and canals, and for an inquiry into the important proposal to dam the Thames and secure for London a tideless river.

THE MINES

I believe that private enterprise is, on the whole, the best machinery for distributing wealth and getting things done : but I am not, like the Socialist, the slave of dogma. The mines may be a special case, as the miners are, without doubt, a specially deserving class of workers in a specially dangerous and important industry. If the mine-owners are unable, or unwilling, so to conduct their industry that the miners can enjoy good wages, I am willing to vote for nationalization. But I suspect the fatal logic of the Socialist and should not hold myself committed to the nationalization of everything. All industries and trades are not the same. What is best for the Navy need not be best for mercantile shipping. It may well be that the mines ought to be considered as a service corresponding to the Navy.

CAPITALISM AND THE SOCIALIST

I am a worker in a precarious trade and know all that can be said against capitalism—the insecurity, the fear of the future, and of old age, the strange inequality of rewards. I have served in the ranks and worked in the East End : I live in a poor part of London, and here, in pubs, in my theatrical work and up and down the London River, have all my life had friendly dealings with working men; and I claim some small knowledge of their lives and needs. But I reject the dogmatic assumptions of Socialism with which Labour has unnecessarily burdened itself. They tell us that Capitalism is doomed : Karl Marx, I believe, made the same announcement 80 years ago. He may still be right : but the old clock ticks on ; and it does not help very much to throw stones at it. It would be surprising indeed if our system had survived quite unshaken the unprecedented upheaval of a world war. But it is infinitely adaptable and has not, I think, exhausted its resources. Capitalism must carry its casualties—it is not

12

doing so badly now and will do better. We should be able to think of unemployment as a triumph of capitalism—the increase of leisure. But that involves more generous unemployment and pension arrangements; and these I should favour, preserving, wherever possible, the principles of contribution and insurance. In principle, there is much to be said for Labour's formula of 'Work or Maintenance': and in practice something like this may come. But we shall not produce equality by turning everything upside-down. My reason, such as it is, reluctantly rebels when I am asked to believe that after thousands of years of a not wholly fruitless civilisation not merely a new but the best and only way of managing this complicated world has been revealed to my old football captain, Sir Stafford Cripps. My instinct bids me distrust those who are so arrogant as to make such a claim. And, practically, I am afraid to entrust them with the government of the country at this difficult time.

Whenever a severe strain comes upon the Socialist Party the fabric totters, and the head falls off. This has happened twice within five years. I am afraid that it may happen again. The residue of the Party complains that it has been betrayed, and throws the blame upon the leaders, not the Party. But when the same misfortune continually occurs to the same motor-car, we rightly cease to talk of ' accidents ' and begin to look for some inherent defect. The essential weakness of the Socialist Party is its rigidity, its passion for fixed mathematical formulae—as if human life were a game of chess. When the wind blows it does not ' give.' When the formula does not fit the facts the leader would like to forget it : but it is too late. His well-trained followers brandish the formula before him and scribble ' Traitor ' on his back. I believe that, whenever a great strain comes, the fabric will split. It follows that, at this difficult and dangerous time, the Socialist Party, however humane in intention and plausible in argument, is not fit to assume the Government of this country. It is relevant to imagine what would have been our position if the excellent Mr. Lansbury and his colleagues had been in office a month ago.

(9) AGRICULTURE

I know nothing about Agriculture.

(10) WAR AND PEACE

I make no apology for touching this question last, and adhering hopefully to what should be the ideal order of things. I shall support

I soon found that his audacity and ingenuity were approved by very old parliamentary hands. To do the thing successfully it was necessary to create a favourable impression: and that was achieved at once. The speech was frank and modest as well as witty: it pleased the House and convinced the House that the speaker was just as much in earnest as if he were a long-haired fanatic.

Yes, but the following year, when I was making a passionate appeal to the Chancellor to double the annual sum devoted (on the Civil List) to authors' and artists' pensions, Mr Neville Chamberlain, a few yards away, kept hissing: 'Say it in *Punch*! Say it in *Punch*!' which maddened me. But the following year there was a new Civil List Bill, and without a word, he did just what I had suggested – and a little more. (One hundred years earlier, in 1837, when the sum I complained against was first fixed, a more important representative of Oxford University, the Duke of Wellington, Chancellor, had complained about it too). I never got to know Neville Chamberlain well (he did not come to the Smoking Room) but I admired him more than most of us did. His short, sharp replies to a nasty debate were admirably done.

Nobody said 'Say it in *Punch*!' during the long divorce battle (for which see *The Ayes Have It*): and from first to last there wasn't a laugh. I glow a little still when lawyers refer to 'the Herbert Act', but I wish it could bear as well the names of my fine team, de la Bere, gallant Arnold Wilson, Mavis Tate, Sorensen, John Withers, William Spens and others. We never had any luck. Time and again the ball bounced fiendishly the wrong way. What a strange chance, for example, that our first two tricky days in Standing Committee fell in Abdication Week! If you fail to get a quorum (20) on two successive days your Bill goes to the bottom of the list (and that would have killed us). On two days the Members, worried to death, and not anxious to discuss the law of adultery and so on, hung about outside, and had to be persuaded to come in. But they did come in. In the Third Reading debate Mr Michael Beaumont, though against us, congratulated us 'as an enthusiastic Parliamentarian', and said that when I introduced the Bill, 'most of us thought the odds were anything up to 1,000 to one that it could never obtain the Third Reading.'

We new 1935 boys were lucky indeed to strike a Parliament so packed with drama. We took the Oath to three different Monarchs, attended a Royal Funeral, Abdication, and Coronation. There was the Hoare-Laval crisis, Mussolini in Abyssinia, Churchill roaring in the wilderness, the war in Spain, 'Munich', the War. What a thing to have heard all the great Churchill speeches on the spot! I am glad too to have seen Lloyd George and Aneurin Bevan battling in that great arena!

In 1945 – another Election – poor Churchill's fall – Attlee's busy

Administration. In the House itself a tremendous change of scene. A good old Tory surveying the justly triumphant invaders is said to have said: 'Who *are* these people? They look like a lot of damned constituents.'

These five years I did not enjoy so much, for the Government took *all* Private Members' Time, which was my favourite form of fun. Still, we did a thing or two. I always had to force myself to make a major speech, but only once did I back out. I can remember a few in which, once on my feet, I felt in form, in command of my subject, the House was warm, and it was fun – Entertainment Tax (many times), the Population Statistics Bill (which, they said, I tore to shreds), Purchase Tax on books, the Lord Chamberlain, Spelling Reform, the 'Oxford Group', Betting Reform and Betting Tax, the public house, Law of Libel, Newfoundland and other themes. But even then I always had a feeling of unreality – 'Is it really me, the mild man of Hammersmith, standing up here and lecturing the Ministers, as if I was their equal?' I always hated the preliminaries, jumping up time and again to catch the Speaker's eye ('bumping' as Mr Baldwin called it), and the sequel, listening to the contemptible speakers who followed, and worse, the summons from the Hansard fellows to journey up, labour through your own contemptible speech, and word by detestable word, tired and thirsty, correct it.

The excellent Euclid, at the end of his merry Propositions, used to say 'I told you so'. Having made the improbable assertion that 'the square on the hypotenuse of a triangle is equal to the sum of the squares on the remaining sides' he proved it, and then wrote modestly: 'Q.E.D.' – Quod Erat Demonstrandum – Which Was the Thing to be Shown. Today they mutter that to say 'I told you so' is not the thing, almost ungentlemanly. I do not agree. So long as it is not said offensively I think it is desirable, almost a duty. For if people are assured that you were right this time they may pay more attention to the next thing you say, and less to the fellow who was wrong. In fact, they don't.

There are few, I imagine, who can read their old election addresses with complete satisfaction. Mine at least show that I was not a one-string (divorce) fiddle. There is some wild and ignorant stuff, no doubt, but also a good many promises, and prophecies, that came true: and most of my subjects were not mentioned in any other Address in the land.

1935

EDUCATION

. . . But I conceive that education for the statesman should embrace the whole wide world of mental enrichment, including literature, art and music, the 'wireless', the press and what is loosely called 'entertainment'. In this wide field I think the State is lamentably idle and unhelpful. It is absurd with one hand to distribute free education, and with the other to lay a punitive tax upon drama and concerts *and the takings of the B.B.C.* The Entertainments Tax (a duty of 20 per cent on receipts not profits[1]) is a barbarous relic of the Great War. It couples blindly the plays of Shakespeare and the exhibition of performing seals, the music of Beethoven and the racing of dogs. Admitting the imperfection of much public entertainment, I regard it as a tax upon knowledge and enlightenment, and the free communication of minds. I shall therefore press for its abolition. . . .[2]

The State, in my opinion should more actively encourage the arts and graces of life, by the assistance of such enterprises as a National Theatre[3] and Opera House[4] . . . the preservation of ancient buildings and national beauties[5] (which should not be left to accident and private charity) and ultimately, by the institution of a Ministry of Fine Arts.[6]

LIBERTY

. . . I am a firm believer in the good sense and robust control of the British people; and therefore, until the contrary is shown, I should prefer to trust and educate rather than restrict. But where, as upon the roads, liberty is abused, I support the firmest measures.

DIVORCE LAW

. . . If His Majesty's Government do not, as they should, accept the responsibility for this reform, I shall myself do what I can.[7]

TEMPERANCE

The time has come to overhaul the Licensing system.[8]

BETTING

The laws relating to betting are chaotic, hypocritical, and unjust . . . I believe that the State should treat Betting as it treats 'drink' – an irrepressible indulgence, which in excess is harmful, but since it cannot be stopped, may be kept within bounds by licence, control and taxation. But it is practically impossible to control or tax betting while a large proportion of it is illegal. All bookmakers, therefore, should be licensed and controlled[9] (in which event the evils of street betting would disappear) and the whole volume of betting be taxed . . .[10]

[1] Like the I.T.V. levy.
[2] Done.
[3] Done.
[4] Done.
[5] Done.
[6] Arts Council, Jennie Lee.
[7] Done.
[8] Done – in part.
[9] Done.
[10] Done.

LAW REVISION

Magna Carta declares: 'To no man will we sell justice . . .' but this should not mean, as it does for too many, that it is impossible to buy.*

The law of libel is full of uncertainty and illogicality and should be drastically reformed.†

The antiquated distinction between felony and misdemeanour should be abolished.‡

ROAD SAFETY AND QUIET

I was, I believe, the first writer to call attention, many years ago, to the slaughter on the roads, to demand the restoration of a speed limit, and the muting of horns . . . I was one of the first members of the Pedestrians' Association and the Anti-Noise League. I shall continue in these beneficent courses and continually deny the false god Speed.

THE MINES

I believe that private enterprise is, on the whole, the best machinery for distributing wealth and getting things done; but I am not, like the Socialists, the slave of dogma. The mines may be a special case, as the miners are without doubt a specially deserving class of workers in a specially dangerous and important industry. If the mine-owners are unable, or unwilling, so to conduct their industry that the miners can enjoy good wages, I am willing to vote for nationalization.§

CAPITALISM AND THE SOCIALIST

. . . They tell us that Capitalism is doomed: Karl Marx, I believe, made the same announcement. He may still be right: but the old clock ticks on . . .

We should be able to think of unemployment as a triumph of capitalism – the increase of leisure . . . In principle, there is much to be said for Labour's formula of 'Work or Maintenance': and in practice something like this may come.¶

'We shall not produce equality by turning everything upside down.'

(Mr Christopher Mayhew, M.P. – Labour – in a book called *Party Games* (Hutchinson, 1969): 'We must cease hoping that individuals who are unequal in intelligence and ability can be equals in power or wealth, or that envy can be eliminated by eliminating class.')

But I suspect the fatal logic of the Socialists and should not hold myself committed to the nationalization of everything . . . My reason, such as it is, rebels when I am asked to believe that after thousands of years of a not wholly fruitless civilization not merely a new but the best and only way of managing this complicated world has been revealed to my old football captain, Sir Stafford Cripps.

(Mr Christopher Mayhew, 1969: 'Many of us hoped nationalization

* Legal Aid – Done.
† Done.
‡ Done.
§ I did.
¶ Done.

would foster a new climate in society. This has not happened. It has failed
to improve labour relations . . . Centralization and monopoly normally
produce inefficiency and complacency . . . What was once the mainstay
of our Socialist faith has vanished . . . Step by step our ideological belief
in planning the economy ebbed away.')

(8) FINANCE, TRADE, EMPLOYMENT etc.
I shall press for the restoration of our inland waterways and canals* and
for an inquiry into the important proposal to dam the Thames and
secure for London a tideless river.†

(9) AGRICULTURE
I know nothing about Agriculture
  (This declaration, I believe, won me many votes, but it was not inserted
with any artful intention. It was a simple statement of fact.)

(10) WAR AND PEACE
I am for Peace with Honour, but not war without Armaments . . . (see
Baldwin, page 299).

But I blush a little when I see what wild head-lines and comments
my modest programme produced when it came to action. My friends
of the Press, on the whole, stood nobly by their lone battling brother,
and gave him perhaps more attention than he deserved.

A. P. HERBERT M.P. SHOCKS THE DIE-HARDS
He's Going To Travel to the House in his Barge
Daily Mirror

HERBERT TWITS BALDWIN
New York Times

'Members are not a little shocked by the terms of Mr A. P. Herbert's
Bill to amend the laws concerning public refreshment . . . There is really
no place in the House of Commons for the professional humourist as
such, particularly when his constituency is Oxford University.'

Spectator

Quite right: the Bill was a joke. But what it said was serious, that
our Licensing Laws should be more like those of France.

'PLAYBOY' TAUNT TO M.P. A. P. HERBERT
Lady Astor's Duel in Drink Battle.

A.P.H. HITS BACK
On occasion sparks flew. Mr Rhys Davies' attacks on Mr. A. P. Herbert
as a man unworthy to represent a university brought a vehement reply
from the victim.

* Done.
† Done.

Mr Herbert retorted that his election address revealed all for which he stood, that Oxford had elected him on that address, and if he wanted any advice from Mr Rhys Davies he would ask him for it.

A.P.H. IN A SCENE WITH CHANCELLOR
Daily Sketch

MR HERBERT ANGRY
(*Civil List Pensions*).

MR A. P. HERBERT
'A PLAGUE ON BOTH YOUR BLOUSES'
The Times

A debate on Black Shirt meetings.

M.P'S ASTOUNDED BY 'A.P.H.' SPEECH
One of the most amazing speeches the House of Commons has heard for years.

The Population (Statistics) Bill.

DID MR A. P. HERBERT GO TOO FAR?
Many members thought that it was too frank; others considered that it had achieved its purpose of killing the Bill by ridicule.
The Times

HANSARD BEST-SELLER
Tuesday's issue of Hansard . . . has been sold out and a fresh edition is being rushed to meet the unprecedented demand.
Daily Mail

TOPSY HERBERT M.P.
Truth

Sir Kingsley Wood, Home Secretary, did me the honour to invite me (a mere new Member) to his room and ask me if I approved his amendments to the Bill, which the new member graciously did. But the fuss went on, and at last I replied to a charge of 'questionable levity' in *The Times*:

Sir – When anyone is accused of levity I suspect that he is right: for it means that the other side has little else to say. And, as a rule, they are confusing heaviness with weight.

In your leading article headed 'A Hidden Peril' you speak not only of 'questionable levity' but of misrepresentation and distortion in the debate on the Population (Statistics) Bill. You then repeat, however, with approval, all the main objections which the alleged misrepresenters made to the form and substance of the Bill, and you record with satisfaction that their arguments (which were much more than mere Committee points) are now likely to prevail with the Government.

But you yourself said nothing about those grave objections in your

{ 191 }

leading article last Monday: and I presume that you had not detected them. We did. The Government had had fair notice of them (three or four weeks) but, misled by persons unknown, had shown no sign of yielding, except on a single point.

In these circumstances the House of Commons then did its principal duty, which is to influence the decisions of the Executive by the weapon of debate, by the statement of argument and common sense, by frank and forcible speech, and, certainly, by ridicule or, if you will, levity. It is nobody's business which weapons we choose, so long as we do our job; and for the manner in which members of all parties did their job that day the House of Commons, I think, has earned no lectures from anyone. Indeed, sir, if I did not love your great paper so well, I should be tempted to suggest that you had committed a breach of privilege by giving a 'false and perverted' account of our proceedings.

As for 'questionable levity', may I add this? If there were more plain language there would be less bad legislation. . . . all these woolly words conceal the truth.

I am, Sir, your servant, but, regretfully, not so obedient as usual.

A. P. Herbert.

The big joke is, of course, that at that time the Whitehall experts were terrified of a fatal *decline* in the population.

MR HERBERT'S CRUSADE
NEED OF LIBEL LAW REFORM

MR HERBERT EXPLAINS HIS BETS BILL
'PAVING THE WAY FOR TAX COLLECTION'

THAMES DAM
Demand In Commons For Inquiry
News Chronicle, 1937

BILL TO CHECK BETTING ABUSES
MR HERBERT PROPOSES REGISTRATION OF BOOKMAKERS

REVERSE FOR MR HERBERT'S BETTING BILL
COMMONS COUNTED OUT
BETTING A NATIONAL INTOXICATION
Mr. A. P. Herbert

MR A. P. HERBERT AND THE AEROPLANE
(My attack on 'Uncivil Aviation' and my Bill to prohibit Air Advertisements. The Government did so later.)

CHURCHILL 'OUTWITTED' BY A. P. HERBERT
LAUGHTER KILLS NEW SANDYS DEBATE

MR CHURCHILL ANGERED
SATIRICAL SPEECH BY MR HERBERT

A.P.H. AND MR CHURCHILL 'STILL FRIENDS'
I was very sad about this: but he forgave me.

'UNCIVIL' AVIATION
Mr. A. P. Herbert's Bill
TO BAN AIR ADVERTISING

BELIEVES HE WAS WRONG
A.P.H's Second Thoughts About Munich

SUPPORT FOR PREMIER

Confessing that he was 'a wobbler' and one of those who had urged a 'stronger line', he says: 'Today, knowing more, and having heard the debates, I think I was wrong.'

ABSURDITIES OF THE LAW OF LIBEL
MR. A. P. HERBERT AMUSES THE HOUSE

MR A. P. HERBERT
'Oxford Group Title Resented'

M.P'S NERVOUS
THE QUEEN SAT LISTENING

Quietly, without pomp or ceremony, the Queen went to Parliament yesterday. It is believed to have been the first time that the Consort of a reigning King has watched 'the faithful Commons' at work . . .

One could perhaps note a trace of nervousness in Mr A. P. Herbert and Mr Walter Elliot, two of the Speakers whom the Queen heard.

29 March 1939.

This was my Bill, which I asked leave to present under the Ten Minutes' Rule, to restore to the L.C.C. the power to provide a passenger service on the Thames – my 'water bus'. Leave was granted, by 174 votes to 132. Nothing happened. Nothing has happened since. But the G.L.C. are now taking real interest in the river – and who knows?

Note the date – 29 March 1939. I never allowed the war-talk to divert me from my small causes. 'Do that' I used to say 'and Hitler has won.'

A.P.H. ISSUES A DARTS CHALLENGE
By *Daily Mail* Reporter

The lovable, the inimitable A. P. Herbert is raising the banner of Personal Freedom and Liberty once again.

He is asking Sir Samuel Hoare, Secretary of State for Home Affairs, this doughty question:

Has the Home Secretary's attention been drawn to the pronouncements of certain licensing Benches against the playing of darts and other innocent and skilful games on licensed premises; what is the statutory authority by which licensing justices are able to veto such activities, and will he draw the attention of all licensing Benches to the Report of the Royal Commission on Licensing 1929–31, which found that games and music and the like have a definite value as a distraction from the mere business of drinking, and expressed the hope that steps would be taken to secure the discontinuance of any policy of discouragement of lawful games on licensed premises.

It is a great mistake to be stampeded away from good small causes because they are not as important as the fashionable Big Thing of the day. It is this habit of thought among statesmen, and aspiring politicians, that causes the neglect of so many good small causes. When I went in divorce-law was a triviality. The students are always making this mistake. Instead of trying to stop Vietnam (which nobody in England can do) why don't they come out strong for the authors in the libraries affair? This is in their department.

THE 'OXFORD GROUP'
MR HERBERT REBUKED

MR OLIVER STANLEY: I have decided to grant to the association a licence under Section 18 of the Companies Act, 1929, to be registered by the name 'Oxford Group' . . . I am informed that the promoters propose to include in the Articles of Association a statement that the group has no official connexion with Oxford University or with the Oxford Society.

MR HERBERT: Is that not a final exhibition of the entire dishonesty of these canting cheats (Cries of 'Oh!').

MR SPEAKER: The Hon. Member must not talk of people in that way. It is only likely to lead to trouble. ('Hear, hear.')

MR HERBERT: I am looking for trouble.

'Double, double, toil and trouble.' One was always worrying about something – often in trouble, often meeting defeat, often doing the wrong thing. Why on earth do sensible men compete for this occupation?

An old hand who loved the place said to me once: 'The House of Commons is a disease.' I should not put it like that, but I know what he meant. There is something there that conquers a man and captures him: and once it has got him it never lets go. I reject that easy picture, 'the best club in London', for it is too much concerned with fleshly comfort (though companionship, of course, is present in both places). What I am thinking of is something deep in the mind and spirit of the Member, something much more powerful than the proper respect and deference that any good man feels for his beautiful club. He has only to walk the clattering stones from the Smoking Room to the Chamber to find himself in a place where history has been happening for hundreds of years, and damn it, where history may happen *tonight* – and even he may become part of history too. It would be very easy for him to pass into history, tonight: he has only to march into that Chamber and do some outrageous thing, carry off the Mace (this has been done), stand by the Table and insult the Speaker: or merely lounge at the Bar and smoke a pipe. He will not do any of these things, he will not think of them, because it would be like doing something outrageous in a cathedral. That, briefly, for me, is why the House of Commons is something more than 'the best club in London'. This feeling, I swear, is not confined to the Members: it fills and fires all those friendly policemen, the dignified Messengers in their chains, the waiters, the girls at the bar. They are not mere club servants – they are House of Commons men and women.

So I was sad when I was abolished and had to go. I missed it, I miss it still. I should not like to have to go there every day: I am not itching to make speeches, but I often wish I had the right, when my subjects come up – or do not come up. I do not miss the Chamber much but I hope my ghost will walk the Smoking Room. It is not, I gather, quite what it was, but in those days it was the best spot in the Palace, and, on occasion, the most important room in the world. All the best Prime Ministers used it. Did not this humble person drink there, and even argue, with Baldwin, Lloyd George, Churchill and Attlee, with Austen Chamberlain and Eddy Winterton, Anthony Eden, Duff Cooper and Bobbity Cranborne (Lord Salisbury now), the twin witty Olivers, Stanley and Lyttelton, Bevin and Bevan, John Simon, Jowitt, and Donald Somervell, three great lawyers, and judges later? All the warm full-blooded men went there, and only the foolish laughed at the place. Almost everything said was 'shop', touching in some way the business of governing men. Here you could hear gossip that could shake the world, send Fleet Street into a fever, if it got out. But it was penned in by a stern unwritten tradition. Collins and White, the two faithful waiters who saw us through the war, must have heard secrets worth a fortune or two. They never got out. Here you could hear the first whispers of big shifts of opinion, plots, cabals, rebellions, that might end in the fall of Ministers or Governments. Here you could pursue your own little plans, suck the brains of the old on strategy and tactics and procedure, and seek their signatures to your amendment or motion. Here the hot enemies of the Chamber had a drink and were friends again. Here you could see Ministers of the Crown, who had just, in the Lobbies, defeated Churchill by enormous figures, sitting respectfully about him while he lectured them upon the folly of their ways. Here, on the other hand, when feeling was high among the Parties, you might see little pools of oil and vinegar, small hostile groups who muttered bitterly among themselves and threw dark glances at each other. I never liked to hear: 'Hullo, A.P., you're in bad company,' when I was sitting with men of the 'wrong' party. A jest,

{ 195 }

no doubt, but it had a rancid flavour, springing from a sour mind. I liked the little groups of men who could relax and forget their creeds and factions, men of all parties, but citizens first and blessed with a broad humanity. Every man in that room, after all (except the University Members) had been through the same sort of hell to get there, many times perhaps, and this alone, as a rule, made respectful brothers of them. The tales they told were never partisan or personal slights, but part of the common store of Parliament men, memorable jests and retorts and orations. I like to think that I may have contributed one or two small memories to that common store: and, whatever you may think of 'the politicians', I am proud that for fifteen years I was one of 'the faithful Commons'.

§11§

BATTLES ABOUT BOOKS

PRAY do not avert your eyes if I speak of Committees, Sections, Clauses, Amendments and so on. The tales in this chapter are as full of incident, effort, action and suspense as the climbing of Everest.

A man is fortunate to be a writer: but that is no reason why he should be knocked about. We envy the swallow but we do not shoot him down. I give thanks every day that this is the state of life to which it has pleased God to call me. I have proclaimed in public my respectful compassion for the man who handles my humble account at the bank. He goes home weary at the end of the day, and his wife says: 'Had a good day, dear?' What can he say but: 'It was just like all the other days – the Herbert overdraft is up again.' But a good man of my craft can say: 'Today all went well. I really felt inspired. I wrote 2,000 words of the novel – I got past that difficult bit. My Boy met Girl.' Or: 'I wrote a poem that will make them laugh.' Or it may be: 'Today, my dear, I finished' (or, more likely, 'I began') 'my masterpiece.' We all, now and then, wallow in such illusions.

I never have to catch the 8.14: and if I catch the 9.15 it is not for my profession but for a public duty, the Thames Conservancy or some damned Conference. I can sit down after breakfast and work at what I will, in the way I will (the only snag is that, unlike most men, I must provide my own raw material). I can work, if my back aches, in a deep armchair, I can work all the week-end, on holiday, in a hotel lounge, on the promenade deck. I am my master, and, though strict, a kind one.

Beyond all these material advantages we all feel, I think, though we do not talk about it, a spiritual satisfaction in our chosen craft, whether we are successful or not. 'We are the music-makers.' We seek at least to be creators; it is our purpose, or hope, to spread light, learning, or laughter, to make the people think, or smile or cry: and so we see ourselves as proud but humble servants of the people.

So we are not rapacious: nor do we claim that any man who calls himself a writer has a right to riches. Indeed, any independent author who makes a living – and there are not many – is surprised and grateful. (I mean by 'independent' the man who lives by his books, without recourse to journalism, the theatre or the world of radio.) But we do feel that in many ways the community takes advantage of our decent feelings, and unfairly uses us.

The great Lord Curzon, in a debate in the House of Lords in 1911, said: 'The trash of one generation is sometimes the treasure of another.' In other words, from a multitude of small scribblers may emerge great Literature. How they would laugh if we employed that plea! Yet it seems to be at the back of the community's mind. Our products – books – are so important that they must be distributed as cheaply as possible, by one statute for nothing: but the producers, authors and publishers, do not matter at all. During one of the innumerable correspondences about the libraries battle a lady wrote to the *Evening Standard*: 'Anyhow, writers shouldn't do too well out of their books: they need to be kept hungry to write more. What good book was ever written on a full stomach?'

I did not take this too seriously, but it seems, alas, to be the attitude of the State

The crazy Selective Employment Tax divided the people into the Sheep and the Goats – the Sheep being manufacturers, especially exporters, the Goats being those engaged in mere 'services'. The Bible of the tax was the blue book *Standard Industrial Classification*. Here all publishers were classed as 'manufacturers', but in the original Bill all were to have been subject to S.E.T. A special amendment, in the House of Lords, exempted newspaper-publishers: but for two years the book-publishers had to pay. This was a monstrous thing: not only are they indubitably manufacturers, but they are, I think, fourth on 'the exporters' roll – they export nearly 50 per cent of their product.* To his credit, Mr Jenkins put this right in the 1969 Finance Act. (For some reason, this good act of repentance was never mentioned in the papers. Perhaps it was feared that any concession to publishers would raise a storm.)

But authors? 'Authors, artists, composers and playwrights' are classified in the blue book as 'services'. They come after 'veterinary surgeons' and not long before 'bookmakers'. So if an author employs a lady secretary he must now pay 24*s*. a week for his crime, the idea being that he will send her off into more productive employment, coal-mining, or the manufacture of 'one-armed bandits'. But authors, artists, and composers are actually manufacturers – they make things with their hands: and an author at least is the one foundation of a flourishing export trade (we also, by the way, patriotically accept lower royalties on books exported). Henry Moore, I guess, must employ at least one

---

* British publishers' turnover in 1968 was £132,724,617 consisting of £73,903,197 in the home market, and £58,821,420 from exports. (Publishers' Association.)

burly man to handle his heavy and highly exportable pieces: if he does, he pays 49*s.* per man, per week.

In a letter to *The Times* (11 July 1968) in which, at the publishers' request, I was glad to set out their case for exemption, I promised not to press the point about authors. I don't suppose there are many authors who can afford a permanent secretary. It would raise a cheer in Grub Street if our status was raised. But then, if doctors are penalized as unproductive 'services' why should we complain? *What* a fiendish, imbecile tax!

But how the State loves books – and the readers (though not the writers) of books! It cannot do too much for them. What a grand and gallant fuss the House of Commons made about books in July and August 1940! It was a historic fuss and I beg to commend it to honourable Members today. The genial but granitic Sir Kingsley Wood, introducing the second edition of the new Purchase Tax (another of those 'purely war-time' taxes – Ha!), said that it would be levied at the rate of 33⅓ per cent on newspapers and periodicals, and books. (The revenue expected was, from newspapers and periodicals between £3,250,000 and £3,500,000, and from books between £1,000,000 and £1,750,000 – Hansard, 1 August 1940: col. 413.)

The newspapers, I need hardly say, were promised exemption almost immediately, but Sir Kingsley stuck his chin out and his toes in about books. The purchase tax on books would remain. (Exactly the same pattern, observe, as Mr Jenkins and the Selective Employment Tax.) The story went that he said to someone: 'I'll show them! I'm going to tell them they're lucky I didn't put books at the higher rate' (66⅔ per cent). The Archbishop of Canterbury led a formidable deputation, but the Chancellor was not impressed. I was down the river, and could not attend that, but from Hole Haven I fired off a letter to *The Times*. (In the *Water Gipsy*'s log I read: 11.15 Searchlights. Wrote letter to *Times* about purchase tax and books. Blowing hard from the North-West. Air Raid Warning. White.) This was a proper arena for University Members, and Kenneth Lindsay, for one, did much more than I did: but I did, I believe, make the first attack in the House, in the general Budget debate, on 25 July (we were in dock).

Sir George Broadbridge (City of London) had said: 'With regard to books and all the fuss that has been made about the suggested tax, I can see nothing to which to take exception. Generally speaking, *reading is a hobby*. Much of the business in books, in any event, is done with libraries. Apart from books and reading, I have a hobby, which is either golf or tennis. Every time I play I have to pay a substantial sum for the pleasure of doing it. If I have to pay for my hobby, surely book readers can pay something for theirs.'*

* Hansard 25 July 1940. Vol. 363, Col. 1025

I 'got in' or 'caught the eye' about an hour later, and among a lot of other things I said:*

I hope that the relations of Oxford and the City of London will always continue to be friendly, but when I hear the representative of the City of London referring to a tax on books, the 'machine-tools of education', as someone has said, of the great craft of literature, the great profession of learning, as a tax upon a mere 'hobby', to be compared with golf, then that is a mind with which I can make no contact, and I do not propose to try. I address myself, with much more confidence, to the Chancellor of the Exchequer. Great qualities, such as geniality and tact, have carried the Right Hon. Gentleman from one office to another, with the good will of all and the hopes of many, as you may see some cheery reveller staggering from pub to pub, emerging from each with such a radiant smile that no one has the heart to stop his passage to the next. But in this affair, without intention I am sure, he has added insult to injury.

After receiving a deputation of the highest authority, led by the Archbishop of Canterbury (Temple) and including men of the greatest light and learning, he dismissed the whole thing as if it were merely a question of 'the publishing trade' having to suffer the same as other trades. There is much more to it than that. . . .

I have been sent a copy of *The Bookseller*, on the front page of which is written:

'*Books are part of the cause for which we fight* – Dear Mr Segrave, I am very glad to know that the list of books to be published here during the summer and autumn is, as usual, going out this year to carry the reminder that freedom to write and read is part of the cause for which the British Commonwealth and Empire fights – Duff Cooper (Minister for Information).'

Which is the right horse here? I am anxious to find out what is in those woolly heads. Does the Right Hon. Gentleman desire, or does he not desire, in his extraordinary language, to '*limit the consumption*' of domestic hollow-ware, brushes, brooms and, as he said finally with that charming smile, books? Does he really desire to 'limit the consumption' of Bibles and Prayer Books? I suppose I can get an answer to that. If he does, there is still a niche in that lobby, and he may go down to history as the first Chancellor of the Exchequer to put a tax on the Word of God . . .

I was reminding the Right Hon. Gentleman just now of a book that I have here, with which I hope the Treasury officials will try to become acquainted, because they seem to have forgotten, if they ever knew, that it is only seventy or eighty years since the great fight against the Taxes on Knowledge was fought and won in this House. They were taxes on the free communication of minds, on the movement of thought and on the free expression of opinion. These taxes were finally wiped out between 1850 and 1870, and the principle was thus established that we would not

* Col. 1040.

put any taxes on the things of the mind. That principle has stood firmly against every attack since then, and has survived two major wars. It has remained for the Right Hon. Gentleman, the Member for West Woolwich (Sir Kingsley Wood) to break it down.

It is a sad and shocking thing that at this time in this titanic conflict, when we are saying and saying truly, that there are arrayed, on one side the spirit of force, and on the other the forces of the Spirit, we should have sunk so low as to be seeking to put a tax upon, and to treat all learning and enlightened literature in the same way as we should treat brooms or something which is kept under the bed.* The Right Hon. Gentleman had a great opportunity. He might have said: 'However many Hitlers are at the door, however many dangers and difficulties confront us, we are not so down and out and so poor in resources that for the sake of £500,000 which is my estimate of the yield of this miserable tax, we are going to do this barbarous thing . . .

Sir Kingsley, later, said: 'I must say that I feel that a good deal of the sound and fury has been unjustifiable.' He may have had my rather brassy peroration in mind:

Well may the shades of Milton, of Caxton, of Sheridan and of Charles Dickens, and of those brave men who in the last century fought and won the principle of free enlightenment, groan in their honoured graves today to think that that lamp which they hung on the walls of Westminster has been clumsily torn down at last by a Chancellor of the Exchequer who, at this hour of civilization, sees no important distinction between boots and books.

Viscount Wolmer (Aldershot) thought that all this was rather narrow – and even selfish, though I had carefully explained that I was writing no more books since the war: 'The consumption of books must be curtailed just as much as the consumption of other things which are necessary to human life as we understand it.'†

The Minister who replied to the Debate (Captain Crookshank) refused to answer my oration.

But something did move Sir Kingsley, I know not what. Nothing was said on the Second Reading of the Finance (No. 2) Bill on 4 August. In these days, by the way, the House does not sit one day into August if it can possibly help it. Note that in that dark and dangerous year the House sat till 22 August. Hitler had the Channel Ports, the Battle of Britain was beginning, mutters about 'Invasion' were to be heard, enemy aircraft had nibbled at the London Docks. Members might well have said: 'This is not the time to bother ourselves about a small purchase tax on books.' But they did. Late in the evening of

* Books and 'domestic hollow-ware' were in the same list.
† Cols. 1047–8.

13 August 1940 they reached an amendment put down by a Labour front bencher, Mr Isaacs (Southwark, North) a printer (later, Minister of Labour). But he had had a 'hint' from Sir Kingsley, and cut short a good speech.* 'Those interested in education are anxious that books should be free of tax. We want all literature free of tax. We have the wireless, but sometimes we are glad to get away from it.'

Sir Kingsley then gave way, but not with his customary good grace. First, the newspapers – 'though I cannot accept the suggestion that the printed word should necessarily be free from taxation.' Then books – 'If the time comes when we have. to choose between money for books, and money for such despised articles as boots, or between magazines and milk, then we shall have to choose boots and milk, and with all due respect to some of my hon. Friends, that choice will be right . . . I think that, on the whole, I should agree that books as well as newspapers, should be exempt from the tax – *at least for the present.*'

Alas, how grudging! Not the smallest concession to principle!

But the Commons won a great victory that day, and long-haired Young who have nothing to say for 'Parliament and all that jazz' should be reminded that out for Parliament's brave stand their books, their slim volumes of verse, would have been paying Purchase Tax at 33⅓ per cent – 6s. 8d. in the £ for the last thirty years.

How the State loves books! Consider Section 15 of the Copyright Act 1911. Here is an entertaining but shocking piece of history of which few know anything. Here is an imposition on the world of books which no other craft or trade would tolerate. Someone described it as the oldest living controversy.

> 15 (1) The publisher of every book published [including new editions] in the United Kingdom shall within one month of the publication deliver, *at his own expense* [this includes packing, postage etc.] a copy of the book to the trustees of the British Museum, who shall give a written receipt for it.

Subsection (1) we do not mind

> (2) He shall also, if written demand is made within twelve months . . . deliver a copy to the Bodleian Library, Oxford, the University Library, Cambridge, the Library of the Faculty of Advocates at Edinburgh and the Library of Trinity College, Dublin and . . . the National Library of Wales.

[Subsection (6) provided penalties:]

> If a publisher fails to comply with this section he shall be liable on a summary conviction to a fine not exceeding five pounds and the value of the book, and the fine shall be paid to the trustees or authority to whom the book ought to have been delivered.

* Col. 364, Col. 747.

In 1968 this Section cost the publishers about £275,000. Authors, naturally, receive no royalties on books bestowed, and they may be said to lose about £45,000.

You may remember what a fuss and fury there was in 1968 against the chance of honest trade unionists finding themselves in the dock for wildcat strikes in breach of contract or contrary to law – 'the penal clauses'. The honest trade unionist in the end was spared this indignity. But, here, behold, a publisher may be taken to Bow Street for the criminal offence of failing to give – *give* – his property away.

This thing goes back to an Act of 1775 and even further. Sir Thomas Bodley, of Oxford, it seems, in 1616 secured a grant from the Stationers' Company of every work printed in the country. According to the Royal Commission of 1878 the other obligations dated from the time of Charles II and an Act of 1662. The Royal Commission, by the way, recommended that these exactions should come to an end, except so far as they related to the British Museum. No one paid the slightest attention. The 1911 section did not become law without protest from authors and publishers, and there were three eloquent and informative debates in the House of Lords. All the great guns were on parade and discharged with dignity. See, for example, Volume X (Hansard, Lords, Column 196):

The Archbishop of Canterbury: My Lords, I stand before your Lordships in an unwonted capacity, as a member of the Board of Trade. I do not know who the other members are, or whether they ever meet.

(A constitutional curiosity. The 'Board' is one of the old committees of the Privy Council which developed into Government Departments. It still exists, on paper, I believe, but like the Archbishop, I have forgotten who the other distinguished members are.)

The Royal Commission of 1878 was mentioned in the debate, but no noble Lord went so far as to suggest that its advice should be followed. Lord Gorell, champion of the book-producers, merely, and mildly, asked that (except for the British Museum) there should be some control or some check upon the right to demand every book published. (Books for the University of Wales, which the 1911 Act added to the Free List, may be limited by Board of Trade regulations.)

Lord Cromer quoted a protesting article written by the poet Southey in 1819: 'The publishers were told that the public bodies would exercise their claims mildly and liberally, that they would take lists and only call for such books as they absolutely wanted, that their main object was to *establish* their right, but trust them, and it shall be seen how they use the power. See, indeed, how they use it!'

'In the course of time,' said Lord Cromer, ninety-two years later, 'it has become the practice . . . to apply for a copy of every book published, including a vast mass of printed matter which cannot possibly be of any use to them, and much that is not really necessary or desirable for the libraries.' (Col. 178.)

The great Lord Haldane said: 'Let them, by all means, have all the books they think suitable, but do not let them appoint *a general agent* to sit in London and call for every book that appears in the publishers' catalogue, irrespective of whether the book is really a book which is useful to the library or not.'

But exactly the same system prevails today, a single agent acts – and demands everything – for all the five libraries.

Earl Curzon of Kedleston, Chancellor of Oxford University, powerfully repelled this talk. How was a librarian to judge between one book and another? In that memorable phrase, *'The trash of one generation is sometimes the treasure of another.'* Had not the Cambridge University Library in the year 1818 'rejected, presumably as trash . . . Beethoven's Sonata for violin, Miss Austen's *Emma*, Byron's *Siege of Corinth*, Shelley's *Alastor*, and Scott's *Antiquary'*?

It was a splendid, stately, battle.

Lord Cromer mentioned the expensive, limited editions which publishers were compelled to give away:

'the *Bridgewater Gallery* . . . the cost price of which was fifty guineas . . . The publishers are making a present of goods which they value at two hundred and fifty guineas, and I think it is asking a good deal of them.'

He was very severe about:

'*The Story of Emma, Lady Hamilton*, published at thirty guineas . . . This work consists of a story of Lady Hamilton's youth and contains reproductions in photogravure of a number of those celebrated pictures of Romney representing this remarkable lady as Circe, Euphrosyne, the Nun, St Cecilia, the Spinster, and several times as a Bacchante. I can hardly conceive a work of a less academic character or one less necessary for the tuition, instruction, and edification either of the authorities at the Universities, or of those students who flood for instruction and study to the Bodleian Library.'

But Lord Curzon vigorously replied:

'The noble Earl . . . spoke of the Bodleian Library as if it were purely an academic institution existing solely for the instruction of Dons and undergraduates. He even put the case of the history of Lady Hamilton and asked what was the good of giving a book of that sort to the Bodleian Library. It would, he said, hardly appeal to the Dons – about which I am not at all certain – and it ought not to appeal to the undergraduates, about which I am even less sure. But . . . the Bodleian is more than an academic institution. It is . . . a great national institution, one of the principal repositories of literature in the country.' (Col. 184.)

He continued, still insisting on the Bodleian's right to have *all* the books, trash or treasure:

'Is it wise, even admitting the special character of the British Museum, that you should treat that as the only great national repository of published books in this country? Supposing some great conflagration were to occur and the British Museum were to be wrecked and its contents destroyed, what a lamentable thing it would be if there were no other institution to which to turn than that which had unfortunately been lost.'

'Fair enough,' as they say. We simply ask why such 'national institutions' should be sustained, or, at least, fed and comforted, by the publishers, and to a much lesser extent, the authors. Our position, exactly. I wonder how Messrs. Rolls-Royce would care to give (compulsorily) six of all their latest models to the State for the instruction of the Young – or even for the replenishment of the British Motor Museum.

The indomitable Curzon said: 'I do not think it is anything more than a slight burden.' But in 1911 perhaps 7,000 books were published. In 1968 21,398 books were published and the average price was 42s. 7d. As production and prices continue to rise so will the 'slight' burden on the publishers.

So far the case for the Section can be heard with good humour. But Lord Curzon next disgorged an argument which entitles us to anger and derision:

'The question is whether it is a burden that they can legitimately be ordered to bear. I think it is for these reasons. In the first place, publishers as a body gain enormously by the privileges (?) conceded to them in the Copyright Act . . . and those privileges are really enhanced under this Bill. Publishers on the whole, and authors with them, are placed in a better position. It is, therefore, not unreasonable to ask that they should make some return to the public for the privileges that they enjoy.' (Col. 185.)

If I had a goat this speech would get it.

The same reply was heard in Whitehall during the passing of the Copyright Act of 1956. 'We are giving you something in this Bill. Why make a fuss about the free books?'

It may be tried again, so let us stamp on it now. The argument is impudent. Everyone, not publishers only, should be duly grateful to Parliament for the laws of copyright, which are directed to the general good: but they do not bestow 'privileges' on anyone (except the six great Libraries). The law provides 'protection' (to use Lord Haldane's word) for all forms of property: but works of art, by their nature, are especially vulnerable to the thief and the cheat and require protection of a special kind. No tribute, I believe, is demanded of scientific inventors who 'enjoy the privileges' of patent law. There have been special statutes concerned with 'poaching', but the grateful landlords were not, and are not, required to send thank-offerings of game, in perpetuity, to the Exchequer.

But then Lord Curzon, leaping like some nimble chamois from one peak of effrontery to another, said:

'If I were a publisher I would rather be disposed to welcome the *gratuitous form of advertisement* for important books which I thus obtained.' (Col. 185.)

God bless my soul! This was the cry of the infant B.B.C., and is now the cry of the Public Libraries. 'Not much cash, old boy – but look at the publicity!' I wonder what the motor manufacturers would say if they were told: 'You will all be compelled by law to give six of each new model to the State. But cheer up! Think of the advertisement!'

In 1961 Mr Nigel Fisher, M.P., took the matter up, in vain.

On 11 July, in reply to a supplementary question in which Mr Fisher 'asked whether the cost to the authors and publishers is about £100,000 per annum', Mr Maudling, for the Board of Trade, said:

'I think that my hon. Friend is possibly over-estimating the burden on the publishers.' (Not at all – it is now, as I have said, about £275,000.) 'In 1952 the Copyright Committee said: "In view of the long-standing nature of the privilege and the obligation and what we feel to be the comparatively slight burden it creates for the publishing trade as a whole in relation to their turnover (!) it did not recommend the discontinuance of the custom."' (But it's not a custom – it's a law.) 'I think,' said Mr Maudling, 'that on the whole I would agree with that.'

So Whitehall stands, unashamed, where it did. The Royal Commission has been ignored for nearly 100 years: we are expected to genuflect to some damned Departmental Committee. But we may observe, perhaps, (1) that if the burden on the publishing trade is comparatively slight it would be unnoticeably infinitesimal as an item in the expenditure of the State, (2) whatever may be thought of the dimensions of the 'burden' we are shocked by the fact that since the Royal Commission of 1878 no official body has admitted the iniquity of the principle.

We are in this affair properly constructive. Years ago I drafted a Bill, which has been approved by the Society of Authors and the Publishers' Association. (1) It preserves the principle of free books for the six Privileged Libraries, but transfers the cost to the State (Ministry of Education and Science): but (2) it extends the Free List to the twenty 'new' Universities (they need books perhaps more than the others) and any similar institution which Whitehall may add to the schedule: and (3) any money granted to them would be in lump sums so that they would not be compelled to take a lot of books they didn't want. I sent the Bill to various authorities and papers long ago. It is a good idea, and, I need hardly say, there has not been the slightest response from anyone.

There was a mirthful episode in 1937 when Eire became a Republic and broke away. The publishers inquired whether they were still expected to send free books to Trinity College, Dublin. Whitehall, I'm told, said it would be a 'cultural' gesture if they did – and, in fact, they still do, though the College is no longer in the Commonwealth. As an Irishman by birth I am glad about this, and Trinity College, I believe, is a faithful fort of the English tradition.

Authors are less affected directly, but everything that touches the publisher touches them, and we should, perhaps, protest more than we do. No individual author loses more than six royalties for each new book (or new edition); but the total loss of royalties must, I reckon, be about £40,000. (Authors and publishers between them receive about one-third of the purchase price of a book. If the total value of the free books is £275,000 we lose one-half of one-third of that.) This is no mean sum, and it would be a pleasing gesture if the State made over that sum to the Society of Authors.

But no, the State loves readers, not writers. One Minister, in 1961, had the cheek to say that the present arrangements 'need not penalize authors at all'! He meant that the publishers should add the cost of royalties to the cost of presenting, packing and dispatching the books. It has always been the custom to exclude from royalty payments books given away whether compulsorily to the privileged libraries, or voluntarily to newspapers for review or public purposes. No author would think of asking for a royalty for them.

Authors use the libraries themselves and are grateful. They have, like the publishers, a strong sense of service. But we favour too fair play and decent dealing. Too often, it seems to us, our gentle feelings are abused by the rulers, or taken too much for granted. This ancient business of the free books is a gross example.

No one, in these days, seems to get anything without making a nuisance of himself. Look at the teachers' unseemly triumph. We are not natural nuisance-makers and there are very few opportunities for nuisance. Here is one of them. One day, I hope, the united publishers will defy Section 15, refuse to deliver except to the British Museum. I at least shall be very happy to stand in the dock beside my publisher.

How the State loves books!

The Public Libraries Act 1892 said: 'No charge shall be made for admission to a library or museum . . . or in the case of a lending library, for use thereof by the inhabitants of the district . . .'*

And quite right too. For those were the days when the Public Library was intended for the education of the 'artisans of the towns and labourers of the villages'.

That Act was repealed by the Public Libraries and Museums Act 1964. But while the Bill was in Committee there appeared on the Order Paper of the House of Commons the following amendment:

Sir Edward Boyle
Clause 8, page 7, line 2, at end insert –
(3) A library may make a charge for the borrowing of *any article except* –
    (*a*) *a book*, journal, pamphlet or similar article, or
    (*b*) a reproduction made by photographic or other means of the whole or part of such an article.

Yes, but this was in 1964, when 70 per cent of the books borrowed were 'fiction', and rich ladies rolled up in their Jaguars and took away whole bundles of bright new books.

Sir Edward Boyle, by the way, was the Conservative Minister in charge of the Bill.

I wish to rub the nation's nose in it: I wish to leave behind me a fair but filthy record of the nation's neglect and meanness. So I must relate the history of Sir Edward Boyle's amendment.

In February 1959 was published the Report of the Roberts Committee, a Departmental Committee appointed by Lord Hailsham (Quintin Hogg) then Minister of Education, in 1957, to consider *the Structure of the Public Library Service in England and Wales*. In all its fifty-seven pages the authors and publishers, foundation of the Library Structure, were not mentioned. The publishers gave some written evidence, but the authors were not invited to testify at all. With the general business of administration we are not concerned, but we are deeply interested in the number of books bought and other matters which were much discussed.

In paragraph 118 the Report said:

'The free provision of books has from the beginning been the primary object of the public library service, and it is in our view, essential that this principle should be preserved.' They went on: 'We cannot subscribe to a discrimination between books and supplementary material. Such things as gramophone records serve the same purpose as books in that they are the media for the recording and communication of information and ideas and artistic experience.

* But it went on '. . . but the library authority, if they think fit, may grant the use of a lending library to persons not being inhabitants of the district, either gratuitously *or for payment*.'

They are a legitimate and valuable addition to the resources of a public library and to make charges for them would be, in our view, a retrograde step.'

Accordingly, they recommended that:

'No charge should be made to borrowers of books *or other material* except for (*a*) notification that a book or other material is available; (*b*) retention beyond a prescribed period.'

Here, I suggest, the Committee strayed from their brief – 'structure' and 'administrative arrangements'. But, having done so, they should certainly have called the authors before them. They were nearly all librarians, I believe, and some at least must have known that far back in 1951 Mr John Brophy had expressed the authors' discontent and suggested 'a penny a loan' as a merited compensation; and that the authors had been muttering and moaning ever since. Either they airily assumed that authors and publishers were perfectly content with the conditions on which their books were supplied to the libraries, or, knowing that they were not, they decided that our opinions and complaints did not matter.

Nor did the Ministry of Education ever consult us during the protracted preparation of their Bill. But their Bill was at least faithful to their Committee's Report. There was to be no charge for any borrowed material. It was the Minister himself, in the amendment I have already recorded, the famous Progressive Sir Edward Boyle, who took the 'retrograde step' his Department's Committee had so strongly deprecated. There can be charges for borrowing gramophone records, musical scores, pictures, catalogues, maps, charts, everything – excepting only books. At one of our deputations to him we questioned the logic of this, and reminded him of the Roberts Committee's view. He feebly replied that some Libraries were charging for gramophone records already and it seemed simpler to make it general. Sir Edward, I gather, is not greatly beloved in his Party but I have always understood that he was brilliant. In this affair the more I saw of him the less I thought of him.

On this point, by the way, the favourite retort of a few is 'But the libraries are *not* free. We pay for them through the rates. We have bought the books already. Why should we pay more to read them?'

There are two answers:

(*a*) A clause in Mr Aneurin Bevan's Local Government Act 1948 (which I supported by speech and vote) empowered local authorities to spend up to a 6*d*. rate on the arts and entertainment. (The Conservatives opposed it.) But though this was a Socialist measure it did not say that the entertainment was to be provided without charge to the ratepayer. You go to a municipal theatre, or concert, which you have paid for through the rates, but you must still pay for your ticket. All books, they rightly say, are educational in a way: so are all plays and concerts. You pay for the municipal swimming bath through the rates, but you must also pay a shilling (or whatever) for a swim. If you did not there would be a grand outcry from non-swimming rate-payers.

(*b*) The 'favourite retort' is not in fact true. The Registered Readers (regular users of the Library) are on average about 25 per cent of the population – sometimes much less. Take the great city of Leeds in 1961. The Registered Readers (85,564) were only *one-sixth* of the population (513,300). The income from the Library Rate (7·23) was £204,548: but roughly, the Registered Readers contributed only £34,091. The expenditure on books was £40,132: but the Registered Readers contributed only £6,688. So it is not true that they paid for the books they borrowed (4,007,078). *Five-sixths of them were paid for by non-reading rate-payers.*

Observe – *4,007,078* 'issues' – books borrowed and taken away. The library *bought* about 40,000 for £40,000. So that for every volume bought 100 volumes were borrowed. For the books borrowed authors and publishers received nothing. For the books bought they earned between them, say, £13,000. At a penny per issue they would have received something like £16,000 more.

Taking the same example, our final proposals set out in our Appeal to Parliament ('Libraries – Free For All?')* 1962, were as follows:

We have made no deductions for non-copyright works, old-age pensioners, or possible diminutions in the number of registered readers. But, subject to these, if the 85,564 registered readers contributed 7*s*. 6*d*. a year, as we propose, the yield would be about £32,000. After deducting £16,000 (1*d*. per issue) for Public Lending Right, there would remain £16,000 for improving the library service, buying more books, or staff salaries. All this without recourse to the rates – and in more 'efficient' cases there might be some relief for the rates. Further, though the principle of collective responsibility would remain, there would be a juster distribution between those who use the public library and those who do not. The Leeds registered readers are *one-sixth* of the population only!

It may be objected that some registered readers carry other inhabitants and provided them with books, on a single ticket. But even if each 'registered reader' supplied two other readers they would still amount to one-half only of the population. The other half may prefer the films, the radio, football, the theatre, to books – even 'fiction': they may even buy their books. But they carry five-sixths of the expense of the public library. Under our scheme the Registered Readers would contribute another £32,000, bringing their total contribution up to £66,000: it would still be only about *one-third* of the total expenditure.

* Institute of Economic Affairs – Hobart Paper 19.

(I cannot tell you on how many pages of anxious logarithmic sums all these assertions were founded.)

This is a classic chapter in the great Whitehall saga 'How Things Do Not Get Done', and I had better go back to the beginning. After ten years of trying to batter the obvious into the brains of Indifference and Illwill I find it hard to write with restraint – but I shall try.

The beginning, for me, was in the autumn of 1959. I had then had five years as Chairman of the Society of Authors' Committee on Obscene Publications. One of our Members was Roy Jenkins, M.P., who did brilliant work in the House and really made his mark over our Bill. In 1958 I did one of my mad things in this cause – Haddock in action. Our Bill was waiting to go into Standing Committee, and, after an unopposed second reading and a favourable verdict (80 per cent) from a Select Committee of the House, by all the rules it deserved to go. But on two – I think three – Friday afternoons Conservative back-benchers exercised their right to cry 'Object!' when the Bill's name was called and we were left in limbo. This is the kind of right by which Democracy may defend itself and Tyranny be defied: but it can be abused. In my very early days I had witnessed a comical example. I was sitting demurely in the Chamber at the beginning of a sitting when the Chairman was formally reading a list of Private Bills desiring a Second Reading. Private Bills are not the same as Private Members' Bills. The latter seek to alter the general law of the land: 'Private Bills' are concerned with local or company affairs. As a rule they go through to Committee without a word said in the House. But if there is some serious objection which the promoters of the Bill have failed to meet any Member may cry 'I object', and the Bill does not then and there get its Second Reading. Up in the Gallery the anxious 'Parliamentary agent' in charge of the Bill spots the objecting Member: he canters down, chases the man round the House, and at last says: 'Why are you objecting, and what can we do?' It may be a farmer objecting to the line of a new road. Some concession or compromise is promised, and next time the Bill goes through.

On this day the Hon. Member next to me was a mild-looking little man, but when the Chairman read 'Wigan Municipal Baths Bill' he cried 'Object!' with splendid vigour. I glanced at him admiringly, a man with a grievance, a man of action. Then came the 'West Middlesex (Improvements) Bill'. 'Object!' again the little fellow cried. 'South Metropolitan Gas Bill' – 'Object!' – 'University of Wessex (Extension) Bill' – 'Object!' – 'London Library Bill' – 'Object!' There were ten Bills, the little man objected to every one, and by the end his vigour seemed to be reinforced by venom. Astounded by this wholesale resentment for reform, I said: 'Sorry – I'm a new Member – but why did you do that?' 'Oh, well,' he said, 'you can't let all the bastards have it their own way.'

What he said to the ten Parliamentary agents, if they caught him, I cannot imagine.

It might be such frivolity that was holding up the Obscene Publications Bill: but we rather inclined to the view that there was a plot – a plot by high-minded Conservatives, who did not want to see the obscenity laws relaxed, to delay the Bill so long that it would have no time to go through the hoops of Private Members' Bill procedure. It was December already. We slightly suspected the Government. This may have been a myth. At all events, we took umbrage. There was a by-election approaching at East Harrow, and at one of our regular committee meetings I said: 'If they're not careful I shall stand as an Independent candidate at East Harrow.' This wild notion was applauded by the Committee, and once more I fell in at the deep end. The seat had been held by the Conservatives, but not, I think, by a large majority. The announcement of my intention caused a great flutter in the Conservative quarters. It was feared that I should split the vote. A Lord Lieutenant sent me an urgent appeal which was flattering, but, I thought, unconstitutional. A gentleman called Heath was Chief Government Whip and he, I was told, was in a great state about it. I can't think why; I did not flatter myself that I had the slightest chance of doing anything effective at the polls. But I went firmly ahead. I visited East Harrow, two or three times. I appointed an agent, Mr Simon Knott, a Liberal, who volunteered for the job. I also wrote a long Address, or 'Letter to the Electors' (more than 7,000 words): and I think it was good. It was called 'I OBJECT'; and it was gallantly printed and published by Max Reinhardt of the Bodley Head. On the back was: 'PRICE ONE SHILLING NET' and 'Two hundred and fifty numbered copies specially bound and signed by the author are available at one guinea each.' Unusual, I agree: but I had no Party funds behind me, and I might have needed the money.

In it I made my main purpose perfectly clear:

Obscene Publications Bill – Here I speak as the reluctant chairman of the Society of Authors Committee assembled in November 1954.

After four years of playing snakes and ladders with the Home Office I am heartily sick of the subject. But it has an important place in the pattern of freedom, and literature, and public morals. Do not suppose that the intention of this Bill is to give new licence to the lewd. On the contrary, it gives new powers to the authorities in the pursuit and punishment of the deliberate merchants of pornography (the new penalties may even be too severe). But its prime purpose was the protection of literature, of honest authors and publishers, from the uncertainty and injustice of the old Victorian law. The meanest burglar, for example, can stand up for himself in court; he can explain that he thought the house was on fire. Authors and publishers, whose only offence may have been an error of taste or judgement, are put in the dock, shut up in cells, and are not allowed to defend themselves: nor is anyone else.

The task of our Committee – and our principal champion, Mr Roy Jenkins, M.P., Labour – would have been difficult and dangerous enough if the Home Office had not blown hot and cold – and finally fallen asleep. At one time, when Mr E. S. Simon, Conservative, was Under-Secretary, we felt that we were collaborating with the Home Office. Twice we accepted amendments that they suggested. We got an unopposed Second Reading but were manœuvred into a Select Committee of the House of Commons, thus losing our place in the ordinary queue. The distinguished Select Committee laboured long and well and reported twelve months later. They accepted 80 per cent of our suggestions. That was on 20 March 1958, nearly nine months ago.

Since then the Home Office have not said a single word about their intentions. You may not care much about books, whether pure or pornographic. But you must agree that this is not the way in which the land should be governed or the laws be made.

On Friday 28 November 1958 when it was reasonably hoped at last to get this long-suffering Bill into a Standing Committee – for *another* bout of detailed examination – two or three Government supporters cried 'Object!' I should hate to think, as I have been told, that this was done by the contrivance of someone in the Government; but I am not concerned to argue about that. Any Member has a perfect right to cry 'I object!' if he thinks that after four years a Bill has not been sufficiently considered. But I too, a modest member of the great calling and craft of literature, have a right to cry 'I object!' as I am doing now.

In short, if Parliament as at present constituted was unwilling to reform the law, I wished to go in and see what I could do myself. This was just what I said about Divorce in my 1935 Election Address: 'If His Majesty's Government do not, as they should, accept the responsibility for this reform I shall myself do what I can.' Many a cause would have done better than it has if its champion had taken the same line. You may attract preliminary attention by marching about the streets or tying yourself to railings, but Parliament in this country is the institution that has the power, and that is where the reformer should make himself heard, if he can.

But I was sixty-eight, I did not really for my own sake want to go back to the Commons, and I had no desire to damage the Conservatives. So, privately, I let them know that if the obstruction to the Bill was ended I would withdraw from the by-election. Meanwhile Mr Knott began the business of distributing my Address. It worked. Mr Heath, I think, must have made some arrangements. When Parliament met again after the Christmas recess no hon. Member cried 'Object!'

and the Bill at last received a Second Reading 'on the nod', without a word. But for that I should certainly have gone on. But Haddock had won; and I duly withdrew. Most of the Press, though, not understanding what mad things Haddock can do, thought that I had simply quitted: interviewers said 'You never intended to stand?' This was quite untrue. They also considered, I think, that the whole matter was trivial. They know better now. Rightly or wrongly, it was our five years of fussing that saved that boring book *Lady Chatterley's Lover* – and a good many others.

Thereafter the Law Officers of the Crown more or less took the Bill over – for the worse, we thought. They were not so much interested as we were in protecting the genuine 'respectable author': they were hotfoot after the 'straight' pornographer (the Soho style) and we were not highly excited about that. So it was an uneasy collaboration. Roy Jenkins showed the prime Parliamentary abilities which have put him where he is. He was in constant conference or conflict with Law Officers and Civil Servants: he reported all to our Committee so we were busy still. The Bill – *a* Bill – became law in the summer of 1959. The sad thing was that after all this effort we were not wildly keen about it. But more of that elsewhere (see page 237).

If it wearies you to read the twists and turns of such a tale imagine how they must have wearied us. They should serve at least to show you how troublesome is the life of a reformer, and how crazy is the literary man, the man of peace and meditation, who lets himself become one.

I now said to myself 'Obscenity's in the bag: no more of that! Damn Causes! Damn Committees! I am going to stay in the "Study".' But Denys Kilham Roberts, then the Secretary General of the Society of Authors, said: 'We want now to tackle the Library affair that you and I have discussed so often. And we want you to go into the figures and all that and start the campaign.'

'No, *no*,' I said. 'A thousand times – No!' And, swearing that I'd ne'er consent, consented. What an ass! 'It would be just,' I said to myself, 'a preliminary survey, with perhaps a sage suggestion or two.' But that very autumn I got out the logarithms and was soon deep down in a swamp of sums and plans. Before the year was out I had completed a Preliminary Memorandum, which was accepted by the Society of Authors and published in March 1960 – ten years ago. It was called 'Public Lending Right', a term which my publisher, Alan White, and I devised over lunch at the Garrick. It is now at least recognized and understood all round the world.

Mr Brophy's article in the Summer number of the *Author* 1951 had developed no details. He simply flew the sturdy kite of 'Penny a Loan' as the kind of compensation the author merited. My Memorandum was an amateur effort, no doubt, but it was a painstaking groping for hard facts and practical remedies: and at the end was a draft Bill, in which I was *much* assisted by my friend and neighbour Stephen Tumim, a barrister.

We were realistic:

2. (*a*) Since X must mean the fairer treatment of authors and publishers it must cost money.

(*b*) This money cannot be raised by making a charge on the reader, as Mr John Brophy suggested. For one thing, it would infringe the 'sacred' principle of free books; for another, according to such librarians as Mr J. P. Lamb, late City Librarian of Sheffield, it would be administratively impossible; most important, it would be contrary to existing law and require new legislation, to which bitter opposition would be certain.

(*c*) The Library Authorities will say that it cannot come from the rates as they have difficulty enough already in getting the money they need out of the local authorities.

(*d*) This leaves us with Government money. The librarians no doubt, will say, 'We shall be delighted if you get a Government grant, go ahead', for they have, we understand, been trying for years to obtain State subvention and inspection on the lines of the Education Services – so far without success. So we shall have to take up the same struggle . . .

10. Observe that these proposals do not conflict with the 'sacred' principle and legislative decree of 'No charge to the book borrowers'. We simply say, 'We are delighted that the community can afford to provide free books for the people. But, not having public money behind us, we cannot afford to supply these books except for a fair reward'. If the Library authorities cannot obtain the necessary money they must be assisted by the Government on, we suggest, the Education Vote.

All this (except for the expectation of 'delight' among the librarians) was precisely prophetic. We did later, as I have related, go back to Brophy and 'charging the borrower' but were duly bashed. We are now in the exact position predicted above – still Waiting for Godot.

But, as we explained in the Memorandum, no private Member can present a Bill of which 'the main object is to impose a charge upon the public resources of the United Kingdom, or upon the people . . .' 'Its introduction must be preceded and authorized by a resolution of a committee of the whole House. This resolution must be recommended by the Crown and must be agreed to by the House before the Bill is introduced' (*House of Commons, Manual of Procedure*, page 159).

Which meant getting the goodwill of the Treasury (and the Minister for Education) before we began – and was most unlikely.

Rightly, we thought that this procedure did not always apply to expenditure that would fall upon the rates. So in our draft Bill the 'Library Authorities' were required to pay 'the annual sums set out in the Schedule', which offered four alternative methods of assessment, each bringing in about £1,000,000.

(Most of my figures, of course, are now out of date. In 1959 the Total Issues (number of books borrowed during the year) were 392,073,021 – in 1960 440,000,000. Today they are said to be about 600,000,000.)

For my part, I never expected to get a penny from the rates. We knew how skinnily the Councils treated them – short of books, poorly-paid librarians – and what it would cost the Councils to reach the standards recommended by Roberts. But it was formally the duty of the Library Authorities, the Councils, to satisfy their suppliers, whether publishers, or milkmen. They must at least, a good case shown, accept the responsibility and if they could not discharge it they must, as we said, go to the State.

You may ask, Who is 'we'? In the first paragraph of the Memorandum I wrote:

> In this old affair it has been customary to speak of the claims of authors only, but it seems to me that no just claims can be made for the author, which do not also, in some degree, apply to his publishers. We therefore feel that authors and publishers should approach the problem hand in hand.

And so we have. At the first meeting of the Authors' Committee (my unfortunate self in the chair) we resolved to invite the Publishers' Association to join us. Alan White, my publisher, who all these ten years has fought like Hector on the plain of Troy, became Vice-Chairman. Certain catty remarks in the Commons required that this should be made clear – the initial move to this alliance came from the Society of Authors, without suggestion or contrivance by any publisher.

Only an idiot will be surprised by this. Neither author nor publisher can prosper without the other; they may quarrel now and then but as a rule they are very good friends. They are the book-producers – not the respected bookseller, not the industrious printer. The Performing Right Society (P.R.S.) has always been an association of composers, authors, and music publishers, and without the skilful organization of the publishers composers and authors might not be enjoying all the benefits they do under copyright law.

Some librarians, and I believe, Civil Servants, and others, have been heard to say: 'Of course we should like to do something for the authors – but we are estranged by the presence of the publishers.' This is either snobbish folly or a specious excuse. In 1951 Mr Brophy said nothing about the publishers: but there was the same acid obstruction or indifference as we suffered in 1960.

On 25 February 1960, then, an Authors' and Publishers' Lending

Right Association (provisional) Committee was formed, hereinafter, as the lawyers say, described as A.P.L.A. Besides authors and publishers it included one or two persons who had had active library experience, an official of the P.R.S., a representative of International P.E.N. (Poets, Playwrights, Editors, Essayists, Novelists), and the Chairman of a Public Library Committee.

From figures kindly provided by Hamnersmith I worked out that at my most friendly library, over twenty years:

1. From my two most successful books I earned 3s. a year.
2. I received 1d. for every sixty issues.

Suppose – a large supposition, and I have no evidence that it is true – that 500 other Public Libraries had bought, issued, and replaced the same book in the same numbers. I should, it is true, have earned £75 a year. Would that be excessive for 90,000 issues a year?

The Water Gipsies was published in 1930 and *Holy Deadlock* in 1934. It may be said: 'These are old books which had a great success in their day. It is unreasonable and greedy to expect a continuing return twenty-five to thirty years later.' Why? There is no age-limit for the earnings of musical works. I am one of the few fortunate authors who have worked in both worlds. Through the Performing Right Society I am still receiving modest but welcome sums from the repeated use of old songs thirty years old and more. A song called 'I Like a Nice Cup of Tea in the Morning', sung by Binnie Hale in a Cochran Revue in 1937, has recently been used by the Tea Council (no less) as a 'commercial' on I.T.V., and this brought in some very welcome money indeed. But even without such a windfall I earn every year more from my old songs and plays than I do from my old books, even if they are in 'constant demand' at the libraries. A repeat fee for repeated use is the simple, reasonable principle. If a talk, song, play, or any other work is done a second time by the B.B.C. you get a second, though not quite the same, fee. I received with excitement £4 the other day, for Zambia, no less, had bought the television rights of some of my *Misleading Cases*. Benjamin Britten will get something whenever one of his works is performed by the B.B.C. till the day he dies. But if every copy of *The Water Gipsies* is read till it tumbles into dust I shall not earn another penny. This is the gist of our grievance. It was plainly declared in the Memorandum:

There is an instructive precedent in the world of music. Musical composers used to live by the sale of sheet music: but the Mechanical Age put an end to that. The united pressure of composers and publishers led to the firm recognition of 'performing right' in the Copyright Act 1911. Thereafter, in 1914, the Performing Right Society (which includes not only composers and publishers but authors concerned in musical work, librettists, lyric writers) was formed for the defence and harvesting of the fruits of Performing Right. When, through gramophone and radio, the sale of sheet music became a shadow of what it had been, it was this great Society which, not without a long and severe struggle, saved the situation; and it is still the main source of revenue for the 'music-producers'. Similarly the author used to live by selling his books. But a great part of the buyers have become borrowers. We are not so foolish as to complain about this. We know that at present prices few can afford to buy the (hard-bound) books: we know that many have not the space for all the books they like. We are not Luddites kicking against the pricks of a new social custom. We accept the change, but ask for new arrangements to meet it – as the composers successfully did. Some idiots have suggested that we should like to abolish the library. What author would be so mad? We simply demand a fair deal.

The Times had put the case very well two years earlier (18 May 1957):

There is something intrinsically absurd in the fact that a considerable portion of the reading public takes its books from a library without benefiting the author in any way, once he has received the royalty on each single copy sold . . . They order this matter better in Sweden. There the Swedish Authors' Union has just announced that some £50,000 will be distributed from the funds of public libraries as a payment to writers for the loan of their books in 1956 . . . *The difficulty of working out a just scheme should not deter us from following, after our own fashion, the Scandinavian example . . .*

Again, on 11 March 1960, on the publication of the Memorandum:

On the face of it, *this is a reasonable proposal. It must be galling to authors to reflect that their earnings, unlike those of manufacturers, or in large part of recording artists, have next to no relationship to the number of people who have enjoyed their product. An author may easily make no more than £250 out of a book which sells a few thousand copies but is read by tens of thousands . . . the notion of a lending fee seems just.*

The prime mischief, and mystery, the great disappointment, was the behaviour of the librarians. I do not mean the rank and file, most of whom, we believe, have in spirit been beside us, but their leaders, the Library Association, and its Council.

We regarded the librarians as our natural friends and allies. They love books, they live with books, they live by books (which is more than most authors can). They, too, want better rewards and conditions and look to the same source, the local authorities. I was shocked when my logarithmic exercises revealed their average salaries: and in all our later schemes for raising more money for the Libraries we imagined benefits for the librarians as well as ourselves.

Now, at the outset, we were eager to meet them. We did not pretend to know all about library machinery; we did not want to suggest anything that would seriously hinder their work; and we wanted their views on practicality and convenience. We expected them to say: 'We couldn't do this or that, but we are on your side. Let us get together and work something out.' You will find it difficult to believe – but *they would not even meet us*. They never have.

We sent them the Memorandum, and we wrote on 7 April 1960 to Mr W. B. Paton (the honorary secretary and later president of the Library Association): 'We should welcome an opportunity of discussing the proposals . . . *or any alternative proposals your Association may have to make.*'

On 12 April 1960 Mr Paton replied:

Your memorandum on the proposed Public Lending Right *has not been considered in detail by the Library Association*, but at the last meeting of the Council the general policy set out in my letters to *The Times* and *Guardian* was approved.

Librarians are not antagonistic to the interests of authors [Amazing! What a concession!] and would be glad to support an acceptable method of increasing the financial return they receive from their writing. The proposed Public Lending Right is unacceptable because in our view its effect would be to reduce the number of books purchased by the Public Library Authorities – a result damaging to libraries and authors alike.*

I will place your letter before them at their meeting next month and I have little doubt that they will *welcome your proposal for a joint meeting* to discuss our respective points of view.

But on 31 May Mr H. D. Barry, the professional secretary, wrote:

The Council asked me to say that having taken note of the correspondence they feel that it would not in fact serve any useful purpose for the Library Association to pursue this matter any further with the Society of Authors.

You will understand now why I said that I might find it difficult to write with restraint. Without the work of authors and their Society the libraries, the librarians, would not exist: yet they cannot condescend to meet us.

Note, too, that our memorandum 'had not been considered in detail'. Our offer to discuss alternative proposals was ignored, and the only reason for their behaviour officially offered was the view that it would reduce the number of books purchased by library authorities.

* Not necessarily to authors, though we never said this. At present, if a library buys 5 books – royalty 1s. – the author gets 5s. If 5 was reduced to 4 and all the 4 were lent 60 times at a penny a loan, the author would get 4s. plus 20s. = 24s.

This arrogant and thoughtless dismissal was explained by a friendly librarian, in a private letter, thus:

> If the Public Lending Right Bill becomes law only a very few enlightened authorities will increase the library rate to compensate for the increased expenditure. The great majority will find the bulk of the money by 'economizing' elsewhere.

And by another likewise:

> Any additional sums which might have to be found for payments to authors would lead to reductions in other expenditure ('we must keep the rates stable') and unfortunately one of the most vulnerable items in a public library's budget is the sum allocated for book purchase.

This argument does credit to the librarians' devotion to the service, but it is hardly a fair comment on the merits of our proposals, and it might just as well be used to deprecate any increase in the salaries and pensions of librarians. It remains on record as the only official reason for the Council's refusal to meet the representatives of British authors and publishers to discuss the practical questions in detail round a table. We had one or two futile bickers with Mr Barry and others on Television and Radio; but to this day we never have 'met round a table'.

But, as I have said, we were not without friends in the library world. Mr W. Handley Snape, lecturer in librarianship at the Liverpool College of Commerce, wrote (*Bookseller*, 1 April 1961):

> The facts are that like librarians themselves . . . authors are asking for more money. Librarians will not help their own cause by refusing some reasonable claim in the cause of our best friends the authors and publishers who produce the raw materials. The Library Association would have been well advised to let the decision about the financial implications rest firmly in the place where it belongs – *with the local authorities*.

A sage remark.

From many letters, interviews, and meetings (especially of young librarians) we had good reason to believe that the main body of librarians was more sympathetic than the Council and its officers. The letters of Mr W. B. Paton to *The Times* and *Guardian*, attacking the idea of authors seeking some compensation from the reader, the local authority or the State, drew a private letter from a Borough Librarian and Curator:

> I was so annoyed at the terms of Bill Paton's letter that I wrote to *The Times* . . . I cannot see why the Library Association should be so unhelpful and unmoved. I for one need no convincing of the worthwhileness of the argument and I am sorry my letter did not get published, for there are others who like myself believe there is a case for the authors. Good wishes.

Yet another librarian wrote to the Press (*Bookseller*, 20 August 1960):

> Quite simply, the Libraries (Public Lending Right) Bill aims at an injustice and I feel that it is most regrettable that Mr —————— and others of my profession should oppose it. Heaven knows library salaries are low enough, but librarians do enjoy modest security, while authors (and not always the least deserving) may literally starve while their books are giving pleasure to thousands through the Public Libraries.

We predicted, rightly, in the Memorandum: '(*c*) The Library Authorities will say that it cannot come from the rates as they have difficulty enough in getting the money they need out of the local authorities.' But if Mr Paton and his colleagues had done us the courtesy to 'consider the Memorandum in detail', or to meet us for ten minutes, they would have realized that we had no hope of getting anything from the rates – so *all the talk of endangering the supply of books was nonsense.* We wanted to get their goodwill and advice, and rough agreement, and then go hand in hand to the Government. If that had happened, we might have got something in two years – and that was my fond expectation. As it is, we have nothing after ten.

But worse, much worse, was to come from Mr Paton, his colleagues, and their irrepressible Secretary, Mr Barry. Having failed in their natural duty they inexcusably stepped outside it. In their proper sphere – the practical details of any scheme they might have to administer – they had every right to be heard and we listened anxiously; but they had nothing to say. Very well – they might then have left us alone. Instead, they sallied forth, horse, foot and cannon, and attacked us in the field of principle and purpose – for example, an alteration of Copyright law – where they had no place.

In 1960 Mr William Teeling, Member for Brighton, Pavilion Division, won a low place in the Private Members' ballot, and he presented our Bill. On 9 December it got a short show at the end of a Friday and was talked out – quite rightly, for there had been only one and a half hours' debate.

But a few days earlier the Library Association had done their malignant best to sink our little ship before it left harbour. They sent to every M.P. a printed document, *The Library Association's Case Against the Libraries (Public Lending Right) Bill.* Consider this piece of impertinence and ignorance:

> A NEW PRINCIPLE: In their claim against libraries the authors and publishers are seeking statutory recognition for a new principle – that when an article is sold outright at a price fixed by the producers he has a right to expect a further payment, related to the number of people who use it.

New? Yet amend the last words to 'the number of times it is exploited' and this is one of the ancient foundations of copyright law. A man may buy a piece of music or a book 'outright', but under the law it is a conditional sale. He may not exploit it in several specified ways – he may not translate it, dramatize it, set it to music, broadcast it, or even, publicly, read it aloud, without getting the copyright-owner's permission, and, if it is demanded, making *a further payment*. Here is the relevant passage in the Copyright Act 1956:

> 2(5) The acts restricted by the copyright in a literary, dramatic of musical work are –
> (*a*) reproducing the work in any material form;
> (*b*) publishing the work;
> (*c*) performing the work in public;
> (*d*) broadcasting the work;
> (*e*) causing the work to be transmitted to subscribers in a diffusion service;
> (*f*) making any adaptation of the work;
> (*g*) doing, in relation to an adaptation of the work, any of the acts specified in relation to the work in paragraphs (*a*) to (*e*) of this subsection.

Copyright in literary, dramatic and musical work.

We simply seek to add one more item to this list, the enormous 'public lending', which is unfairly damaging the value of our copyright. Our original Bill said:

> 2(1) The Copyright Act 1956 shall be amended by the addition to Section 2 of the following subsection:
> '(*g*) causing the work, being a work in which a public lending right exists, to be made available to the public in a public library or lending library.'
> (2) The Public lending right shall be vested solely in the owner of the copyright of a book.

(Later, we confined the provision to 'lending books to be taken out of the library'; excluding, that is, the use of works of reference on the premises: but this is still a debatable point.)

Then, said the illustrious bookmen: 'It is misleading to represent books as being in a category of their own. If the public must compensate the producer when they hire books, why not also when they hire cars, agricultural machinery, and washing machines?'

We were appalled, ashamed, to see such thoughts presented to Parliament by the governing body of the librarians, respected members of the family of books. Fancy telling Parliament, which has made I know not how many copyright statutes, that 'it is misleading to represent books as being in a category of their own'! Two hundred and fifty years earlier Parliament had put books 'in a category of their own', by the Act of Queen Anne. The preamble to the Act of 1842 declared that: 'It is expedient to amend the law relating to copyright and to afford greater encouragement to the production of literary works of lasting benefit to the world . . .' But the lords of the libraries, have the cheek to tell Parliament that they see no difference between books and washing-machines. *Washing-machines!* All comparison with other articles is foolish. If the librarians still saw no spiritual difference between the two, let me explain that no special conditions are attachable by law to the sale of a washing-machine: but in the world of copyright, of art and entertainment, the conditional sale is a commonplace. I cannot believe that head librarians, serious bookmen, composed this document. It must have been the work of Mr H. D. Barry the secretary. This gentleman may know something about books by now, but evidently he did not know much then. He had recently, they said, been professional adviser to the dentists. He is, I believe, a barrister: but he can have made no prolonged study of the law of copyright.

Here is another prize example of, shall I say, a failure to understand: 'An average increase in price in the order of 6*d.* on all books published would produce more than the one million pounds a year originally budgeted for by the promoters of the Bill.'

This one constructive suggestion missed the mark altogether.

(1) It would not even work. Authors and publishers are not the only people concerned in the sale of a book. They get, between them, if they are lucky, about one-third of the price of a book. So to secure the said £1 million for us the price of every book would have to be increased by 1*s.* 6*d.* – not 6*d.*

(2) And the method suggested is inequitable and absurd. The ordinary *buyer* at home and abroad would be asked (but could not be compelled) to pay an artificially higher price in order that the *borrower* should continue to get his book for nothing. And the Public Library would presumably continue to enjoy a privileged discount of 10 per cent under the Net Book Agreement.

(3) In any case, we were complaining not of the terms on which books are bought and sold, but of the elephantiasis of *borrowing*, and the terms on which books are lent and borrowed.

Since we were not able to answer this contemptible document in full before the debate it may well have carried weight in the minds of the uninformed.

Then on 10 March 1961, there was another brief debate (eight minutes only) but none of our supporters had an opportunity to speak.

We battled on, with as much effect as a bird or bee trying to penetrate a window-pane. Some of it was funny. In July 1960 I had led a deputation to Sir David Eccles, then Minister of Education. He had invited us to go and see him, but we could not imagine why, for he had nothing at all to offer. He courteously expressed the ritual sympathy with authors, but easily concealed any sympathy he may have felt for the publishers. Before we had had a chance to utter he carefully named and dismissed the possible sources to which we might look:

(*a*) The Government could do nothing;

(*b*) Anything like 'charging the borrower', he warmly said, though nobody had mentioned it, was out of the question – against Government policy;

(*c*) There remained the local authorities – here he had no influence; but he advised us to seek out their representatives.

There was some friendly talk. On his 'charging the borrower' ultimatum I inquired whether the 'free' Public Library was to be regarded as a corner of the Welfare State. After some hesitation he seemed to me to assent (though others do not agree). It evidently is: and I then observed (as I have many times since) that in other corners of the Welfare State the community recognized that it had some responsibility for the welfare of those who served as well as for those who received. You could not have a free Health Service without considering the doctors, or Free Education without providing for the teachers. I cannot recall that there was any answer to this. That is the worst of deputations: while you are waiting for an answer, someone pops in a question about something else and your quarry escapes.

The Minister told us that he was preparing a Public Library Bill, and we should be able to move amendments. That was in 1960 – we did not see the Bill till 1964.

The Minister, *à propos* of what I forget, said: 'The librarians will have to do what they are told.' We have never taken that line: but the remark should be noted by Messrs Paton, Barry and Co.

Our campaign was never slap-dash or slothful: we did our best to leave no stone unturned. We at once, on 27 July 1960, followed the Minister's advice and approached the associations representing local authorities. But it took us eleven months to turn this particular stone. After a long and cautious correspondence, some of which was funny, we met representatives of the Association of Municipal Corporations, the County Council Association, and the Urban District Association on 21 March 1961.

It took them *ten weeks* to reply. On 1 June 1961 the Secretary of the Association of Municipal Corporations (A.M.C.) wrote: 'The Libraries Committee . . . have asked me to say that . . they remain opposed to the principle of Public Lending Right.'

(Local authorities were equally opposed to 'the principle of Performing Right' when that began, but they have been paying for it for fifty years.)

In 1965 I resigned the Chairmanship of A.P.L.A. but remained on the Committee. This was mainly to disperse the notion that the whole campaign was a one-man A.P.H. affair. David James of Burns and Oates, publishers, and M.P. for Brighton (Kemp Town) succeeded me. Apart from his personal qualities, and experience, it was most useful to have a chairman in the House.

There were endless speeches, lectures, meetings, bouts of correspondence: but nothing much happened till 1964.

'How Things Don't Get Done.' On this theme there must be a million Whitehall memories, tales of folly, deceit, conspiracy, frustration. But here, I believe, is a classic. In all my years of battles about the Libraries this was the deepest disappointment, the most miserable 'might have been', Whitehall at its worst.

Early in 1964, the story goes, the Conservative Chief Whip was looking for some mild measures to occupy the Commons before the General Election. Scrabbling through a pile of aspiring Bills he picked out the Ministry of Education's Public Libraries and Museums Bill: 'Well, this,' he said, 'should not be controversial,' and put it down for Second Reading in ten days' time.

A Bill, we had heard, had been hanging about for a long time, but we were never consulted about it, and had almost ceased to believe in it. Suddenly, without a word of warning, it appears on the Order Paper; and we have less than a week to study the Bill, get together, discuss policy and draft amendments. David James was enraged by his own Government's scurvy behaviour, but there was no time for complaints. We set to work.

The situation was complicated by a sort of Musical Chairs at the Ministry. Mr Quintin Hogg, an old friend of mine (I should have made him Conservative leader) had been Minister of Education, but had left the place, I forget why, for two years and Sir Edward Boyle had stepped in. Now Mr Hogg had just returned as Minister, and Boyle had stepped down to No. 2. But, I suppose, because he had been in charge during the preparation of the Bill he remained in charge of it now. This was the first bad bounce of the ball; for Quintin Hogg, I happened to know, was far more likely to favour our views than the brilliant Sir Edward Boyle.

So the brilliant Boyle moved, and obtained without difficulty the Second Reading. David James, who did fine work all through, Mr Iremonger, and others, made all our points, but we had no hope there.

The Bill was fundamentally absurd and boneless. I drafted a 'reasoned amendment' (always an interesting literary exercise) but I don't think it was put down.

That this House declines to proceed with a Bill which

(*a*) for the first time lays upon local authorities a statutory duty to maintain efficient public libraries but with no material assistance from the State or contribution from the beneficiaries;

(*b*) while purporting to improve and develop the public library service makes no financial provision for the purpose, but imposes the entire cost of the service on the local ratepayer, whether he uses the library or not, fails to secure the substantial sums that might accrue from a small charge upon the borrowing of books, records, and other articles for use in the home, and compels the local authorities to distribute books, including fiction, on unremunerative terms not applied to any similar pleasures such as music, plays, films, radio and television;*

(*c*) makes no provision to improve the remuneration and supply of librarians;

(*d*) makes no provision for the compensation of authors and publishers, who are the true foundation of the service, but are ungenerously and unfairly treated;

(*e*) places the Minister of Education in charge of a service of which the main activity is the free distribution of works of fiction.

Before the Act the Public Library was a voluntary affair. Now the Local Authority is compelled to maintain one, and is answerable to the Ministry for the way in which it is run. New duties and standards are laid down – the number of books to be bought, the ratio of librarians to registered readers, and so on. By Section 7, as I read it, they are required to provide any book that anybody wants:

(1) It shall be the duty of every library authority to provide a comprehensive and efficient library service for all persons desiring to make use thereof...

(2) In fulfilling its duty under the preceding sub-section a library authority shall in particular have regard to the advisability
(*a*) of securing, by the keeping of adequate stocks etc., that facilities are available for the borrowing of books and other printed matter ... sufficient in number to meet the general requirements and *any special requirements both of adults and children.*

No more, therefore, of 'No you can't have a Blyton book. We don't approve of her.' If Blyton is wanted they must buy Blyton – and Bunter too.

I don't suppose the new standards and duties are being severely enforced, but there they are, on the Statute Book.

* In 1948 I supported and voted for, the Section in Mr Aneurin Bevan's Act allowing Local Government Bodies to spend up to a 6*d.* rate on entertainment. But we did not say 'The entertainment must be free' because the plays of Shakespeare, Herbert and others are *educational.*

The Government that decreed all this compulsory expense not only offered or arranged for no new money; by Section 8 they debarred the Libraries from the only source of new money open to them, that is, from charging the borrower for the use of books. The only people who tried to make new money available were the authors and publishers: but the brilliant Boyle would not listen to us.

We had many amendments down for the Committee stage. I do not think we won a single coconut. We proposed that authors and publishers should have two members at least on the new Library Councils the Bill created. This was brushed aside. Why should anyone in the Library world require the opinion of people who wrote books?

There were others, which I forget. But the prime affair was 'charging the borrower'. The Act says (8(3)): '. . . the authority shall not charge . . . for borrowing (a) a book, journal, pamphlet or similar article, or (b) a reproduction made by photographic or other means of the whole or a part of any such article.'

Our amendment was two-fold. First, an addition to 8(2): (c) for books on loan taken from the library premises. Then a new clause: 'Charges made under Section 8(2) (c) may include a sum approved by the Minister either contributed from time to time on the enrolment of a registered reader or readers for any specific category or all categories of books stocked, or in respect of the borrowing of an isolated book:

Provided that a person in receipt of an old age pension, and other persons at the discretion of the Library authority, may be exempted.'

Observe, this was permissive only. It permitted any Authority to make a charge, but compelled none. Also we provided for the exemption of old age pensioners – and students. I now think that the last concession was feeble. Why should authors alone have to subsidize the student? Do milkmen, grocers, allow him special rates?

David James took some of us to see the brilliant Boyle twice. Though hotly against any charge for the borrowing of books, he himself put down an amendment to his Bill to permit a charge for the borrowing of *any* article not being a book etc. This was especially aimed at gramophone records. When we politely suggested that this was a touch of inconsistency (and contrary to the sacred Roberts Report) he answered feebly that a few Libraries were charging for records already and the simplest thing seemed to be to make it general. (The charge for borrowing records, by the way, goes into the general library funds, and does not do authors or composers any good.) Once – it may have been this very point – when he seemed to be listening to our arguments with an open mind David James discovered that he had already put down an amendment against us.

If Quintin Hogg had been at the helm I am sure that we – and the

Libraries – would have fared much better. This was a Conservative Government Bill, with a built-in Conservative majority on the Standing Committee – 17 Conservatives, 12 Labour, 1 Liberal. The Minister in charge could have done what he liked, whatever the Civil Servants said. Moreover the vocal Conservatives were all behind David James. There were six or seven of them, mostly young men, and good men too – Mr Channon, Mr Iremonger, Sir Randal Russell, Sir Arthur Vere Harvey, Mr Nicholas Ridley, Mr Denzil Freeth, Sir Charles Mott-Radclyffe.

They were primed with facts and figures we had laboriously collected or calculated. The Library Association in those days issued an admirable Annual Report with many columns of figures concerning almost every one of the 536 Public Libraries. Indeed their records were evidently so precise and thorough that we were inclined to suspect the protestations that to record the kind of facts the authors wanted would be an impossible and inhuman task. Most of the Libraries published their own reports and accounts too. From all this it was possible to put many two's together, and I spent weeks, months, of logarithmic labour at the job. How many libraries were living up to the standards recommended by the Roberts Committee – the number of books bought, the ratio of librarians to readers, and so on?

What was the book-expenditure per head of population? (2s. to 3s.) Average salary of non-manual staff in Libraries? (Wretched – Top Boroughs £656 – Leading Counties £669 – London Boroughs £796.)

What proportion of the population were the Registered Readers? (Generally about 25 per cent.)

What proportion of the Total Issues was Fiction? (About 70 per cent.) How many books a year did the average reader borrow? (30 – in London.) How many books were bought and how many borrowed? (The answer to this was 'For every one book bought by the Public Libraries about 100 were borrowed'.)

Charged with full information and solid conviction the seven Conservatives made some splendid speeches. No Labour man had taken so much trouble. They contented themselves with antique and erroneous generalities – 'This would be a retrograde step' – 'This will be a tax on education' etcetera. (It was, of course, no more of a 'tax on education' than the purchase-price of a book or theatre ticket.) The voice of the seven Members was, I am sure, the voice of the Conservative Party, which even then was beginning to mutter about the cost of social services undemanded and undeserved. But the brilliant Boyle would not listen to his men. One could blame the Civil Servants behind him: but I blame Boyle. The debate on our amendment lasted for two mornings. It was defeated on 28 April.

Three years earlier, through the Institute of Economic Affairs,

A.P.L.A., had published our 'Appeal to Parliament – Libraries – Free For All?' I had compiled the long war-cry myself but every word was examined, questioned, and passed by the whole Committee. Here we set forth the whole history of the argument, and explained our most recent practical proposal for the raising of new money. This was to bother no more about how many books were borrowed by this person or that. Every 'registered reader' would pay an annual subscription, as to a club, of 7s. 6d. to 10s. a year, which would entitle him to borrow as many books as he liked. (I added, relevantly, I think, that the average *weekly* subscription to the Pools was 5s.)

I sent a copy of this document to Quintin Hogg. He sent me a note of thanks and added: 'I will read your personal contribution with interest. I have always wondered what in *principle* public free libraries were for now that there are no deserving poor. Perhaps your bit will tell me.' He did not, of course, mean 'no deserving poor': but he did mean what we had always said, that the free library, intended in the last century for 'the artisans of the towns and labourers of the villages' but now used by the rich rolling up in Jaguars, was a hoary anachronism.

I now remembered this letter, dug it out, and showed it to David James. He thought it was clear evidence of a conflict at the peak of Education Mountain. As a good party man he thought it was not for him to confront the two, so he tried a deputation to the Prime Minister, Sir Alec Douglas-Home instead. Unhappily – and here was another vicious bounce of the ball – the Prime Minister could not receive us until the evening of the day on which our 'charge the borrower amendment' was voted down. The division was at 1 p.m. – we met the Prime Minister at 5 p.m.

Here, I suppose, it may be said by regular politicians, that I behaved badly: but if this is said I do not care a damn. Whitehall had behaved wickedly: and why should I sit good and gracious? At the long sunny table David James and Alan White sat opposite to the Prime Minister, and I was on the left flank opposite to the brilliant Boyle. Sir Alec seemed genuinely interested in our pleas. After some general discussion the question of money was mentioned and that brought up 'charging the borrower'. I piped up in this manner (I cannot swear to the exact words): 'I should like to ask what Minister is ultimately in charge of this Bill, for I have reason to believe that on the proposal defeated in Committee this morning the Minister of Education holds very different views from the right honourable gentleman opposite to me.' Boyle said, 'Oh, we are in constant touch.' I then took from my pocket Quintin Hogg's letter and passed it across the table to the Prime Minister. (Naughty, without a doubt: it was a private letter and years old.) The Prime Minister read it, smiled wryly and returned it. At the end of the talk I felt that he was more warm towards us than any other Minister we had met. He had not, of course, been drugged by the High Priests at the Ministry of Education. He said that he did not see how we could be helped within the framework of the present Bill now but he wished us well and hoped there would be other ways.

The very next day I was invited to that fine feast the Royal Academy Banquet. I like to get there early and wander about looking at the pictures before the ribboned, medalled throng arrive. On this night I met the Prime Minister strolling solitary too. I did not badger him – that would have been outrageous – but I did thank him for receiving the deputation. 'Not at all,' he said, 'I enjoyed it.' And then he said these shattering words: *'I wish I'd known all that two or three months ago.'*

I could not pay close attention to the speeches that night. I sat and sadly masticated our misfortunes. After one interview, it seemed, the Conservative Prime Minister was on our side. The Conservative Minister of Education we presumed to be on our side. The seven active Conservative members of the Standing Committee were on our side. Our Leader, a member of that Committee, was a Conservative. Why all this scattered goodwill had never found a centre, never worked up to action at the top, I could not tell. Why did no one ever tell the Prime Minister about 'all that', and ask for a ruling? There seems to have been a failure in the signal system. But the man on the bridge was the brilliant Boyle and the brilliant Boyle is the man I blame. Indeed, he is the man I curse – and about no other man in politics have I ever thought of saying that. But for the brilliant Boyle this bitter business would have been settled six years ago. The authors would be content at last, the readers would be content, for after the first splutters not more than one in a million would have objected to paying ten shillings a year – twopence a week – for the right of entry to all the books in the world. The libraries would be better off, for the said ten shillings would produce much more than authors and publishers ask – something like £5,000,000. We grin when we meet but politically my curses are on the brilliant deplorable Boyle.

But I wrote to the Prime Minister in a more bonhomous vein:

29 April 1964

Thank you very much for receiving us yesterday and for suffering our plaints so patiently.

There is one thing I forgot to say, though I said so much. Last week I listened, with interest and admiration, to two debates in Standing Committee E on 'charges'. There were seven of your young men supporting our side, and they put up a splendid show. They were well-armed with facts and figures – and logic – and, I think, with sound Conservative feeling. Prejudiced though I was, of course, I thought the weight of the debate was theirs, and you would, I am sure, have been proud of them. The Opposition were armed with such old pieces as 'a retrograde step' and a 'free library doctrine' which is wildly out-of-date (as the entertainment clause in Bevan's Act shows clearly). The librarians (most of them) still mutter the same incantations and I was sorry that your Minister seems to have fallen under the spell – unlike the Minister of Education who, according to the Act, is to administer it.

Apart from my particular interest, I was glad, as an old Commons man, to see a Standing Committee in action again. This one, very well handled by the Chairman, Dr King, was a model of good temper and solid, though inconspicuous, toil – the Parliamentary machine at its best. It is a great pity that the critical electors hear and know so little of this sort of work.

I hope that you may find a moment to glance at the orange Appeal to Parliament I thrust upon you. The case was very fully argued, and there is very little to add to it now. As you will see, we have by no means been thinking only of ourselves. Indeed, I think we have done more to put the case for the librarians than the Socialists (or even their own Union).

The decision on charges, I suppose, is final and must be democratically accepted. This by no means diminishes our case for a Public Lending Right, and, pending that, some form of library compensation payment. On the contrary, Tuesday's decision (if confirmed by Parliament) puts the Public Library more firmly still into the realm of the Welfare State, and, as I have said to two or three of your Ministers, it is, it must be, a canon of the Welfare State that those who serve are considered and cared for not less than those who receive. You could not have a free health service without making arrangements for the doctors. So far, in this affair, after nearly five years of struggle and argument, deputation and debate, we, the producers, the suppliers, have not encountered any genuine goodwill or consideration anywhere. Even the Socialists, the great friends of the 'producers' and the 'toilers', regard us as no more than battery-hens, who should be delighted to supply free eggs, whatever the conditions. So we turn, with rather more hope, to you. Tuesday's decision was, I think, a calamity. The charges we had in mind (£5,000,000 or more) could have done good for everybody, the customers, the librarians, and, in the end, the authors and publishers. They would have put the public libraries on a firm financial footing. But the State is saying to the local authorities: 'You shall not manage your business in a business-like way. You must rely on the rates for all things.' Sir Edward himself now seems to realize that it may take a long time for all his expensive improvements to emerge from the rates. We, it is clear, will never get justice from the rate-payer and the Councils. We must now look to the State; and I do hope you will give our appeal a little thought. My Arts Council suggestion might be worth considering – it would dodge some difficulties, as the financing of Covent Garden in that manner does. You, at least, could say – which nobody has said yet – 'Look here, these fellows have got a case. Let us see what we can do for them.' And do not, please, be put off by talk of administrative difficulties. We have got answers to them all, and, if we had ever got round a table with anyone who mattered, with goodwill and money assured, we could have worked out something long ago. But, quite apart from money, there has never been goodwill. We thought we saw a glimpse of it yesterday, and thank you again.

Next comes a rather comical interlude; and for once the ball bounces our way – Haddock triumphantly in action.

Far back in 1957 I had written (in *Punch*) a Misleading Case, *Haddock* v. *The Arts Council of Great Britain**

Mr Justice Lark, giving judgement today, said:
'This captivating bicker began with a polite writ of *Quaere Transgressit* requiring the Arts Council of Great Britain to show cause why it has exceeded the instructions and conditions which govern its existence.

The Council was incorporated by Royal Charter on 9 August 1946:
for the purpose of developing greater knowledge, understanding and practice of the *fine arts exclusively*, and in particular to increase the accessibility of the fine arts to the public . . . to improve the standard of execution of the fine arts and to advise and co-operate with . . . Government Departments, Local Authorities and other bodies on any matters directly or indirectly concerned with those objects . . .

'The sixteen Members of the Council are appointed by the Treasury, from which it receives an annual grant. Among other laudable activities it finances the performance of Grand Opera and Ballet at Covent Garden and Sadler's Wells; it supports the London Philharmonic, the Halle and other symphony orchestras; the Old Vic and Nottingham Theatre Trusts, the English Stage Company, the Birmingham, Repertory and other repertory theatres all over the country. The public funds, we were told, between 1945 and 1956 contributed £1,778,000 towards the losses sustained by the Covent Garden Opera House, so that the questions raised in the case are of more than academic interest.'

'A notable omission from the objects of the Council's aid is "literature" – and this is one of the plaintiff's grievances. But in recent years a slightly helping hand has been held out to Poetry. In 1961–2 the total expenditure was £1,598,201. Of this sum £1,216,937, or 76 per cent, went to Music: £256,007 (or 16 per cent) to Drama, and only £79,000 (or 4·9 per cent) to Art. Poetry got £4,581 (or 0·3 per cent): the small remainder went to Festivals and Art Clubs.† Thus 92 per cent of the money went to Music and Drama and less than 5 per cent to Art . . .'

My Mr Haddock argued that the bulk of the Council's money was

---

* See *Bardot M.P.* – 'What are the Arts Council Up To?' and *Wigs at Work* (a Penguin) – 'Good old Scire Facias!'

† See *Government and the Arts*, a pamphlet issued by the Conservative Political Centre, 1962.

not being spent on the Fine Arts. The court agreed. The Fine Arts, it seemed, had never been defined in any statutes. But, said Mr Justice Lark, 'I find that in law the words have the same meaning as they had, *I think*, in 1843, that is painting, sculpture, engraving and architecture – the French Beaux Arts . . . Accordingly all the activities of the Arts Council other than those I have named are *ultra vires* and must be abandoned . . .'

No one, of course, paid the slightest attention. Five years later, though, in 1962, the Conservative Arts and Amenities Committee (in the House of Commons) in an enlightened pamphlet, *Government and the Arts*, took up the same tale.

'The Arts Council's terms of reference confine them to the "fine arts" which by an outmoded definition do not include literature (except for poetry). This arbitrary limitation should, in our opinion, be abolished and a Literary Panel set up in the place of the existing Poetry Panel. This new Literary Panel, covering the whole field of creative writing, would be widely representative and reinforce the diverse efforts of the many existing literary bodies.'

No one disputed their statements of fact: no one paid the slightest attention to their advice. (Yet the Conservatives were then in office.)

The little bee was always buzzing about at the back of my mind and in February 1964, at a dining club, I discussed the problem with two agreeable lawyers I had not met before: Haddock's writ of *Quaere Transgressit* was an invention of my own; but was there not some real writ that would fit my purpose? Two days later I had a kindly note from one of them – he turned out to be a High Court Judge – indeed a Lord of Justice of Appeal: 'What about proceedings on a *scire facias*? (Halsbury 3rd Edition Vol. IX pages 62, 97, 99).'

My barrister friend, the ever helpful Stephen Tumim, dived into Halsbury and came up delighted. *Scire facias* ('you should make to know') is a very ancient writ. When a corporation created by Royal Charter was shown to have abused or exceeded its terms the Clerk to the Petty Bag used to take the Charter out of the Petty Bag and snip off the pretty seals and ribbons. That was the end of the corporation.

The Clerk to the Petty Bag had been abolished but, on the recent authority of Lord Goddard, the writ retained its power: so we considered plans to fire off a *scire facias* and get the Arts Council (in a friendly way, and for its own good) snipped out of existence. But we were not seeking unnecessary trouble and expense: so I wrote politely to the Chancellor of the Exchequer, Mr Reginald Maudling, and explained our view of the legal position. Assuming that he agreed, I suggested that he should have the Charter revised, make honest women of Opera and Ballet and let Literature in. If he did not agree, we said, we should be very willing to co-operate in a test case, by way of *scire facias*, the costs, of course, to be the business of the Crown.

To my astonishment Mr Maudling replied, on 18 March 1964:

'Having thought about it and taken advice, I do not find I can accept your argument that the expression "Fine Arts" used in the Charter does not include poetry and literature, or that it is dubious whether it includes music, drama, opera and ballet.'

Later, he wrote to Sir Hamilton Kerr, M.P., Chairman of the Arts and Amenities Committee:

'I am satisfied that "Fine Arts" is used in the Arts Council's Charter in its wider sense, so that literature is not excluded. It follows that I would not regard the Charter as preventing the Arts Council from devoting part of their resources to the literary arts or to music.'

Well done, Chancellor! And well done, Haddock! The extraordinary thing is that the Treasury should not have revealed this verdict before. *Government and the Arts* was published by the Conservative Political Centre, by Mr Maudling's own party. Nobody said to its authors: 'You're barking up the wrong tree – Literature is in already.' Nor did the Arts Council know. The Secretary, Mr Abercrombie, in a friendly correspondence, said that he did not want to be involved in litigation. But he did not say: 'Anyway, there'd be no point in it.' It remained for the interfering Mr Haddock to extract the truth.

Never mind. The Arts Council met the Society of Authors and the Publishers' Association: and in December 1965, under the splendid new Chairman, Lord Goodman, that orchestra of a man, it set up a Literature Panel, with Mr C. Day Lewis in the chair. I can't help thinking that without good old *scire facias* all this would never have happened: and the world of books should be duly grateful to the learned Judge – Sir Charles Russell.

Before that, in the summer of 1965, there was a great day. Miss Jennie Lee, M.P. – Minister of State at the Department of Education and Science and Princess of the Arts – was the Guest of Honour at the Performing Right Society's annual lunch, always a populous and stirring affair. In her speech she said to the composers: 'You have worked out a very excellent scheme of mutual self help. I am hard at work trying to work out a similar scheme for authors . . . You have shown me that if it can be done for writers and composers we ought to be able to contrive the right kind of scheme to help authors.'

This was a great day, because here was the first public admission from anyone in Whitehall of the parallel between Performing Right and Public Lending Right. Miss Lee, I believe, is a friend of Lord Goodman. At all events she handed over her hopes to him.

The new Literary Panel of the Arts Council appointed a special working-party to prepare a scheme for Public Lending Right. (It was intended to represent all the interests concerned (but the librarians declined their invitation). This was fine news. The working party were given two vetoes – nothing to come from the rates, and no charge to the borrower. They laboured for two years. Victor Bonham-Carter (Society of Authors) and Alan White (publisher) visited all the Scandinavian countries to study their methods.

They produced a Report and a Plan. I will not weary you – or myself – with all the details; for it has died once, and, who knows, may not be seen again. Roughly, it was founded on the Danish model – payments according to number of books in stock, not loans: method, a sampling system, covering three or four typical libraries. The money would be reckoned on the basis of 15 per cent of the annual sum spent by Library Authorities on books – would come from Central Government Funds, and amount to about £2,000,000 a year.

The plan was full and detailed; a Bill could have been drafted at once. Miss Lee had been looking over the working party's shoulders, and, so far as was known, had nothing to say against it. So it was with high hopes that I heard that it had gone to the Department of Education and Science, in the autumn of 1967. Silence fell.

For eighteen months nothing was heard – except some assurances from Miss Lee that the report was being studied, and some good firm speeches from Lord Goodman.

On 15 February 1969 Mr Michael Holroyd wrote a powerful, memorable article in *The Times Saturday Review*. '*Oh Lord, Miss Lee, How Long!*' I had heard nothing about it till I saw it in print. It began: 'Authors are angry now. The patience, the politeness, of years has been exhausted. In the history of modern literature their mood is unique, and the sort of action they are now being forced to take is without precedent. Most of them feel that they have been betrayed. For this they blame, personally, Miss Jennie Lee.'

He brilliantly sketched the whole story from Brophy and 1951. But the main motif was the bitterness of disillusion with poor Jennie Lee – the fall of an angel. 'We have flattered you (my God! how we have flattered you!) and you have not smiled on us; we have spoken well of you, even behind your back, and you have merely turned away from us; we have trusted in you, and you have failed us.'

And now:

We are exasperated; we are sickened. The anger that was dammed up and diverted over four years ago has now swept back with redoubled force. It is almost impossible adequately to convey the anger that is felt for you, personally, Miss Lee, without some drastic change in the law of libel . . . For us there is nothing left to say. We have thought of the librarians, of Parliament's objections, we have thought of everything, and we have grown hoarse speaking about it. We decline absolutely to discuss it further for anyone's entertainment. Everything that can be said by us has been said and is available in print. The time has now come for abuse, for bloody-mindedness. That is the only new authentic contribution left for us to make.

Whitehall is not accustomed to such able abuse, especially from the sheepish well-behaved writers. Distinguished friends rushed to Jennie's aid. Mr Holroyd was 'hysterical' and 'venomous'. Lord Eccles (I think it was) said that it was unfair to blame Miss Lee for what must have been a Cabinet decision. But there was no evidence at all that the plan had ever been put before the Cabinet (I thought myself that Miss Lee was stopped by her own Civil Servants). On 22 March 1968, after a discouraging story in *The Times*, I wrote to the Minister (Mr Gordon Walker) and put the question directly. 'Has the Arts Council's plan been approved by you, has it been considered by the Treasury, has it in fact been vetoed by that Department, or has this been assumed by your own?' I got no answer to any of these questions. Jennie Lee replied in her usual friendly style. 'As I think you know both Arnold Goodman and myself are keen to find an answer to the legitimate claims of authors. A charge on books borrowed from libraries is out. The scheme prepared by the Arts Council is estimated to cost the Exchequer £2 million a year. At the moment, apart from the merits of the scheme, this cannot be a Government priority.

But I do assure you that as the financial situation eases I shall continue to press the claims of authors – and keep in touch with you.'

Which I took to mean that her advisers, of whom I had heard a good deal, were not agreed about 'the scheme'.

I was a witness at Jennie Lee's wedding to Nye Bevan and have always had a soft spot for both of them. Michael Holroyd's basic facts were undeniable, but I should not myself have shot the pianist quite so severely.

But there was worse to come. In March my fears came true, and on the 15th I wrote to *The Times*, as President of the Society of Authors: I told the story from that happy day in 1965:

... Then suddenly in the House of Commons (March 6 Col. 657) Miss Lee said 'There are alternative proposals. There are alternative ideas affecting copyright and a good deal more. A working party is to be set up'. *Another* working party! I nearly cried.

I have not abused – and shall not abuse – my old friend Miss Jennie Lee. But I must say, remembering her declaration of faith in 1965 and all the fine effort that has followed, it is disappointing to hear her say: 'We will now start all over again.'

Let her stick to the original plan, to which she herself has found no objection. Let her draft a Bill, present it to the Cabinet, and if they reject it, resign. Let Mr Jenkins on April 15 (the Budget) say that he is willing to provide up to £2 million for any scheme that Parliament may approve.

The Government, Mr Philip Howard tells us (March 13) sees three snags: (a) £2,000,000. This is less than the State provides for Covent Garden and Sadler's Wells: (b) The Librarians were not represented on the Arts Council working party. Whose fault was that? They were invited but refused to come in and help, as they have been refusing since 1960. (c) The publishers are to have a quarter of the money. Why ever not? For forty years I have been sharing 'Performing Right' with musical publishers, without whose services – and risks – my 'right' would be worthless. The only question is in what proportion, and that is our affair.

None of the 'snags' is new. All were present in the minds of the Arts Council Working Party. Pray, dear Miss Lee, get back on your excellent, well-charted course.

I do believe this letter may have had some effect. We heard no more about the new 'working party' or the crazy tinkering with copyright law which, we were told, was in the air. During the summer hope, like a wounded creature, stirred slightly again. A deputation to Mr Jenkins, that distinguished author, had a kind and encouraging reception. At the Annual General Meeting of our Society in July (Winston Graham about to leave the chair) I was told of a portent – the Ministry itself had prepared a scheme.

Victor Bonham-Carter, the Society and the Arts Council still work nobly away. Scheme follows scheme. As this book goes into the oven I hear that Miss Jenny Lee has gathered all concerned together again. This time the Library Association and the Local Authorities graciously attended – but said nothing. No money is being asked from the rates, no labour from the librarians: yet their leaders still declined to assist, or even to comment, being still opposed to P.L.R. – that is, to a fair deal for authors – 'on principle'. God help us! But after all these years the world at least knows what we want, and why, and, I believe, is with us.

I return reluctantly to the Battle about Obscene Publications, which, like Divorce, wearies me. There are some very good books about it – see the excellent *Obscenity and the Law** by Norman St John-Stevas, M.P., a member of my 'Committee' and the recent *Books in the Dock*† by C. H. Rolph.

To the first meeting of the Society of Authors' Committee, into the chair of which they had thrust me, I took a very rough draft of a Bill, in pencil. 'It is no use passing powerful resolutions,' I said. 'They will be thrust into the nearest pigeon-hole. But a Bill is a weapon. You can wave it about – and suddenly, perhaps, go into action with it.'

* Secker and Warburg, 1956.
† André Deutsch, 1969.

Not much of my Bill remains, but a lot of it got into the first Bill we presented to Parliament. I was all for the protection of works done 'with honest purpose and due care': but not of the dirt-for-dirt's sake – those who 'for purposes of wickedness or gain deliberately or recklessly publish or purvey corrupting matter'. In other works, I wanted 'intent' and 'the dominant effect' to be the test. So did Bill 17 printed by the House of Commons in 1956.

'The question of guilty knowledge is declared to be relevant . . .' So we threw out the absurd 1858 definition about 'a tendency to deprave or corrupt'. But the Law Officers, with whom Mr Roy Jenkins had to deal, insisted on its going back – and there it is.

A frequent criticism of the present law (the Act of 1959) is that it is obsessed with sex and says nothing about 'violence'. That is not our fault. Our first Bill said:

> 2. Any such matter shall be decreed to be obscene . . . if:
> (b) whether or not related to any sexual content it crudely exploits horror, cruelty or violence, whether pictorially or otherwise.

But we had to take that out too.

But our five years' fight was not in vain. The Act of 1959 contained many improvements, though, in my opinion, fundamentally at fault.

Some are for scrapping it altogether, notably a committee appointed though not, I think, supported by Lord Goodman of the Arts Council. It is difficult, perhaps impossible, to devise a wholly satisfactory law: but I think we must have something. I distrust the stories about Denmark. The Theatres Act 1968 is not a happy precedent for having nothing. As I understand the law, you can still be prosecuted for indecency if you take all your clothes off in a public street, or even on a public beach. The stage of a theatre is in a sense more public than either: yet, I believe, the whole of the cast can lawfully be naked from the rise of the curtain till its fall. I may be square and stuffy, but I am against this. I see no point or purpose in such liberties. The attractions of nudity are greatly exaggerated, as anyone knows who has used a Turkish Bath.

As President of the Society of Authors, I have another thought in mind. In my memorandum to the Select Committee of the House of Commons I said, I see: 'Pornography spoils the respectable market.' How brave is the novelist today who does not litter his book with homosexuals and photographic sex-scenes! Some, a publisher told me, have given up writing because they do not want to write that sort of book. At one time, I remember, I wanted to call our Bill THE PROTECTION OF LITERATURE BILL. I still find it attractive, and reasonable. Literature requires protection:

White margin X

Double spaces

(A 'skeleton' . Bill)

CORRUPTING PUBLICATIONS

A Bill to repeal or amend the laws relating to
obscene libel : to amend *(and define)* the language of the law; to make
new provision for the prevention and punishment of corrupting
publications. For the protection of works of honest purpose; and for
purposes connected therewith
(*spens*).

Preamble

Whereas it is established that works of art, music,
literature, science and history are not only a pleasure
and instruction to the present time but a *(a blessing)* support *(in causes)*
for the future, and accordingly there should be set no
undue limits to the freedom of those who with
honest purpose and *proper* care devise, or publish or
distribute such works; but it is expedient that those
who for purposes of wickedness or gain deliberately
or recklessly publish or purvey corrupting matter
should be prevented or punished; and the laws in
this respect are at present uncertain, vague and
inimical to honest and harmless work:

Be it enacted therefore by the Queen's most
Excellent Majesty etc.

{ 239 }

(*a*) from unfair prosecution by the law;

(*b*) from unfair competition, from 'adulteration'.

'Adulteration' is defined as 'the corrupt production of any article especially food', indictable at Common Law.

The 'dirt-for-dirt's sake' writers are 'corrupt producers' just as much as the man who unlawfully sells margarine as butter. They seek to enjoy the freedom of literature without deserving it. When we say that Art and Literature must be free we mean honest Art and Literature. When we say 'Speech must be free' we do not include seditious or blasphemous or, now, 'Racial' speech. So, if we want to, we should condemn 'dirty books', not as corrupting, but as 'corrupt', punishable, like a bad penny. This would make more logical the business of exemption in border-line cases.

But I should not expect this argument to go far in the House of Commons. Indeed, if I were there again, I should think much more than twice before I introduced a Private Member's Bill on the subject.

Authors do not, I think, resent the taxes (excepting those on wine and whisky) more unreasonably than the rest of us. But our peculiar craft breeds peculiar grievances and burdens. Patient work by the Society of Authors and an occasional compassionate glance from the Treasury have dislodged an occasional straw from our backs. It was Lord Waverley, I think (then Sir John Anderson), who gave us the first instalment of 'the Three Years' Spread'. If you have a sudden success you can spread the tax over three years, provided the research and the labour took at least twelve months. This at first applied to lump sum receipts only, but in 1954 was extended to royalties. My greatest financial success in the theatre was C. B. Cochran's *Bless the Bride*. Such an accretion of cash never happened before: also it followed about ten theatrical productions from which my earnings had been modest. But the spread did not apply to royalties then, and in one year I paid £8,000 in income tax – at the rate of 19*s*. plus. It worries me now if they ask me for £80. Still, the Treasury did something for us: and if Fortune did smile heartily again I should be grateful.

There is one deafeningly just complaint which Authority switches off contemptuously. That is the taxation of capital sums as if they were income. Here is an example. While *Bless the Bride* was still running successfully dear old C. B. Cochran rang up and said: 'Alan, I've got an offer for the amateur rights of the *Bride*': and he mentioned a sum – I think it was £2,400 – which would be divided between C.B., Vivian Ellis and myself. It did not strike me as enormous, but for me £800 was £800. I imagined that the great old man had been properly advised and knew what he was doing. Also, I supposed he was building up funds for the next production on which we were already at work. So, I said: 'All right, C.B., anything you say.'

Too late, Vivian and I agreed that the transaction was mad; but at first we did not know just how mad it was. We thought *The Bride* would be attractive to amateurs – and so it has turned out: but you never know; it might be too big and ambitious. We had the sort of choice that occurs to landowners or farmers. The copyright in a work can be divided into sections, like an estate or farm. You can keep the professional stage rights, but sell the amateur rights. The Long Field at the end of a farm may yield a good crop for a long time – or not: but it is inconvenient, a neighbour wants it badly, and the farmer sells it for £2,400. That £2,400 will not be taxed as income: here is a capital transaction. In the same way, C.B.C., Vivian and I had sold the right to charge a fee whenever amateurs performed our work as long as we lived and for fifty years after our deaths. It was an outright sale: never again could we draw a penny from the amateur rights. But, blow-me-down, my £800 was treated as *income*, and taxed as income, so that, at the rates I was then paying, I got something like £150 for the rights of seventy or eighty years. Does this appear to you to be just?

Any crumb that comes our way is income. Or as a learned judge put it:

> Professional earnings are comparable to the profits of a trade. But . . . in the case of a professional man such as an author or actor one is not concerned with the contracts under which he worked or the rights in his work as an income-producing asset, but *only with the receipts when they come in,* whether as *proceeds of the sale of those rights or being retained and income coming therefrom.*

But why, my lord? But why? Put all that, as I have done, into terms of farmers and fields, and it makes no sense whatever.

The doctrine was born, I believe, in a case of 1944, but other judges have followed it. Mr Justice Danckwerts, who was at Cook's with me, said in 1950 that many people thought it was unjust, and seemed to suggest that he did too, but he had to administer the law. I have tried hard to understand the reasoning behind it. 'You see,' say the learned men, 'the trader has stock in trade but the professional man has none . . .' I still fail to follow – I believe it to be Judge-made law, and Parliament should change it.

But there is an ending to this tale that made me very happy: for it displays the most generous conduct I have ever encountered in my professional life. The firm that bought the rights was the famous Samuel French, who do great work in the assistance and supply of amateur companies. One of the firm, Mr Hogg, now dead, invited Vivian and me to lunch. He had heard about our tax misfortunes, thought that Fate had used us hardly, and said – astonishingly – that his firm proposed to pay us something *ex gratia*, for all amateur performances of *Bless the Bride*. And so, ever since, they have. I do not know how the sums are calculated, but they are very, very welcome. We pay income tax upon them as if they were regular income. We are not entitled to a penny. The race of gentlemen is not dead yet.

Observe now how the Treasury changes its tune, or rather its weapons, when an author dies. It is like a thug who fights with his feet but has a knife ready behind his back. While the author lives, as we have seen, everything that comes into the till is taxed as 'income'. The State will not recognize that the sale of the amateur rights in a play is the outright sale of a capital asset, a receipt that cannot be repeated and therefore should not be accounted as income. 'A live author,' says the State, 'has *no* capital assets, no field like a farmer, no stock-in-trade like Harrod's Stores. We cannot go into this contract or that, this section of copyright and the other.' But when he dies that is just what they do. All his copyrights become one large capital asset. The State, in harsh consultation with his agent, or executor, assesses the 'principal value' of the whole, on the basis of 'likely receipts'. Judging by the last three or five years, they say, the amateur rights are likely to yield x pounds. Here is a contract to make a film of the play and that is likely to yield £5,000. Having done the sum they charge the estate, that is, the widow, Death Duties according to the schedule, 25 per cent of the total 'value' on £10,000 to £20,000, 45 per cent if it is £30,000 to £40,000 and so on. Observe that she has got to pay this before she can get anything that is due to her under the will. There may be nothing in the bank, but she has been left the house. She may have to sell the house to pay the Death Duties; she will have to pay Death Duties on the house, in any case, and perhaps Capital Gains Tax if she sells it. Further, the 'principal value' of say the amateur rights is supposed to include 'likely receipts', but if she receives any royalties from them, 'actual receipts', she will have to pay income tax upon them, so she pays twice. My agent tells me that the Treasury vampires are getting tougher and tougher. An artist told me that they are now valuing and taxing everything they find in a dead man's studio, and some artists are clearing their studios in consequence.

In 1967 I was elected – '*nem con*', they told me – President of the Society of Authors. This made me feel both proud and puny. For my five predecessors were Alfred Lord Tennyson, George Meredith, Thomas Hardy, J. M. Barrie and John Masefield: and what was I doing on such a list? But I was there, I supposed, not for my books but my battles: I had probably battled more than those great fellows, and had some struggle in me still.

This fine Society is officially eighty-six years old. It was born on

26 May 1884 when Lord Tennyson, Poet Laureate, accepted the Presidency. There was an eightieth Birthday Party in 1964, and I steal shamelessly from the account that Victor Bonham-Carter prepared for the occasion. The first stirrings in the womb were in March 1843, when a small group of writers met informally at the British Hotel, Cockspur Street to found the British Society of Authors. It was fathered by Charles Dickens, who was infuriated by the pirating of his books in America and by the rapacity of his British publishers. But Dickens dropped the baby after the second meeting and it lived for less than a month. He even scorned some of the brave men who had made the pilgrimage to Cockspur Street. 'If it were the best society in the world,' he wrote, 'the grossness of some natures in it would have weight to drag it down.

'You may suppose, from seeing my name in the printed letter you have received, that I was favourable to the proposed Society. I am decidedly opposed to it. I went there on the day I was in the chair after much solicitation, opened the proceedings by telling them that I approved of the design in theory, but in practice considered it hopeless. I may tell you – I did not tell them – that the nature of the meeting, and the character and position of many of the men attending it, cried "Failure" trumpet-tongued in my ears . . . In practice I feel sure that the present publishing system cannot be overset until authors are different men . . . Having seen the Cockspur Street Society I am as well convinced of its invincible hopelessness as if I saw it written by a celestial pen-man in the Book of Fate.'

Dear, dear!

Another discouragement was the universal hostility to 'unions' and collective action. In 1852 the Booksellers Association, supported by certain publishers, tried to enforce 'net book agreement' (such as exists today and – years ago – was approved by the Restrictive Practices Tribunal). It failed; it was undermined by undersellers and vigorously condemned by a whole battery of public men, including Carlyle, John Stuart Mill, Mr Gladstone, and, rather strangely, Charles Dickens. Free Trade was the thing and the Association collapsed.

Thirty years later the authors tried again. By this time Dickens, Carlyle, and other faint-hearts were dead. The copyright laws were as confused and inadequate as ever. There were some sound and respected publishers but the trade was infested with sharks who preyed upon all but the few established writers. But now, enter a fine new champion – Walter Besant. He was a prolific novelist, a historian, a philanthropist, a warm friend of France and a pioneer of inexhaustible energy and courage. He was a practical man too: having been secretary to the Palestine Exploration Fund for nearly twenty years, having helped to found the 'People's Palace' in the East End, he knew the tricks of running societies. He knew too about the *Société des Gens de Lettres*, which had been in action since 1837 and done great service to writers. He was a lively fellow, enjoyed good company, good food, and the club, and fought his battles with relish and resolution. 'His big beard,' says Bonham Carter, 'was not a screen but a banner.'

The campaign opened on 28 September 1883 when Besant took the chair at a meeting at 3 Sheffield Terrace, Kensington. Eleven others attended and all resolved to found a Society to be called 'The Company of Authors'. The aim was to protect and advance the interests of authors, principally by defining and defending literary property, at home and abroad, through copyright improvements. After twelve more sessions for the preliminaries a public meeting was called at 1 Adam Street, Adelphi, a fitting address, on 18 February 1884. A Council and a Management Committee (Besant in the chair) were formed, just as today. A constitution was drafted and duly completed by the end of June. The title registered at the Board of Trade was The Incorporated Society of Authors. An impressive list of Vice-Presidents, drawn from every branch of science, literature, and art, included Lord Lytton, Matthew Arnold, Thomas Huxley, J. A. Froude, Wilkie Collins, Charles Reade, John Ruskin, R. D. Blackmore, W. S. Gilbert, Charlotte Yonge. At the second shot Besant got Tennyson to accept the Presidency, and this triumph was announced on 26 May 1884: and at a Lord Mayor's Mansion House banquet (a speech by Gilbert) 'the Society was dragged out in the light and exhibited to the world.'

But for some years there was a struggle to survive – only sixty-eight paid subscriptions in 1884: no permanent offices till 1887, no full-time Secretary till 1892 (G. H. Thring). The Society roared into action, though, and came under fire. They attacked the objectionable publishing practices then in use: the automatic surrender of the author's copyright, usually for a trifling sum; the half-profit system (where the author 'shared' the profits with the publisher, who commonly concealed or inflated the true costs of production); or the plain fraud where the aspiring author was induced to pay for the full cost of a book, which might then never be distributed to the trade or even appear at all.

Besant and his brave band came under fire. They were 'trying to be a Trade Union', encouraging strikes; setting contented authors against their publishers; generating baseless hatred of Paternoster Row, attempting the impossible.

There was internal criticism as well. Some authors thought business beneath them and would not read the contracts they signed – and then blamed the Society when they asked for help too late. Some would not join for fear of offending publishers.

Many years later, in 1932, George Bernard Shaw wrote:

What a heartbreaking job it is trying to combine authors for their own protection! I had ten years of it on the Committee of Management of the Society of Authors: and the first lesson I learnt was that when you take the field for the authors you will be safer without a breastplate than without a backplate. They will not combine against the crook publisher and the sweating editor: but they will combine against you and the Society with the fervour of crusaders. They loathe an interfering fellow who, with a soulless eye to business, reminds them that when it comes to selling their work, and incidentally feeding their children, they must come down from romance to vulgar trade commission, and not indulge in splendid gestures at the expense of their profession.

I think we are more loyal and sensible now: but I know what the great man meant. Now and then, in the library battle when we have had a good correspondence, and perhaps a supporting leader in one of the papers, some author would butt in and throw cold water at our efforts. He might be quite obscure, not even a member: never mind, he was an 'author', and a great satisfaction to our enemies. But we have not much to complain of.

There are now 4,000 members. For the last seven years the presiding genius has been Miss Elizabeth Barber, General Secretary, recently honoured by Her Majesty. She has a small but skilled platoon of assistants, and meets her Management Committee, all active authors, once a month. The agenda at these meetings is astonishingly extensive.

The Society is always ready to advise individual members, on the rights and wrongs of contracts, to take up suitable battles with publisher, papers, the B.B.C., and to resist any assaults on copyright or fair practice. The Society worked for twelve years to extract from the B.B.C. the admirable principle of a repeat fee for repeat performance. They were standing by to aid the gallant Hammond Innes in a shameful persecution by the Inland Revenue. In good faith he gave a book to his old father who took all the profits, and presumably was taxed upon them. The Revenue wanted the author to pay tax on the sum he would have received if he had not given the book away – 'notional income'. He won at every stage, but the vultures forced him up to the Court of Appeal. If that Court had not nobly and unanimously defended him, his costs alone might have been £8,000.

There are generally as well one or two major campaigns simmering or boiling – obscene publications, the libraries, some desired amendment of copyright law, a brush with the publishers, or a drive against the Treasury about taxation: and such affairs need long discussion of principle, policy, and tactics. Under Miss Barber many quiet victories have been won.

The Society issues useful leaflets on practical matters, taxation and so on. We are not a society for reading literary papers, but for getting things done.

The magazine, *The Author*, made its first appearance in May 1890, with Walter Besant as 'conductor', as a monthly, on a budget of £6 per issue. From the start it was full of lively news and articles, written by such men as Edmund Gosse, Rider Haggard, Wilkie Collins, Andrew Lang and, of course, Besant himself, who filled number after number with aggressive reasoning and challenging facts. Oscar Wilde contributed inadvertently to the fourth issue, which contained his speech at the Annual Dinner that year. Now edited by Richard Findlater, *The Author* still makes a lively and combative appearance every quarter.

The author sits alone in his little study, scratching his head: but it is a citadel, he is a captain of thought, and a master of men. Who else in the world has had such fine thoughts as these? What man has ever set down, with such style and spirit, such a tale as his? But he is alone, and all the other captains of thought are alone. They seldom meet; they do not feel the fire of company, the surge of common action. When they do come together it is rarely to discuss their own rights and problems and complaints. They assemble in clothes they do not like, to salute some great man who died a hundred years ago: and mostly they do not know the faces of the other captains who are alive.

I can remember only one occasion when the scribbling battalion gathered on parade with fire in their bellies, bent on battle. This was in 1928 and the *casus belli* was the prosecution for obscenity of a book, Miss Radclyffe Hall's *Well of Loneliness*. This was a sincere, courageous, but to me at least, unexciting plea for a tolerant understanding of the unfortunate Lesbians. When I read it I could not understand what the famous fuss was about: as Norman Birkett said later at Bow Street: 'Nowhere is there an obscene word or a lascivious passage.' The book received praise in respectable places. 'This is a truly remarkable book. It is remarkable in the first place as a work of art finely conceived and finely written. Secondly it is remarkable as dealing with an aspect of abnormal life seldom or never presented in English fiction – certainly never with such unreserved frankness' (*Daily Telegraph*). 'Sincere, courageous, high minded, and often beautifully expressed' (*The Times Literary Supplement*). Arnold Bennett wrote: 'It is honest, convincing, and extremely courageous.'

But one James Douglas of the *Sunday Express* had set himself up as the Savonarola of the city. A month after publication he wrote:

The decadent apostles of the most hideous and loathsome vices no longer conceal their degeneracy and degradation . . . This novel forces upon our society a disagreeable task which it has hitherto shirked, the task of

cleaning itself from the leprosy of these lepers and making the air clean
and wholesome once more . . . It is a seductive insidious piece of special
pleading designed to display perverted decadence as a martyrdom
inflicted upon those outcasts by a cruel society. It flings a veil of sentiment
over their depravity. It even suggests that their self-made debasement is
unavoidable because they cannot save themselves.

And he added: 'I would rather put a phial of prussic acid in the
hands of a healthy girl or boy than the book in question . . . What
then is to be done? The book must be at once withdrawn.'

Savonarola was supported in some corners of the Press. Jonathan
Cape, the publishers, consulted the Home Secretary (Joynson Hicks,
the celebrated Jix) and offered to withdraw. Jix said that would be
best, and Cape withdrew at once.

But a new edition was printed in Paris and the first consignment was
immediately seized by the Customs at Dover. On 9 November the
Government applied at Bow Street for a destruction order under Lord
Campbell's Act of 1857.

Two days before the hearing authors and artists and others assembled
in protest at a studio in Chelsea. There must have been two or three
hundred of us. We were to be addressed, they said, by the great Bernard
Shaw who would, no doubt, with eloquent words throw us the Torch
of Liberty. (He had written to the *Daily Herald* that he had read the
book carefully and it ought not to have been withdrawn.) But where
was the great Bernard Shaw? Half an hour – three-quarters, passed:
but still no Torch of Liberty. Nor were there any refreshments. We
stood about and smoked and made rude remarks about Jix and James
Douglas; but boredom threatened, protesters started to slip away, and
it was decided to hold the meeting without the great Bernard Shaw.
One or two speeches were made, and we were all asked to go to Bow
Street and give evidence against the destruction of the *Well of Loneliness*. A lot of us held up our hands and said we would.

At that time this was no slight undertaking for a struggling young
writer especially if he had no great interest in Lesbians: we all expected
to appear in a James Douglas black-list, heavily printed, THESE
ARE THE MERCHANTS OF FILTH. But we were determined,
however dubious, and felt slightly heroic. Then the great Bernard
Shaw arrived. He told us some tales of his own scuffles with censor-
ship: but then he said that we were all making fools of ourselves. The
resolution we had carried was useless, and our proposed action would
be quite in vain. As things turned out, he was perfectly right, but it
was not an inspiring address from our major prophet. We all went
out with our little tails between our legs.

The rest of the story is well told in Norman St John Stevas's excellent book *Obscenity and the Law* – Secker and Warburg. The friends of justice attended Bow Street in swarms. 'We came,' said Sir Norman Birkett, 'from every conceivable walk of life . . . A more distinguished body of witnesses has never before been called in a court of justice.'

But the magistrate, Sir Chartres Biron would not hear a word from any of us. 'I don't think,' he said, 'people are entitled to express an opinion upon a matter which is for the decision of the court.' The first witness called was Desmond MacCarthy, the editor of *Life and Letters*. Norman Birkett asked him (the wrong question, some say): 'In your view is it obscene?'

The Magistrate: 'No, I shall disallow that. It is quite clear that the evidence is not admissable. A book may be a fine piece of literature and yet obscene . . . I shall not admit the evidence.'

Nor would he 'state a case' for a higher court on the question of the expert evidence which Birkett wished to call.

The author, who was present in court, was not allowed to say a word, for the book, not she, was in the dock.

The book was burned. But in 1949 it was published again without a word of protest, and is, I believe, freely available today, at its original price of fifteen shillings.

So the valiant massing of the authors may be said to have come to nothing, as Shaw had predicted: and the captains of thought retired to their lonely citadels. On the whole I think it best that they should be allowed to stay there. I, at least, should never ask them to march down Parliament Street in columns of four, even to denounce the brilliant Boyle or the Library Association. They are not that sort of creature: they do not work or dwell together, and they will never be good at getting together. But the less able they are to aid and agitate in numbers the more necessary it is that a faithful, skilful few should carry their hopes, their cares, their consciences for them: so that though they stay in their citadels scratching their heads they will not in effect be dumb or undefended. This is the task, the lofty duty of the Society of Authors. Here is a quiet elephant that never forgets. It was not till 1954 – twenty-six years after the *Well of Loneliness* that the Society appointed a Committee to attack the obscenity laws in ordered fashion and we began the drafting of a Bill that was knocked about but contributed much to the Act of 1959. Many other later cases had worried us – even more – but the corporate memory had carefully stored that futile morning at Bow Street. Three or four points of injustice and folly in the law that had shocked us that morning were strongly pursued in the very first draft of our Bill: and we fought for our remedies, successfully, to the end of the long bickering with the Law Officers of the Crown. Whether we were right is another matter. I am simply saying that the voice of the scattered scribblers, scratching their heads in their lonely citadels, was heard at last in Parliament, and so, I am sure, it will be on many other matters. So I am proud to be the President of the Society of Authors. I may be not much more than a figurehead, but the ship is a real ship. God bless her and all who sail in her!

No sooner had I retired from 'the leadership' in the Libraries campaign than they asked me to be Chairman of the British Copyright Council. 'No,' I said, 'a thousand times, no!' 'But there's nothing in it,' they said. 'It will only mean taking the chair at a few meetings a year.' The usual happened and I have been the unworthy Chairman since September 1965. We meet in fact once a month: and never can a Chairman have presided over so many discussions so little of which he really understood. Fortunately, he has a most able secretary, Reynell Wreford, who understands everything. It is a fine old body, recently restored to life by Royce Whale, for so long the King of the Performing Right Society (at whose offices we meet – damn it, by the way, I am Vice-President of that as well).

We consist of delegates from eighteen bodies whose members are actively interested in copyright as makers or users – but chiefly makers – thereof, authors, composers, musicians, publishers, photographers, *et hoc genus omne*. Our object is to foster and maintain respect for the principles and practice of copyright, which are being assailed and eroded by enemy waters everywhere. On this account we had prolonged labours over the 'Radio Pirates' – 'Free Radio ' means, among other things, 'Free from Royalties'. Some 'developing' countries expect everybody's books and music for nothing and pass impossible new laws if we don't spot and dissuade them. All sorts of international conferences require understanding and attendance; papers by the mile must be read. Mr Ronald Barker, Secretary to the Publishers' Association, a high authority on all the mysteries, commutes from Continent to Continent. Angry, incomprehensible letters must be written to *The Times*. New 'technological' blessings multiply problems – tape-recorders, copying-machines, the computer. Education, we say, is greedy – not to mention the B.B.C. Authors and composers, for their contribution to gramophone records, still get the only 'statutory maximum wage' on the statute book. We are toiling at amendments all over the Copyright Act. We are constantly consulting, or abusing, the Board of Trade, which for some strange reason is our Papa. We have, I believe, made a name for ourselves as a benevolent nuisance.

Lofty literary men may have been surprised on 1 January, to see that I had been appointed a Companion of Honour 'for services to literature'. They cannot have been more surprised than I was. But I suppose my 'services' were the various efforts to aid the author which

I have described in this chapter. If so, those with whom I have worked must have said a kind word, and I thank them (also Mr Harold Wilson, who can recite some of my songs in *Big Ben*).

A Companion of Honour is invested privately; he is not mixed up with a mob of mere Knights Bachelor; and I had a charming quarter of an hour with the Queen. Strangely, on this occasion, I was able to do one more literary service. Her Majesty, clearly, has a special feeling for this Order. 'This is unique,' she said as she gave me the beautiful Badge; and then, when we had sat down, 'I like the words, but I don't know where they come from.'

Nor did I: but I went home and hunted them down for Her Majesty. They come from Alexander Pope's Epistle to Addison:

> Statesman, but friend of Truth! Of soul sincere,
> IN ACTION FAITHFUL AND IN HONOUR CLEAR
> Who broke no promise, served no private end,
> Who gained no title and who lost no friend.

§ 12 §

BATTLES FOR BRITAIN

READ carefully, pray, this repugnant sentence:
'Modern technology has brought us to the point where *change is going to be the norm of everyday life*. The educated man, the socially useful man, indeed the happy man of the future will be the man educated to *constant change*, educated to adopt, to initiate, to enjoy, embrace change . . . . .'

(Mr Jack Straw, then President-elect of the National Union of Students, delivering the first Granada Guildhall Lecture 1969.)

God knows, I am not dangerously allergic to change. All my life I have been advocating changes which I thought necessary and reasonable. But I have no congenital itch for change. I often say, as we all do: 'Why not leave things alone?'

Mr Jack Straw is a very different fellow, and his doctrine daunts me. 'Constant change . . .' 'Change the norm of everyday life . . .' Nothing about 'wise' or 'reasonable change . . .' Nothing about 'desired' or 'desirable' change. This is change for the sake of change: we must constantly dump our institutions, our weights and measures, as women change their hats, or men cross their legs. Any new toy that the accursed tyrant Technology imagines must be without question admitted to our happy bosoms, embraced and enjoyed, whether we like it or not.

The Straw school of thought seems to have powerful cells in Whitehall. Year after year we hear of some new assault on the customs and arrangements with which we were perfectly content. We are not asked if we should like the change; we are not told what the reasons for it are; if we complain we are ignorant and 'insular': if our Members complain the Government puts the Whips on. I do not pretend to know anything about coinage, and I am quite willing to accept the opinion of experts. But I do wish that someone had troubled to explain to me what mischief our old coinage, our dear sixpences and half-crowns, was causing, and what will be the great advantage of the new. Mere decimality does not impress me. Twelve is a much better number than ten. More important, I know that in the House of Commons there were many knowing Members of all Parties who were ready for a change but thought that the change proposed was the wrong one. In such a case, on such a subject, the vote should be free and the majority have their way. But no, the Government 'put the Whips on', and so I suspect this change.

I suspect too any change which seems to be based (*a*) on a desire to make us 'uniform' with Western Europe and (*b*) the assumption that European methods are bound to be better than ours. We have been in business much longer than those little fellows: and sometimes the real question is whether they should not come over to our superior ways.

'Time' is a sharp example. The most fatuous reason advanced for our adoption of British Standard Time (which is in truth Central European Time) was that it would 'bring us into line' with Western Europe, that Greenwich Mean Time was an 'insular whim' and so on. Classic forms of this ignorant assertion were heard from business men. Sir Richard Powell, of the Institute of Directors, said: 'We have been out of step for years. It is about time we abandoned this insular attitude, and conformed with the rest of Europe.' One Mr Peter W. Johnson in the *Financial Times* (22 July 1967) did even better: 'The British Isles must have introduced *their type* of G.M.T. and summer time at some period later than the rest of Europe – how, otherwise, would it have come about?' The truth is quite the other way, as I have explained again this year in my pamphlet *In the Dark*.* Far back in 1884 at a Conference in Washington, the nations chose the meridian of Greenwich as the initial meridian of longitude – the Prime Meridian – 0° – and appointed Greenwich Time as the standard time of the world (it is now known among the scientists as Universal Time). The globe was divided into twenty-four Time Zones, each 15 degrees of longitude wide (the distance covered by the sun in one hour). Zone 0 straddles the Greenwich Meridian from $7\frac{1}{2}$ degrees West to $7\frac{1}{2}$ degrees East longitude. In that Zone lie London, Dublin, Paris, Brussels, the Hague, Geneva, Madrid (and very nearly Lisbon). In the next Zone eastward (Zone minus 1) are Berlin and Rome. Their time is one hour ahead of Greenwich Time, because the sun gets there one hour earlier. Manchuria is in Zone Minus 9 – 9 hours ahead of Greenwich. A business man in Manchuria who wishes to ring up Lombard Street at a convenient time subtracts nine hours from Manchurian Time and gets Greenwich Time at that particular moment. New York is five hours behind, Zone *plus* 5, so to get Greenwich they add five hours to their time: all this is a simple but useful arrangement – anyone who knows about the Zone system can tell what time it is anywhere.

Now between 1892 and 1911 the West European countries all

* The Bodley Head 6*s*.

adopted the Zone system, even that slippery fish France, which meant that Holland, Belgium, Luxemburg, France and Spain all kept Greenwich Time. But now – it was when the Common Market began, I think – they have deserted the Greenwich Zone and gone into Zone minus One with Berlin and Rome. As the sun flies the distance between London and Paris is still sixteen minutes: by the Greenwich clock it is seventy-six minutes.

So, the suggestion that *we* are 'out of step' and 'out of line' is sadly laughable and our acceptance of it in the British Standard Time Act 1968 was criminal folly. I cannot believe that Parliament will permit it to continue. It means that *for civil purposes* there is at present *no world standard time*. No man in New York, no man in Manchuria, no man anywhere will be able with confidence to play the useful trick I have described because the king-pin has been shifted. Greenwich Time means nothing now for ordinary men: it is reserved for astronomers and navigators.

The Clock at Westminster, the great bell Big Ben, used to keep not only London's Local Time but World Standard Time, Universal Time. We were the only country that could say such a thing. It was a cosmic compliment, an international trust: our rulers want to throw them away. What other country, I wonder, would do so?

You may well say: 'But what does this amateur know about it?' I shall not blame you: but I must then quote proudly from a letter in *The Times* of 24 October 1967 from the Presidents of the Royal Astronomical Society, the Institute of Navigation, the Royal Geographical Society and the Royal Institution of Chartered Surveyors.

'. . . We do wish to press most strongly that the provisions of the Bill shall not diminish in any way the unique status of Greenwich Mean Time or of the Greenwich Meridian which are used universally for astronomical, navigational, and allied purposes; we concur in the arguments so brilliantly adduced by Sir Alan Herbert (3 June – *The Times*).'

I will not here repeat the whole of the argument. You must read *In the Dark*. But briefly, I conclude:

(1) we must abolish British Standard Time which (quite apart from practical objections in this country, is an ignorant affront to Nature and Science) and return to Greenwich Time.
(2) having done that we can secure Daylight Saving:
   (*a*) by going back to the old 'Summer Time' drill, for longer periods, if you like, but *never* between 15 November and 15 February.
   (*b*) by the Painless Plan – no clock changing, but Government example and exhortation and, where convenient and reasonable, popular compliance.

(3) ideally, Western Europe should come back to Greenwich Time. 'If I were King' I would refuse to enter the Common Market till they did.*

(3), I agree, may be considered ambitious – but why not? It is high time that the United Kingdom gave a lead instead of trotting obediently behind France and Co.

In one area at least, we are standing fairly firm: and that is a large area, the sea.† We are saddled with decimal coinage already, and we're doomed, it seems, to metrication. Indeed, without most of us noticing it's been creeping up for some time. In May 1965 Mr Douglas Jay in the House of Commons said that the Government considered it 'desirable' that the metric system should become the primary system of weights and measures for the country as a whole. In September 1969 the primary schools went metric – this is the cunning way of conquering us – 'pharmaceuticals' went that way on 1 March 1969. 'M-days to come' says Mr Nigel Calder in the *New Statesman* of 30 January 1970, 'include cement and paper and printing 1971; marine and building industries 1972; road speed limits 1973; electric appliances 1975; general engineering 1976.'

'The Americans', says Mr Calder, 'are beginning to feel isolated *following the British decision to metricate*: their National Bureau of Standards is currently investigating the prospects, and it is probably only a matter of time before they follow suit. Then the inch and the mile, the pound and the bushel, will finally go the way of the farthing and the fardel ...'

What a pity we did not stand together! The Americans have had decimal coinage without metrication and flourished: could we not have done the same? The Americans have 'rationalized' some 'Imperial measures' – the ton and the gallon, I believe. Could we not have done the same, could we not still do the same – getting rid of any resented absurdities – poles? perches? I do not know what they are – but keeping to the old names and measures which after all were good enough to get Apollo 11 to the Moon.

'The inch and the mile will go . . .'

Not so fast.

Here are two rather contradictory statements of 1969:

(1) In the *Times Saturday Review*, 30 May, Major Oliver Stewart Sailing Correspondent, told us that '*feet and fathoms, nautical miles and knots are on the way out* . . . Seamen may not take kindly to the idea of thinking in *metres per second* instead of knots' (nautical miles per hour) 'but *they will be obliged to do so.*'

'Why?' I spluttered at once, 'and by whom?'

* I do not want to enter it on any terms, as I warned the world far back in 1961.

† But see the sad postscript to this chapter.

I appointed myself President of the Friends of the Fathom and began, I think, a useful correspondence which *The Times* called *The Fathomless Sea*.

(June 4th) My information may be imperfect, but I hope that Parliament will inquire just what is being done and by what authority the seamen are to be 'obliged'. The Friends of the Fathom believe that here is a case where we should for once resist our rulers' mania for masochism. Let the English-speaking mariners stand together and refuse to be stampeded by the unnecessary novelties of European 'scientists' who want to tidy the world, but do not sound like seamen.

The foot and the fathom have been used in marine measurement for three or four centuries;* and the big joke is that the metricalizers are asking us to abandon a respectable decimal system of cosmic importance. There are 6 feet in a fathom, there are 600 feet (or 100 fathoms) in a 'cable'. There are 10 cables (or 1,000 fathoms) in a sea mile. A sea mile is the length of a minute of latitude and there are 60 minutes in a degree of latitude. So that anyone who cares can calculate in a second or two how many feet (or fathoms) there are in a degree of latitude.

I do not suggest that such sums are of much practical importance (or will always be precisely accurate). But they are the kind of tricks for which the metric system is commended. On our charts the nautical mile is divided into 10. On a French chart before me, which has a scale in metres, the nautical mile has 12 divisions, which makes me laugh.

After endless labour I reckon that a ship doing 30 knots is travelling at 15·4 metres a second; but even if it were right what sort of picture does it give the ordinary man?

(2) There was a glorious answer to Major Stewart's information and my complaints. A letter – private – from the Department of the Hydrographer of the Navy, a few days later, said:

The 41 member states of the International Hydrographic Bureau use nautical miles which are related to a minute of latitude, therefore *there is no point* in changing that or abandoning the knot. For that reason the new British Admiralty charts are changing to metres *only for heights or depths*, and the Admiralty *has no intention of doing away with either the nautical and sea mile or the knot*.

Note, by the way, the strange procedure. It was extremely courteous and kind of the Hydrographer of the Navy to give this important information privately to this humble person. But why not give it publicly to the great community of British seamen? Why for that matter, was it left to me to chase Major Stewart's alarming assertion? Why did not

* Someone said that I should have gone back much further, to the Acts of the Apostles XXVII 28: '. . . the sailors deemed that they drew near to some country and sounded, and found twenty fathoms. . . .'

some Member of Parliament ask Ministers to state the position clearly?

The position, then, in 1975 it seems, if all parties continue on their present courses, will be:

(1) lateral distance on land in the United Kingdom will be measured in millimetres, metres and kilometres.

(2) lateral distance on the waters surrounding these islands will still be measured in feet, fathoms and nautical miles (6,080 feet to a nautical mile).

(I am not so mad about uniformity as some of these change-mongers. At this moment the Thames above Teddington is measured in 'statute miles': the Thames below Teddington – the Tideway – is measured by the Port of London Authority in nautical miles. No great mischief results, so far as I know. But I have a major exercise in uniformity to suggest. *Why do we not bring the nautical mile (2,000 yards) ashore?* Then our land and the water round it would have the same measurement – and we should be spared those tiresome kilometres.)

But 'the position' will not be quite so simple as I said. Our dear Admiralty, laterally, is sound; but vertically, in my humble judgement, they have gone a little mad. For they have begun a long process of 'metrifying' – or rather semi-metrifying the splendid and famous Admiralty charts. I have a couple. *Heights and depths* are measured in metres: but the horizontal scales are still in old-fashioned feet, cables and nautical miles, and there is nothing about measuring distance in metres. 'Metric Charts' is therefore a misdescription – I threatened a nice sailor at the Boat Show with a prosecution under the Trade Descriptions Act.

I call them hybrid or semi-metric charts. It is like measuring a girl's height in centimetres and her bosom and belly in inches, or playing tennis on a court concrete at one end and grass at the other.

Height, depth and distance [I remarked in my second letter] often work together at sea. Using a hybrid chart a ship may be ordered to anchor on the 10 metre line 200 yards (or 1 cable) from the ship ahead. An anchor cable measured, and marked, in fathoms may descend in waters measured in metres. Till every chart in use is semi-metric there will have to be two different lead-lines in every ship and I suppose convertible echo-sounders. 'Tidal Information' will give the heights of tides in metres and their speed as a rate of knots.

A Yachtsman seeking to establish his position off a dangerous shore may use the method called Distance Off (e.g. a lighthouse) by Vertical Sextant Angle. He will get his answer – in distance – in metres for the height of the lighthouse is shown in metres, but he will then have to convert it into nautical miles: then he must switch his mind back to the other measure to get the depth of water. Some of these may be mere incongruities: but some may be opportunities for delay and error. Moving from one chart to another may dangerously confuse. ('Under no circumstances should a seaman be put in the position of changing from fathoms on one chart to metres on the other, and back again' – *Journal of the Institute of Navigation.*)

Not one seaman wrote to *The Times* that I was talking nonsense. But the courteous hydrographic officer defended the hybrid chart persuasively:

(*a*) it will aid in the approach to 'international charts' in certain areas;
(*b*) it will save civil servants in the field of hydrographic survey from the labour of 'converting' metric material into feet and fathom material:

(I do not like the smell of (*b*): is it not better that the labour of 'conversion' be done by civil servants safe ashore than by sailors in doubt, darkness or danger?)

(*c*) If we were to be the only country not producing metric [? semi-metric] charts (and the U.S. Oceanographic Office already includes metric charts on its lists) we should soon lose our overseas customers.

What is the evidence for this apprehension? Knowing men in the chart-trade tell me there are no complaints from the numerous nations who use our present charts; on the contrary the seamen are content, they are conservative, and will be irritated by the change. And, anyway, is the Admiralty a profit-seeking department?

Another officer told me that metrical depths and heights are wanted by the 'scientists', meaning, I gathered, biologists, engineers etc. But the first purpose of an Admiralty chart surely is to serve the seamen, not to save the civil servant labour, please the miscellaneous scientist, or make a profit.

Then on 13 June I flushed another hydrographer, across the Atlantic, Captain T. K. Treadwell of the United States Naval Oceanographic Office. He was not very polite, criticized arguments I had not used, and finished rashly by suggesting that I was trying to be funny. But I let him off.

Now, the United States Navy still use the foot and the fathom etc. on their own charts of their own enormous coasts. Here then the main body of English speakers (and a great many foreigners too) think that our way is the best way: and here I should like to see them give an active lead to the world, refuse to follow the European landlubbers:

But Captain Treadwell, I thought, was in a defeatist mood.

He 'sympathized entirely,' he said, with my 'adherence to *tradition*', but 'the fathom-lovers', the United Kingdom and the United States

'are in the insignificant minority, and in the interest of simple consistency . . . we must simply face facts'.
I replied:

The 'fathom-lovers' are not moved by 'nostalgia' or 'tradition' but by an
affection for efficiency. The metre, however useful to engineers, indus-
trialists and others ashore, is not the best thing for the navigator. One
thousand eight hundred and fifty-two metres to the mile, divided into
twelfths – what clumsy nondecimal figures! The metre is not like the
fathom, 'related to a minute of latitude'.* It did not, like the fathom,
help to make the maps of the world. At its birth, during the French
Revolution, it had cosmic pretensions too. It was supposed to be – what
was it? – 1/10,000,000 of the distance between the Equator and the Poles.
This has since been found to be erroneous. 'The now widely adopted
international metre is not of precisely the length it was intended to be'
(Charles Cotter, Forum, Institute of Navigation, July 1968).
So on the world stage the metre has been a flop from the first. There
is no magic in it and it is just as much an arbitrary measure as the
fathom. The difference is that the fathom has been a success at sea, and
fits into the world system as the metre never could.

No one corrected or reproved me.
Captain Treadwell, in his letter, had said:

As a matter of interest, the United States Naval Oceanographic Office is
currently publishing almost half its charts *in the metric system*. This
is an inevitable result of our exchange agreement with some 21 countries,
under which each hydrographic office has authority to publish the other's
products. Since the vast bulk of the material we receive in these exchanges
is *in the metric system* we do not convert it to fathoms but publish it as
received.

(Yes, but what does the gallant Captain mean by 'in the metric
system'. Does he mean totally metric charts – or hybrid charts, as I
have described them. This professional is singularly lacking in professional precision.)
I replied:

Captain Treadwell's office, he confesses, is acquiring quantities of
'metric' (or does he mean 'semi-metric') foreign charts and selling them
just as they are . . . Is this 'simple consistency'? Is it true to the doctrine
and practice which the English speakers believe to be the best? Should
our hydrographers do anything that encourages the proliferation of the
inferior metre at sea, and must increase the dangers of confusion?
The Captain says that Britain and the United States are 'an insignificant
minority'. So they are at the United Nations. But the charts they sell are
multitudinous and dominant. They are of the very few who have a world

* See the R.N. Hydrographer Officer's letter.

chart coverage. If we stick to our standards they will prevail. Where necessary (I am told that at sea it isn't) we should be seeking to convert the foreigner to the fathom. Our hydrographers, I respectfully suggest, look like the Pope selling Protestant pamphlets, to save trouble, or make money.

The Captain did not reply: nor did anyone else. But see the post-script on page 266.

On 18 June 1969 in the *Daily Telegraph* I began a small battle about Centigrade, another matter where we are deserting the Americans and other English-speakers.

Sir – The most modern piece of machinery in the world, the Apollo 11 rocket, stands 363 *feet* high (two feet lower than the Cross of St Paul's), weighs 6,000 *tons*, and will travel so many *miles* (nautical) to the moon. Its fuel, you tell us (July 11) includes '344,500 *gallons* of liquid hydrogen at —425 Fahrenheit'. Yet Britain, who sent these weights and measures to America, is being slowly bullied, in the name of modernity, into metres, litres, kilogrammes, kilometres, Centigrade, and so on. How odd!

I was told at once – but I knew it already – that the United States ton and gallon both differ significantly from those of the United Kingdom. 1 short ton = 2,000 lbs., instead of 2,240 lbs. and so on. The foot (which was written large on the Moon), the pound, and Fahrenheit are the same in the United States.

How is dear old Centigrade getting on? In 1961 the B.B.C. began its twin predictions. In 1962 we were told that 'eventually' Fahrenheit would be dropped. After eight years of publicity I meet few Ordinary Men who give Centigrade any serious attention. We are not impressed by its decimal tricks – 0 degrees the Freezing Point of Fresh Water and 100 degrees the Boiling Point of Fresh Water. Indeed, they seem rather silly; for it is often colder than the F.P.F.W. and if you name that 0 degree anything colder must lead you into tiresome minuses. Clever Fahrenheit (1686– 1736), a Fellow of our Royal Society, avoided this trap and made his F.P.F.W. 32 degrees. His 0 degree represents the freezing point of a mixture of water, ice and sal-ammoniac, which Fahrenheit thought to be the extreme of cold. He was wrong about that, but he was on the right lines.
The Ordinary Man is seldom concerned with the temperature of boiling water, or with more than 32 degrees of frost. He wants to know how hot or cold it is in home or garden, and Fahrenheit with his larger lens, more numerous degrees, tells him that more clearly and closely than Centigrade with no bothering minuses or decimal points. Our doctors, by the way, buy four Fahrenheit clinical thermometers to one Centigrade.
But we shall be told, as usual, that the O.M. doesn't matter, that Science and Industry are itching for uniformity with Europe. Should we

not, then, say to Europe: 'Why don't you come over to the superior Fahrenheit? Then you will be one not only with Britain but North America, not to mention Australia and other English speakers. And, as for efficiency, what is good enough for the Apollo should be good enough for you.'

. . . Note the little F's wherever 'Temp.' is mentioned on the instrument panel of the Lunar Module, or Moon Bug. Fahrenheit will be the first temperature scale Man takes to the Moon: and we must have uniformity, mustn't we?

It is not often, in these Whitehall affairs, that one can discover who started it. But now I flushed a distinguished meteorologist, Sir Graham Sutton, Director General of the Meteorological Office from 1953 to 1965. He wrote on 22 July:

I was partly responsible for the decision to introduce this scale into public statements about the weather.

First, may I say that the decision was that of the Ministry responsible for the Meteorological Office [Air Ministry] acting on the advice of the Meteorological Committee . . .

Sir Graham said that my letter

was, I fear, more emotional than factual.

The most important temperature for all human activities is 0 deg. C. (or 32 deg. F) . . . In the Fahrenheit scale this temperature is denoted by the *unremarkable* figure 32: in the Centigrade scale it marks the division between positive and negative temperatures and so is at once forced on the attention of the listener.

. . . The degree Fahrenheit is too small for specifying air temperatures near the ground . . .

He ended with a useful rough translation of Centigrade:

0 deg. C. and all minus temperatures	Freezing
5 deg. C.	cold
10 deg. C.	chilly
15 deg. C.	mild
20 deg. C.	warm
25 deg. C.	hot
30 deg. C. and above	heat wave

I replied (July 29):

I am grateful to Sir Graham Sutton. But I get from him no compelling reason why we should abandon Fahrenheit. The word I heard from the Moon was 'Fahrenheit' not 'Centigrade'.

[I did hear the words in one of those extraordinary talks, while the heroes were dressing for their 'step' on to the Moon's surface.]

Distances, heights, and speeds were stated in feet (not metres) or nautical miles (founded on the foot and the fathom). The stones picked up weighed so many pounds (lbs). Is it not a wonder that with all these derided out-of-date tools the Americans brought off 'Man's greatest technological triumph'?

Yes, yes, I know that the Americans have 'rationalized' the 'ton' and the 'gallon'. But it follows that we should do the same, not that we should panic off into dubious Continental practices. In all these affairs (B.S.T. for example) we think too little of English-speaking America and too much of one small corner of Europe.

When we protest, the 'scientists' who keep butting into our lives accuse us, like Sir Graham, of 'emotion', sometimes 'nostalgia'.

Not at all. I am for efficiency, and British ways are often best.

When an American, a Canadian, an Australian, or a Briton says: 'It's 80 in the shade', they mean the same thing. I call this good and efficient for there are 260 million of them, and we talk to them much more than we talk to Belgians and Italians. China uses Centigrade. Who cares?

I am against the abandonment of Greenwich Time because it is not only our local time, but the World Standard Time (it is now called Universal Time). Not emotional – but scientific.

The British and Americans agree that the fathom is a better measure for the surface of the sea than the metre. Not nostalgia – but efficiency.

For many years in an amateur way I have been constructing sundials, requiring high precision. I find on various rulers, with divisions of 1/8, 1/10, 1/12, 1/16, 1/32, the versatile inch more helpful than the rigid centimetre. 12 is a good number: the virtues of 10 are greatly exaggerated.

Are we irrevocably committed to the costly unpopular change to the metric system (or S.I.)? I meet men of industry and business who hate the prospect. Yet we all sit mum, terrified of being called 'insular'. Is America insular?

P.S. Sir Graham, by the way, scorns 'the unremarkable number 32'. Unremarkable? 32 points of the compass – 32 chessmen – 32 pages in a standard printer's 'sheet' – 32 on the Stock Exchange – 32 bars in a popular song – 32 in that 'gravity' formula – 32 pages in the *Daily Telegraph*. It's a magical number; and as Fahrenheit's freezing point it has been remarked – and remembered – by the English speakers for about 250 years.

Then, on August 1, came a shattering letter from Mr James W. Oswald:

KELVIN SCALE

. . . It is only fair to Sir Alan and others of like mind to point out that not only are degrees F out but degrees C are also doomed. In the new *Système International* units the unit of temperature is the degree Kelvin.

This certainly rids us of the 'tiresome minuses' as 0 deg K is *absolute zero* below which temperature cannot drop. [But what will you bet? Fahrenheit thought that too.] I wonder how Sir Alan will feel when freezing point is 273° K and his normal body temperature is 310° K.

I shall feel furious.

Celsius (or Centigrade) runs from 0° (freezing) up to 100°: Fahrenheit from 0° through 32° freezing to 212° boiling. Kelvin from 0° (absolute zero) to 1,273°.

If this information is correct, if Kelvin is to be our final fate, why is the Air Ministry, aided by the B.B.C. and some of the Press, wasting its time on teaching us Centigrade?

See, by the way, into what confusion they have thrown the newspapers.

The Times in the text of its weather reports and predictions puts Centigrade first – 18 C (64 F): but in its map of the British Isles it gives Fahrenheit figures only.

The *Daily Telegraph* puts Fahrenheit first, both in text and map.

The *Guardian*, consistent too, but contrary, puts Centigrade first and shows Centigrade only on its map.

The *Daily Mail* puts Centigrade first.

The *Daily Express* gets my prize: for it does not mention Centigrade at all.

The B.B.C. Television Weathermen show Centigrade figures (in rings) on their maps but do not attempt to explain them.

Here we had better say a cautious word about this mysterious *Systéme International d'Unités* – referred to by the experts as S.I. You will not find it in the telephone book. I have no idea where it is based. But it seems to be the latest God – a God without an address.

Major Stewart, in one of his Fathom letters to *The Times*, wrote:

Although Ministers and others persist in calling it the metric system, it is, as the British Standards Institution has made clear [where?] really the Système International d'Unités to which we are changing, and this . . . is a very different thing.

The International System, or S.I., is not a system at all. It is divorced from the traditional metric system and is *almost as much a collection of arbitrary standards as are British imperial weights and measures* [Well, well?] It has the fatal defect of admitting different grades of accuracy, one first class, the other second. Thus the *litre* is not included among S.I. units: but it is graciously allowed for expressing low precision measurements. Kilometres per hour are excluded from the S.I., but may be allowed for those who do not like metres per second.

[Splendid!]

It would be useful [Major Stewart concluded], if the distinguished people who have been selected to guide the current meteorological reform were to give up talking about the metric system when they mean the S.I. They might also clean up S.I. terminology, sort out, and systematize its decimal units, and give the whole thing a less dreary and indeterminate title.

Yes, but who are THEY? Where are they to be found?

Mr Nigel Calder, in the *New Statesman* (30 January 1970), writes: 'Existing metric nations have the task of adapting to S.I. units, without the incentive of wholesale conversion. For this reason, Britain may well be ahead of the rest of Europe by the late 1970's.'

Stranger and stranger. I thought that whatever we are doing was to put us into glorious harmony with Europe.

Mr Calder tells us more about S.I:

The metric system being adopted by Britain is not the old lot that for long decorated the back of school exercise books: it is the official new international system of 1954, S.I. for short, based on the man-sized metre and kilogramme, rather than on centimetres and grammes. Force is measured in newtons (the weight of an apple is roughly one newton), power in watts, energy in joules and temperature in degrees Kelvin – a fair string of British physicists by the way. The aim is to restrict multiple and sub-multiples of units to steps of 1,000: micrometre, millimetre, metre, kilometre. The centimetre is to be tolerated as an aid for schoolchildren, rather like the initial teaching alphabet, but adults will be expected to call it 10 millimetres. The litre, though not an S.I. unit, will be allowed. The S.I. System has immense advantages of simplicity and consistency, and everyday electrical units (volts and amps) are fitted into it precisely.

Sometimes, though I have never met it, I feel that, if we must have all this change, I might like the S.I., as against the rigid 'metric system'.

Mr Thomas J. Campion wrote to *The Times* on 11 June 1969:

Although the S.I. system derives nearly all the quantities needed in technology from only six base units (metre, kilogramme, second, ampere, kelvin, candela) it does not preclude the use of other units which are commonly used. Sir Alan Herbert's splendidly coherent nautical mile is listed for use in the United Kingdom, although not yet included in the I.S.O. draft recommendations, as is also the unit of velocity, the knot.

Well, *well*? Does this mean bringing the nautical mile ashore, as I suggested earlier?

But, I repeat, where *is* the S.I.? How can I write to it? I should like to make one point. Will the learned people in charge bear in mind that many measurements which seem plain and sensible to them may be unfitted and difficult for ordinary citizens who will have to use them. Mr Calder, talking of 'the transition period', says airily: 'It is better to know that 940 – 630 – 960 (millimetres) is a shapely figure than to stop and convert it to 37 – 25 – 38.' Some of us have been making apprehensive jokes about 'vital statistics' for some time, but generally in terms of centimetres. But, under S.I. centimetres are as much 'out' as inches. The aim is to restrict multiples and sub-multiples of units to steps of 1,000, as Mr. Nigel Calder has already told us. 'The centimetre is to be tolerated as an aid for children, rather like the initial teaching alphabet, *but adults will be expected to call it 10 millimetres.*' Oh, will they? Well, I can tell S.I. at once that no British maiden is going to describe her breast measurement as 940 millimetres.

Large figures are not appropriate for small objects: all figures should be such as to give an intelligible picture.

At the monthly meetings of the Thames Conservancy (more than 100 years old) the Chairman begins by giving us the latest figures of rainfall, always in inches. He will soon be expected to give them in *millimetres* – not centimetres, for he is an 'adult'. Now I can imagine a sheet of water two-and-a-half inches deep, but I cannot see one 60 millimetres deep. I could perhaps imagine 6 centimetres (not very easily) but that will not be allowed. Such figures are intended for the ordinary man as well as the clever scientist.

In these 'battles', I am well aware I was 'sticking my neck out', a layman challenging high experts with limited information: but no one has successfully twisted it. Many, I know from my letter-box, are with me. What saddens me is that more people, with better title and resources, do not stick their necks out. I may not always be right, but at least I have teased some of our remote masters out of their holes. But this is the job of Members of Parliament.

By the way, I have a challenge for our dear decimalizers. Why don't they have a go at the Calendar, and muddle us a little more? This has been a settled thing for many centuries: but so have the foot and the fathom. What about – *fasten your belts* – a 10-day week?

Why? First, because it would be one more genuflection to the decimal, the tyrannous ten. But there are weightier reasons.

The 7-day week has respectable authority – the Book of Genesis and the Fourth Commandment. But what does the Commandment say? '*Six* days shalt thou labour and do all that thou has to do . . .' How many citizens labour for six days in this age of welfare (except authors, who labour for seven)? In high quarters there is a bit of dwindling at each end of the five-day week. Try starting important business on Friday afternoon. So that rest on the seventh day no longer seems as well-deserved as it did, in hot countries, to the Creator.

Why seven anyway? It was 'a mystical number among the Jews', I read, 'it was the perfect number and denoted completeness'. But is this great technological, modern world to be governed by mystical numbers in practical affairs?

In the Garden of Eden 'productivity' and 'growth' were not the problems that they are today. What will history say of us if Man at last produces himself too much and other things too little, and so is in peril of passing away? History will say: 'What can you expect? He laboured only 5/7 of a week instead of 6/7 as commanded. Instead of 52 days of rest he had 104 (not counting Bank Holidays and special feast-days). It was not till 1970 when a British *savant* gave the world the 10-day week, that Man recovered and started marching on to the sunny uplands.'

I am sorry but the months, I think, should still be 12. Those old Romans began with 10, but they had to add January and February. The first 11 months will each have three 10-day weeks, 30 days in all. (I see now that ancient Egypt had this idea too – I thought it was my invention.) So at once we eliminate those tiresome differences between the months – 'Thirty days hath September etc.' – and the absurd February with its 28 (or 29) days. Eleven months of 30 days will come to 330. That leaves 35. Splendid. December will also have 3 normal 10-day weeks – with 5 days over (December 31–35) for Christmas *and* the New Year, which will be sensibly celebrated together, thus avoiding two consecutive national hangovers.

No attempt will be made to interfere with the behaviour of the heavenly bodies, or the accepted calculation of 'the year', so every four years there will still be a 'Leap Year' with an extra day. But the extra day will be added not to the ridiculous February, but to December, the 36th. This will add one day to the big December holiday and make Leap Year a positive joy to look forward to.

A few administrative details remain. For how many days of the ten should we labour? I leave this to Parliament, the T.U.C., and such authorities. But I feel the principle of elasticity should prevail. In time of crisis we should labour for 8 days, with weekends of the present length. But when we saw the end of the tunnel we should make it 7, with lovely 3-day weekends. That, I reckon, would give us 108 weekend days, 4 more than now; but even then, I am sure, the increased continuity of toil on the one hand, and leisure on the other, would yield economic and psychological benefits by no means to be excluded from the consideration of our rulers. The business of beginning and ending the week must always cause economic wastage, so bigger weeks will cause less waste.

Pray remember, whatever your practical objections, that it will be one more triumph for *the decimal system*, Man's chiefest hope.

We might, of course, pass on to the 10-hour day. I cannot myself see the slightest point in this reform, but it should please the powerful tribe of Decimen. Noon and midnight would be glorious *10* o'clock instead of 12. Between them there would be the same number of minutes, namely 720. So each hour would be 72 minutes long, and each quarter

18. No, would it not be better to go the whole hog and reform those out-dated institutions the hour and the minute? Should there not be 100 minutes to the hour, and 100 seconds to the minute? A quarter of an hour would then be 25 New Minutes, which, when you come to think of it, would be the greatest fun. A whole day, then, from midnight to midnight, would consist of 20 Hours, 2,000 New Minutes, and 200,000 New Seconds. How tidy, how decimal, how delightful! At present, it is (I *think*), 24 hours, 1,440 minutes and 86,400 seconds. And a 10-day week would have 200 Hours, 20,000 New Minutes, and 2,000,000 seconds. Just what we want. It fits in beautifully with the nautical mile which is 2,000 yards (and a bit). This, as I have said, when we are really reformed, will be our land mile too. What a four (old) minute mile would mean in New Minutes and New Miles I cannot tell you, but you may be sure that it would make running rational at last, and a New Age would dawn in international sport.

But there would still be some loose ends about. Look at the old circle – look at the compass – with their 360 degrees. Why 360°? Because, I believe, the Babylonians made it so. But surely, surely, this brilliant technological age is not content to take its circle from ancient Babylon! On the compass 90 degrees from north is due east, and 90 degrees on the other side is due west. How laughable! Obviously it should be 100 – which would make the whole circle 400 degrees. This, I expect, astronomically, would fit in nicely with the 20-hour day, the 100-minute hour, and the 2,000-yard mile: but I can't go into that now.

You think I am trying to be funny? The reform of the circle was discussed at a scientific conference at Rome in, I *think*, 1883: and there are some folk, I believe, using a reformed circle already. So go to it, decimalizers! Demonstrate, Mr Straw!

POSTSCRIPT – Sadly – back to the Nautical Mile. On June 5 Mr G. Littleton (who turned out to be a Board of Trade man) released an important cat in the *Daily Telegraph*: 'All the Government Departments concerned' have agreed that 'the nautical mile will no longer be 6080 feet but 1852 metres.' The Admiralty letter quoted on page 255 clearly means that the n.m. is to remain in the form familiar to English-speaking seamen. But there must have been a surrender. A friendly hydrographer (of the Navy) says that 'eventually' the scales in feet, yards and cables will disappear from our charts. What our practical seamen will think of this, I do not know, but I can guess.

But charts are not changed as easily as cash-registers. Even before this decision the hydrographers estimated that it would take 15 years to do the 'important' new charts – 34 years to change the lot. So for sea-minded Britons feet and yards will be 'required knowledge' for a long time, perhaps a generation.

⧼ 13 ⧽

NOT SO DEAD AS ALL THAT

HERE is a cause of mine which may well drive many readers to the television den. But you will, I hope, remain with me, for it concerns every one of you: and at the end of the chapter there is a long funny story of high constitutional importance.

In my first Election Address (1935) I wrote:

Having educated four children myself I am acquainted with the difficulties of clergymen and professional men with families. I think that they should receive more generous income-tax allowance in relief of the expense of education. If it is said that they may send their children to the free State schools, the answer is that there are certain desirable studies which can only be kept alive by the continued existence of private schools for particular sections of society.

I have in mind, especially, the study of Latin and Greek. I believe that a little Latin at least, should ultimately form part of the studies of every citizen and, whenever opportunity arises, I shall vigorously defend the advantage of classical learning as part of the *practical* education of all who employ the English language.

I did not forget this election pledge: I suppose I should have put down an amendment to the Education Bill 1944, but that year we were rather busy down the river. The Americans had invaded the Thames: and the Thames was making ready to invade. But I had already drafted an Education (Latin and Greek) Bill, and tried to present it at the opening of the 1945 Parliament. Here is the Preamble. In all my many Bills, from the Marriage Bill onwards, I used the now neglected Preamble. In your Memorandum you may state in cold terms the machinery of your Bill, but you must not be controversial. In the Preamble you can let fly with facts and arguments. Also, ages later, you may let baffled judges know the purpose of the enactment:

Whereas the English language has been much enriched and is every day expanded by the adoption of Greek and Latin words and roots, and some knowledge of Greek and Latin is an undoubted aid to the right use and understanding of the English language and English literature, and a practical aid in many crafts and callings: and although a full study of these languages is not possible or expedient for every student some elementary instruction must assist all citizens to an understanding of the events and controversies of the day:

Be it therefore enacted etc.

Latin and Greek are called the Dead Languages; they have been buried by most of the schools: but they grow more lively every day. Latin is the foundation of many tongues. Greek is still spoken by a live nation of nine million people. It is 'Modern Greek' now: but it is written and printed in the same characters as Ancient Greek, and I can see in the newspapers of Athens, and over the shop windows, the same words that as a boy I studied in Euripides and Homer.

Every new thing we do or make strikes a spark from the dead languages. The latest thing is Space (from the Latin *spatium*), and Space is as full of dead words as it is of *defunct* sputniks. There were *Jupiter, Mercury* and *Gemini programmes*. But it was a *Saturn* rocket that put the most *famous astronauts* into *orbit*, and an *Apollo vehicle* that carried the *'lunarnauts'* round the moon. They defied *gravity, magnetism,* and *solar radiation*. From time to time they *corrected* their *lunar trajectory*. Near the moon they did a *Lunar Orbital Insertion*. Later they changed their *altitude* to sixty-nine miles above the moon. On the way round they inspected the *Mare Tranquillitatis*, the *Copernicus* and other *craters* (G.). Some of the *craters*, they judged, were of *volcanic origin*, others were caused by the *impact* of *meteors*. They gave *television exhibitions* and took *numerous photographs* which were *transmitted* by *artificial satellites* all over the *globe*. They safely *penetrated* the Earth's *atmosphere* at a *specified angle*. A *helicopter* took them to the aircraft carrier *York*. Thus ended a most *efficient* and *heroic mission*.

The next thing was a manned *expedition* to the moon. Here a small *vehicle* called the *Lunar Excursion Module* left the *parent* aircraft and *descended* to the moon with two men aboard.

All this was *organized* by the *National Aeronautical* and *Space Agency*.

The doctors – and the lawyers – can hardly open their mouths without dropping a Greek or Latin word. Almost every part of the body, every complaint and cure, is Latin or Greek. My doctor, dear Hugh Browne, does not even have a cold: he suffers from *coryza*.

What are the words most frequently used by the fashionable Young? 'Mini' and 'pop' – both Latin. Next come 'fantastic', 'fab', 'super', 'disc', 'telly', 'radio', 'audio', 'video', 'stereo', 'mono', 'mike', 'record', 'rhythm', 'scene', 'orbit', 'biotics', 'demo', 'irrelevant', 'participation', 'prejudice', 'psychedelic', 'sex'.

{ 268 }

All of them spring from 'dead' Latin or Greek. Yet if you told the same young people that it would be no bad thing to learn a little – a very little – about Latin and Greek there would be a chorus of resistance and derision. 'We don't have to go to school,' they might say, 'to learn the meaning of "pop", "mini" and "sex"!' True, but suppose some silly elder offers you a new word like 'psychedelic', which smells strongly of a dead language? Wouldn't you like to know something about its history and pretensions – what, for example, it is supposed to mean – before you admit it to Carnaby Street and the King's Road, Chelsea? You can hardly avoid using such dead words as 'mini' and 'mike', for minimum and microphone have long been established. It is quite another thing for your advanced and electric generation to accept without question a perfectly new and noticeably stinking dead word, and spread it among your innocent juniors.

But that is just what they did, bless them. Though an old friend of the dead languages it took me some time to make a firm guess at 'psychedelic'. Most of us know that 'psyche' (*Greek*) means 'soul, spirit, or mind' – we have heard so much about 'psychology' and 'psycho-analysis'. We know too 'psychiatrist' – *psych* – and *iatros* (G.) (healer). I sought, in vain, for a word like 'edelic'. Then, suddenly, I remembered δηλος – deelos – clear. The word must mean something like 'clearing the mind'. Then someone told me, truly or not, that the word was invented by an American doctor to describe such drugs as L.S.D., which are said to 'release the consciousness'. This seemed to fit. But why must Modern British Young go to the Dead Languages to find a name for the Most Modern Drug? Why not call it a 'Soul-searcher' or a 'Mind-sweeper'? Still, if you must have a dead word for such a drug, it fits the purpose pretty well (though by the rules it should be 'psycho –'). It is a well-bred word – that is, both halves are Greek – which is more than can be said for 'television' or 'breathalyser'. But then, bless me, it is switched from drugs to entertainment, to lighting, to furniture, clothing and anything else that the young people thought gay, hip, way out, turned on, etc. I *think* I have seen a reference to psychedelic trousers. Very well; let them enjoy themselves. But I still think it funny that such enemies of dead tradition and obsolete thought should be led into loving such an evidently dead word.

Now, any man can invent a new word and start it whizzing round the world, and many a good word or saying has been started by simple men. Thus the language is enriched and kept alive. But too many simple men think it is easy to dig a good new word out of the dead languages: and it is not. Consider the dreadful word 'breathalyser', an instrument which performs, I suppose, breathalysis. The man who first breathed this poison into the air supposed, no doubt, that 'alysis' was the important part of analysis, and he had only to add 'breath' to 'alysis' to get what he wanted. Unfortunately, he divided analysis in the wrong place, 'Ana - lysis', like 'cata - lysis', and 'para - lysis', is - lysis (λυσις), from the verb λυω (loose, loosen, detach) preceded by a preposition ana- (ἀνά) – like cata- and para-. Every simple Briton cannot be expected to know this sort of thing, but if he does not he should not dare to fashion new words from Latin and Greek. This ignorant invention should have been strangled at birth. Why not breath-tester?

'Biotics' is fashionable now among high and low. I read in a Sunday paper that 'the king of weirdies', from his youth 'a rebel trying to find a cause', a 'hippy leader of the "revolution" which preached the gospel of universal love, became involved in a way-out Macrobiotic restaurant, an ultra-vegetarian establishment. . . .' 'Macrobiotic', μακρος (long) plus βίος (life) – both words are in use in Athens today – does not shock me, but it makes me laugh to see it used by hippy rebels. What can the word mean to the average customer? Why not a Long Life Eating Place?

But why blame the hippies? In *The Times* of 5 January 1969, Mr David Wood, distinguished political correspondent, writes of 'the evolution of the peculiar *symbiotic* relationship Mr Wilson has created with the Labour left'. This, I suppose, means 'living with', in the sense of 'enduring' or 'getting on with'. If so it is a mere translation of English slang into dog-Greek, and has much less excuse than macrobiotic.

All this was begun by '*anti-biotic*', invented by some eager chemist to describe penicillin and other magic concoctions which destroy living foes of the body. It has always seemed odd to me that any remedy for human ills should bear the name of 'anti-life', even in medical circles. It is odder still when you hear a charwoman (sorry, 'lady cleaner') happily announce: 'I'm better now. They've put me on the antibiotics.'

'Charisma' and 'charismatic' are recent upstarts which are employed in a vague way with small excuse.

Words travel so fast and far today that it is difficult to catch and kill a bad one: and those who must invent words in a hurry may have nowhere to turn for advice and charge ahead without it. This independent race would not, I think, accept a British Academy which examined and authorized new words as the College of Heralds examines a new coat-of-arms. It would take too long and be laughed at too easily. But there should be some sort of Word Watch, always on duty, ready to pounce at the first appearance of a 'breathalyser', 'psychedelic', 'symbiotic' or 'productivity'. They could inquire into the breed, authority, and purpose of the word and announce their conclusions. These of course could not prevent anyone from using a bad word, but at least we should know what we were doing.

The Word Watch might be a branch of a larger, perhaps commercial, body, the *New Names and Words Society*. This would be run by retired scholars and well-educated business men. Anyone with a new invention or product, anyone wanting a good new political phrase or catch-cry, anyone with a new boat or mansion, a thoroughbred colt or a racing greyhound could go to *New Names* for learned but practical advice. The doctors even – for the medical student, I believe, no longer learns any Latin or Greek.

But then there are the innumerable old Latin and Greek words, mostly in disguise, but often naked, with which English books and papers (even the 'populars'), political and industrial affairs, are peppered. How often is the average man halted, and sometimes baffled, not only in his reading, but at his work, in his everyday life, by a word of Latin or Greek descent at whose meaning he can only guess? As the years roll on the halts will be more frequent; for the Lords of Education have surrendered the fort and only a very few of the young so much as catch a glimpse of the Lively Languages in their schools and colleges. I say that all should have at least a glimpse. I would not inflict on every boy and girl such long and detailed labours as I endured, the writing of Latin prose, the anatomy of the irregular verbs and so on. By the few such studies must always be pursued for the sake of scholarship, history, and mental enrichment. The rest, I urge, should be taught enough to make it easier for them *to read the newspapers with understanding*. I would permit no one to regard these languages as something remote from the ordinary man. 'One hour in every school in every week,' I proposed in my Bill. I recommend it more strongly still today.

In the *Daily Telegraph* of 29 April 1969 I read that 'Latin learners rose from 2,589 in 1938 to 7,519 in 1966'. Hooray!

But my 'one hour' would be for every boy and girl. The hour would begin, I suppose, with an explanation of the latest arrivals in the news – 'psychedelic' 'breathalyser' 'multilateral', 'moratorium', 'audio', 'video', 'antibiotics', 'orbit', 'satellite' etc. Then the teacher (who need not be a classical scholar himself) would turn to his little 'Not So Dead' book. I began such a work myself last year, but I have not had time to finish it. It began by compiling four lists of words, and it is surprising how long they are already. The first is 'Naked Deads' – actual Latin and Greek words in common or fairly common use among laymen. I have more than 500 of them already. There are sixty-six 'A's' – from A.M. to asphyxia. Then there is a Doctors' List – there are fifty 'A's' in that. How is the ordinary man to know what is meant by 'a renal condition', by 'aphasia', or 'alopecia'? Then there is the Lawyers' List, whose numerous 'naked dead' words are always popping up in the law reports – 'alibi', 'ultra vires' 'fiat', 'de facto' and so on.

Then there will be a big list of 'Deads in Disguise', English words which are purely Greek or Latin in origin, 'memento', 'monarchy', 'metronome', 'metaphor', 'binoculars', 'quadruped', 'antipathy', 'diarrhoea', 'automation', 'discotheque'.

There would also be a page or two of general instruction on the strange way in which we use the 'dead' languages – prefixes like ana- and dia-, hypo- and hyper-, suffixes like -ize, and -itis, and that mysterious negative initial a-. How, again, is the ordinary man to know that the 'a' (or 'an') in anodyne, aphasia, amnesia, astigmatic, anarchy, anaemia, agnostic, means 'not' or 'without', that 'amoral' is not another form of 'amorous' but means 'non-moral', and what's the difference between 'aseptic' and 'antiseptic'?

My Bill was never printed. Here comes a very odd Parliamentary episode. All through my fifteen years in that place I made whatever use I could of Private Members' Time (for this was the best arena for an Independent) and I defended our 'rights' whenever they were attacked or diminished. Even during the War, when they inevitably were taken away, with one or two others I made an annual protest like someone formally asserting a right of way.

When the 1945 Parliament opened we expected, after the Allies' Victory for Freedom, to get all – or at least some – of our rights back. But on the first or second day Mr Herbert Morrison put down a Motion which took them all away again. The excuse now was the Government's great legislative programme of reconstruction. No one but Ministers must have an idea, or occupy a moment of time. Mr Eden, Mr Churchill, the Father of the House (Lord Winterton), W. J. Brown and others spoke against the ban: but in vain.

I was genuinely disappointed and aggrieved. I had been working very hard and had eleven Bills ready, in case the old Government story should be heard that the private Members had no ammunition, no Bills ready. (This was what Mr Baldwin had said ten years earlier on the first day of my first Parliament.)

My Bills were not mere names, or 'dummies', as they could have been within the rules, they were fully drafted. Also, my indignation was constitutionally well founded. At the start of a new Session the Commons go to the House of Lords to hear the Gracious Speech from the Throne outlining Her Ministers' programme for the new Session. They troop back to their own House and the first thing they do is to give a first reading to something called the Outlawries Bill. This is simply to assert the right of the Commons to discuss what they like whatever the Queen's Ministers say. (In theory, I believe, at that moment it would have been in order for me to move the first reading of all my eleven Bills and lay them on the Table; but this was one of the madnesses I never committed. One day, I hope, some rebel will try it.)

After the swells had made their protests I 'caught the Speaker's eye', and faced one of my stormiest audiences. The triumphant surge of Socialism into that Parliament was something to see. The mere numbers of the victors, justly jubilant, was physically formidable. There was not room for all of them on their own benches, and on a crowded day they overflowed onto the Opposition side, so that if you were speaking there you might have chi-yiking and interruptions from flank and rear as well as in front.

Not only the 345 new Members, but many others had never seen the private Members' ancient rights in action, and it was necessary to explain them, and our pride in them: but they were not easy to impress. 'A man called Samuel Plimsoll,' I reminded them, 'who wrote the Plimsoll Line on all the ships of Britain, began his great career of reform by presenting – unsuccessfully it is true – a Private Member's Bill in this House.'* I do not think they laughed at that.

I reminded them of my own good fortune, and the contribution that Labour men had made: 'I am not boasting but I am trying to tell hon. Members what is the scale of these things that we are asked to throw away . . .'

'Private Members' Bills also bring about a charming camaraderie between the Members of one party and another.' How they laughed at that! Camaraderie with Tories? In their victorious mood they could not imagine it. 'I had most ample support from Members of the party on the benches opposite . . . and I shall always be grateful for it. On such occasions Members of all parties get together.' They laughed again. So I said: 'Well, if I were to introduce a Bill to abolish the Decree Nisi, I feel sure it would find a great many supporters on the benches opposite.' And indeed, a year or two later, the Labour Lord Chancellor, Lord Jowitt, did practically abolish it.

The odd thing was – and I was duly thankful – that nobody laughed when I flung my eleven Bills on the floor. I suppose, by then, I had persuaded them that I really had something to say and meant what I said:

Lastly, these Standing Orders which we are asked to suspend are part of the great apparatus of Parliamentary freedom for which we have been fighting. What was the first thing we did this afternoon . . .? We gave a First Reading to the Outlawries Bill, a most extraordinary proceeding. It is a Bill not recommended or introduced by any Members, it is not printed, and it is quite impossible to find a copy of it in the Library. I am not laughing at it. It is a very serious thing. The purpose of that queer procedure was to establish the right of this House to discuss what it likes quite apart from the programme of legislation laid down in the Gracious Speech.

This Motion is taking away a right which we laboriously established this

* 16 August 1945, col. 140.

morning. Hon. Members are against monopolies. Do they suggest that the Government have a monopoly of wisdom? I am sad about this. I have worked very hard. Hon. Members may laugh at my little Bills, but I believe they will be more popular with a great many people than some of the proposals which will later be laid before us . . . Look at what this House is doing to me after all the things I promised to my constituents, and all the things I have promised to the constituents of other hon. Members. I get a hundred letters a week, not from my own constituents but from poor people who are worried about their divorces. (*Laughter*.) There is no laughter about this. They write about the Poor Persons' Procedure. I have a Bill here dealing with the provision of legal aid and assistance for the poor. That is something fundamental, but there is not a word about it in the Gracious Speech. What am I to say to all these people who write to me? I must tell them to stop sending their letters and to save their stamps, because I can do no more to help them if this Motion goes through: I might just as well be a Member of the German Reichstag or a stuffed exhibit in the Natural History Museum. If the House will not have my Bills on the Table I cast them on the Floor, as a monument to Parliamentary liberty and a challenge to despotic power.

·

And so I did. It was, I dare say, a crazy melodramatic thing to do: and, as I tossed the bundle into the middle of the Floor towards the Table, I thought: 'This will be the biggest laugh of the lot, the biggest laugh for centuries.' But there was no laugh – not a sound.

I continued, more mildly and now in silence, asking for some compromise or concession. I finished with a prophecy which was nearly true: 'If this Motion is accepted today I believe that next year the right hon. Gentleman will come forward with some other reason why Private Members' time should be taken, and not only in this Session but in all the Sessions.' In a later year I accused my friend Herbert Morrison of wanting to abolish the whole thing, and he did not shake his head. Today he was polite and complimentary ('a very interesting, witty, eloquent and quite relevant speech') but adamant. We fought the same battle at the beginning of every Session and got nothing till 1949. But every battle helped to keep the cause alive, and so many people remembered my 'Bills on the floor' that I do not think they were flung in vain.

Their themes were not all so 'far-out' as Latin and Greek. Indeed, eight out of the eleven tasks were tackled later, and mostly much better, by this Government or that. They were:

A Legal Aid and Advice Bill.

A Judicial Appeals Bill.

This contained the 'leap-frogging' proposal I first made in a *Misleading Case* in 1933 – that certain cases should go straight from the High Court to the House of Lords, 'leap-frogging' the Court of

Appeal, and it was adopted by the Evershed Committee in 1953 and included in the Administration of Justice Bill 1968: and blow me, the new arrangement *'came into force' on 1 January this year*, 1970. What a pity that I was not allowed to put this reform 'on the Table' twenty-five years ago..

A Decree Nisi (Abolition) Bill.

In 1946 six months was reduced to six weeks.

A County Court (Extension of Jurisdiction) Bill.

This, I *think*, has been done.

A Law of Slander Bill.

I think I wanted to abolish slander. It has been modified.

A Sunday Entertainment Bill.

This dealt with the theatre only. Lord Willis, last year, presented a more general measure in the Lords – but it seems to have disappeared.

A Fair Voting (Proportional Representation) Bill.

Nothing doing.

A Hotel and Restaurant Bill.

This was not my own Bill, but one that others had presented in 1936, when I had my first clash with Nancy Astor. Towards the end of the 1945 Parliament three things were done about which the private Members had yattered then. The 'hours' in London were standardized by Mr Chuter Ede's Bill. Midnight refreshment was made more civilized and free, very much on the lines of the Hotels and Restaurants Bill. And, by another Bill, members of 'the Trade' were no longer excluded from the Licensing Benches.

An Air Advertisements Bill (to prohibit them).

This was a Bill I had presented in 1939. Later the Government did prohibit them.

A Betting and Bookmakers Bill.

This was a Bill that I had drafted, formally presented and expounded in 1939. It was the first proposal to license and register bookmakers, which later was done. But my Bill had nothing to do with the 'betting-shop' which was, I think, a great mistake. I wanted the 'letter-box' outside the bookmaker's premises in which the poor man could deposit his little bet in the morning – this was proposed by a Royal Commission and approved by the police.

An Education (Latin and Greek) Bill.

Who knows? One day some enlightened Minister will put that through too.

A SALUTE TO SOME SWELLS

I LIKE the word swells, not meaning rank or riches, but people who are high in their Leagues. I have been looking with amazement through a large collection of letters from friends of all sorts, many of them from swells long dead. Some of the letters I would have sworn did not exist – but here they are. I am amazed not only by the kind things said to me, but by the trouble and time these busy men gave to saying them. Most of us tend to bottle up our praise in our bosoms. Someone sends us a book. We thank him and say we 'look forward to reading it': but when we have read it how often do we write and say how much we enjoyed it, and why? If we do we probably dictate some simple praise and have it typed. But the great scribes of the '30's sat down and wrote what they thought in pen and ink: moreover they gave to their private casual communications some of the style and stamp of their public work. I have told a friend or two how J. M. Barrie once said to me: 'There's a new pirate called Herbert in Peter Pan. He plays skittles,' but I had no idea where this distinction was recorded, in a new edition, introduction or what: so I may well have been suspected of unreasonable name-dropping. But, behold, here is a letter of 16 August 1928, in the spidery, left-handed, but tidy writing, about an invitation to Stanway – and at the bottom:

'Stop Press news – You Alan have been made a pirate in P. Pan. Promptly killed.'

I feel shy and slightly guilty about printing some of these letters: but they throw a warm light on these generous men. Also, I do not expect to get high posthumous marks from the literary judges of today, and perhaps the evidence of these dead swells may be admitted.

Why should Hilaire Belloc, one of my prime heroes, bother to write this pleasing letter? It came from King's Land Shipley, Horsham, where, I am glad to hear, the Windmill still stands. I had sent him a book, *Still More Misleading Cases*:

18 X 33

My Dear Herbert,

That's indeed kind of you! I'd just got home and found it and I devoured it at a gulp and am vastly refreshed. Your gift is unique and the sudden unexpected – e.g. 'as we all should be soon ' on page 20 – are like currants in a bun. It's an amusing thing to contemplate what the decaying lawyers guild will look like in fifty years; it will be a strong thing, but stricken. What a run it has had for its money, and what a lot of money for its run. Every yard of English railway pays a (?) tribute of a shilling a year to the lawyers – or to those who inherited or filched their money. There is no more to take in that line: but they will still have, for a long time, the income paid out of the taxes. Haddock has 3 qualities, wealth, courage and inflexibility (or continuity).

May he live.

Thank you again! I read hardly anything, but reading of *this* kind is different.

Yours

H. B.

I'm not in town for a fortnight – but I shall insist on drinking with you then. I shall show you a wine.

Reform Club

24 VI 33

For God's sake and your own come sailing with me for a week. I leave Poole on Friday 7 July. Oh! Do come and fail not; it's much the best way of passing a week and we will visit strange places. Desmond McCarthy's son, an expert sailsman, will be aboard and another, Tony Gibbon. So come. I enclose a card: write on it anyhow and post it.

Yours

H. B.

Join me at the Antelope Public House Poole any hour on that Friday.

I was not able to obey that summons: but I did, some other year, have the honour to travel in Hilaire Belloc's famous *Nona* from Torquay eastwards along the Channel. The other passengers were J. C. Squire, Hilary and Peter, the Belloc boys. We had two or three preliminary conferences in Fleet Street taverns, where the main topic was always Portland Bill and the dangerous Portland Race which rages off it. Belloc was a good sailor and had a wholesome respect for the sea. He seemed to be obsessed by 'William' [The Bill]. He drew elaborate plans reminding one of his Land and Water articles in War One. There was, it seemed, in every tide a safe period, a narrow eddy-like smooth passage, 'the tail of the Race', close under the cliffs of the Bill. The time of this had to be calculated from High Water Dover, and the whole voyage, date of departure, and so on, was planned to circumvent the Bill at a convenient hour of day.

We duly sailed from Torquay at last, one evening in July, taking away with us, for some reason, a harbour-master's boat. Belloc looked exactly like a character in W. W. Jacobs's books – with a peaked cap, unadorned by any badge, an old blue jersey and jacket. I loved the great man but he alarmed me a little. We called at Lyme Regis to try to get a 'jorum' for water. No 'jorum' was to be found, and Belloc stumped about the town explaining angrily how England had run down since the Tudor times, when jorums and other simple necessities would have been available everywhere. We sailed on. I don't think he ever admitted anyone else to the tiller. He sat there, happily muttering or declaiming. When the sun shone and the wind was fair there might be a little lecture on the glories of the Tudors: when it was foul we heard about the machinations of the Jews. 'William', undoubtedly a Jew, punctually stood up, stark and dark, from the sea, about twenty miles away. But as we drew nearer black clouds assembled in the east and the wind freshened from the south. Belloc, sage and cautious, decided that this was no day to round the Bill. Abreast was Bridport, a small harbour he had never visited. Fortunately the tide was high so there was no trouble about water. The harbour has a long narrow canyon of an entrance and we bowled down it under full sail, alarmingly. But we rounded up safely inside and anchored.

Jack said at once: 'Let's go and see Hardy.' So the three of us crammed into a taxi and drove up to Dorchester to see Thomas Hardy, whom I had never met. Max Gate was a modest villa with a small suburban crescent approach round a shrubbery. It was wonderful to see Belloc who had been lording it along the coast, bullying harbour-masters and all we met, enter the little drawing-room, hat in hand, and bow reverently before the Master. I forget what the three talked about. I never said a word. Hardy, they told me, was not in his best form, for he had heard about another octogenarian bicycling, and had, just to show the world, bicycled over to some member of his family, and was now recovering from this excess.

Next day we sailed on again, but again we failed to round the Bill. It may have been the wind falling away, or it may have been the Transfiguration of the Virgin Mary, which was near. At dusk, I was ordered to stand by the anchor as we nosed into the Chesil Beach corner where the storms of ages have built a mountain of shingle and the water is formidably deep, a shocking place to anchor in. I remember reading in the Channel Pilot something like: 'In 1886 three transport vessels foundered here. No small vessel should anchor in these waters.' As Belloc called 'Let go!' some unseen fellow ashore called, 'Oy! You can't lay there.' But we did. The Catholics, Belloc and the two boys, went ashore to celebrate the Transfiguration, leaving Jack Squire and myself to pump out the *Nona* which needed it every day. We lay there two nights. Then the wind rose and they said we must go soon or we should be on the beach. I rowed ashore to fetch the great man. I found him at breakfast at the little Portland Hotel writing verse in the Visitors' Book. He turned the pages back and found an entry he had made a year or two earlier when he had come to Portland from the east. He had written – and this I swear:

> We made the passage of St Alban's Race
> And came to anchor in this bloody place.

A good breeze took us round the Bill. But that day 'the tail' of the Race did not seem to be working. It was a strange experience, the most confused sea I ever saw. Waves charged each other from different directions and some stood up like hillocks and collapsed alarmingly. My faith in the *Nona*'s rigging was not absolute, but it stood up well to the extraordinary strains and at last we lumbered out of the Race into civilized water. We all felt better, St Alban's Race was child's play, Jack Squire, 'spinning', caught some delicious mackerel. Belloc steered himself all through the night, refusing aid, and whenever I woke grave mutterings came down into the cabin. We were making for Ryde: it was the first day of Ryde Week; and about breakfast time we were sliding past the luscious yachts making ready for the Day. We rowed ashore, windswept, weary and hungry. At the hotel smart people in white skirts and trousers were about already, and at first the hotel refused to give the great Belloc any breakfast. But Jack Squire whispered a word and the literary mariners were allowed to eat behind a screen. I enjoyed this very much.

Belloc and Squire left us there, and with the two boys I was charged to take her over to her mooring in the Hamble River. I am sorry to say that I laid her for an hour or two on the Hamble Spit.

Dear Herbert,   13 X 27

Your book makes me laugh and laugh. It is bloody funny! Write some more books like that (*Misleading Cases*) I sit at the lawyer's table at this club at Dinner it is huge fun hearing them describing how they condemn the innocent and cheat their clients. I wish I were a lawyer, then I should have more money.

                                        Yours

                                                    H. Belloc

H. G. Wells was one of my early heroes. We used to meet him at literary parties in the Thirties, and once he came to the Boat Race. But I can't pretend that we knew him well. The chief thing I remember is the fluty voice and the flow of words. I was highly surprised to find this letter in the file:

Dear Herbert,   24 Oct. '30.

You are the greatest of great men. You can raise delightful laughter and that is the only sort of writing that has real power over people like me. We secretly hate to be impressed by any other sort of work, even 'sheer loveliness' is highly irritating at times. But when we have really been got at and made to cackle, we want to follow the divinity about as a cat follows a catsmeat man. This is not only for *Misleading Cases* but also for the *Water Gipsies* which I read in Paris. Human and true.

My homage I may add is entirely compatible with the utmost scorn and contempt for your limited, (?) litigious prejudiced political and social views.

I sat next Inge* the other night. He is a great lad but at his age he ought not to prefer Benedictine to old brandy. There are some boys that never grow up.

My salutations to Mrs Herbert.

Your friend and well wisher

H. G.

Malcolm Sargent

Like all the world (except a few of the musical world) I was very fond of Malcolm Sargent, and I saw much of him just before the end. Whatever the high critics say, he made music exciting, and I loved to watch him conducting, erect, electric, whatever he was at. He could be as solemn as a musical Pope in talk as well as action – you should have heard him in the Savoy Grill, on the Dream of Gerontius. But he did not mind making music fun. Some of the Cardinals of Music used to shudder at the antics of the Young at the last night of the Proms. To me it was always a moving and stimulating occasion, one of the best nights of the year. There was fun and feeling, but there was always music: and the same noisy boys and girls stood in respectful silence during works which I could hardly bear to hear. What struck me most was not the din but the discipline. As for the complaints against the patriotic songs, 'Rule Britannia' has a fine tune and some very fine words, and we are as much entitled to sing 'Land of Hope and Glory' as Frenchmen are to sing the 'Marseillaise.' Neither is topical but both are on target.

Malcolm always gave a birthday party for his faithful henchwoman Sylvia Darley who served him for so many years. One of these was at the charming home of Joe Cooper, the excellent pianist, on Barnes Common. That gifted girl Joyce Grenfell (whom I knew when she was so-high) was there. After dinner the two men and Joyce gave an impromptu but marvellous musical exhibition. They played piano duets, at two grand pianos, in the style of this or that great composer: they did 'cod' Grand Opera (Joyce singing) and folk songs, everything. Joe Cooper can do instant Beethoven, and many other Masters. I have seldom laughed so much or enjoyed an evening more. But music was the foundation, profound love and knowledge of music.

* Dean Inge.

Ap 24 . 30

Dear Herbert .

You are the greatest of great
men .   You can raise delightful laughter
& that is the only sort of writing that has
real power over people like me . We secretly
hate to be impressed by any other sort grunk
, even "sheer liveliness" is highly irritating at
times . But when we have really been
set at triumph to cackle , we want to
follow the divinity what is a Cosh bellows
a calm meet man . This is not only
for nine leading Cases but also for the
whole Species which draws in Paris
            Humanum & true .

My homage I may add is something
compatible only the utmost scorn &
contempt for your limited, iniquitous
prejudices political & social views

My salutations to M₍s₎ Herbert
Your forever Wells-wards

In one of the many turns I played a humble part myself. In 1951 Malcolm and I were both members of Gerald Barry's Council for the Festival of Britain. One morning after a protracted meeting Malcolm took me back to his great flat by the Albert Hall. While he signed letters I wandered about and found a large room with two grand pianos. I sat down at one of them and, all alone, began to play my 'party piece', Handel's Largo. Malcolm stole in, sat down at the other grand and joined in. Then I began to 'sing', astonished secretaries came in (he had three at least) and we set the Festival of Britain afoot in no mean style. Whenever opportunity arose thereafter – if we had no more than one piano, and that not grand – we played Handel's Largo together. Always, and this is the point, I wondered how many other musical swells would have condescended thus.

I shall never forget the inaugural Festival Concert at the Festival Hall. King George VI and his Queen, and some of the Family were in the Box. First I think, came Sir Adrian Boult with some properly 'serious' music. Next was Malcolm with his new version of 'Rule Britannia'. He had a huge choir (from, I suspect, Huddersfield) and high up above them, a battery of trumpeters in some fine old rig. He had found Arne's original manuscript somewhere. This disclosed some stirring trumpet passages between phrases and between verses. It showed too that the refrain was not the lumbering dirge we had so often heard, but quick and gay, full of dotted notes, a real comic opera number – sung by King Alfred in the Masque *Alfred*. This fortunate audience heard 'Rule Britannia' as none of us heard it before. We all went mad. We insisted on encores. At the other end of my row I could see Nye Bevan clapping like a Churchill.

A few days later, Malcolm said, he met the King. His Majesty told him how much he had enjoyed 'Rule Britannia'. 'Whenever I come to one of your concerts you must play it again, just like that.' 'I should love to, sir,' said Malcolm. 'But it might not be suitable.' 'Not suitable, Sir Malcolm? What do you mean?' 'Well, sir, I might be playing the Matthew Passion.' 'That's all right,' said His Majesty. 'I shouldn't be there.'

Malcolm, I found with surprise, was sensitive to the charges of musical frivolity. I was one of a television party to celebrate his seventieth birthday. He gallantly appeared himself, heavy with flu. At a preliminary conference the tone was rather loftily musical, and out of my range. I thought at least that I might say something of his lighter side, but I was warned – I think by Bob Boothby, who knew Malcolm, and Music, very well – that Malcolm did not want to draw heavy fire from the Friends of Solemnity. But I did manage to get in a word about 'Rule Britannia', and for the first time in public he told the King George story. No harm, I think.

I saw him twice in the Nursing Home that last August. I remember how he laughed when he said: 'Bob Boothby came in yesterday. He said: "Malcolm, I've just been preparing a magnificent obituary for you for the B.B.C. The only thing is, I don't get anything till it's delivered."'

I saw him again when he was back at his flat. The first time I think he knew the worst, and he was a little low. The second time was on the Sunday, two days before he died. Now he was cheerful and lively, you would have said he was at the end of convalescence for some mild trouble. Some Shakespeare play was in rehearsal with an all-male cast. We had both seen pictures in a Sunday paper, and we were both, we felt, against it. Suddenly, with great energy he said: 'It makes me so angry when people say that Shakespeare was a homo. I can prove that he wasn't! I can *prove* it.' He rang his little bell and asked sweet Sylvia to find the Sonnets of Shakespeare. She did. 'Here you are,' he said and turned, I *think*, to Sonnet 22. He read the whole thing, firmly and strongly, which is quite a task for a healthy man. Half-way through he stopped and repeated a line. 'That's it,' he said and read to the end. 'So you see,' he said, 'that proves it. The way things are going,' he went on, earnestly, 'they'll be saying this more and more, so you see, Alan, you must tell them it's nonsense.' This hint that he might not be about to tell them himself was the only moment of its kind. I was so amazed and moved by the scene, by the energy of the dying Maestro, by his concern for Shakespeare's reputation, that I did not really take in the point he was making. I am not sure it was Sonnet 22: but so, imperfectly, I pass his message on.

He was a great host, whether at the flat after a concert or at that table by the door in the Savoy, after a Gilbert and Sullivan opera. He seemed to sparkle with the joy of life, of his friends about him, of the work just done. He liked to give you Château Yquem instead of port. I did not see him very often but I miss him very much. We even, in a small way, collaborated. He made me write two carols for tunes, I think Czecho-slovakian, that he had arranged. They were performed at his Carol Concert, and one is published, 'Star In the South'. I am glad to think that there is a work by Herbert and Sargent.

Sir Robert Menzies

I am highly proud to be able to address that great man Sir Robert Menzies, for so long Prime Minister of Australia, as 'Bob'. But he is such a democrat, such an Australian, that uncountables can say the same. Massive, I think, is the word for him. He has a massive head, a massive mind, a massive character. It is not for me to classify statesmen, perhaps, but Bob, I dare to say, is one of the most solid English-speaking statesmen of the century. I said to him, long ago, as he mixed some splendid Martinis in that room over the river at the Savoy that he loved so well: 'You've done enough for your dear Australia. Why don't you come over and help us?' He confessed that he had toyed with the temptation to settle in our land – but not to retire. He would not, like some predecessors, have sought a seat in the Lords: he would have tried for a seat in the House of Commons. But he decided that he must stand by Australia. What a pity! What a pity he was not about when Harold Macmillan had to retire (not that I have anything against Sir Alec or Mr Heath). He would have made us a fine Prime Minister. He would, I am sure, have dominated our House of Commons as I have seen him dominate his House of Representatives, with weighty guns of speech and all the light artillery of rebuff and repartee, loaded always with wisdom, wit, wide experience and the arts of a practical advocate (our present Lord Chief Justice, Lord Parker, I believe, was his pupil in Chambers). He is as near to Churchill as God has given us. He is the most human of massive men. He has an unfathomable fund of fun and fable – and is a mimic too. He would have been a great Smoking-Room man (all the best Prime Ministers are). If they pressed him (as I used to) I can see him making glorious laughter with his imitations of Willie Hughes, a famous past Prime Minister, and tales of sharp exchanges in the Chamber or the Courts. He is a devoted member of the Melbourne and the London Savage Clubs, and you learn good mixing there. He told us that whenever he went to see Nasser on that fruitless mission to Cairo he wore his Savage Club tie. But I believe he was happiest when he had two Test Teams, Australia and England, to dinner. What recollections, what nice assessments of this hero and that! Once I had the honour to sit next to Lindwall, the illustrious, graceful fast bowler. I asked him if he was really excited when they gave him 'the new ball' of which the commentators speak with such portentous awe. 'No,' he said, 'I know that everyone's expecting me to get a wicket – and I don't know that it makes all that difference.'

The last time I was in Canberra Sir Robert wrote a poem, a skilled amusing poem, in my honour on the Treasury Bench in the Chamber during Question Time. It is not every Prime Minister of whom a man can say that: and so my best salutes to Sir Robert, not forgetting the charming Dame Patty – and his daughter Heather.

Bernard Shaw

I think I once crossed palms with Bernard Shaw, but cannot remember where. We crossed pens more than once in the columns of *The Times*.

In 1950 – or 1951? – there was a public search for a name for the riverside area of land captured for the Festival of Britain next to the Council Hall. 'South Bank' won. I wrote, I think, my shortest letter to *The Times*:

Sir,

What about 'Waterloo Shore'?

I am, sir,

A. P. Herbert

Shaw wrote:

Sir,

South Bank is by far the best name for the new embankment: and it involves a very beneficial change of the present name, The Thames Embankment, which is no longer distinctive, to North Bank. Whichever name be chosen will be written, printed and typed every day, every letter costing a huge sum in human labour and every letter saved saving that sum. There are 16 letters in Thames Embankment [but there is no such place – he was thinking I suppose, of Victoria Embankment] and nine in both South Bank and North Bank. In Southward Side and Middlesex Side there are 13 letters each. South Bank and North Bank will thus effect a saving of manual labour that will soon run to millions of saved man-power.

The suggestions of Sir Alan Herbert and other of your correspondents ignore this enormous consideration, and should therefore be ignored as thoughtless flights of fancy.

G. Bernard Shaw.

I replied:

If we are going to choose our names by Mr Shaw's queer letter-saving system we had better call Waterloo Station 'South Station' and 'Waterloo Bridge' 'Bridge W'.

And what of 'G. Bernard Shaw'? 'Why 'Bernard'? Seven letters. What a waste of man-hours and letter-miles! By the way, geographically 'East Bank' would be nearer to the truth than South Bank; and that would save another letter. [The river here runs North and South] But 'Waterloo Shore', I submit, runs easily, sounds well, and shows the stranger what we mean.

I am, sir,

Alan H.

Mr Shaw wrote:

May I ask Sir Alan Herbert for his estimate of the valuable working time he saves by spelling his Christian name with one 'l' instead of two?

Yours etc.

G. Bernard Shaw.

{ 285 }

But this was not my first bout with the great man about brevity and the space wasted by a single letter. In 1949, in the House of Commons, I made a long and, I believe, effective speech against Mr Follick's Spelling Reform Bill.* The Bill was defeated by three votes only, and Mr Shaw wrote to *The Times*. He spent a haughty paragraph on me and ended with a challenge which could hardly be ignored.

In the debate Sir Alan Herbert took the field as the representative of Oxford University, the university of Henry Sweet, greatest of British phoneticians. After debating the stale tomfooleries customary when spelling reform is discussed by novices and amateurs he finally extinguished himself by pointing out that a sample of Mr Follick's spelling saves only one letter from the conventional Johnsonese orthography. This was the champion howler of the debate. I invite Sir Alan to write down that one letter, and measure how long it takes him to get it on paper, and how much paper it covers: say, a fraction of a second and of a square inch. 'Not worth saving' is his present *reductio ad absurdum*. But surely a University Member must be mathematician enough to go deeper. In the English-speaking world, on which the sun never sets, there are at every fraction of a moment millions of scribes, from book-keepers to poets, writing that letter or some other single letter. If it is superfluous, thousands of acres of paper, months of time, and the labor of armies of men and women are being wasted on it. Dare Sir Alan now repeat that a difference of one letter does not matter?

The rest is poppycock . . .

I replied:

Sir – 'Dare!' indeed? I eagerly accept Mr Bernard Shaw's challenge. I still think nothing of one letter (in 31 words) to be saved (perhaps) by the Follick plan however many millions are now writing or printing it. Nor am I worried by the millions who are spending time or space this morning on shaving their chins or spelling God with a capital G.

I am sorry to say, by the way, that I may have been too generous about that one letter. I have done again the long title of the Bill into Follick English, as I understand it; and this time I make the scores equal (145 letters). I may be wrong; but look, sir, at the following phrases, set down at random:

'The United Nations need a philosophy.' (31 letters)
'Dhe Iunaited Neishuns niid ei filosofii.' (34 letters)
'No sage is as wise as he looks.' (23)
'Nou seij iz az waiz az hii lwks.' (24)
'You are going round in a circle.' (25)
'Iu ar gouing raund in ei serkel.' (25)
'No elephant is a Socialist.' (22)
'Nou elefant iz ei Soushalist.' (24)

* 11 March Hansard Vol. 462, Col. 1599.

Here, if Ai hav dun it rait, Mr Follick is six letters down. It is easy to see why. He pulls out the 'ph' from 'elephant' and says 'What a good boy am I!' But what does it profit a space-saver if at the same time he spells 'go' 'gou' and 'a' 'ei'? Now for the time-saver. See what he has done (above) to such words as 'United', 'nations', 'circle', and 'Socialist'. Such words, at present, are easily apprehended by millions of the Latin (and the English) speakers. Let Mr Shaw, the great mathematician, consider how many trillions of important seconds are going to be wasted by Frenchmen, Italians, Spaniards, and Americans wondering what on earth the English mean by 'serkel' or 'neishun', which are related to nothing they know, and do not even represent phonetically the way we say 'circle' and 'nation'. As for our children, Mr Shaw and his like are distressed by the time spent in teaching them that 'nation' and 'national' are not pronounced the same way. But how much time shall we have to spend on teaching them that 'neishun' and 'nashunal' are really the same word and spring from the same root?

Of course, as I said in the debate which Mr Shaw seems to have read, you can save paper (though not, I think, much printer's or student's time) if you have a thorough-going phonetic system with an enormous alphabet and a lot of weird signs that make the printed page look like a bowl of tadpoles. Both Mr Shaw and Mr Follick, I gather, shrink from this. But Mr Shaw and others want to use several of our letters upside down. Imagine the trouble of teaching a child to write 'c' or 'e' upside down! How many adults are likely to do it efficiently? And in print, as Sir Harry Johnston has remarked, how should we be sure that it was not a printer's error? The reformers, it seems to me, are in a dilemma which they will not face. Either they save no space worth mentioning, or they make the page repulsive and the sense obscure.

Going back to the challenge, even if I were persuaded that Mr Follick was going to save that one letter, I should not be impressed. What is the hurry? If we wish to communicate swiftly we have shorthand, morse, the telephone and loud-speaker. The printed page is read at leisure: and other qualities get marks. We could save much time if we all wore beards and no collars. It would save time if Black Rod ran up the floor of the House without the stately gait and bows. We could save street-space if the Colonel marched in column of threes and there were no intervals between the companies. We could save paper if we cut out stops or ranthewords-togetherlikethis. All books, no doubt, could be printed in shorthand, and all citizens compelled to learn it. But in all those cases there would be a loss to elegance and understanding and the pleasures of the mind and eye which no mere saving of space, time or trouble could justify. For example, it does not upset me to see Mr Shaw spell 'Labour' 'Labor'. Let him carry on. What a wonderful saving! But suppose the one letter were the 'y' in 'you' (Mr Follick wants to abolish 'y'). I do not find it any easier to write 'iu' (try it, Sir): it is not so legible in cursive script and might be taken for 'in': it does not seem to me to be quite the same sound; and I, for one, should miss the word 'you'. So, with due apologies to the children and foreigners, I hope the letter 'y' will be spared, not 'saved'.

{ 287 }

Mr Shaw should be almost old enough to know that you prove no case by shouting words like 'tomfoolery' and 'poppycock'. My own 'tomfooleries' I believe to be facts. From Mr Shaw we get nothing but dogmatic assertion and vague invective. But I hope that the writing of this long letter shows my proper respect for our oldest writer. Mr Follick wants to represent the 'aw' sound in 'paw' by the letters 'oo'; and I was tempted simply to say 'Pw! Mr Shoo!' It would have saved much time.

I am, Sir, your obedient servant,

A. P. Herbert.

Twenty-one years later I feel that that was not a bad retort to the intellectual tyrant of the day. I expected a tempest, a tornado, in reply: but none came.

How sad, though, that only one year later he was on his old one-letter horse about the South Bank!

I wish I had met him.

Arnold Bennett

Belloc frightened me a lot, Galsworthy a little, Arnold Bennett never. He was the most human and natural of the literary swells whose names I am just entitled to drop. We met first, I think, at Nigel Playfair's, for he was on the Committee that ran the Lyric, Hammersmith. But before that he wrote a wonderful review of my first book *The Secret Battle* in his *Evening Standard* column, or rather two columns – 'a masterpiece' he called it, slightly to my surprise. He loved the theatre and the tribe of Bohemia, properly admired C. B. Cochran, Noël Coward and Oliver Messel. He was on the Committee of the Gargoyle Club in its sedate early days. My wife and I used to celebrate our Anniversary there, on New Year's Eve, with some of the family; and Arnold often joined us. Always that day he would count the number of words he had written during the year, and how much per word he had earned – a pardonable pleasure. We would be sitting at a table on the fringe of the dancing floor, gay girls and boys shuffling behind him. 'T-t-his year, Alan,' he would begin, fighting that embarrassing impediment in his speech, 'I have written s-sev-' a passing dancing girl would bang the old gentleman on the head with a balloon, but he did not mind, 'I have w-w-r-itt-en sev- enty –' He did not mind, and we did not mind, how long the triumphal message took to battle through the din; it came at last, and a fine brave signal it was.

With his wife, Dorothy Cheston, the actress, he gave charming little dinners in the Cadogan country. I remember, at one, while the wine went round, he gave us a little lecture in praise of French wine in general, and this one in particular: but he added a warning against

{ 288 }

taking too much of it. It was a cruel stroke that this careful man died of drinking French water.

I got him once to throw a cheese at the Black Lion Skittle Club. But I remember him most vividly at one of our family sing-songs. Most of us had been gathered round the piano singing bits from the Beggar's Opera and so on. Elsa Lanchester and Harold Scott had given some of their Cockney numbers, and one or two of mine. Arnold sat quiet in an armchair, I think enjoying himself among the young. At last there was a lull, no more 'turns'. Arnold rose without a word, walked over to the piano-stool and carefully disposed himself – he was not being funny, he wanted to be comfortable. The noisy young were hushed. Then, accompanying himself, he sang, in a high little voice, this deathless ditty:

> The prettiest girl I ever saw
> Sat sucking cyder through a straw-aw-aw-aw-aw –
>> The prettiest girl etc.
>
> Her young man cried 'What do you for
> Sit sucking cyder through a straw-aw-aw-aw-aw –?
>> Her young man cried etc.
>
> The maid replied 'There is no law
> 'Gainst sucking cyder through a straw-aw-aw-aw-aw –
> So cheek to cheek and jaw to jaw,
> They both sat sucking cyder through a straw-aw-aw-aw-aw –
>> So, cheek to cheek and jaw to jaw,
>> They both sat sucking cyder through a straw.

That is one of my warmest memories.
A few nice letters:

This one is in careful, tiny long-hand. Barrie, and Wells, wrote tiny too.

My sweet Alan,
    My august views on 'M.C.' [Misleading Cases]
    I have read over ½, and shall read the remainder in due course. I think it is very good, very good indeed. Close-woven, and extremely humorous. In a word sound satire. But read in the mass, all at once, it has a certain effect of monotony, quite new though the 'vehicle' is. As regards the public, I think it may fall between two stools, being a bit too restrained and even austere – inadequately farcical. The touches of farce are fine, but for the B.P. they should have been more frequent. The small public it will undoubtedly ravish. In saying 'fall between two stools' I now perceive that I didn't say what I meant. Mais vous comprendez.
                              Yours
                                        A. B.

My dear A. P.,

Dorothy reads it out loud to my intense annoyance, because I should prefer to read it myself – and quietly. Shrieks! and many of Topsy's adjectives! Many thanks. It is highly hilarious and very good.

My love to you both

. y ever

A. B.

Here is an earlier one, consoling, because few seemed to agree with him:

I have not time to do a holograph letter. I like your play [*The White Witch*]. I think it is much too long towards the end, and rather old-fashioned in construction, but I like it. The general 'feel' of it is fine. Some of the scenes, I think, are very good indeed. Duff and I are convinced that you are a dramatist, if that is any use to you. Personally I always feel compassion for a man who is a dramatist.

Some of the acting was good and some of it was hellish.

Yours always

Arnold Bennett

How kind – how kind!

Rudyard Kipling

I met Kipling only once, which was exciting, but in the circumstances, embarrassing. Thereafter I extracted one nice letter from him by writing a book (I don't think I sent it to him and he doesn't say so), and another by being elected to the House of Commons.

This is in long-hand:

Bateman's
.Burwash
Sussex
May 16 '34.

Dear Herbert,

Just back from France after three months out; and I've read your 'Holy Deadlock'. It made me sick. I knew things were pretty heathen in that department of our 'Civilization', but I didn't realize that they were worse than heathen. (The heathen, at least, had a working-plan in their social arrangements, but this muck of ours seems like the elderly hysterics of Bishops and Inquisitors.)

It won't be the book that will do the trick of working reforms; but it will be the reference work, as well as arsenal and magazine to draw on, for future work by men and women who have been driven more than half crazy by the existing state of things. Anyhow, that's how I look at it.

I like the Judge's soliloquy (in his bath) best, as a bit of work; and I saw from the reviews that that made people wince most. So I expect I'm reasonably right here.

Your mail, by now, ought to be interesting. Are the women cursing you very much: or is it the Church? You've a pleasant year ahead of you!

Ever sincerely,

Rudyard Kipling.

Private and own type-writing on a new hard-mouthed machine

Bateman's
November 17/35

Dear Herbert,

If our valley wasn't flooded, you'd be hearing loud and continuous cheers from it. I am more pleased that I can decently say over the news of last night. Also, more surprised; for I did not know that the Seats of Learning kept so much sense at the unused ends of their bodies.

You won't be able to *do* a thing; but you will be there to 'sting the faces of men' re 'Holy Deadlock' and Gambling (I can see from here the joy of your running-mate* over these questions) *and* Thames –
Traffic! Now you'll have to evolve a decent type of penny-steamer. All the luck of the Practical Gods be with you.

The letter ends with a delicious paragraph in business – and official-ese (evidently he had read my *What a Word*).

Trusting your good self has not been unduly affected *qua* your esteemed health by the political events which have transpired subsequent to your entry into the Public Arena.

Always yours sincerely

Rudyard Kipling.

Our meeting was at a dining-club of which I am still proud to be a member. It began as one of those oases where statesmen who had been hunting each other in the desert all day met soothingly at even. But there were other big public men, and servants of the State. I was only elected, I am sure, because my editor Owen Seaman was one of the secretaries. The only other literary members were Barrie and Kipling. Today there are many, and that fine writer, friend and Englishman Arthur Bryant, is the secretary.

My first attendance was all terror. At the preliminary sherry stage Kipling kindly took me under his wing, and at dinner I sat between him and Seaman. It was a long narrow table, and on the other side was a formidable row of stars of the State, an Archbishop of Canterbury, a

* Lord Hugh Cecil.

☩ BURWASH
⚒ ETCHINGHAM

Rudeard Kipling

BATEMAN'S
BURWASH
·SUSSEX·

May. 16. 34

Dear Herbert

Just back from
France after three months
out: and I've read your "Holy
Deadlock." It made me sick.
I knew things were pretty
beastly in that department of
our "civilization"; but I didn't
realize that they were those I know
beastly. (The beasts, at least,
does a working-plan in their
social arrangements. but this
muck of ours seems like the
elderly hysterics of Bishops and
Inquisitors.)

It won't be the book that
will do the trick of working
reforms - but it will be the

reference work, as well as arsenal
and magazine to draw on, for
future work by men & women
who have been driven once than
half crazy by the existing state
of things. Anyhow, that's how I
look at it

I wrote the Judge's soliloquy (in his bath)
last, as a bit of work: and, I found
from the reviews that that made people
wince most. So I expect I'm reasonably
right here.

Your mail, by now, ought to be
interesting. are the women cursing Yothe
very much: or is it the Church?
You've a pleasant year ahead of
you!

Ever sincerely
Rudyard Kipling

✝ BURWASH

ᚺᛞ ETCHINGHAM

BATEMAN'S
BURWASH
SUSSEX·

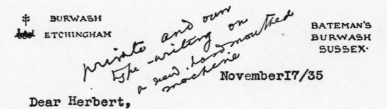

private and own Type-writing on a new loud-mouthed machine

November 17/35

Dear Herbert,

  If our valley wasn't flooded, you'd be
hearing loud andcontinuous cheers from it.

I am more pleased than I can decently say over the
news of last night.Also, more surprised; for I did
not know that the Seats of Learning kept so much
sense at the unused ends of their bodies.

You won't be able to <u>do</u> a thing; butyou will be
there to "sting the faces of men" <u>re</u> Holy Deadlock
and Gambling(Ican/s ee from here the joy of your
running-mate over these questions) <u>and</u>Thames-
Traffic! N_ow you'll haveto evolve a decent type
of penny-steamer.All the luck of the Practical Gods
be with you.

Trusting your good self has not been unduly affected <u>qua</u> your esteemed health by the political events
which have transpired subsequentto your entry into
the Public Arena

  Always yours sincerely

   Rudyard Kipling

   — · —·

Viceroy of India, an ex-Viceroy, Ministers, ex-Ministers, members of both Houses, high Civil Servants – the genial Austen Chamberlain is the only one I remember. Kipling seemed to regard the gathering with small respect – he and I, it was clear, were the only honest men there – and kept up a flow of political comment which was far from friendly to our rulers – we did not talk about 'the Establishment' then. I don't think he actually said 'They'd sell their souls for a mess of pottage' but that was the general message. I could not think of anything to say, feebly assented now and then, and fumbled with my food. Suddenly, about the port stage he rose up, tapped me on the shoulder said: 'Good night, my boy,' and strode out. 'Heavens!' I thought, 'I've bored this great man away.' But Owen Seaman must have read my thoughts, for he turned and said, looking at his watch: 'It's all right. He has to be home by ten. Always.'

Stanley Baldwin

That great, that unfortunate, that much-maligned man Stanley Baldwin was always kind to me in the House of Commons. We had many a gossip in the Smoking Room (where I don't think I ever saw Mr Neville Chamberlain). I remember one day when I came from the Chamber exhausted and cross after an afternoon failing to catch the Speaker's eye, he gave me a philosophical and practical talk about 'bumping', as he called it. How often, after all, when an eager young Member did 'get in' he afterwards regretted it.

But he was kind to me long before that. Once or twice we spoke at the same public dinners (in those days I was much in demand); he asked me to speak at his Worcestershire Society Dinner and we had a breakfast about this, at No. 10.

Then in 1928 I received, from the same address, this charming letter:

> I am going to risk being cut by you next time we meet and losing the Freedom of Hammersmith. But you are young and I am old and I am thinking of the future.
>
> I want you to take heed to the delivery of your speeches. It is at present without form and void.
>
> It is like an intermittent machine-gun fire, rapid, but dropping at the end almost into inaudibility. Ordinarily this wouldn't matter, but your stuff is A.1.
>
> When you can put it over you will be in the top flight of after-dinner speakers. Study method. To my mind, at his best, Gordon Hewart* is a model; every word and every phrase tells. And so might your stuff: it is good enough but it doesn't get across properly.
>
> You may say what business is it of yours? or Mind your own speeches.

* Lord Chief Justice.

{ 295 }

31. x. 1928.

10, Downing Street,
Whitehall.

My dear A.P.H.

I am going to risk being
cut by you next time we meet
and losing the Freedom of Hammersmith.

But you are young and I am
old and I am thinking of the
future:

I want you to take heed to the
delivery of your speeches. It is
at present without form and void.
It is like an intermittent machine
gun fire, rapid, but dropping
at the end almost into inaudibil-
-ity. Ordinarily this wouldn't
matter, but your stuff is A1.
When you can put it over, you
will be in the top flight of
after dinner speakers. Study method

To my mind, at his best,
Gordon Stewart is a model: every
word and every phrase tells. And
so might your stuff: it is good
enough, but doesn't get across
properly.

You may say what business
is it of yours? or mind your
own speeches. True, but you can
be a 1st-class coach without being
a 1st-class man (Ranji and others)
and I can judge a speech.

You have it in you to be
so good and that is why I
have butted in. ♡
    That's all.

                        S. B.

True; but you can be a first-class coach without being a first-class oar (Rudie Lehmann) and I can judge a speech.

You have it in you to be so good and that is why I have butted in.

That's all

S. B.

What a wonderful thing that a Prime Minister should take the trouble to write so beneficent a letter to a young man he hardly knew! I glowed with gratitude, obeyed the advice and, I believe, improved.

Whatever you thought of his policies you had to admire his command of the House of Commons, his plain, persuasive, and often moving speeches. How unfairly he was treated by Fortune and his fellow-men! How tragic that such an honest man, such a loving servant of his country, should go to his death under a cloudy suspicion of deception and betrayal!

The legend is that in 1935 a dumb Mr Baldwin led a blind people to the polls, that nobody had heard of Hitler, that nobody thought about re-arming and the people, itching to be at the dictators' throats, were held back by cowardly statesmen in power.

This is utter nonsense. There was confusion maybe, but no shortage of concern. Remember the wicked words 'East Fulham'? Two years before the Election, in October 1933 the Opposition (Labour) won the East Fulham by-election with a 'war-bogy'. Mr Lansbury said that the Conservatives were 'leading the country to war'. The *Daily Telegraph*, on 27 October, said: 'Alderman Waldron's support of the action of the Government and his plea that our Navy and Air Force were not at present sufficient to defend our seaborne trade were twisted to serve as an attack upon him *as a war-monger*.'

Sir Archibald Sinclair, in the debate on the Address, at the opening of the 1935 Parliament, said:

It is very difficult indeed for us to tell on what scale the Government are intending to ask us to re-arm ... On the one hand we had the [Conservative] Bournemouth Conference, we had compliments – deserved compliments – paid to the Prime Minister by Mr Churchill, we had the most generous replies from the Prime Minister, *we had demands for great armaments made, rather oddly, by the Chancellor of the Exchequer* (Mr Neville Chamberlain) *and were told that the verdict of the country on the question of re-armament was the most important issue of the election* ... But as the campaign proceeded, the soft pedal was introduced. . . .

Soft pedal? If it was employed one can easily imagine why. Someone approached perhaps, and said: 'For heaven's sake don't forget *East Fulham*! You'll be a war-monger again.'

But after the Election the King's Speech let the pedal up:

The fulfilment of our national obligations under the Covenant, no less than the adequate safeguarding of my Empire, makes it *urgently necessary that the deficiencies in My Defence should be made good.* My Ministers will in due course lay before you their proposals, which will be limited to the minimum required for these two purposes.

'The deficiencies . . .' – *'Urgently necessary . . .'* Plain enough, surely. Indeed, on the second day my friend Arthur Greenwood (Labour) was crying 'Warmonger!' again:

Yesterday we had a little quite genteel applause for peace sentiments, but *vociferous applause from the other side of the House at the mention of increased armaments.*

It is interesting to see how, within the last year, aircraft factories whose work is primarily intended for war purposes have been extending . . . They are not building those factories because they believe in the peace Prime Minister. They are building those factories because they know that *this country is about to enter on another armaments race . . .*

(Interesting – and this is the Prime Minister who has since been accused of dragging his feet.)

Mr Radford (Rusholme, Manchester) said (and others said the same): 'I wish the Government to realize that the country is not in favour of our being parties as members of the League to action which would result in war.'

Mr Neville Chamberlain summed up the Labour position curtly but correctly: 'There are the intellectuals who say "Get on with your sanctions" [against Mussolini] whatever the cost, and the hon. Members who say "The Tories it is who want war". But all join together to say: "Above all do not let us have any armaments".'

Indeed, almost to the outbreak of war they voted against the Service Estimates. They voted against Conscription in the Spring of 1939. They thought that if everyone muttered 'Collective Security' three times after meals all would be well. If Labour had won the General Election of 1935 we should not have re-armed at all; it is no wonder if Mr Baldwin and his men trod delicately. Poor Mr Baldwin! I was in the House at the Abyssinia *cum* Hoare-Laval debate when, getting up late and reluctantly, he said: 'I shall be but a short time. I have seldom spoken with greater regret, *for my lips are not yet unsealed.*' These strange words had nothing to do with Hitler or re-armament.

He said later that 'it was one of the stupidest things I ever said' but he was 'morally certain that Laval had been bought by Mussolini' and to reveal the truth would shatter the tenuous basis of Anglo-French unity'.* I am no historian, and cannot speak about that sad and complicated affair. But the legend that 'Old Sealed-lips' deliberately suppressed or ignored the truth about the Hitler menace is, it seems to me, cruel and untrue.

As I said in my Election Address of 1945: 'It may be observed that the aircraft which won the Battle of Britain, the ships which held the seas in 1940, were not designed or begun in that summer.'

He never failed, when I sent him a book, to write a real letter, in long-hand, about it. He was a great lover of Topsy too.

10 Downing Street
13 April 1924

Dear Mr Herbert,

How grateful I am to you for sending your dear Topsy to spend her Easter at Chequers, I am quite unable to express.

I had of course met her, perhaps once a week† but only in a crowd. But now I feel I am really getting to know her. We missed her the first day or two she was here, and I found what indeed I had suspected, that she had been borne off to my daughter's room. They understand each other so thoroughly and are delighted after a hebdomadal glimpse during the season to have a real talk during whatever it is that women do now they have no hair to brush.

You will recognize the impression she has made on me next time you have the misfortune to hear me speak.

Yours sincerely and gratefully
Stanley Baldwin.

19 December 1931
11 Downing Street

My dear Herbert,

You are a kind friend and I am very happy to have your latest poems. We *must* see if anything can be done to get the beer duty lowered but even a National Government can't improve its quality.

I hope to take to beer again when I have finished with politics and can get exercise.

It is a soul-satisfying sight to see elderly gentlemen drinking out of tankards, but I don't do it. But I don't boast: I am conscious of my own inferiority.

All good wishes for Christmas.

yours sincerely
Stanley Baldwin.

* *Baldwin* – Keith Middlemass and John Barnes – Weidenfeld and Nicolson, p. 889.
† In *Punch*.

Austen Chamberlain

Everybody in the House of Commons, I think, would have agreed that 'old Austen' was a dear man. A statesman but human, unpompous. There was always a happy ring about him in the Smoking Room, enjoying his old slow tales. I met him first at Oxford, where we had both been speaking, between the General Election of 1935 and the opening of Parliament. He gave me long and earnest advice about the Maiden Speech. Don't rush it. Sit in the Chamber for six months at least, get the feel of the place, study the good speakers, and the bad as well. Excellent advice. But then I went and exploded on the second day of Parliament. He was pained, I know, but he said nothing.

One evening after he had made a successful speech in the Chamber I was asking about his methods – how much preparation? What sort of notes? He took a card from his pocket with a few headings written on it in the common fashion, in ink. But in pencil some subject, I forget what, was written large across the card in capitals. 'But,' I said, 'you said nothing about that.' 'No', said the statesman ruefully, 'it was the one thing I was keen to say, so I made that special note. And then I forgot it.'

Comforting to hear that the old hands could do it too.

18 Oct. 35

Dear A.P.H.,

Thanks for your book (*What a Word!*) You are a bold man and should have made many enemies by your 'aggression' though I suppose you will plead that it was not unprovoked. I forgive you your reproof and thank you for your praise, but if I meet with 'ticketeer' in any future work of yours I will do my best to 'sabotage' its circulation until it has been submitted to a repeated process of 'redecontamination'. How could you?

Do you know Roosevelt's phrase: weasel words? A good one, I think, for words which suck the meaning out of those which follow. They are much used by politicians in trouble and by some others.

yrs sincerely

Austen Chamberlain.

J. M. Barrie

My dear friend E. V. Lucas, who knew everybody, first took me to see Sir James in his lofty flat at the west end of Adelphi Terrace, and thereafter I went often. I retain the impression of a benignant gnome or elf – very small and slightly twisted. He loved cricket and I once played in the team he used to get up at Mells, Lady Horner's beautiful place. He bowled very slowly, left handed I think, exactly like a gnome. There was a famous croquet game too at Stanway, his own home –

Barrie, John Galsworthy, E. V. Lucas and little me. All the others, I thought, were guilty of sharp practice. He came down to Hammersmith once or twice, threw a 'cheese' at the Black Lion Skittle Club, and dandled our small son John on his knee. The boy was said to be backward, couldn't read soon enough etc. 'Don't worry,' said J.M.B. 'It's all there, I can see.' And it was.

But most I remember him in the Adelphi Terrace eyrie. He had a great log-fire and a deep – is it ingle-nook? There he sat, far back in his dusky corner, smoking pipe after pipe and coughing his heart out. The enormous coughing made you wonder how so small a frame could survive it. I always wondered why he wanted to see me for I was not, I felt, cut out for Barrie dialogue, and often found myself wondering what to say next. You remember, in *Mary Rose*, 'the island that likes to be visited?' That was himself I feel. He talked a lot about *Peter Pan* and Eton, which seemed to be always on his mind – and of course, the boys whom he had adopted. He told me too that he got his characters' names out of the telephone book, and sure enough, you will find many Smees and Starkeys in the London book. (How lucky that *Peter Pan* was written in 1904 and not in 1954! For by the new libel law of that year an author is expected to look up the pirates' register and make sure that he is not defaming a real pirate.) He would tell me too of his larks with Bernard Shaw, who lived in a flat across the narrow street – flipping cherry stones at Shaw's windows, and so on.

Once, at dinner, just the two of us, we were discussing the meaning and pronunciation of some word or other, when the butler, serving the fish, murmured over my shoulder the Greek origin of the word and the correct pronunciation. The Admirable Crichton, I supposed. There was much fun in that large lovely flat but not, one felt, much happiness. The failure of *David*, which Cochran put on (Elizabeth Bergner), shook him severely. It was sad to feel sorry for this rich and famous man.

I have just seen for the first time a sentence in C. B. Cochran's *Cock-a-Doodle-Do*: 'For my friend A. P. Herbert, Barrie had a great regard and admiration. Even before I came in close association with Barrie, he never missed a revue or musical play which had been written by A.P.H.'

This surprised and pleased me greatly, for though the intellectuals may brush him aside he did know something about writing for the stage. I cannot remember that he ever discussed my little works in conversation: but now I have been looking gratefully at letters which I had ungratefully forgotten:

In December 1924: 'Let me wish great success to King of the Castle. I have long wanted you to have a shot at play writing. J. M. Barrie'.

29 March 1925

My dear Herbert,

Here is a compliment to you. The copy of your book you so kindly sent me (*The Old Flame*) is at present going the rounds in a nursing home, and one of the nurses tells me that when laughter is heard from anywhere they know which room that book is in. Before it reached there (whence it shall be recovered) it had given me some gay hours, and my verdict is that nothing of its kind has been better done since 'The Dolly Dialogues'. You have a very rare and delicious way of saying things and I was 'happy of you'. There is also another Herbert that I guess we shall see more of in your work by and by.

With warm regards
Yours sincerely

J. M. Barrie.

21 Oct. 1926

I have been enjoying 'She Shanties' so much that I won't swear I haven't been humming i.e. practically singing them, I who never sung before though when hands are clasped in Auld Lang Syne (which I expect is by you) I can look uncommonly like it.

2 May 1928

My dear Herbert,

There was a kind of book I always wanted you to write, and now I find you did it years ago. Can't understand why I hadn't read 'The Secret Battle' before – of course I knew about it – ? ? ? to you. I have read it now, and can assure you with great admiration. The good qualities of this writer ?used by the man behind this writer came out abundantly, and I never was so pleased with you in my life.

Yours

J. M. Barrie.

And here is a happy one:

24 June 1928

My dear Herbert,

Or rather, Alan my son, I hope you remember a half promise you made to come to me for a week-end with your wife to Stanway in Glouces-tershire. Any Friday to Monday in August that suits you would be the thing, and I'll lure you to shovel board on the classic scale and other devilries.

Yours

J. M. Barrie.

Went to a political meeting the other day – slipped out to the Fair. By time meeting ended had won one silver watch, some wrist watches, two ?pepper pots, three rings, four necklaces, various scent bottles and eight cocoa-mats. Searched in vain for the pig in poke.

ADELPHI TERRACE HOUSE,

STRAND, W.C.2.

24 June 1938.

My dear Herbert,

Or rather Calais my son, I hope you remember a hasty promise you made to come to me for a week end with your wife to Stanway in Gloucestershire. Any Friday to Monday in August. I think surely you would do this thing, and I'll love you on the Stanned bread on the classic scale and other dentries.

Yours

Jm Barrie

Went to a political meeting the other day — slipped off to the Fair. By time meeting ended had won one silver watch, some wrist watches two puppies polo three mugs four necklaces various scent bottles and eight coconuts. Searched in vain for the pig in poke. Address, Rue Thming Oprar Cari Abaile Lira Egypt.

14 Oct 1927

My dear Herbert,

. . . When doctors are not at me I am reading your works, of which the two latest are delicious specimens. You give me more sheer joy than anybody, and you are also as wise as wise . . .

Winston Churchill

I have written miles about Winston Churchill in *Independent Member*, and elsewhere, and must not repeat myself. But there are one or two things I should like to say. The Royal Naval Division was Winston's own creation. (It included many who joined to serve as sailors but found themselves compelled to serve as soldiers). We were sent to 'the Dardanelles' which was an enterprise designed but not, alas, entirely controlled by Winston. It was a gallant but grim failure. Our Division suffered terrible losses. We might have been forgiven, then, if we had followed the example of the official and the common world and shown some coolness towards the man who was responsible for our existence and our misfortunes. There was no coolness. First and last we believed that it was a grand design. Fate, and many faults defeated it: but it was not a Winston folly. One or two of us went up to Leicester to speak for him at a by-election where the corner-boys were crying: 'What about the Dardanelles?' For many years he came to the Division's Annual Dinner and had a hero's welcome. Two years running in the early twenties, at the Café Royal, he proposed 'The Royal Naval Division' and I had the honour to respond. 'Keep together', was always his message, and bless me, fifty-six years after he created us, though there are not many of us left, we are still holding our annual dinners, as near as possible to 13 November, anniversary of the Battle of the Ancre where our great Freyberg won his V.C. We keep too a happy relation with the Admiralty. Our War Memorial had to leave the Horse Guards' Parade when 'Lenin's Tomb' was built but it is respectfully tended in the grounds of the Royal Naval College at Greenwich and the Admiral President and Captain of the College at Greenwich are very welcome guests at our dinners. Our continuous affection was, I think, one comfort to Churchill in the long dark years.

Here is a tale of those days I do not think I have told elsewhere. In 1933 we were invited to lunch at Chartwell, but my wife could not make it. The only other guest was William Nicholson, who was at work on a portrait of that great lady 'Clemmy', Mrs Churchill. It was a wretched day, raining hard. After lunch the artist went off with his model. Winston said to me: 'Let's have a look at the estate.' There was a great business of arming me against the rain, a sou'-wester, scarves, big rubber boots. Winston carried a large basket full of bread for his water birds.

{ 305 }

'We have plenty to occupy ourselves,' he said as we halted outside and looked down at the lake.

From the house there is, to my recollection, quite a steep slope down to the water. Zig-zag across the slope ran a small waterway, recently constructed, I believe. 'We had fun with this,' he said. 'The water, you see, begins its march over here, and here, like a stage army, retraces its step and crosses the scene again.' We moved down. 'Yes, we have plenty to do. But when you consider that the reins of this great Empire are in the nerveless hands of Stanley Baldwin and Ramsay Macdonald, you wonder sometimes whether one should not be otherwise engaged.'

I was no politician, and no apt reply occurred to me. The National Government were in power, Ramsay Macdonald at No. 10, Stanley Baldwin at No. 11. Neither of the Parties would have anything to do with Winston. He was many leagues away in the wilderness. And here was the poor man trying to pretend that he didn't mind. I felt deeply sorry for him – but I could think of nothing to say.

We reached the lake, the birds made for him, all kinds of ducks and fancy geese, and he began to distribute bread. He had, it seemed, some favourites:

'Come on, ducky! come on! come on, ducky – this is for you. No, not *you*. Go away, you! Go away, you've had your ration. That's the most formidable bird on the pond. He always reminds me of that pestilent Liberal – what's his name? Go *away*, you. Come on, ducky! Pringle? No, not Pringle. It's Hogge, the other one. Go away, Hogge.'

We moved along the waterside. 'As I was saying, when you consider that the reins of this great Empire are in the nerveless hands of – Come on, ducky! Come on! There's Hogge again. Go *away*, you! No it's Pringle. You agree, Hogge, I hope, that the reins of this great Empire should *not* be in the nerveless hands of Stanley Baldwin and Ramsay Macdonald? Come on, ducky. No, I don't suppose you do. Can't count on 'em – never could! Go *away*, Pringle.'

There was at least one more bird-encounter like this and then, the basket empty, we walked up the hill to a sort of kiosk or summer-house where, I think, he did some painting. The walls were covered with his works and very gay and good they looked. He was very modest about them, 'I don't call myself an artist,' he said, 'but at least there's a little joy and sunlight here. So much of this modern painting seems joyless to me – no sunlight.' At last I was able to say something, and I said it warmly. Under that small roof was a fort of joy and sunshine. I selected my favourites and praised them, and for a minute or two we both forgot about Ramsay Macdonald. The rain had stopped, we walked on up the hill, and sat down on a low bench at the top. On our left front was the orchard round which he had himself built the brick wall. On our right was the pleasant house where he was writing, I think, the last volume of his 'Marlborough'. 'Yes,' he said at last with a sigh, 'I should be very content. There is much to do. I have my birds – I have my bricks – I have my books – I have my dear family. But when you consider that the reins of this great Empire are in the nerveless hands of Stanley Baldwin and Ramsay Macdonald—' Then I think, there was a pause and he said, 'Shall we go in?'

At that moment, sadly, I would have betted 10,000 to 1 against his ever becoming Prime Minister. And so, I believe, would he.

We all know with what grandeur his war-leadership began and with what glory it concluded. But few remember the horrid half-way house, 1942, when it seemed to some that Fate, and Parliament, might strike him from the heights as they did in War One. It never became a catch-word, thank God, but in May and June 1942 'Churchill Must Go' was in the minds of many important and influential men. This is worth re-membering, I think, because his response was one of his high peaks of courage and the result was a fine mark for the House of Commons.

On 19–20 May there was a two-days debate on the war in which criticism of the Prime Minister was severe and loud: and six weeks later we gave two days to a Vote of Censure, moved by Sir John Wardlaw-Milne (a Conservative) and seconded by Aneurin Bevan (Labour), in these terms:

CENTRAL DIRECTION OF THE WAR

That this House, while paying tribute to the heroism and endurance of the Armed Forces of the Crown in circumstances of exceptional difficulty, *has no confidence in the central direction of the war.*

And you can't say plainer than that.

On 20 May, for once, I popped up in a general debate and, I am glad to see, defended my earliest hero:

In the long catalogue of British misfortunes, for which the Prime Minister is said to be responsible, I do not think that the Hon. Member omitted a single episode, except the Battle of Hastings and the wreck of the schooner *Hesperus*. He might, I felt, have dwelt a little longer on the Battle of Crecy . . . It was said that in Napoleon's time every soldier had a field-marshal's baton in his knapsack. How much more fortunate are we in this House, where almost every Member has the flag of an Admiral of the Fleet in his pocket as well. [For my more solemn remarks see *Independent Member*] I ended: I believe the people know that they have a great man; they are determined to keep him and determined to deserve him – and so am I.

Obvious, you may think, but in those unhappy days it was enough to get you the reputation of a 'Yes-Man'.

Sir John Wardlaw-Milne had said: 'I say quite frankly that it is the

Prime Minister I am criticizing . . . As Prime Minister and Minister of Defence he is trying to carry too heavy a burden, and the country with all its belief in him, which many of us share [many!] with all its trust, with all its gratitude, is beginning to feel that it would be well if he were to share that burden with somebody else.'*

Mr McGovern said: 'Everyone is asking [in the country] when this Government is to come to an end.' He also said, in the later debate: 'So far as I am concerned, if I had to choose between Hitler and the Prime Minister I should not know exactly on which the choice had to fall.'†

Those were the days.

Churchill rose to reply to the Vote of Censure on 2 July. He could hardly have had a worse day for the job. Tobruk had fallen the week before. On the very day the debate began Rommel had opened his assault on the South Africans at the gates of Alexandria. How in all the anxieties and duties of those two days he had been able to prepare and polish a long speech at all seemed a mystery to lesser mortals. Indeed, he said himself, while he was listening to Bevan's 'diatribe' about things that he did, or should have done eight months ago, 'I found it very difficult to withdraw my thoughts from the tremendous and most critical battle now raging in Egypt'. What was happening there at the door to the Suez Canal, while all these know-alls yattered away?

I should not wonder if those days were reckoned among his worst. He must by now have had the sense of his own destiny strong in him. Surely he had not emerged from all those years 'in the wilderness' for nothing? Yet here were men of all parties, important men, serious men, men who had clamoured for him in 1940, joining in the hunt – not only the malignant whipper-snapper from Wales, but Wardlaw-Milne, strong, patriotic Tory, Clem Davies, sober leader of the Liberals, Lord Winterton, Mr Shinwell. Either he had done too much or he had done too little: they were against him. It was by forces no stronger than these that Neville Chamberlain had been cast down: and Chamberlain had only one defeat to his account – he had a dozen. He may well have thought: After all that I have done – is this the beginning of the end? Was it in vain that I displaced those 'nerveless hands'?

Yet the old lion roared robustly for twenty-six columns of *Hansard* – about ninety minutes.

At one point Mr Hore-Belisha interjected: What about the 'Churchill' tank?

THE PRIME MINISTER: At the present moment I have not got there. But he did.

'This tank, the A22, was ordered off the drawing-board and large

* 19 May 1942 – Col. 148.
† 1 July 1942 – Col. 433.

numbers went into production very quickly. As might be expected, it had many defects and teething troubles, and when these became apparent the tank was appropriately re-christened the 'Churchill'. These defects have now been largely overcome. I have no doubt that this tank will prove, in the end, a powerful, massive and serviceable weapon of war.'

I remember how we laughed at that – full, human, sympathetic, happy laughter. It was a true 'stroke of genius'. I often said that if Churchill had done nothing else he would still, at least, be England's greatest humorist. For, on any subject, before any audience, with no fault of taste or tact, he could make laughter when he would. Who can say more? Time and again, in those immense war-speeches, full of detail, defiance and dignity, there came the sudden jest that made the whole House happy. Here, in (to my mind) the most difficult speech of all, he had the nerve, the time, to pop in a little joke that was against himself and yet, obliquely, was an answer to the harsh debate. Old hands said that that jest, that laughter, altered the whole tone of the affair. The hard tension had gone.

He also said, in the same vein:

I have never made any predictions except things like saying that Singapore would hold out. What a fool and knave I should have been to say that it would fall! I have not made any arrogant, confident, boasting predictions at all. *On the contrary, I have stuck hard to my blood, toil, tears and sweat, to which I have added muddle and mismanagement and that, to some extent, I must admit, is what you have got out of it.* *

The final roar was this:

Every vote counts. If those who have assailed us are reduced to contemptible proportions and their Vote of Censure on the National Government is converted to a vote of censure upon its authors, make no mistake, a cheer will go up from every friend of Britain and every faithful servant of our cause, and the knell of disappointment will ring in the ears of the tyrants we are striving to overthrow.†

Still, 25 resolute men voted for the Motion – but 475 voted No.

While the Commons yapped at the Minister of Defence the Army, under Auchinleck, was pushing Rommel back.

Aneurin Bevan had said: 'I say that the Prime Minister has great qualities, but obviously, picking men is not one of them.'‡

But next month Montgomery was on his way to Egypt; and three

* Col. 603.
† Cols. 609–10.
‡ Col. 539.

months later the Battle of El Alamein took place. There were no more Votes of Censure.

I remember too a Vote of Confidence a little more than a year earlier, on 7 May 1941. It was carried by 447 votes to 3. Patriotic persons might say: 'Who are these beastly three? Ought to be shot.' But 'they' were the tiny Independent Labour Party, led by the popular James Maxton. Afterwards in the Smoking Room Winston would call across to Maxton: 'Thank you, Jimmy. "Carried by 447 to 3" looks much more drastic and dramatic in print than "Carried unanimously".'

His peroration that day is not as well-remembered as some others, but for many reasons it is memorable. After a long, detailed speech about military matters he said:

It is a year almost to a day since, on the crash of the disastrous Battle of France, His Majesty's present Administration was formed. Men of all parties, duly authorized by their parties, joined hands together to fight this business to the end.

[Observe 'joined hands together' – not 'agreed to co-operate', or 'consented to a Coalition'.]

That was a dark hour, and little did we know what storms and perils lay before us, and little did Herr Hitler know when he received the total capitulation of France, and when he expected to be master of all Europe in a few weeks and the world in a few years, that ten months later, in May 1941, he would be appealing to the much-tried German people to prepare themselves for the war of 1942.

When I look back on the perils which have been overcome, upon the great mountain waves through which the gallant ship has driven, when I remember all that has gone wrong, and remember also all that has gone right, I feel sure we have no need to fear the tempest. Let it roar, and let it rage. We shall come through.

'We shall come through' – the words are short, as ever: the metaphor is old and simple: but I remember what a trumpet-call it was. They were the last words he spoke in the old Chamber. That was Wednesday 7 May. On Saturday the 10th, an apt reply to those defiant words, the Germans utterly destroyed the Chamber of the House of Commons, and dropped a shell, unexploded, through the roof of the House of Lords.

You will not, strangely, find any reference in Hansard to the destruction of the House of Commons on 10 May 1941. You will find this:

8 May 1941

Adjournment

Resolved 'That this House do now adjourn' (Mr Munro)*

* Col. 1050.

Tuesday 13 May 1941
(Mr Speaker in the Chair)
'Let it roar!' The House sat on, at the other end of the building.

Field-Marshal Viscount Montgomery
A long time ago I answered the front-door bell, and there was a shy young man who said 'Is Betty here?' He was after Betty Carver, a great friend of my wife, who lived in Chiswick Mall. Years later we stayed with the couple at Alexandria. The shy man was now the Colonel of a battalion of the Royal Warwickshire Regiment. Very quiet and precise; he liked the meals to be punctual: evidently respected; but there was no sign of a world-beater. Betty died tragically before War Two of a silly bathing cut, and we did not see the shy man for many years. But we read about him. One day our shy friend announced publicly: 'The battle which is now to begin will be one of the decisive battles of history. It will be the turning-point of the war. The eyes of the whole world will be on us, watching anxiously which way the battle will swing. We can give them their answer at once: "It will swing our way".'
The shy man was right, for the battle mentioned was the Battle of El Alamein.
At the end of July 1944 I received one of my most exciting letters.

Dear Alan,
Thank you very much for your latest book, *Less Nonsense*. Two copies arrived. I think you must have sent me a copy before I asked for one.
Would you care to come over to Normandy and stay a night with me – or two? If you can arrange it I will send my aeroplane for you . . .'

I got leave from my kindly officers and went – in my Petty Officer's uniform. I visited him also at a grand house in Brussels (where he sang a song at the piano), and a poor house in Holland, and at last in Paris where de Gaulle embraced him, right and left, and invested him with the Grande Croix of the Legion d'honneur, and the crowds went mad, and the shy man, invited to urge them to clear the British Embassy said, '*Merci – et maintenant – allez vous en*'. ('Alan,' he said afterwards, 'they say I said the wrong thing . . . *Allez vous en* means "Go away" doesn't it?' 'Yes, sir.' 'Well, that's what I wanted. And that's what they did.') And so to Luneberg Heath, the scene of Victory, where Monty wrote his *High Command in War* and I wrote my Election Address 1945.
I have filled large canvases with Monty in *Independent Member* (you should read that – it is a good book): but some special corners stand out in my memory – Monty at the fantastic Peter Pan camp in the

Bois de Cerisy, the ferns, the dogs, the tame rabbit, the caravans, the sunshine and the shade – Monty, before dinner, saying to young Johnny Henderson, a delightful A.D.C., 'Give Alan a drink – give Alan a drink. Don't make him tight – but give Alan a drink.' Monty after dinner, in the map caravan, explaining quietly the plan for the Falaise Pocket – no boasting, no 'We've got 'em in the bag', but a modest 'It will be very interesting to see the outcome' – and Monty driving round the countryside with many cigarettes and old copies of *The Times*, which he would press on astonished Traffic Control men. It was hot but I remember how half-naked Pioneers sweating with picks at the side of the road, would look up and recognize and lift their heads high and salute, sometimes with special contortions, as if to say: 'This is *my* salute for *my* general' – one realized what saluting is for. I remember him standing on the deck of a Royal Naval vessel in Hamburg and saying: 'Commodore, I should like if I may to say "Splice the main brace"' – an extra tot of rum for all hands. The Commodore was all for it, and 'made it so'. This was at my own innocent suggestion. After all, he had just accepted the surrender not only of the German Army, but the naval and air forces as well: he was in supreme command, and these were the first two British ships to come up the Elbe. But for him they could not have come: and I *think* he could have told them to go away. But the Admiralty took a pedantic view and rebuked him on the ground, I gather, that only the Monarch was entitled to request 'a special issue of spirit'. 'Admiral Cunningham complained to the War Office that I was not entitled to "splice the main brace" and asking that I be told not to do it again. I was duly told!!' I took a very poor view of the Admiralty, and do so still. There is – or was – nothing about the Monarch in King's Regulation 1825 (11). It simply says, 'The order "Splice the Main Brace" is to be regarded as authorizing etc. etc.' (I knew this because I had recently had to look it up. I had myself made an extra issue of spirit to the crew of the *Water Gipsy* when we had rather skilfully rescued another small vessel on a rough cold night: it was approved by the Admiral.) It was the Commodore, not Monty, who 'authorized the special issue': and he, no doubt, should have been hounded out of the Service. But to Monty in the very special circumstances, the descendants of Nelson, I should have thought, might well have turned a blind eye. He never reproached me, and apologized to the sea-lawyers.

Monty is not the fiendish foe of human pleasure he is sometimes painted. He likes a little bet. The mess betting-book was full of entries like this: 'General Eisenhower bets General Montgomery that the war with Germany will end before Christmas 1944.'

He goes to bed at 9.30, if he can, but does not expect the world to do likewise. He does not drink himself because he does not like it, and no doubt, in the way of duty, he is severe in this department of conduct. But at a dinner in London, though he swills his orange drinks, his staff may have what they like. I don't think I ever saw one of them smoke in his presence – that is a strong dislike. When we sat talking after breakfast in the mess I would always (heroically) defer my first, and finest, pipe till we were outside. But once or twice he said suddenly: 'Smoke your pipe, Alan, smoke your pipe' – a still more heroic effort, I believe.

One morning in the small Holland TAC headquarters, where the doodle-bugs roared over and the tanks roared by, I was sitting in the ante-room waiting to fly home. Enter the Field-Marshal bearing a bottle of brandy across his breast. 'A bottle of brandy – captured from the Germans. A present for Gwen. Would you like it?' 'Thank you very much, sir,' I said, and muttered something silly about the Customs. 'Oh, the Customs?' said the Field-Marshal. 'I must write you a letter,' and he disappeared.

It was just before Christmas, true, but I was somewhat surprised by this generous gesture. For the Field-Marshal had started a small battle that morning – only a small battle, I gather, to clear away the last pocket of Germans on our side of the Meuse. I knew something of his methods. He made his precepts clear to his subordinate commanders, they were steeped in his principles and he had faith that they would follow both; so when the thing began, unless crises intruded, he left them to it, relaxed and wrote letters home. Still, all this effort for Gwen and me, and a bottle of brandy!

I went up to my room. There Johnny Henderson and a batman were struggling on the floor with my small bag. In Brussels we had gone shopping. I had bought some toys for grandchildren and a little red wine for the home. Also Johnny had thrust upon me two of those large bottles of 'Bols' gin – again captured from the enemy. The problem of packing then was dismaying, and when I produced the bottle of brandy, looked desperate. In comes the Field-Marshal with a letter he had written: 'I have presented my friend A. P. Herbert M.P. with a bottle of brandy, captured from the Germans. I hope the Customs will take a kindly view of this. I am sure they will.' I was so staggered by his care and kindness that I did not know what to say: but I did get out something about 'the two bottles of gin the boys have given me'. 'What, gin? What, gin?' said the Field-Marshal. 'I must write it again.' He went away, and came back with a new letter including the Bols.

At Northolt the two Customs officers on duty happened to know me for they had recently been serving with the Water Guard on *The Harpy*, off the Customs House at Billingsgate, where I sometimes cadged a berth for the *Water Gipsy*. 'Well Mr H,' they said. 'Have you anything to declare?' 'I have,' I said, and showed them the letter. There was a lot of nudging and chuckling as they read it, and at last one said:

'Well, that will be all right, Mr H – only, you know, we shall have to keep this document won't we, just to make all shipshape,' or something of the sort. I would much rather have paid double duty, or surrendered my cargo, and kept 'the document'. But that would have made a vain thing of all the Field-Marshal's toil and trouble. So I let him have it. And some damned Customs Officer has the finest autograph of a Field-Marshal that ever existed. I insist that he sends it to me at once. I will pay the duty.

Well, there is your 'inhuman martinet': and that is the point of the story. Some have been 'shocked' by it. To them I say: 'You can't have it both ways.' But they do. All the legends are wrong. 'Only a show-man – conceited fellow', they used to growl in the clubs – much resented by his friends and, I should say, by his soldiers. You can't be a showman without something to show: and his chief audience was the enemy. And what the growlers had in mind in those early days was done, I feel, with a purpose. When he took high command the Army had little to show and few to show it. He blew the Army's trumpet not his own. It was not in conceit but confidence that he made that astonishing prophecy before Alamein. Humourless? No. There is plenty of quiet fun. One of his personal staff – they all seemed to revere and love him – told me he never saw the Chief 'more magnificent' than he was during the Rundstendt offensive in the Ardennes. At the height of the crisis – and it *was* a crisis – he could come to breakfast and say: 'This is awkward. We can't go out through Dunkirk this time. The Germans are there.' When things were bad, he was at his best. Those about him used to welcome my visits, because, they said, I cheered him up. If a match can assist a furnace I am proud indeed. As for me, he always gave me a strong desire to be a better man.

John Astor

Most people, I find, are confused about the great Astor clan, and wonder which Astor is which? In my lifetime there have been two tribes prominent in England, the Cliveden Astors and the Hever Astors. I have been privileged to know them both and saw most of the younger generations when they were prancing round Christmas trees: but they often muddle me. At lovely Cliveden, by the Thames, reigned Waldorf Astor, husband of the famous Nancy M.P., eldest son of 'the old man' William Waldorf Astor, and heir to the Viscountcy. At lovelier Hever Castle in Kent reigned his younger brother, John Jacob. He lost a leg late in War One, with the 1st Life Guards; served in the House of Commons as Member for Dover for many years; rescued *The Times* from under the feet of the Northcliffe dragon and modestly but powerfully presided at Printing House Square for nearly forty years; and became a peer under his own steam, Lord Astor of Hever. He was

Chairman and 'Father' of the Middlesex Hospital, his prime pride for a
long time. He was the beloved President of the Press Club too and the
Commonwealth Press Union. He loves organs – and presenting organs
(he played himself the beautiful little organ in the hall at Hever, and
with his one leg did wonders on the pedals). He married Violet,
daughter of the Fourth Earl of Minto and war widow of Lord Charles
Mercer Nairne; and they had three fine children, Gavin, Hugh and
John.

I met John and Violet first in 1925 when all three of us went to Melbourne for the Third Imperial Press Conference. Through the genial
machinations of Sir Harry Brittain I represented *Punch*. One Anthony
Eden, making his first public appearance, represented the *Yorkshire
Post*. Led by Lord Burnham, we went round the world, picking up
Commonwealth and Empire journalists on the way – Canada first, the
formidable Dafoe – Honolulu – Fiji – New Zealand – Sydney – by ship
all the way. In Australia we spent three jolly months and in Melbourne
two days, conferring. (After that I delightfully 'did' Ceylon with John
and Violet.)

May I pause at Hawaii, to recall one of the magical mornings of my
life? We came to Honolulu one evening, now about sixty newspaper
men and magnates strong, we had a swim on the famed Waikiki beach
and, for once, an unofficial dinner. But the morning's programme was
hideous – inspect a Pineapple cannery – visit the industrial district of
Pali and the Naval Base – and sail after a big official lunch. I said to
myself, naughtily: 'I am not Lord Burnham, Lord Iliffe or Major
Astor. I am not important. This is the only morning of my life that I
shall spend at Honolulu. I am blowed if I am going to spend it inspect-
ing a Pineapple cannery – or an industrial district – or even a Naval
Base.' After breakfast I hid in the lavatory. A fleet of cars arrived. I
heard Harry Brittain and others marching in and out, crying 'Alan!
Alan! Where's old A.P.?' But I kept quiet and they went off without
me. Then I crept down to the beach and found a Hawaiian 'boy'. 'I
want to surf-ride,' I said. 'I teach you surf-ride,' he said. I put on the
long 'University Costume' which gentlemen then had to wear in the
sea, a long dark clammy garment that stretched from the shoulder
almost to the knee. He brought a huge, heavy board about 8 ft long.
You lie over the end of it and paddle out but, of course, he assisted.
About 300 yards out he turned and pointed my missile to the shore. The
expert then looks over his shoulder and chooses a good wave. But the
boy said 'When I push, you kneel.' I said, 'Oh yes?' Presently I felt a
great heave and I was whizzing to the shore at about 30 knots. Mindful
of orders, I crawled into a kneeling position. Not content, the boy said
'Now you stand'. 'Oh yes?' I replied, but by Poseidon, I did! There I
stood in the middle of the board, stooping slightly in my inelegant

raiment, but in command and speeding for the shore. No rope, no motorboat assisted: there were just my body, a board, and a wave. If you stand a centimetre too far forward the board, and you, plunge into the deep. An inch too far back and your stern collapses. Off-centre you ignominiously sink on one side or the other. The sensation was blissful, one was flesh no more, but the spirit of power and speed. But I had done a mere 300 yards. Safe ashore, I gazed out to sea at the experts showing their fantastic skills half a mile away, standing on each other's shoulders, standing on their heads, on the roaring enormous rollers. I grabbed my board and feebly paddled out to sea. My boy was pleased with me and pushed me again and again: but the magic had left me and I did no more standing, though I knelt for a few brief passages. I won a burned and blistered back, but it was worth it.

We steamed on to Fiji and charming New Zealand (where many said they recognized the 'Selwyn Nose'). Tall John Astor with his tin leg always won the First Class Deck Quoits competition; and then he would take on the champion of the Tourist Class, and defeat him too. He also, to my mind, made the best of the innumerable speeches we made on that trip (we even had speeches at breakfast in the bush after a long night journey in a most noisy train). Under cover of a hesitant air and a gentle voice he deployed some penetrating wit and wisdom.

As Chairman John attended many such Conferences, demanding faultless tact and fatiguing toil: and for very many years he kept that valuable body, the Commonwealth Press Union, in healthy being. It was started by that inhuman wonder Sir Harry Brittain, now a sprightly ninety-seven. We shared a carriage all across Canada. I remember him telling me how he stood with the original Mr Rolls and someone else at the lowest point in the valley of Piccadilly and debated whether they should try to get their car to go up the hill as far as the Ritz (where the red flag waited for them). I think they succeeded.

John and Violet were magnificent hosts at Hever. The original castle, still complete with moat and drawbridge, belonged to Anne Boleyn's father. John's father added the long and lovely Italian garden and the lake, and behind the Castle is the artful 'Tudor Village', designed by F. L. Pearson, where the guests were entertained. Never can American money have been better spent in England. A sunny weekend at Hever was an enchanting experience. Plenty to do – do what you will. Superb flowers, grandchildren, tapestries, and Editors of *The Times*. I confess that *some* Sundays I used to watch them walk off to the church through the woods, hurry to the organ and joyfully fill the empty castle with Handel's Largo, Jerusalem and favourite hymns.

After the war John took to yachting and we had the first of numerous delicious voyages with him. From Venice – to be anchored at Venice!

– the *Ceto* took us slowly down the fair coasts of Yugoslavia to Corfu. But the fair coasts of Yugoslavia were jumpy after the war. There were challenges in Morse from hill after hill, and it was difficult, in port, to explain that the Yacht Squadron's White Ensign was the flag of the Navy yet *not* the flag of the Navy.

The *Ceto* was succeeded by the *Deianeira*, designed by John himself with his habitual touch of understatement, comfortable but seemly, five passengers only. When an Onassis or a Docker ship entered the bay she looked a very modest maiden. Nor was she one of the stay-at-homes in Cannes or Monaco. She made long passages and was seldom at anchor two nights in one place. But much could be done in a day – painting, swimming, sailing the small boat, 'sights' – John and I worked out our sextant sums and I even wrote, thousands of words. She has had many a rough ride and nasty bouts in the Bay. She knows every island between Gibraltar and Asia, many in the Adriatic and most in the Aegean. She has steamed through the Dardanelles to Istanbul, south to Rhodes, to Tripoli and Ceuta. More than once we have flown the only White Ensign in Gibraltar Harbour. Now that the Navy is everywhere no more it is a pity there are not more *Deianeiras* to show the flag in foreign parts.

One year the *Deianeira* sailed from Falmouth with her owner and two passengers, Sir William Haley and myself. We had a reasonable passage through 'the Bay' and were steaming south off Portugal. It was my habit to be up at 8 o'clock, check the time by the BBC with Captain Behenna and hear the first news. One morning, when I had done this, I walked along to the small staircase that leads down to the dining-room, and looked round the corner. There in quiet contented talk sat the Proprietor of *The Times* and the Editor of *The Times*. 'Ha'! I said roguishly. 'I bet you can't guess what the news is this morning.' They couldn't. '*Nasser has pinched the Suez Canal.*' We were still about thirty-six hours from Gibraltar and the ship had no means of transmitting a message. It was a fairly frustrating moment for the top levels of the *Times*. I remember how we listened to the 9 o'clock news – '*The Times*', said the News 'describes it as the action of a bandit' – and I remember how William Haley leapt out of his chair and applauded. But he could neither say nor do anything. The *Deianeira* has a radio-telephone now.

I have seen John dance with one leg in a rolling ship, I have seen him play a smart game of tennis with one leg, climb steep hills and long stairs (doing sights) with his one leg, stump round endless cathedrals and all round Jerusalem with his one leg, always, I suspected, in pain but never complaining. In his later yachting days he would take off his tin leg once or twice a day, do a graceful dive from one leg, swim round the ship (till we stopped him) and kneel his way aboard unaided. As I have said, he played the organ very ably with one leg. Altogether, an accomplished man.

In 1961 the tin leg nearly caused an international incident at Amman. We flew from Beirut to Jerusalem and drove from there to Jericho. We had a halt at noon at the head of the Dead Sea. I was determined to bathe in the Dead Sea and I was gallantly joined by Sir William Haley, then Editor of *The Times*. It was difficult to reach the Dead Sea, so hot were the stones underfoot. Then there was a long wade through shallow water. Soon one met large underwater shrubs and bushes, victims, I supposed, of the punishment of Sodom. At last, more venturous than the Editor, I reached deep water and essayed a swim. But your legs fly to the surface, something takes hold of you, and you find yourself lying on your back. It is a battle to thrust your legs down, you feel a helpless thing and I was glad to paddle back to the shallows. You are enjoined to shower thoroughly lest you become a 'pillar of salt', but it was high noon and the first water the shower discharged was nearly boiling. A memorable swim.

We drove north a long way to Jerash, some excellent ruins, then south again, exhausted with heat, for Amman, where we were invited to cocktails by the British Ambassador. The Embassy is one of the buildings in the Royal enclave, surrounded by walls and armed guards. Trouble of some sort was afoot or feared, as sometimes happens in those lands, and our taxis were thoroughly searched, for bombs, by a very stern and militant Jordanian sergeant. He tore the driver's papers from their lockers and savagely threw them everywhere. He searched the engine, he searched the boot: then he peered at our feet and rattled his cane under the seats. When he came to John there was a loud metallic click. The sergeant's face darkened with fear and fury, he yelled to the guard-room and two men came running. 'Imprisonment,' I thought, 'is certain.' But John said softly, comfortingly: 'That was me.' The sergeant stared and peeped under the seat. 'That was me,' said John again, patting his tin leg. The sergeant was persuaded, and almost smiled: but it was a near thing.

He is an eager and, to my untutored eye, a very good amateur painter. Churchill would have liked his pictures: they are full of 'joy and sunshine'. Moreover, when I look at old ones, modestly ranged round the floor of his studio, I can say: 'I can remember *that* – that's Formentor, that's that pretty place in Corfu – that's Mykonos, that's Rhodes' – and a dozen places in the Mediterranean, the Adriatic or the Aegean. He works very hard in blissful oblivion of heat, flies and peering children. Laurence Irving, a brilliant wit with his brush, did a beautiful series of John, erect and dedicated, painting on and on, the world against him.

In 1962 the Treasury – and Parliament – struck a cruel blow. I do not fully understand it but the Treasury, I gather, directed its grasping hands towards settlements of American money made in America forty-three years earlier by his father, the first Waldorf, on grand-children and beyond. If John had died a resident of the United King-dom the Treasury would have grabbed 80 per cent of these American settlements. Not for his own sake, but to honour his father's wishes, he was compelled to depart, abandon his beloved Hever, and find a home abroad. Violet was a keen and gifted gardener, but where on the con-tinent could they expect to replace the glories of Hever and such fond causes as the Middlesex Hospital, *The Times*, the Commonwealth Press affairs, and others? Yet, at the second shot, they did find a fine place in the hills near Grasse, with a blue swimming-pool surrounded by unbelievable oleanders.

Violet did not live long in exile; after her death John himself created a splendid garden and park and added to the beauties of France as his father had added to England's. Till this year the *Deianeira* has come out to comfort him each spring. Family and friends make happy pilgrimages – nurses and doctors from the Middlesex have generous holidays there. It is a pleasant exile – but it is an exile.

Only once has he discussed these troubles: 'The fools!' he said rue-fully, 'I am richer than I was before, and they have lost God knows what in taxes which I should have paid with pleasure.' Whatever the Treasury case may be, I am sad that we should drive abroad one of the finest Englishmen I have known, and one of the best unofficial servants of the State.

John Galsworthy

Simpleton that I am, no doubt, I have admired John Galsworthy's work since my youth: I even maintained, and do today, that he had a good sense of humour. Some of the Forsyte dialogue makes me chuckle still. Remembering how lofty intellectuals dismissed him it makes me laugh heartily to see him a cosmic success today.

I cannot now remember how and where we first met – perhaps at Robert Lynd's in Keats Grove, Hampstead – but I know that he was good to me in many ways from the early '20's. In 1921 he kindly read my second attempt at a post-war novel (in type) and wrote two long and elaborate letters – four pages of longhand – within three days, about it. This was a remarkable thing, for in spite of compliments and some wise advice: 'I think the book *could* be put right by etc. etc.,' he clearly did not have much hope. I felt he felt it were better scrapped, and scrapped it was. He said in one letter: 'By the way I shouldn't read any more Conrad. Not that there's any sense of imitation, but I feel as if he would lure you along an unnatural path and ? your line.'

He took just the same trouble about my play *The White Witch* which appeared at the Haymarket for four or five weeks only, though it had Fay Compton and Leon Quartermain:

July 1 1925

My dear Herbert,

I gather that you've been spending a gloomy evening with my play; and I've been spending a gay one with yours. (He had been reading *The White Witch*). It's a curious play – most of the first act should be very amusing; and the second should be dramatically effective if well enough played. The cross-examination scene in Act III is very clever – and, like your *Punch* satire on the same subject, badly needed. You take a big risk in the actual arrangements by drowning the girl and bringing her to life again. I'm not sure that the audience shouldn't be allowed to know from the beginning of Act III that she isn't really drowned. But all this is a little by the way. The real comment begins when one says that the characters are very well realized and rather curiously alive; and yet I'm not sure they ought to be. This sounds cryptic. The question is, however, whether the theme doesn't kill them a bit. When a man feels as strongly as John feels for Jenny talk fails; and in the play it doesn't. Platonism gets its full advocacy as in life somehow it wouldn't. That's the devil about choosing play form (which is all talk) for the treatment of such a theme. You hang a little, I think, between reality and the stage. But with really good playing I can see you issuing with your skin. Anyway I enjoyed the reading, and that's the main thing.

I'm glad you had a go at Shaw, for he really wrote a silly and unworthy letter.

Personally I regard the Epstein tablet as a piece of unrealized affectation. It's curious – or rather very natural – that all his defenders are writing men. They are often very silly when they deal with what they believe to be art.

Well, he's invented a new bird anyway by crossing the duck with the vulture. He's also invented a new kind of hip-joint based on the merry-thought. I'd like to have seen you again before you go. But if I don't best of luck to you in Australia! All greetings to you both.

Always yours,

J. G.

Later, before the first night, he wrote: 'Very very best wishes for the success of *The White Witch*. You needn't worry about the Platonic point so far as the public are concerned or even the critics. It's one for a much higher conscience than theirs – like yours and mine.'

But 'the Platonic point' did worry almost everybody. Nobody 'made love' and that was fatal.

Then, in glowing terms, he wrote an introduction to the published edition of *Riverside Nights*. He was as generous with praise as he was just in criticism.

We dined often with John and Ada at the big house on the Hampstead heights: and we stayed one weekend at a delightful house in Sussex near Pulborough. John was a keen tennis-player: and Gwen and I, who were young and almost tennis-mad, were itching to get on to the beautiful courts. But there was no tennis before lunch on Sunday, and after lunch Ada had to have her croquet. It was a tantalizing day for the suburban couple – all those hours denied to tennis. But that is my main picture of the great man, John G. about to serve, clean-shaven, handsome, neat, all-white. He took tennis as seriously as he took the world, and there was often a prolonged argument about the score when we reached the '40' zone. It generally turned out to be 40–15: but what did we care? It was bliss to be playing tennis at all, and double bliss in so fair a place, under the green downs, with a revered writer.

I recall little of our conversations: but suddenly one day at lunch 'the sense of property' came over the soup, and I remember thinking 'I suppose the Forsytes are always with him'. He seemed to be a most considerate husband. We were at Stanway one weekend when the Galsworthies were there. Most of the husbands got down to breakfast before their wives, helped themselves, grabbed a paper perhaps, and happily settled down. When their wives arrived we let them help themselves, which was what, we thought, they preferred. But when Ada appeared up leapt the good John and hurried to the long sideboard. He picked up one dish-top after another. 'Would you like this? How about that? Kedgeree? Sausages? Let me make your tea.' The other husbands heard all this, with one ear, in guilty dismay. John, we agreed later, had let the side down.

But I have always been proud and grateful that John Galsworthy was good to me. He was a New College man too and his last room in the Garden Quad was immediately opposite mine. The legend was that as an undergraduate he was idle and slightly wild: which shows that there is hope for us all. I hope that the Young of today may sometimes draw as much encouragement from the Established of today as I did:

19 April 1928

My dear Alan Herbert,
     Thank you ever so for 'The Trials of Topsy'.
     You are 'For the best humorist we have had for ages'; and if those words which come from my heart are of any use to you at any time, on any book, or anywhere or when, for every sake make use of them. You ought to be read throughout the land. Not that anyone pays attention to what I think. How are you both? And how's the family? And aren't you coming down to have a look at us?

Always yours

John Galsworthy

My dear Alan Herbert,

The rhymes are delightful, but the 'Misleading Cases' are (is) lovely stuff – rich and precious in the Victorian sense of the words. Young Sir, you are a valuable fellow.

> Grove Lodge
> The Grove
> Hampstead.

A most excellent and pathetic book [*The Water Gipsies*] my dear Alan, and full of strange and very real living. It has that quality which I look for and so seldom come on – the breath of life. Jane and Ernest and Fred and Bryan they're all genuine creations, and the humour is precious and subordinated, and all is well. The Derby and the skittles match, and many other parts are priceless, and the whole is a triumph and I congratulate you. Poor little Jane!

Our love to you – Ada will now get the treat.

> J. G.

21 Sept 1927.

My dear Alan Herbert,

Delightful of you to send me those two books. As ever, I revel in your writings . . .

How kind! Enough to keep a fellow going for another forty years.

Edward Heath

I am not keen on the Common Market: but I admire that brave sailor, Mr Edward Heath. I have mentioned that the 'University Members' did mean something to the politically-minded undergraduates, though they had no votes. In 1939 I was heartened by a letter from the President of the Oxford Union:

> February 25th 1939

Dear Mr. Herbert,

I have to inform you that the following resolution was passed unanimously by a crowded House at the Presidential Debate here last Thursday:

'That this House desires to express its support for the endeavours of the Senior Burgess of this University to prevent the name Oxford Group being used as the title of a limited liability Company, seeing that whatever be the merits of this organisation, its association with Oxford is not sufficiently close to warrant the appropriation of such a name.'

I hope you will be able to use this expression of undergraduate opinion and that you will be successful in your efforts.

> Yours sincerely,
>
> E. R. G. Heath

{15}

'A GOOD RUN'

WHEN good friends ask me how I am or do, with serious intent, my favourite reply is: 'As well as I deserve – and much better than I expected.'

When I get to bed at last – this takes some time because of my exercises – I give thanks that I have come through one more day safe and well, I say to myself how fortunate I am to have escaped, so far – who knows what is to come? – the dire troubles that have struck down so many younger and better men!

When my mind reels round from one worry to another and Sleep refuses duty I play a trick upon that flighty fellow. We should not, by the way, feel so guilty or distressed as we do when Sleep does not come quickly. One should say: 'Well, what does it matter?' turn on the light, and read a book (I accept the corollary that objections to reading in bed should be a matrimonial offence amounting, if persistent, to cruelty).

If that fails try my trick. I despise your counting of sheep at a gate. It is too much of an intellectual exercise, and by the time you have done ten sheep, I find, the mind is wandering. Where is the sheep-dog, you wonder, and miss several sheep looking for him. Then the question arises: 'Allow five sheep or start again?' For that matter, where is the farmer? And why don't I see any rams? Why are these sheep all the same size? And by the way why are these sheep going through this damned gate, anyway? By this time you are wide awake.

My method is spiritual and less of a strain. You open and close the eyes so that you can see the chink of light at the edge of the window. This alone will take the mind off the whirling worries. Then, on Open, you whisper to yourself '*Fear nothing*': that removes all worries about the future, even that serious operation tomorrow. On Close, you whisper: '*Thank God*'. That puts all the past in its place. *Fear Nothing – Thank God*. I don't say it will work if you have incurable cancer, I am thinking of the fortunate ordinary man: for him, for a time, it really does induce a sense of content and calm and drives the worries away. You can if you like, at the start, take a deep breath on each Open and

Close: that helps. Sometimes I use more words:

> Fear Nothing –
> Thank God!
> You're not in pain –
> You're not in quod.

There's a thought to bring content and calm. How lucky you are!
Yet you take it for granted.

If you wish, here is a second verse:

> Fear Nothing!
> What the Hell?
> Why worry?
> All's well.

But this may be too much of an intellectual effort.

I do not fear death, but I shall resent it, as I resent the assaults, so
far reasonable enough, of age. How I miss my boat and all the water-
business! How much I should love to play lawn-tennis again! I dream
of both. I serve my terrible American service. I do great trips in the
Water Gipsy. But 'though much is taken, much abides': I enjoy life,
fortunate fellow, I can be useful still, there are things I want to do, I
still sing on the way downstairs in the morning, I like to talk to pretty
ladies and amusing men, to hear music, read books, sit in Gwen's fine
garden, ply my pencil – and I wish for more.

I do fear a painful and protracted ending and, pain or not, I fear to
become a recumbent nuisance. May I never be tied to a bed or chair –
and if I am, may some kindly doctor take note of my objections! I was
always puzzled by the passage in the Litany: From battle and murder,
and from sudden death – *Good Lord deliver us*. Except for the deeply
religious that should surely be 'from lingering death'.

I have no expectation of an after-life: nor do I hope for one. It has
never been described in terms that made it attractive. Are we angels
going to be conscious spectators of the world which we have left? Shall
we look down and see our wives dying of cancer, our children going to
jail for drugs or devilry. England conquered and occupied by the
Russians? London a forest of topless towers? What sort of Paradise
will that be? On the other hand, an after-life which bears no relation to
this one seems to me to be a contradiction in terms.

I never worry myself, as many do it seems, with the question: 'Why
am I here? What is it all about?' I regard the question as idle curiosity
of the kind that sends men to the Moon to find out how it was made. I

do not care twopence how or when the Moon was made. I liked the Moon when it was a handsome mystery. Now they have spoiled it with their wretched photographs, their ridiculous dust and pebbles (though, of course, I greatly admire the brain-work and the bravery and I don't miss a moment on the telly). In the same way there is pretty good evidence that I exist, and I am ready to accept the fact without argument or complaint. Life, I feel, is like a country walk. It may have a purpose, to get somewhere, to go to church, to shop, to swim. Or you may be merely enjoying the sun and the scene. In neither case do you stop from time to time and say to yourself: 'Why on earth am I walking about the country?' The walk may be safe and successful, you may get home for tea and crumpets: or you may fall down a well. It is still a country walk.

This wandering work has left out many things, and I have a guilty feeling that it contains no powerful moral message. Let us try. We might begin with some good old words: 'Fear God! Honour the Queen! Love your country and defend her institutions' (for, when all is said, they are pretty good). 'Love your neighbours, be kind, be courteous. Honour the Old, encourage the Young. Be thorough, be careful, be punctual and proud of your work. Be grateful – and say so. Confess when you are wrong. Say what you have to say over and over again, for no man listens. Never give up – you may become a bore, but even then. . . .'

A footnote or two. '*Love your country.*' I don't mean merely love her now, but be proud of her past which is now unfashionable. We have done wonders all over the world. 'The building and administration of the British Empire was one of the most astonishing achievements in human history, much greater than the journey to the moon.' Who wrote that? Someone whose name is not clear in my diary (it looks like Gudrun Tempel). She was right. Wherever we went men and things were the better for our going, for our laws, our liberties, our language. We put some of the boys into trousers too soon – and some into ill-fitting trousers – but everybody said they must have trousers, and there it is. But see how many are happy in their trousers.

How glad I am that I have made three long tours of Australia, the mightiest of islands, the friendliest. I have seen the sheep-shearing, I have rounded up cattle (a single cattle), I have heard Bob Menzies speaking in the House, I have been called a 'dinkum Aussie'. And Ceylon, that lovely jewel! I have seen all the Dead Cities, the jungle, the elephants, the monkeys, the fields of tea. I saw the long procession for a beloved Speaker's funeral on a torrid afternoon. A white-robed chanting group approached bearing a portrait of the dead Speaker – and he was wearing the Speaker's wig – *our* Speaker's wig.

'*Be Kind.*' Kindness in little things has great merit. The English, I like to think, are good at this. One test is the treatment of foreigners or strangers who ask you the way in the streets. In some foreign lands there may be nothing but a rude stare without words. In these parts the stranger may get a 'Sorry don't know' or 'Stranger here myself'. I like to see the little Londoner accosted, stop, think, fix the desired spot in his mind, lead the stranger round the corner and with generous words and gestures set him on his way – probably in the wrong direction.

When some weary man rings me up and it is 'wrong number' – perhaps the third he has suffered – and sighs 'I'm sorry', I try not to give an angry grunt, as many do: instead I say with sympathy 'I'm sorry for *you*'. This may seem smug or silly, but I like to think that it lights a momentary gleam, a glow, in the harassed man's mind. Who knows? He may be a lover.

My wife is a lifelong addict to kindness. Every Christmas, like so many good women, she nearly kills herself with kindness, scouring the town for the exact thing wanted by the smallest grandchild. In between Christmases she remembers all the other birthdays and is not really happy if she has no excuse to send flowers or a beautiful plant to somebody. It ruins me but I admire too much to mind.

I forget if I said '*Be thorough*'. I do. Ecclesiastes had it: 'Whatever thy hand findeth to do, do it with thy might' – all thy might. I do nothing for the garden but weed the grass that extrudes between the crazy-paving stones. I should think very poorly of myself if I left the captured weeds for someone else to remove: but the world is full of poor wretches who would. *Au pair* girls who after a hasty clean leave dust-pans, brushes and dusters on the stairs reveal, of course, the natural inferiority of continental races: but I have known a similar Briton or two.

I do not write well – I write too much – but my signature is always plainly legible, even on a cheque. I get few letters from men in business or politics whose signatures give me a clue to their names. At a lunch club I belong to, but do not often attend, I meet members whose names I am eager to learn: but the list of signatures at the door is untranslatable. Ecclesiastes, I feel, wrote his name with care.

If you are to be a writer, my boy, you must carry this counsel into your work. You must do many things that I have often failed to do. For one thing, while you are writing, or typing your masterpieces, you must give thought to the printing of it. Not your business, you may think, but in these days it is. Every publisher has his own 'style', a set of rules – what to do about capitals, hyphens, 'quote' marks, and many other things. Also in the old days they had skilled and industrious fellows called 'printer's readers'. These with infinite pains and eagles' eyes went through the proofs of your work before they were sent to you. They spotted all the silly 'literals' which you might easily miss –

'Jerusalen', for example – they enforced their 'style', and corrected all your inconsistencies. Those hateful hyphens! As your theatrical novel bounds happily along you may write stage door in one chapter, stage-door in the next, and perhaps on the same page, stagedoor. You will have to-day, today, tomorrow, to-morrow, tonight, to-night. At the moment it does not seem to matter – and in the good old days it didn't. The printer's reader, with his red pen, put everything right.

But the printer's reader – I know not why – is not what he was. He misses more misprints than you do, he fails to help on the hyphen problem, very often he does not seem to exist. So you must be your own reader, must achieve consistency so far as you can before you send your masterpiece to the publisher. Myself, I hate hyphens. Often they are necessary; but I avoid them whenever I can: what problems! The man who guards the stage door? 'stage door-keeper' is clearly wrong – 'stage-door-keeper' is horrible – *two* hyphens – stagedoorkeeper? Rather long – I *think* I go for stagedoor keeper: but the best thing is not to write a theatrical novel. I hate 'to-day', 'to-night', and 'to-morrow' – so I think, do the great papers: but, behold, those are the forms recommended in my 'Authors' and Printers' Dictionary' – Oxford University Press 1950. The big rule is, boy, make up your own mind, and stick to it. This will save you pain and the printer pence, at proof-reading time. I remember a sad affair in which I took out about a million hateful hyphens, and the printer put them back again. So if you have any special fad or plan consult the fellows.

You may write with a pen or pencil, you may dictate into one of those machines, you may compose straight on to the typewriter. Better men, men of style, St John Ervine and Harold Nicolson, have done that comfortably and well. I can't. Nor could I dictate. I can only compose with a pencil (some india-rubber at the other end). 'The moving finger writes' and ideas flow. Often I have sat down to write 1,200 words for *Punch* or someone on a given theme, thinking 'Have I got enough to say?' and the next thing is I have written too much.

Whichever your method there may come a point in Chapter 2, the family scene, when you seem to be stuck. You are not sure how the conversation is to go, who is to say what. It is often then a temptation to leave a gap and gallop on to Chapter 3 or 4, the bathing scene, which you are longing to do. It may be a single sentence that will not come sweetly, a single word that will not emerge. Why not leave a gap and go on? The word will come in the bath. Unless you are writing up a tree, as Beethoven did, without a dictionary; unless you are short of some fact or figure which is now unobtainable the temptation should be resisted. One will come back and revise, of course, many times: but I try to leave everything as if this was the last edition, ready to print if I meet a lorry tomorrow. Jumping ahead to another chapter is much to be discouraged: women change the colour of their eyes – men even change their names. Things happen in Chapter 4 that you can't be sure about till you've done Chapter 3. Ecclesiastes, be sure, would have been against it.

Be thorough, too, as I have already hinted, if you are rash enough to leave that old 'last' and take up causes. An experienced dramatist advised me long ago. 'Anything important you want to say in a play you must say at least three times.' The first time there may be a loud coughing fit which can drown even your leading man, the second time there may be the tinkle of tea-cups or a doodlebug approaches. If a long correspondence in the papers produces no result, you must bide your time and start another – or write a little book.

I don't think I said '*Keep fit*'. I do. On this I have a tip or two, not for the Young, bless them, but for the forties, fifties and over. In 1937, after the Divorce Bill, *Home and Beauty, Paganini* and other labours I was evidently wilting (I was then forty-seven). Sir Percy Harris, the friendly Liberal Member for Bethnal Green, said 'I will take you to a man'. The man's name – bless me, I have forgotten; but in spite of my advice, I will go on till I remember it. Mr X was not a doctor, but he had spent much time in Africa and studied what I think were still called 'the natives' then. The secret of life, he said, was the abdominal muscles, especially the V of muscle that leads down to Man's middle. Man was not intended to walk erect, he said; he was meant to go on all fours like a horse. You never saw a horse with a middle-age spread. But since Man insists on going about in this absurd fashion at about my age all the gooseberries start making for the bottom of the bag. Mr X's Africans never had a middle-age spread because they did so many ventri-something, or stomachy dances. His name was *Hornibrook!*

So the secret of life is to strengthen the muscles already mentioned. He gave me two exercises which I have been doing every night ever since – that is, for thirty-three years.

The first is very simple. You stand up straight and press the buttocks together. I do this 100 times every night. You need not even stand up straight. You can do it in the bath, or in the bed, waiting for a train or speaking in the House of Commons (yes, I have done that). This exercise not only fortifies the said muscles, it presses the lower part of the trunk against the upper, up against the ribs, and so (this is my case) massages the liver of a sedentary man, and, I suppose, the other organs in that part of the forest.

The second exercise is a little more clever and requires practice. It does the same thing in reverse, and it is called 'Rolling the Abdominal Wall'. It is not, as novices suppose, a simple matter of pushing the abdomen in and out. There must be a downward movement. When you have mastered it you can really see in the mirror a rotary downward wave passing over the dear abdomen. You can do this exercise too, erect or recumbent. I do it 100 times every night in the garden and after that I do my deep-breathing exercises.

The liver-massage claim, I should say, is my own invention, and I have no medical authority. But it must, I feel, have the same effect as horse-riding on a medieval liver. Certainly, knowing the history of my liver, I am gratefully surprised that it has lasted so long and, so far as I know, is functioning still.

My second secret of life is Vitamins which I have studied for many years. Far back in the twenties I wrote a poem which began:

> There are three vitamins, not four:
> I have no doubt there will be more . . .

God knows how many there are today, but I take most of them. I must not go down to history, though, as a literary man addicted to 'pills'. I take no pills, no Benzedrines, no sedative or stimulator: no – God forbid! – psychedelics. Vitamins are mere food-supplements: they exist, or should, in the body already, but are diminished or destroyed by this and that. Vitamin C, I see, is greatly reduced by smoking, other vitamins by cooking, Vitamin B by what they call 'alcohol'. It seems only sensible to replace them; and since they are such innocents they need no doctor's prescription (so I have to pay for them). My third daughter Lavender Clarke started me, years ago, on Desiccated Liver tablets. They owe a lot, I believe, to 'the livers of selected oxen', bombs of Vitamin B; they contain also edible bone phosphate and raw sugar; they furnish energy and, I am told, a good complexion. Then there is the blessed Vitamin C, not your mere orange juice, or apples, though these are grand, but special C from Scandinavian rose-hips, no less. I take the magical mineral magnesium, with calcium, straight from the Dolomite mountains, and these do good to my inside, both departments. Oh yes, and there are A and E. I get these boons, not cheaply, from the Organic Vitamin Company at Berkhamstead, run by a learned gentleman called Rodale. They send me a fascinating monthly magazine, which proves that almost everything that ordinary people eat or do is fatal. If you can read it without ordering another vitamin or two you are a strong fellow.

Then, for the brutes who like wine or whisky, the prime necessity is Vitamin B1. This restores whatever it is that wine and whisky burn away. Take it, say 25 milligrammes, before a City Banquet or Wedding Feast, and you will have no hangover.

Since the breath-testing began my conscientious doctor never comes to my 'local' and takes his wine, moderately, at home. One day he was to take me to see a specialist in Harley Street about 6.30 p.m. I said:

'Leave your damned car at home and dine with me afterwards, we'll travel by taxi.' We had a reasonable meal at my club, two martinis perhaps, some wine, and he had a brandy. During dinner I said, 'You're not used to this sort of thing, try one of these,' and I pressed a Vitamin B1 tablet (25 mg.) into his hand. Next day he rang up to thank me and said: 'Alan, what was that marvellous pill you gave me? I feel fine. Where can I get it?' 'At any chemist,' I said, 'without prescription.'

Some folk, some of the family, laugh at my exercises, my vitamin addiction. I often say: 'Old boy, when you're in your eightieth year, I shall be glad to hear what you have to say. Till then, pray refrain from unseemly mockery.'

Observe, by the way, that my régime demands none of the tiresome exercises, press-ups, arm-waving, or leg-lifting. I have high evidence about mine. One day, after a heart-scare, a charming heart-specialist who was prowling about my frame said: 'I say, this man's got jolly good abdominal muscles.' Few utterances have pleased me more. For about twenty-five years I had been privately 'doing my exercises' and said no word to the world about my abdominal might. At last, uninvited, an expert discovers them and pays this generous tribute. It was like a publisher stumbling on some early MS and saying, 'I say – I must publish that!'

The same kind heart-specialist, I am sorry to say, died a month later of a heart-attack. I told the sad tale to an irreverent young doctor. He said: 'Ah, yes! Dear old —— You know what happened? He'd just finished with a lady-patient. "Madam" he said. "Goodbye. Don't worry. Your heart is just as sound as mine" – and fell dead at her feet.'

The third secret of life is to believe in the manipulative surgeon, osteopathy – or, as we rudely say, the bone-setter, especially, if, like many great men, he is a qualified medical man as well. My old body has had a bang or two, beginning with that Civil Servant who dropped me on my head on a fender. I have had many an -itis and an -osis or two. I started my intercostal neuritis rehearsing for the 1939 War, pulling sacks out of the river (they represented the dead). At Oxford I was one of the first Englishmen, I believe, to imitate the special 'American service' that one McLoughlin brought across the Atlantic to Wimbledon. This rash act produced a 'tennis elbow' that, combined with the Civil Servant's mischief, has grown in stature through the years. At one time it was promoted to *cervical spondylosis*, a magnificent name. It means, I believe, something like Necky Spinery. My trouble deserved a great name, for at its worst it reached, very painfully, from the back of the neck through the starboard shoulder, down through the tennis elbow and into my writing hand. I could not shave, hold a pipe, or some days even rest my forearm on a table, much less write. I began seriously to teach myself to write with my left hand (which I did very badly) and so I saw myself ending my days, as J. M. Barrie did. But how many thousands of words have I written comfortably with my right hand since then! This I owe to the great craft of osteopathy, manipulative surgery, what you will. My first man, who roasted you before he racked you, died. A fellow Member of the House recommended me to poor Stephen Ward, and I attended him off and on for a year and more, about ten years before the Profumo troubles. He did quite a good sketch of me one evening, over sherry (which, rather embarrassingly, was exhibited at the trial). I saw nothing naughty, but he did not impress me professionally, so I went round the corner to the man who, for me, is the King of Bones, my friend Guy Beauchamp. No Harley Street pomp here: one day he brought out his box of tricks and relieved my trouble just before the Boat Race.

The first visit you may find alarming, but don't. 'Relax', they say (which makes you taut all over), the head is bent to one side, then firmly thrust to the other. CRACK! goes something at the back and you are fairly sure that your head has come off. But all is well. What is bad is when you feel that your head has *not* come off successfully, for then they do it again.

They go down the spine like a gardener sowing peas and with one finger and a squeeze do something beneficial to all the vertebrae. They firmly prod a spot down here and the pain departs from a spot far away up there. They stand you in front of them and give a slight jerk and that blasted lumbago is a thing of the past. My own Wizard has worked very hard at the Elbow – now promoted to Arthritis (first class). He told me from the first that I should 'have to live with it', and so I have, for ten years and more. But the wonderful thing is that at my great age I have to see the Wizard much less than I did. I faithfully do his 'exercises' – yes, more exercises, about 100 which, with the abdominals, tots up to say 400 a night. I am careful: I do not wantonly carry heavy tea-pots in the starboard hand, and whatever the urgency, I try not to screw reluctant cork-screws. I must avoid sawing or screwdriving ('repetitive action') which is a pity, because of my sundials; if I am silly, if I recklessly saw a semicircle for a sundial, if I wildly weed too much, if, as I did last year, I madly take John Astor's delicious two-sailed dinghy out in a sharp Mediterranean breeze, all alone, the Elbow will declare savage war again and my Wizard must give me an 'injection'. But in ten years I think I have had only four injections: and all those years I have been scribbling like a mad thing with my rightful writing hand. There were days at the beginning when I thought I never should start again. It is now 12 midnight 25/26 January 1970, and thank God and the Wizard, I am scribbling still, in my little bed.

Now, the regular doctors, bless them, are still I believe, officially at war with the wizards; but they are not themselves much use in the kind of trouble which the wizards tackle so willingly so well. 'Rest' – 'light' – 'pain-killers' – 'take its course' – has your dear doctor anything more to offer for lumbago? One nice lofty man wanted to put a great collar on me for, I think, six months. I jibbed at this, so did my wizard: 'I believe in motion.' 'Keep her going' as the sailors say. So, thanks be, we rejected the collar. Privately, I know, some doctors agree that there is a place for the wizards. Two at least, have said to me, in an unofficial manner: 'Well, perhaps this is a case for "your man". You believe in him, don't you?' To be fair, they have also told me sad tales where wizards have gone wrong and their patients to hospital. But what body in the world is not capable of error? I at least wish to offer my humble but grateful testimony to the wizards.

Should we not all, by the way, be ashamed to be so un-ambidexterous (what a word!) as we are? Whenever my right arm is partly out of action I am shocked by the feeble behaviour of my left. Shaving is difficult, even brushing the teeth; and my left-hand writing is slow and infantile. Should we not all, in spare minutes, practise the left hand in the common, necessary actions, especially writing? We are not all doomed to arthritis, but we may all have a motor-accident and break an arm, or simply fall down on an icy road.

Do not, after this lecture, tell me that I am a 'hypochondriac'. For one thing, I don't suppose you have the slightest notion what the absurd word means, and why. No, I believe in Mother's ancient cry to her young: 'Take care of yourself.' This does not mean 'Fuss about your health', still less 'Imagine you have complaints that you haven't got'. It means what it says, 'Take care'. Look the right way in a One-Way Street. Take nothing for granted. If a man of my age does not 'take care of himself' he is either idiot or idle.

I am offering no advice about Sex. There has been too much about it, and it has become a bore. Anyhow, you know.

I have never itched to take part in the Radio programme called 'The Time of My Life', where some swell chooses some prime period of his career and talks about it. I have often asked myself what slice of my life I should select if I were so invited. It would be difficult; there have been so many slices: and some of them have run parallel, like the layers of the old Vanilla ice. Some period in youth? No. Odd – when I come to think of it, the ladies and gentlemen never do elect to talk about their youth: Youth cannot be such a prime time as we say. Should it be my life in the theatre – and then what part of it, the modest Lyric days or the grand times in the West End? Parliament – the struggle to talk entertainingly, but to be taken seriously, the few speeches where I really felt in form and at home? – the excitements of

Private Members' Fridays – that jolly, friendly chatter in the smoking-room – the plans and plots? Or should it be the merry twenties and early thirties; what I call our Bohemian period, when I had won quite a name with books and plays, my wife was painting busily, charming pictures of canal boats, and somehow we seemed to have good friends, high and humble, in all the arts. High company at Lady Horner's, Lady Colefax's, the Maughams, the Courtaulds, John Galsworthy, Arnold Bennett's (how we all raved about Lydia Lopokova, the wife of Keynes, at the Ballet! I could hum every note of *La Boutique Fantasque*). My wife even rose to the height of tea with Edith Sitwell. Livelier parties at Gerald Barry's in Brunswick Square (Gerald was a great friend – and Gladys too – I worked with him on the *Outlook* and the *Week End Review*); Charles Laughton (before he became too famous: later, Hollywood rang him every ten minutes which became a bore), his friend and later wife Elsa Lanchester, that droll attractive creature, Harold Scott, her accompanist, the Baddeleys, Angela and Hermione. Lance Sieveking, one of the Savoy pioneers, Natalie Denny who married him, but is now Mrs Robert Bevan, John Armstrong, the artist. Livelier too at the Etoile in Charlotte Street, at Rules, in Maiden Lane, at the Cave of Harmony where Elsa and Harold Scott performed, at the Gargoyle, then a very small, respectable night-club, at the great Brasserie of the Café Royal, where some swell from any of the arts, a writer, a composer, an actor, an artist, might stroll or stride in at that distant door at any minute. Jimmy Agate always strode.

Heavens, how many ghosts crowd up through the mists as I try to recall those days! (They are not all dead, but we hardly ever meet the survivors. Nor did we know them all well.) The Huxleys, Aldous, lofty and charming, Julian and sweet Juliette, dear Rose Macaulay, dear Robert Lynd of the *New Statesman*, and Sylvia, his lady, 'Jack' (J.C.) Sir John Squire, a neighbour of mine, very kind to the young man, editor of the *Mercury*, captain of the Invalids cricket team, for which I once made 53, top score, against a team of Authors – dear Edward Wadsworth the artist, and Fanny in their delightful Sussex nest – Ivor Brown – still alive and writing, St John Ervine, full of good talk and kind to a young struggler too – Walter Peacock, my agent, as quiet and charming as the poet – Brother Savage Mark Hambourg – Hubert Eisdell the light but electrifying tenor, Gwilym Lloyd George and his Edna in later days, tall, quiet, sage and amusing, Gerald Fitzmaurice, now a judge at the Hague, wise Ralph Hamlyn and Harry Strauss.

Most of them came to our Boat Race parties. At one time we had up to 200 guests for that mad gathering. If they were driven out of the garden by rain or cold the little house almost exploded. They came in crowds even before television was invented, when those on the ground could see as much of the race as you see of the Derby from the wrong side of the course. But from the upper stories or the roof we have a wondrous view, from Hammersmith Bridge to Chiswick Steps. I used to take Bill Mabane, my great Commons friend and supporter and Douglas Fairbanks, an athletic fellow, on to the roof to see the tiny boats come through the Bridge, pursued and menaced, it seemed, by the launches and the mighty steamers. In the early days the tow path on the other side was black with people, the noise was tremendous – a mystery the whole thing, but moving. Clem Attlee was a keen and regular attender. I put them in the Swell Stand, my bedroom, with Arthur and Edith Salter, who never missed, Charles and Evelyn Cochran, H. G. Wells, perhaps, Gerald Kelly, who loved it.

Many came who made no attempt to see the race, but sipped their mulled claret and enjoyed the young things next to them. Some of the guests had come to the wrong house, some were utter strangers who thought it looked like a house where the sandwiches would be good and just walked in.

One great day the formidable Speaker Fitzroy was in the Grand Stand. I took the *Water Gipsy* down and embarked him at the Speaker's Stairs under the Clock Tower, a unique occasion – he had never set foot on his Stairs before. On another great day both Monty, the Field-Marshal, and Charlie Chaplin came and they were the first two guests to arrive. I had to leave them together by the river-wall, and much regret that I did not hear the talk. Monty, when he left, said proudly: 'I won my bet with Mr Chaplin.' He had staked 6d. on Cambridge. Chaplin said: 'I made the Field-Marshal give me change.' He was a model guest celebrity. He arrived first and left almost last, he did not seem to mind how many mothers brought up their little Margaret or Simon to introduce, and he must have stood for two hours. At our few meetings I have always been struck by his courtesy and charm. I sat next to him at dinner at a Douglas Fairbanks party in the Boltons. He told me the entire plot of the new film that he was preparing. I said at one point: 'Should you be telling me all your secrets? They might get out' – but he went on. After dinner Danny Kaye came in, and two little courts were formed. Danny went first, but Chaplin stayed on till about two in the morning, sitting on one of those backless stools before the fire, while four or five of us discussed, of all things, the theory of humour, the making of laughter, and so on. I remember piping up myself with my favourite quotation (which I have probably got wrong) from William Hazlitt 'Man is the only animal that laughs and weeps, for he is the only animal that perceives the distinction between things as they are and things as they ought to be.' This, I maintain, is better than the theory that all humour is founded on misfortune – which makes the funny man a callous fellow. Chaplin, I kept thinking, maker of cosmic laughter, might well decline interest in our little theories, especially those who dared to disagree. But no, there he sat, patiently listening, answering, questioning. Never did he say, 'Well, the way I work is this . . .' If he had been behind a screen he might have been some don discussing for the first time a new enthralling theme. He is a great family man. His Christmas cards, with all the family 'sized' in military style, are a joy.

Then there was that long exciting slice of my life, World War Two. The story of 'The Port at War' is a great one, and I have told it in *The Thames*, but mine was a modest part, and I should not choose that.

My dying dreams will be strange I am sure, and beautiful I hope. I have some strange dreams already. The *Water Gipsy* is always in them, though she perished many years ago. She has magical qualities now. She needs no petrol. I keep saying to my crew: 'What about petrol? Will one of you see if we have enough? If not where can we get some petrol?' No one pays the slightest attention, but we steam on happily. Moreover, she has acquired the properties of a D.U.K.W. or 'Duck'. There she is, at Low Water, high up on the sloping foreshore; we take on passengers, food, drink (but never petrol): and then I touch the button (there is only one button now) and I steer her down the slope into the water. Once I steered her round Piccadilly Circus. This was enjoyable. Also, she is much bigger than she was and infinitely expandable. She can take on anyone who wants to come, but all the time she keeps her tiny, intimate character, and I am alone on my diminutive bridge with the White Ensign flapping behind me. Yet with her magical power she can hold easily Gwen and the entire tribe of Herbert, the four children, Crystal and Jocelyn (the theatre girl), Lavender and John (of Christie's), the fourteen grandchildren and some of the five great-grandchildren, with all their wives, husbands, boy-friends, heirs and assigns. But there are some welcome friends of the tribe, golden girls from Cochran days and others, as young and fresh as they were in the time of *Helen*. Charles Cochran, proud and beaming, is aboard and now the great ghost has no arthritis. In the fore-peak Vivian Ellis sits at the piano. Now and then Evelyn Laye, looking still as lovely as she did on the Walls of Troy, sings 'O God of Love'. Then we all sing 'Is That the Face . . .' Dear ghost Malcolm Sargent stands on the top deck and conducts. Once every hour Wendy Toye, our superb producer, bangs the great bell in the bows and calls 'Quiet please' for the millionth time, Georges Guétary and Lizbeth Webb, still in her first girlish bloom, sing 'This is our Lovely Day'. Wendy strikes the bell again, looks aft, and cries 'Lights burning brightly, Skipper. All's well' – a sailor's cry true, but is not the theatre as teasing and treacherous as the sea? I think we have just had a sparkling conquering First Night, a cross between *Helen* and *Tantivy Towers* and *Derby Day* and *Bless the Bride*, what a night, the Queen came, and

Bob Menzies and Monty (but Johnny Henderson took him home at ten), when they cried 'Author!' we all went on the stage, Cochran, he can do it now because that damned arthritis has gone, and Vivian Ellis and Tony Vivian, and Nigel Playfair and the other composers, a sweet little speech I made, how they laughed, I kissed all the chorus except some of the altoes, then we had a grand supper at the Savoy, we took the whole of the restaurant floor, lots of neighbours from the *Black Lion*, George Bull, the Tumims, Hugh Browne, Sue, Penelope, Rosemary, and the Bevans, Natalie and Commander Bob, with Randolph Churchill *bonhomous*, and of course Derek and Jean, the Tangyes, up from their Cornish citadel and Peter Saunders and Pamela Charles, Dora Bryan, and Emile Littler, Reggie Pound and half a dozen Savages, then we all adjourned to the *Water Gipsy* at Charing Cross Pier and there in the cockpit was dear old E. V. Lucas with a great case of Piesporter carefully preparing his winecup as he loved to do, lots of lemon, beautifully carved, he and Bob Menzies got on splendidly, I have some of my old crew Connolly and Tom Cheesman, the fisherman, joint mates, Stan Atkins, the St Helen's glassmaker, and Eddie Elsbury, now practically king of North Thames Gas, joint stokers, the engines are working wondrously eighteen whole horses, faithful Priscilla and three or four of my past regiment of secretaries are passing drinks and delicious dainties but *no* champagne, extraordinary, even after the supper everyone was madly hungry and thirsty, how do you account for that, so we cast off and proceeded, but as the last line went there was a great roar from the shore and who do you think ghost Richard Tauber plunged out of the darkness and did a pierhead jump, the moment he saw Evelyn he burst into 'Girls were Made to Love and Kiss' from Paganini, well, first we went up to Westminster to fetch Gwilym Lloyd George, Charles Taylor and Connie, dear old Harry Fildes, telling endless stories and looking precisely like Punch, Maurice Petherick, Roy Wise, Paddy Hannon, and some others, the fools had an All Night Sitting about some unutterable nonsense, I laid her cleverly alongside the Terrace, a policeman protested mildly but I rose to my full height at the wheel and said 'Mr Speaker sir, Mr Speaker sir the right honourable policeman is *wrong* as I am prepared to show the House. God Save the Queen', then he was all right, he was my favourite policeman anyway, oh and Nye Bevan came too and Jennie, and Megan Lloyd George, whom I once kissed in the Members' Lobby of the House of *Lords*, my buddy Jim Callaghan and Roy Jenkins, quite an all party mission, and George Brown who loves the Tangyes, before we left we all made a joint speech, Wendy Toye produced us, Mr Speaker sir the right honourable gentleman is wrong so are we, God Save the Queen, we made such a noise that all the police rushed out, we thought it best to proceed and proceeded, so now we are on our way down the mighty river, we stopped by the way at Cleopatra's Needle to pick up Hugh Wontner the charming king of the Savoy, Robert Hannay a director, Bridget D'Oyley Carte, Freddy Lloyd, who manages those pests Gilbert and Sullivan, and a great ghost his predecessor Richard Colet, how I miss him, oh and I forgot a friend of ours that wonderful ghost from Canada Brockington, he was a Welshman really, is with him, pouring quotations and bits of poetry in all directions, Noël Coward came with them with Celia Johnson and Peter Fleming, that superb couple, I always claim I introduced them, and by the way, I've only just noticed Bob Newton still sober and that long-suffering angel his Ann and Bernard Delfont with his Carol Lynne singing 'I want to see the people happy' and there's Trefor Jones singing 'Let us go down to the river' from *Big Ben*, well, we're on our way now, I made Wendy call for silence while I asked if anyone else had seen Charing Cross Bridge and Waterloo Bridge on fire at the same time, as I had, Malcolm said Yes. He'd put one of them out which rather spoilt my effect, it's a Full Moon and St Paul's looks rather a fine Cathedral, I make them all stand to attention as we pass my revered *Times* to which I have written more letters than any man alive or dead, by the way, it's rather splendid they've nearly finished the Barrage, dam to you, at Woolwich which I've been yapping about for more than thirty years, the tides, the the sea at last will *not* intrude into the City, we're on a gentle current of about one mile an hour, the river's full and shiny with full moon and you can't see mud anywhere, not a pram not one dead cat, what's more, they've whisked all those warehouses and architectural riff-raff in front of St Paul's away and you can see the entire thing as old Wren saw it when he lived in that little white house opposite, Evelyn Laye is singing her point-song from *Helen* about Leda and the Swan, that was a good job mine I mean, we're stopping at Tower Pier to pick up Lord Simon king of the Port of London Authority, wonder what he'll have to say about the Dam they've been against it for ever, over there is Hay's Wharf where old de la Bere is king brave lad he gave his place for my Divorce Bill in 1937, here's dear Tower Bridge, best bridge anywhere, I remember the morning a doodlebug came straight through it on to the Tower Bridge tug, killed both crews I believe, they were relieving, what a lesson is this bridge to modern planners, the grey stone doesn't clash with the Tower at all, from a distance a stranger might think they were built together, if they built a replacement now suppose it would be all glass and concrete, I say the *Water Gipsy* has swollen to such a size they're raising the bascules for us, I've always wanted that to happen, thank you, sir, have you ever been up to the top bridge, the view is ruined by all those horrible topless towers, thank you again, here we are in the Pool, that's Rotherhithe Church where the captain of the *Mayflower* is buried.

There's the old Prospect of Whitby, miraculous, I've seen it with a big fire both sides, Gwen's birthday, 1940, and here's the Surrey Docks, you couldn't see *them* at all that night because of the smoke, half a mile of it, and here's glorious Greenwich, what did Frank Carr call it, the most unaltered view, how damnably they've treated Frank!

After Blackwall Point where we cross into East longitude, the most extraordinary thing, we suddenly pass into true-blue, deep blue, velvet skirt Mediterranean water, suddenly the *Water Gipsy* seems to have turned into something like the *Deianeira* and we're all aboard her, I hand over to Captain Behenna, best captain in the Med, and here's John Astor himself, but goodness he's got *two legs*, at last, he's been hauling that tin leg round too long, 1915, a Life Guard, I think, fifty-five years too long, but he never complained, now of course without a tremor he orders 100 of those infallible dry martinis, and the next thing while they're brewing, we're all diving into this blue perfect impossible water, I never saw him dive on two legs before, what a chap, the swim is miraculous, and over the cocktails my crew sing all their songs, John is delighted, the *Water Gipsy*'s piano has come aboard somehow and Malcolm and I play Handel's Largo which is a stupendous turn, Bob Menzies diving is a magnificent spectacle, all the golden girls have fallen for him, and they swim round him like a cloud of nymphs round the rock of Gibraltar which, of course, is just what he is, the situation now confused, except it's clear that we are whizzing through the Med at a preposterous speed, John and I take sextant sights now and then to make sure where we are, but we are not sure, we seldom were, I know we whizzed past delicious Elba, I should have liked to go in to Porto Ferraio again and go up to Napoleon's poor little garden over the sea, my *Why Waterloo?* began in the *Deianeira*, we whizzed round Italy, popped in at Corfu and Ithaca, Ulysses came aboard, a nice man, he and John and Bob Menzies had a tremendous chatter, all this time either Malcolm or Vivian is playing the piano which is a joy and somewhere Joe Cooper came aboard, dear old Tauber hardly ever stops singing and I think Guétary's spirit is broken, but Trefor Jones gets a song in edgeways now and then, every three hours we all plunge madly into the impossible blue water and damn the sharks, here we are in the Corinth Canal, we did Delphi very good, and by Apollo here's the same kingfisher we had before guiding us through, there he goes darting from side to side, the dear little green thing, what's his name Halcyon, Halcyon, lovely word, Ulysses has gone back to Ithaca, we lent him the sailing dinghy, he said he couldn't stand Athens, nor can I, we're not going there, they should put the Parthenon somewhere else or just eliminate the town, Bob Menzies told Ulysses he should take it over but Ulysses said You should have taken England over. Too right, he'd have been a prime Prime for us, I've taught all the golden girls and

the grandchildren the stars and they love them but I wish Capella
would not come up so late, we have both Jupiter and Venus in the
evenings now, cocktail time, and the other morning I saw a portent not
a green flash like sunset but the sun rising like a green apple, Captain
Behenna says that man and boy he never saw the like, it *was* a portent,
because that day we caught the Onassis yacht and simply left her
standing, I waved to Jackie but she simply ignored me, damned old
Tauber was singing 'Girls were made etc.' we looked in at Rhodes and
saw the butterflies, rather a hurry now because we're going to drop
Bob Menzies and the Dame at Melbourne, he has to speak on Burns
Night at the Savage Club as we both did once, should have liked to
call at Rangoon and Bangkok, those names have always been a magnet
but John says better leave them for another trip, but I insisted on my
beloved Ceylon, we all went up to Kandy, the children saw the Temple
elephants bathing, we did two of the Dead Cities, Anuradhapura and
Polonnarua, though personally I'm always more excited by the
monkeys and the birds than the historic ruins, and we had the hugest
Bungalow Curry at a planter friend of Malcolm's, well here we are off
Sydney we dropped the Menzies sadly, no it's not Sydney damn it, it's
Southend looking jolly tropical in the sun, we're in the old *Water
Gipsy* again, how cosy, Sea Reach looks splendid, strong south-
westerly all the buoys a-bouncing, but the tribe of Abraham are all good
sailors, not so sure about some of the guests, Sea Reach, children, my
hat here comes a Barge Race roaring down before the wind, twelve of
them, there's *Veronica* in front as usual, *Cambria* and *Sara* not so far
astern, Sea Reach, children, the road to London, this is the way all
those damn foreigners came the Vikings and the Danes and the Dutch,
there's Canvey Island, this is where the great fleet of ships were lying
the day before D-Day ready for France, the little *Water Gipsy* did odd
jobs for them and very proud she was, there's Hole Haven, there's the
Lobster Smack, that was our little harbour, this was the way at one
time we thought that fellow Hitler would come, we seriously did, that's
the Creek, see the bawley boats, they catch shrimps, yes there was a
string of mines just here to annoy him and torpedoes farther up, the
Water Gipsy had two cutlasses and one rifle, we were nearly sunk by
that jetty, later we had two machine-guns, imagine, in this little boat,
most heavily armed vessel in the Navy, I couldn't use either of them
but Tom and Stan could, I fired the rifle once, Sea Reach over there
there's the Dickens country, Gadshill and all, and there's Gravesend the
Gateway of London River, hoist the Q flag Tom, and stand to attention
children, half the history of England has gone this way, here come the
Customs and they've got a good ghost with them, my old friend Captain
Owen Ruler of the Pilots, good morning Captain coming up with us, he
says he will because he's got a letter for me from the Prime Minister, I

say this is wonderful he says the Cabinet have decided to abolish that damnable B.S.T. and go back to Greenwich Time, Hooray, also they are going to give the poor authors what they want about the libraries, Hooray again, what's more he promises to cancel all schemes for metrication and other continental fiddle faddle the coinage has been a lesson to him, well that's very handsome, Mr Speaker sir the right honourable Gentlemen are right at *last*, and there's a P.S. You've got a surprise coming what's more? and do you know what it is, when we get to Woolwich there's the Barrage absolutely finished, they've been pretty quick, I must say, and the shipway for the big ships too on the east side of Gallions Reach, we go modestly through the small lock at the end of the Dam, but the other side the whole river has gone Mediterranean, John Astor water again, there's a gentle current coming down, much clearer, a glorious day, all the people are rowing or sailing little boats and swimming and we're all singing 'I Want to See the People Happy', most moving God bless the London General Council and the Minister of Forget What, well, here we are back at Westminster at last, there's the great Clock Face the lighthouse of London and Big Ben booming the hour it's rather like the last night of a play, everyone embracing everybody and darling, darling like church chimes in the morning, you know how one says when it's come off a little sooner than we wanted, a pity darling but we've had a good run, well I do think we've had a good run so goodbye darlings, bless you, love to all and God Save the Queen.

OTHER WORKS

Verse
PLAY HOURS WITH PEGASUS 1912 At Oxford (Blackwell)
HALF HOURS AT HELLES 1916 War Verse (Blackwell)
THE BOMBER GIPSY 1918 War Verse (1919 New and enlarged) Methuen
LAUGHING ANN 1925 (Fisher Unwin)
SHE-SHANTIES 1926 (Fisher Unwin)
PLAIN JANE 1927 (Ernest Benn)
BALLADS FOR BROADBROWS 1930 (Ernest Benn)
A BOOK OF BALLADS Omnibus of the four preceding books (Ernest Benn)
'TINKER, TAILOR . . .' For children Illustrated by George Morrow (Methuen)
THE WHEREFORE AND THE WHY For children Illustrated by George Morrow (Methuen)
WISDOM FOR THE WISE The two preceding books together
SIREN SONG 1940 Mainly war (Methuen)
LET US BE GLUM 1941 War (Methuen)
BRING BACK THE BELLS 1943 (Methuen)
LESS NONSENSE 1944 (Methuen)
LIGHT THE LIGHTS 1945 (Methuen)
FULL ENJOYMENT 1952 (Methuen)
A.T.I. 1944 (Ornum Press)
SILVER STREAM 1962 Long poem about a greyhound and greyhound racing (Methuen)

Novels and Near-Novels
THE SECRET BATTLE 1919 (Methuen) 1970 New edition Chatto & Windus
THE HOUSE BY THE RIVER 1920 (Methuen)
THE OLD FLAME 1925 (Methuen)
THE WATER GIPSIES 1930 (Methuen)
HOLY DEADLOCK 1934 (Methuen)
THE TRIALS OF TOPSY 1928 (Ernest Benn)
TOPSY M.P. 1929 (Ernest Benn)
TOPSY TURVY 1947 (Ernest Benn)
THE TOPSY OMNIBUS 1948 (Ernest Benn)
NUMBER NINE 1951 (Methuen)

WHY WATERLOO? 1952 (Methuen)
MADE FOR MAN 1958 (Methuen)
THE SINGING SWAN 1968 (Methuen)

General
INDEPENDENT MEMBER 1950 Time in Parliament (Methuen)
THE AYES HAVE IT 1937 Story of the Marriage Bill (Methuen)
THE THAMES 1966 (Weidenfeld & Nicolson)
SUNDIALS OLD AND NEW 1967 How to make sundials (Methuen)
WHAT A WORD! 1935 Use of English (Methuen)
'NO BOATS ON THE RIVER . . .' 1932 (Methuen)
THE POINT OF PARLIAMENT 1946 For the Young (Methuen)
NO FINE ON FUN 1951 Case against entertainment tax (Methuen)
THE RIGHT TO MARRY 1954 (Methuen)
WATCH THIS SPACE . . . 1964 First seven years of Space (Methuen)
A BETTER SKY 1944 Re-naming the stars (Methuen)
POOLS PILOT 1953 Football Pools (Methuen)
MR PEWTER 1934 A series for the B.B.C. (Methuen)
IN THE DARK 1970 Summer Time Story (Bodley Head)

Pamphlets
LET THERE BE LIBERTY 1940 (Macmillan's War Pamphlets)
ANYTHING BUT ACTION? 1960 On Royal Commissions (Hobart
    Paper 5, Institute of Economic Affairs)
LIBRARIES – FREE FOR ALL? 1962 An Appeal to Parliament, for
    Authors and Publishers (Hobart Paper 19, Institute of Economic
    Affairs)
THE WAR STORY OF SOUTHEND PIER 1945 (Southend-on-Sea Cor-
    poration)

Election Addresses
OXFORD UNIVERSITY 1935
OXFORD UNIVERSITY 1945
EAST HARROW 1958 'I Object' (Bodley Head)

Law
MISLEADING CASES IN THE COMMON LAW 1927 (Methuen)
MORE MISLEADING CASES 1930 (Methuen)
STILL MORE MISLEADING CASES 1933 (Methuen)
UNCOMMON LAW 1935 (Omnibus of three) New edition 1969
    (Methuen)
CODD'S LAST CASE 1952 (Methuen)
BARDOT M.P. 1964 (Methuen)
WIGS AT WORK 1966 Selected cases (Penguin)
MR GAY'S LONDON 1948 (The London Sessions 1732–33, Comments
    and Extracts.) (Methuen)

Collections

LIGHT ARTICLES ONLY 1921 (Methuen)

HONEYBUBBLE & CO 1940 (Methuen)

THE MAN ABOUT TOWN 1928 (Heinemann)

MILD AND BITTER 1936 (Methuen)

GENERAL CARGO 1939 (Methuen)

SIP! SWALLOW! 1937 (Methuen)

'WELL, ANYHOW . . .' 1942 (Methuen)

LOOK BACK AND LAUGH 1960 (Methuen)

Dramatic and Musical

DOUBLE DEMON 1923 One-act 'absurdity' – Four One-Act Plays (Blackwell)

TWO GENTLEMEN OF SOHO 1927 One-act play – A Book of Ballads (Acting Edition – Samuel French)

FAT KING MELON For children – *Dennis Arundell* (Oxford University Press – libretto and music)

THE POLICEMAN'S SERENADE 1926 *Alfred Reynolds* – One-act (Chappell's)

PERSEVERANCE 1934 *Vivian Ellis* – Gilbert and Sullivan one-act parody (score – Chappell's)

PLAIN JANE 1929 *Richard Austin* – One-act (score – Samuel French)

THE BLUE PETER *Armstrong Gibbs* One-act

RIVERSIDE NIGHTS 1926 (libretto – Fisher Unwin)

LA VIE PARISIENNE 1929 *Offenbach* (*A. Davies Adams*) (Score – Boosey & Co)

HELEN 1932 *Offenbach* (*E. W. Korngold*), (Libretto – Methuen)

DERBY DAY 1931 *Alfred Reynolds* (Libretto – Methuen, Score – Elkin)

TANTIVY TOWERS 1931 *Tom Dunhill* (Methuen and Cramer)

PAGANINI 1963 *Lehar* – New version (Francis Day and Hunter – Glocken Verlag)

BIG BEN 1946 *Vivian Ellis* (Libretto – Methuen)

BLESS THE BRIDE 1947 *Vivian Ellis* (Libretto – Samuel French, score – Chappell's)

'COME TO THE BALL' 1951 *Johann Strauss*, Die Fledermaus adapted (Libretto – Ernest Benn)

THE WATER GIPSIES 1957 *Vivian Ellis* (Chappell's)

INDEX